Writing

with
Contemporary
Readings

BARBARA BAKER
BAKER RESEARCH AND CONSULTING

CATHERINE BAKER
PLAIN LANGUAGE COMMUNICATIONS

EMCParadigm

Senior Editor	Sonja Brown
Consulting Editor	Mary Reichardt
Art Director	Joan D'Onofrio
Design and Composition	Bolger, Inc.
Copyeditor	Gretchen Bratvold
Proofreader	Kay Savoie
Indexer	Beverlee Day
Permissions	Susan Capecchi
	Tari Cliff
	Desiree Faulkner

Acknowledgments

The Publisher, Authors, and Editors thank the following instructors for their insightful evaluations and suggestions during the development of this text:

Dr. Johan Christopherson
Minneapolis Community and
Technical College

Kathryn L. Cid
Lincoln Technical Institute

Ted Krize
Rasmussen College

Janet McGregor
Draughons Junior College

Dr. Carol Pemberton
Normandale Community College

Janet Walker
West Tennessee Business College

Laura Wallace
Drake Business School

Library of Congress Cataloging-in-Publication Data

Baker, Barbara A.
    Writing with contemporary readings / Barbara Baker, Catherine Baker.
      p. cm.
    Includes index.
    ISBN 0-7638-0209-3
    1. English language--Rhetoric. 2. English language--Grammar. 3. College readers. 4. Report writing. I. Baker, Catherine, 1956- II. Title.

PE1408 .B264 2000
808'.0427--dc21   99-057735

Contents

Preface

What You Can Get from Writing

In a writing class several years ago, students were asked to write an essay responding to this statement: "Some friends bring you up, and some friends pull you down."

One student, William, wrote about his girlfriend. He described how she encouraged him to drink excessively, despite the fact that he was a prison security officer with the goal of joining the police force.

"You ought to get rid of her," the other students counseled William. A few months later, when the classmates asked William how he was faring with that girlfriend, he quietly replied that he had broken off the relationship.

Of course, William did not enroll in the writing course for advice. He was there because he needed to improve his writing to advance in his career. Yet it is possible that the act of putting his situation into words on paper helped William make a decision. It is possible that writing helped him see his goals more clearly and recognize how his friendship was interfering.

We tell this true story about William (who did become a police officer) to remind you that the act of writing can benefit you in unexpected ways. You know that writing is a useful skill for making it through college and for succeeding in the workforce. You may not be aware that the act of writing can help you become more conscious of your thoughts and actions. It can help you observe and interpret the world around you. These processes can transform you. They really can give you more power and control over your life.

We also should mention that writing, in its own way, can be a lot of fun.

How This Book Is Organized

This textbook has been designed to take advantage of the ways that you, as an adult, learn. If you are like most other adults, you learn best when you can connect what you are learning to what you already know. You also learn best when what you are being taught is interesting or can be put to immediate use.

This is why each chapter opens with an illustration. Each one is an interesting conversation starter, designed to provoke you and fellow students to think about and talk about the knowledge you already have on the chapter's topics. These illustrations appear under the section title *Picturing Meaning*.

In the text itself, the presentation of each new concept is immediately followed by a writing activity labeled *Write Now*. These activities are done individually, in pairs, or in groups. They are designed to help you retain what you have just read and also to apply it. We advise you to read thoughtfully through each *Write Now* activity even if you have not been assigned to do it, because this can help you remember and make use of the material later.

Writing-related terms appear in the text in boldface on their first appearance. These terms are usually defined in the text itself, or you can look them up in the Glossary near the end of the book.

Computer Tips appear in the margins and are intended to make the transition to writing on computer comparatively easy and efficient.

The questions that appear in a box labeled *Second Thoughts*, at the end of each chapter, are intended to draw your attention back to the opening illustration. This is to help you make stronger connections between what you knew before you started the chapter and what you have learned through reading and your writing practice.

The final section of each chapter, entitled *Summing Up*, asks you to recall what you have learned and, just as importantly, apply it to your own practices as a writer.

Following each chapter is another section called *Read and Reflect*. This contains a contemporary reading that illustrates the chapter's concepts. For example, the reading after the chapter entitled "Narrating" tells about a trip through a used auto parts lot. Each reading is followed by questions, discussion topics, and writing ideas. These are intended to help you retain what you have learned and to apply that knowledge in your own writing, using the reading as a model.

This textbook has a companion book called *Writer's Journal*. Many of the *Write Now* activities direct you to write in this journal. If you do not have a copy of the *Writer's Journal*, you can use any lined notebook. You can even keep your journal on computer. What is important is to do frequent writing on topics of your own choosing and to experiment with several kinds of journal writing.

Acknowledgments

Writing a textbook about writing is a humbling experience. Though between us we have more than fifty years of professional writing experience, it was no easy trick. We went through the same process of writing that we talk about in this textbook: thinking, planning, drafting, revising—and especially revising. We learned two important lessons from this project. One, there is no such thing as writing—there is only rewriting. Two, writing well requires the help of others. Therefore, we would like to thank the many people who have contributed to the development of this textbook:

Jim Bell, Nancy Goudreau, Steven Philleo, Phil Shapiro, and Lisa Swanson, the friends who stimulated our thinking and gave us good ideas;

Tally Morgan, our friend in the book publishing industry who helped us understand the process;

Dan Walsh, who brought to our attention two of the featured artworks;

Stephon Gray, who generously allowed himself to be interviewed for this textbook and whose own efforts as a writer are an inspiration;

Queen Brown, Andre Lyles, Jean Shade, Thomas K. Wynn, and Kevin Summers, the writing students who allowed us to use their first drafts;

Mike Fox, the teacher who connected us with his students and who provided us with frequent good counsel;

the many authors of books on writing, public speaking, college success, and English skills that we consulted;

the wonderful people at EMC Paradigm who know how to make a rough manuscript into a polished book, including Jan Johnson, our dear friend and colleague whose brainchild this book was and who shepherded it from idea into reality; Sonja Brown, senior editor at EMC Paradigm, whose calmness prevailed; Mary Reichardt, our reviewer and consulting editor who skillfully encouraged and coached us through the final phases; and Tari Cliff, Desiree Faulkner, and Sue Capecchi, who worked doggedly on obtaining the many permissions for excerpts and artwork;

Johan Christopherson of Minneapolis Community and Technical College, whose suggestions were on-the-mark and witty at the same time;

the writing instructors whose generous contributions of time and opinion helped shape the book; and

David Baker, John Baker, Susan Buie, Carolyn Reser, and Greg Sherrard, our family who helped us directly and indirectly.

Finally, we would like to thank the people who taught us most about writing and about teaching: Marjorie Bailey, Mike Fox, Marcia Harrington, Peter Klappert, Michael Mott, Audrey Parish, and Alan Reiter. This book is dedicated to them.

Barbara Baker
Catherine Baker

UNIT 1

THINKING ABOUT WRITING

What exactly is writing? How is it different from talking?
What are the secrets to writing well? What makes writing enjoyable?
What steps are involved in the process of writing? This introductory
unit explores these questions. Goals of the unit are to help you:

- Define writing and become familiar with the skills that go into it.

- Learn to take advantage of your experiences when writing.

- Explore your academic and personal writing goals.

- Identify what makes writing effective.

- Understand what an essay is.

- Recognize that you can learn to write effectively through
  training and practice.

- Become aware of the steps involved in the writing process.

Activities in this unit will help you become accustomed to using
a journal. They also will help you establish a writing folder for storing
works-in-progress. Eventually you may select from this folder to create
a portfolio demonstrating your progress as a writer.

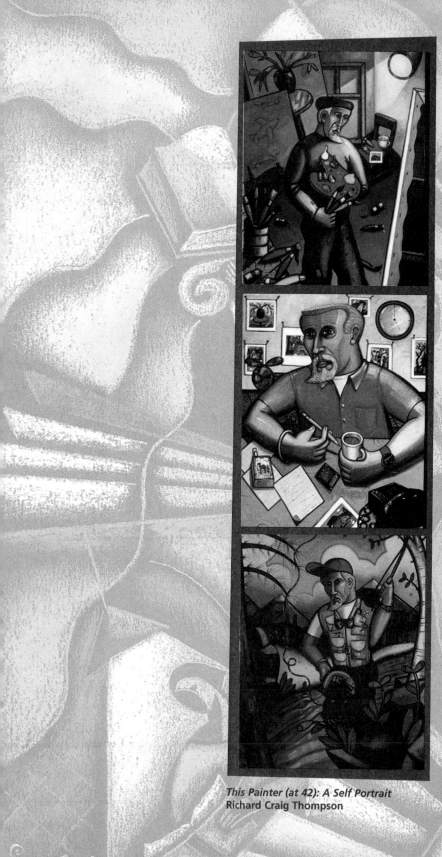

This Painter (at 42): A Self Portrait
Richard Craig Thompson

CHAPTER 1

Defining Yourself As a Writer

These are the **key ideas** of this chapter:

- Writing is a creative activity that requires a lot of energy.

- Writing is also a skill that anyone can learn to do well through training and practice.

- You can become a better writer by adopting these habits: observe, read, be organized, write often, and have goals.

Picturing Meaning

Examine the set of self-portraits on the opposite page; then think about or discuss these questions:

1. What do you see the person doing in each picture?

He is thinking. about life in these pictures.
He is boggled down with the what ifs in life
He is thinking about what if he could make things differently
mow would he are

2. What do you think the person enjoys about each of these activities? why.

In each different activity he does
it helps bring out the good qualities he has as a
person. It helps relax him, while thinking about his life

3. How do these different activities connect?

They are all talents he has mastered
throughout his life.

In the *Responses* section of your journal, write down your thoughts about these self-portraits.

Write Now (1)

Every person has many different identities. Child, parent, learner, teacher, worker, friend—one person can have all of these identities and more. What are *your* identities? Is "writer" one of them? How is writing involved in each of your identities? Write down your responses to these questions. Keep this work because you may use it in a later activity.

What Is Writing?

You are enrolled in a **writing** course, and you are at this very moment reading a textbook on writing. So a good place to start is with a definition of the term:

> Writing is the act of organizing your thoughts into recorded words. The purpose (usually) is to communicate your ideas to others. Writing is a creative activity. Therefore, it requires energy, and it draws out many feelings, such as frustration, fear, satisfaction, and joy. Writing is also a skill. It is something that anyone can learn to do well through training and practice.

Perhaps you are a person who already enjoys writing. Perhaps you are not. Perhaps you feel anxious or even resentful about writing. You may think of writing as something that other people do easily, but not you. However, even professional writers find the work challenging. The journalist William Zinsser confesses:

> I don't like to write, but I take great pleasure in having written—in having finally made an arrangement that has a certain inevitability, like the solution to a mathematical problem. Perhaps in no other line of work is delayed gratification so delayed.
>
> *Writing to Learn*

If you want to become an effective writer, you have to embrace the challenge. You have to think of yourself as a writer. What does this mean? It means, first of all, to be clear about what a writer is. Based on the definition of "writing" that you just read, a writer is "someone who organizes [his/her] thoughts into recorded words." At the very least, then, you are a writer because you will soon be producing pieces of writing for this course.

Yet this definition is not complete. A writer is someone who is willing to say, "Writing is what I do." When you are a writer, however, writing may not be all that you do. Writing may not be what you do best, but it is a craft you practice. It is a set of skills you exercise and develop.

A writer is someone who finds satisfaction from the process of forming words into an object of value and significance. Like wood, thread, or clay that can be worked, woven, or sculpted, words are a material that can be shaped into many forms and for many purposes. The work itself may be difficult, time-consuming, and even tedious. However, for the writer, the end product makes the struggle worthwhile.

In conclusion, if you want to develop effective writing skills that will serve you throughout life, you must do these things:

- You must write.

- You must define yourself as a writer.

- You must discover the satisfaction that comes from working with words.

Write Now (2)

Move into pairs. Ask your partner these four questions:
1. **What is your name?**
2. **What kind of writing do you do?**
3. **What kind of writer would you like to be?**
4. **What do you like about writing? (Don't take "nothing" for an answer!)**

Use this information to write a short description of your partner. Use the description to introduce your partner to the class.

Write Now (3)

1. **Think of something you do well. Name it:** _____

   _____

   Example: *soccer.*

2. **List three strengths you have in this area:**

   • _____

   • _____

   • _____

   Examples: *I have speed, I am good at teamwork, I practice hard.*

3. **How might you be able to apply these strengths to your work as a writer?**

   • _____

   • _____

   • _____

   Examples: *I can think of writing as a kind of running, to give myself good feelings about the work; I can give help to and take help from others; I can apply my hard-working attitude to writing practice.*

Keep this work because you may use it in a later activity.

Habits of a Writer

As a practicing writer, you will want to cultivate the following habits:

✔ Observe.

✔ Read.

✔ Be organized.

✔ Write often.

✔ Have goals.

Observe. Your daily life is rich with material that you can use in your writing. The trick is to notice and to remember—to be wide awake to what is going on around you. Train your mind to hunt for topics, to gather examples, and to remember interesting happenings and situations. Observing is an acquired skill. However, the more you do it, the easier it becomes.

Read. The importance of this habit should be obvious to you. By reading, you collect ideas and facts that you can use in your writing. Just as important, when you read you learn by example how to write. Through reading, you expand your vocabulary and internalize the structure of language. Reading is a much more enjoyable way to learn these essentials than through studying. So read broadly. Read fiction. Read biographies. Read articles about subjects you enjoy and articles about subjects you know nothing about. Read advertising. Read poetry out loud. Listen carefully to song lyrics. Pay attention to how each writer strings words together. When you are reading something you admire and enjoy, reflect on why it pleases you.

Be organized. Organization may strike you as not particularly necessary to writing. However, you will not write well if you are stumbling around looking for a pencil every time you are ready to start working. You need to have a system for keeping all your paperwork organized so that when you are ready to work on a particular piece, you can find it. You need a place to write that has good lighting and an uncluttered surface upon which to write. You need the tools: pencils and paper or a computer you know how to run. You need a place that gives you freedom from interruption. Finally, you need to be organized in your approach to writing. This begins with the recognition that writing involves several stages of effort (you will read more about this **writing process** in Chapter 3).

Write often. You cannot become fluent in a new language without practicing. You cannot perform well on the piano without practicing. Likewise, you cannot become a skilled writer without practicing. So practice, practice, practice. The activities in this textbook should give plenty of writing practice, but you also can practice on your own: writing letters, scribbling in a **journal** (see more about the journal below), drafting poems and songs, making lists—whatever it is you can do that has you recording words.

Have goals. Know where you are trying to go as a writer. Think short-term and long-term. Completing a writing assignment might be a short-term goal, while making your writing more interesting might be a long-term goal. By setting goals, you turn a vague desire to improve your writing into a directed activity with tasks and, ultimately, rewards.

Write Now (4)

Complete the sentences below.

1. One way I can become a better observer is to _____

_____

2. One thing I can do to increase the amount of reading I do is to

_____

3. One thing I can do to become better organized for writing is to

_____

4. One way I can begin to write more is to _____

_____

5. One thing I can do to focus on my writing goals is to _____

_____

On computer, create a folder with a name such as "Writing Folder." Create another folder *within* this folder for each separate writing project. Also create another folder *within* this folder for miscellaneous files that you may use in future writing tasks. Be sure to save work into the proper folder.

Keeping a Writing Folder

As a writer, you will generate a lot of paperwork that you will not want to lose. For example, certain Write Now activities in this textbook advise you to save your writing from those exercises because you may use them in future activities. In addition, when you are writing something important, you will want to hold on to all your different copies of it until you have finished. To keep track of all these papers, you should create some sort of a **writing folder.**

One way to organize a writing folder is to keep a three-ring notebook with multiple dividers. Another organizing method is to store material in three pocket folders: one folder for your most current writing project, one for completed projects, and one for miscellaneous work.

Besides keeping yourself organized, a writing folder serves another purpose. It stores the material that eventually you will draw from to create a **portfolio.** A portfolio is a collection of your best writing. It also may include samples of a work through all stages from start to finish. Some instructors require you to submit a portfolio at the end of the course. Even if your instructor does not do this, a portfolio can become a useful record of progress to keep for yourself.

Write Now (5)

As a class, discuss different ways to set up your writing folder. Then answer the questions below:

1. **What different types of paperwork will you be generating for your writing class?**

   _____   _____

   _____   _____

   _____   _____

Put a check mark next to the types of paperwork you will want to keep in your writing folder.

2. **What method will you use to organize the papers you want to store?** _____

   _____

3. **What materials will you need?**
   ___ three-ring notebook   ___ pocket folders (quantity ___)
   ___ dividers (quantity ___)   ___ paperclips
   ___ three-hole punch   ___ stapler
   ___ other items _____

Keeping a Journal

Keeping a journal is one simple thing you can do to help you practice all five of the habits of a writer. A journal is simply a private book for you to record your thoughts and ideas. A journal will help you *observe* because in order to put anything in it, you must pay attention to your impressions and experiences. A journal will help you *be organized* because it can help you shape your random thoughts into order. It also can serve as a central storage spot for random ideas and scraps of information. A journal can get you to *write often* because journal writing is an unthreatening, even pleasant, kind of writing that you can do on your own schedule. Finally, a journal can be the place where you *set goals*, record them, and measure progress toward them.

Consider keeping a word-processed journal. Create a file, name it "journal" or something along that line, and save it into your Writing Folder. Type the date and start writing. Save the file when you are finished. The next time you open it, scroll to the bottom, type in your new date, and start writing again.

A portable journal is available with this text. It is offered to encourage you to give journal writing a try over the next few months. If you have skimmed through this journal, you have seen that the main section is for recording your everyday thoughts and observations, like a diary.

The journal also contains sections in which you can react to writings and artworks, keep a list of words you want to learn, make notes of good topics for writing, and record your goals.

You should also note that the journal has a section in which you can record interesting quotations or paste in small clippings. Your journal can be like a scrapbook or like the "commonplace book" many professional writers keep. ("Commonplace" is an old-fashioned term for quotations of common interest.) Here is how one writer keeps and uses "commonplaces":

I keep a folder, a yellow folder with pockets. For a long time it had no label because I didn't know what to label it: WHATCHAMACALLITS, filed under *W*, or also under *W*, STORY-POEM-WANNABEs. Finally, I called the folder CURIOSIDADES, in Spanish so I wouldn't have to commit myself to what I was going to do in English with these random little things. I tell my students this, too, that writing begins before you ever put pen to paper or your fingers down on the keyboard. It is a way of being alive in the world. Henry James's advice to the young writer was to be someone on whom nothing is lost. And so this is my folder of the little things that have not been lost on me; news clippings, headlines, inventory lists, bits of gossip that I've already sensed have an aura about them, the beginnings of a poem or a short story, the seed of a plot that might turn into a novel or a query that might needle an essay out of me.

Periodically, when I'm between writing projects and sometimes when I'm in the middle of one and needing a break, I go through my yellow folder. Sometimes I discard a clipping or note that no longer holds my attention. But most of my curiosidades have been in my folder for years, though some have migrated to new folders, the folders of stories and poems they have inspired or found a home in.

Something to Declare
Julia Alvarez

Within this textbook are many journal-writing activities. These are intended to prompt you to develop a journal-writing habit. If a particular journal prompt fails to interest you, do not respond to it. Do, however, use it as an opportunity to write in your journal about *something*.

Write Now (6)

In small groups, page through your journals. Discuss how you can use each section of the journal to improve your writing skills or to collect writing ideas. If someone in your group is interested in keeping a word-processed journal, discuss how to re-create these sections on computer. Then, in the *Observations* section of your journal, write an introduction of yourself. In that introduction, describe how you plan to use the journal over the next few months.

Making the Most of Technology

If you have not yet made the transition from pen or typewriter to computer, the opportunity to do so is probably available or close at hand. Consider the advantages of using a computer to write:

- You can make changes without recopying the entire document.
- You can easily alter a document's format such as from single-spaced to double-spaced.
- You can use your word processor's spelling and grammar checking functions.
- You can use other specialized functions, such as word count, readability, and auto-correct.
- You can produce a professional looking document.
- You can incorporate graphics.
- You can automatically add page numbers and the date to your documents.
- You can cut and paste sections from one location to another in a document (or from one document to another).

If you have used a computer, chances are good that you are familiar with the **Internet.** However, you may not yet have used it to full advantage. The Internet is the worldwide network of computers that enables anyone with a connection to access and exchange information. Initially developed by the U.S. Defense Department, it is now highly utilized by the general public. One of the most popular aspects of the Internet is the **World Wide Web.** The Web contains linked sites that you can leap back and forth between with simple keystrokes. Consider the many ways that the Internet can help you in your writing:

- You can find out what is available at different resource centers, such as libraries and bookstores.

- You can obtain answers to grammar and style questions.

- You can do research without leaving home.

- You can contact experts.

- You can converse electronically ("chat") with writing colleagues and instructors.

- You can receive assignments from and transmit completed work to instructors.

- You can exchange materials with colleagues for comment.

- You can collaborate with others without meeting physically.

In the margins of this textbook, you will notice tips about using computers and the Internet. These tips are intended to make you a better, more efficient writer with these technological tools. Always keep in mind, however, that whatever can be done on computer also can be done the old-fashioned way—sometimes with more satisfaction and success. It pays to keep a level head about technology. Technology can help you write, but it cannot do your writing for you.

Write Now (7)

In small groups, discuss and answer the following.

1. What is one advantage, not listed above, to using a computer for writing? _____

   _____

   _____

2. What is one disadvantage? _____

   _____

   _____

3. How can you overcome this disadvantage? _____

   _____

   _____

4. What is one advantage, not listed above, to using the Internet as a writing tool? _____

   _____

   _____

5. What is one disadvantage? _____

   _____

   _____

6. How can you overcome this disadvantage? _____

   _____

   _____

Write Now (8)

Below are listed some technological devices that can be of service to writers. For each one, list an advantage, a disadvantage, and a way to overcome the disadvantage. The first item has been done for you as an example.

Technological Device	Advantage	Disadvantage	How to Overcome Disadvantage
cell phone	can make it easy to get in touch with classmates for a group project	calls can be distracting	turn off cell phone when writing
handheld spellchecker	_____	_____	_____
photocopier	_____	_____	_____
zip-drive	_____	_____	_____
CD-ROM	_____	_____	_____
pager	_____	_____	_____
networked computers	_____	_____	_____
tape recorder	_____	_____	_____
television	_____	_____	_____
fax machine	_____	_____	_____
handheld computer	_____	_____	_____

Write Now (9)

Divide into groups and research these questions.

1. What opportunities are available at your educational institution to use computers or to take computer courses?

   _____

   _____

2. What opportunities are available in the community to use computers or to take computer courses?

   _____

   _____

3. What software programs or books teach word processing and Internet skills, and where can they be obtained?

   _____

   _____

4. Where can you purchase inexpensive used computers (or obtain them for free)?

   _____

   _____

5. Which classmates would be good mentors when learning how to use word processors or the Internet?

   _____

   _____

Course Goals and Your Goals

Your instructor has goals for students enrolled in this course. This textbook was written with certain goals in mind for its readers. Course and textbook goals affect you because they are used to help you learn, and they will be used to measure your effort and progress. However, they may not be *your* writing goals. Have you thought about what those goals are?

Write Now (10)

Complete the Inventory of Your Writing Habits which appears in Figure 1-1. Your responses can help you identify your personal writing goals. Are any of your "X's" near the left end of the lines? You may want to set goals that will help you move those "X's" over to the right. Keep this inventory. You will be retaking it and comparing your responses at the end of the course.

Write Now (11)

Working in small groups, do the following tasks and answer the questions.

1. Read your course syllabus (the course description your instructor hands out on the first day of class). What are the instructor's goals for you?

    _____

    _____

    _____

2. Review the table of contents for this textbook. What are the authors' goals for you?

    _____

    _____

    _____

3. Finally, exchange ideas on personal goals you have for writing over the term of this course. What is one of your goals?

    _____

    _____

    _____

Figure 1-1: Inventory of Your Writing Habits

Instructions: Put an X on each line somewhere between the two endpoints. For example, on item 1, if you dislike writing, put your X close to the left end of the line. If you like to write, put your X close to the right end of the line. Put your X somewhere in the middle if your feelings about writing are somewhere between like and dislike.

1. I dislike
   to write.
   _____   I like
   to write.

2. I write only when
   required to do so
   by others.
   _____   I often write for
   my own purposes.

3. For any writing
   task, I write as little
   as necessary to get by.
   _____   For any writing
   task, I write until
   I am satisfied with
   my work.

4. I live each day
   without looking for
   writing ideas.
   _____   I collect writing
   ideas from the
   events in my day.

5. I read very little
   each day.
   _____   I read a great deal
   each day.

6. I have no specific
   place for writing.
   _____   I have an
   organized location
   where I can write.

7. I write very little
   each day.
   _____   I write a great
   deal each day.

8. I do not keep
   a journal.
   _____   I keep a journal.

9. I do not use
   a word processor.
   _____   I effectively use a
   a word processor.

10. I do not use
    the Internet.
    _____   I effectively use
    the Internet.

11. I have no
    particular goals for
    myself as a writer.
    _____   I have clear goals
    for myself as a
    writer.

12. I do not think of
    myself as a writer.
    _____   I think of myself
    as a writer.

Summing Up

1. Complete the following sentence: I am a writer because:

   _____

   _____

2. Consider again the five habits of a writer discussed in this chapter: observe, read, be organized, write often, and have goals. Underline the one habit you do best. Why is it easy for you?

   _____

   _____

3. Circle the one habit that gives you the most difficulty. What is one thing you can do to overcome this difficulty?

   _____

   _____

Second Thoughts

Review the set of self-portraits that opened this chapter; then think about or discuss the following questions:

1. What do you think are the habits of an artist?

2. What is the artist's equivalent of a journal?

3. How do you think this artist might organize his different sketches, drawings, and paintings?

4. How do you think this artist might make use of technology?

Based on what you have learned in this chapter about the art of writing, what new insights do you have about these self-portraits of a visual artist? Write your thoughts in the *Responses* section of your journal.

4. Describe the functions of each of these for you as a writer:

   journal _____

   writing folder _____

   computer _____

5. Name one situation in your life outside of school where you write for yourself, and one situation where you are required to write.

   _____

   _____

6. As you start this writing course, what is one new habit you will try to adopt, and why? Write this resolution in the *Habits for Life* section of your journal.

Write Now: Defining Yourself as a Writer

Review any writing you have done in your journal or have stored in your writing folder, for example, your responses to Write Now (1), (3), and (4). Also, review your responses to Write Now (10) and (11). Then write a letter to yourself. Describe the kind of writer you are today and the kind of writer you hope to be. State the writing goals you have set for yourself over the term of this course. Express your hopes. Encourage yourself. Seal the letter inside an envelope, put your name on the envelope, and turn it in to your instructor. The letter will be returned at the end of the course.

If you and your instructor are on networked computers or both connected to the Internet, you can e-mail your letter to the instructor.

Peaches and Prose:
Keeping a Journal

by David Mas Masumoto

Check out David
Masumoto's
home page at
www.masumoto.com.

With his parents, wife, and children, David Mas Masumoto operates a small peach orchard in the Central Valley of California. He also has written what one book reviewer calls "generally peachy books about his commitment to farming and family tradition." His book, Epitaph for a Peach, *tells the story of his journey away from farming and back again. In a later book,* Harvest Son, *Masumoto explores the history of his Japanese-American parents and grandparents.*

    When Masumoto was asked to contribute to a book about journals, he created his submission in the form of a journal itself. (The book is called The Writer's Journal: 40 Contemporary American Writers and Their Journals.*) As you read the following excerpts, take note of the many reasons he gives for keeping journals. Also, consider how Masumoto divides (or multiplies) his energy between his work as a farmer and his work as a writer.*

What are the
purposes of
journal writing,
and what are
the dangers?

March 8

A journal about keeping a journal. This could be dangerous, venturing into the private world of a writer and exposing a vein. But isn't that what journals are all about? Another danger lies in analyzing journal writing—the writer becomes too self-conscious, overly critical and the words lose their freedom. For me, that's what keeping a journal is about: thinking freely.

    Because I farm, my field work is often woven into my journals. But do records on when the peaches first bloom or the grape shoots peek out at the spring sun or the early signs of worms in my peaches—do they belong in my journal?

    Yes and no. They are part of what makes a journal important—a documentation of where you were and what you felt at a specific time and place. But do worms and metaphors belong on the same page? I've written some of my best stories about worms—but I keep a different type of farm journal in addition to my writing journal. No one said I couldn't have more than one.

March 17

Journals capture my ideas, my emotions, the smell of
the mowed grasses, the taste of a wildflower lemon
stalk, the images from the farmhouse porch on a cool
spring morning. My farm journals do the same; they
record my feelings about a spring storm on peach
blossoms or the fear of invisible diseases growing on
my grapes.

Writing and farming share a common tie—
neither is done well by using formulas. Good stories
are not based on recipes, a juicy peach cannot be
grown by following "how to" books. Nor does
technology automatically improve my work. Riveting
characters and moving themes are not created by word
processors and new software; bigger machines and new chemicals
do not equate to better produce.

So I write and farm drawing from experiential knowledge. I need to
dirty my hands to write about farm work. I need to feel the tightening of
stomach muscles when a dark storm approaches in order to understand a
sense of helplessness as I bow before nature.

My journals take many forms. Some are scribbled notes I write while
on a tractor and then jam into a file folder. Later I'll pull out the pieces of
paper like leaves in a family album, each tells a story of a moment in time
and the emotions captured in the words and shaky handwriting. I keep
another journal of one-page entries with headings that sound like short
story titles. Some will grow into manuscripts such as a journal entry
entitled "Five Worms" that later became a story about the meaning of
finding worms in your peaches and my learning to live with nature.

My journals allow me to integrate my ideas with who I am. My
words are not removed from the real and everyday. And that is precisely
what I strive for in my stories.

April 8

I do not write in my journal every day, though I am disciplined enough
to write daily. On days where the words cease to flow or my thoughts
are jumbled, I can return to my journals. They help soothe and calm and
provide a forum to "think out" ideas and issues.

What does
Masumoto use
instead of
"formulas" to write
and farm?

My journals often do not make sense. I have a rule: there can be no wrongs in my journals. I misspell words frequently, use wrong verb tenses, create sentence fragments. I can check the facts later, I can verify quotes some other time. Some thoughts ramble, others remain disconnected and out of place, I enjoy nonlinear thinking, jumping from idea to idea without worrying about how they may be connected and coherent.

What's important is to get it out on paper, to commit feelings to words, to write and capture the creative spirit. I seek a freedom of expression, for no one will read these journals verbatim, my words are not intended for writing teachers or editors. No one will ever write in red ink "Who cares?" over my words. I care and that's all that matters.

Why does the April 25 journal entry have a different appearance?

April 25
Poetry and prose.
Some of my journal entries are written in the form of single-line entries.
I like to think of these as poetic prose.
Like good poetry,
the single-line format invites reflection.

Here's how it works.
I begin with a single word or phrase.
Then I brainstorm and am soon bulging with thoughts.
I need to get them out before I lose one.
That's when the ease and simplicity of a journal shines.
My writing resembles a random list of ideas.
Some stand independent of each other,
some are clearly connected,
but they all reflect how I think at the moment,
complete with the excitement of creative energy.

Later I'll add more details
Some ideas blossom into longer stories.
Others need to be clarified,
I bundle the thoughts into a package
that I can ponder when I'm out in the fields.
A few remain loners.
I'll wrestle with them
and try to figure out why they were even mentioned.

I seek to establish a series of connections,
thoughts that relate to each other
and give life to one another.
I search for those meaningful connections.

April 30

I often reread my old farm journals, retracing my footsteps over familiar ground while renewing past friendships. The passing of time contributes to a refreshing perspective—I no longer have high ownership of my words and ideas.

Why was I so preoccupied about summer pruning of peaches in '92? Did it really make a difference when I found some worms in my peaches? "Where I was" helps orient me to "where I am now." Journals date me because my memory too easily lies.

Future stories often begin in the passages of my farm journals. An old neighbor drops by and shares his invention for drying grapes into raisins. My nine-year-old daughter drives the tractor by herself—my little girl is now big and strong enough to push down the clutch—a modern-day rite of passage for farm kids. We fertilize a young orchard as a family working together, we all have our jobs as we nourish life for the future. Raw ideas for good stories, like an artist's sketches.

In my journals I show what once happened so I can later reread the passages and learn. The bad writing will reek terribly, I'll be amazed I even wrote such garbage. The good entries will ring with honesty and they will be fun to revisit.

May 21

Soon my journal-writing will become lean. Farm work takes center stage, 80 acres of vines and trees demand my attention. I am torn by the dilemma, to stay inside and write or to go outside and prepare for the harvest. A writer must do both, no? But like farming, my journals will be here for the next season and if I'm fortunate, for the season after that too.

Postscript: Every family needs a writer, a family journal writer. Who else can document and save family histories? Who else can pass on the voices and characters for the next generation? Stories honor the legacy of a family for an audience of the living and those not yet born.

What reasons does Masumoto give for rereading old journals?

What two things is Masumoto referring to when he says a writer must do "both"?

THINK AND RESPOND

1. What different identities does Masumoto have?

    _____

    _____

2. What "habits of a writer" does he have?

    _____

    _____

3. How does farming help Masumoto write?

    _____

    _____

4. How does writing help Masumoto farm?

    _____

    _____

5. What do you think might be Masumoto's goals as a writer?

    _____

    _____

6. Provide **synonyms** (words or phrases with essentially the same meaning) or definitions for these words from Masumoto's journal, and add at least two of the words to the *Words Worth Remembering* section of your journal:

    riveting _____

    experiential _____

    integrate _____

    verify _____

    nonlinear _____

    verbatim _____

rite of passage _____

reek _____

lean _____

legacy _____

7. If you liked this reading, make a record of it in the *Readings Worth Remembering* section of your journal.

COMPARING VIEWS

Masumoto says, "I need to dirty my hands to write about farm work." What does he mean by this? In what ways does experience affect writing, and vice versa? What work do *you* do that might find its way into your writing? How can the writing *you* do assist you in your work and other life experiences? After discussing this topic with others, continue to explore it on your own, in your journal—if it interests you. You may be able to use material from the discussion and your journal in a future writing activity.

APPLIED WRITING

Write a journal entry in the style of Masumoto's April 25 entry. Do you agree that "the single-line format invites reflection"?

Summer Hats
Brenda Joysmith

CHAPTER 2

Recognizing Effective Writing

These are the **key ideas** of this chapter:

- Talking and writing draw on many of the same skills, though there are key differences between these two forms of communication.

- Effective writing is writing that succeeds in its purpose.

- Effective writing has these characteristics: a main idea, a logical organization, and an appropriate presentation.

Picturing Meaning

Examine the picture on the opposite page; then think about or discuss these questions:

1. What do you see the women doing in this picture?

   _____

   _____

2. What do you think they might be talking about?

   _____

   _____

3. Besides using words, how are these women communicating?

   _____

   _____

   In the *Responses* section of your journal, write down your thoughts about this picture.

Write Now (1)

What kind of a talker are you? Write a description of your voice, your mannerisms, and your style. Keep this work because you may use it in a later activity.

Writing versus Talking

Many writers get words on the page by imagining that they are talking to someone. This can be an effective device for getting started because most people are comfortable conversing. It also works because conversing and writing draw upon many of the same skills. Good talkers, for example, do not ramble on and on. They talk with purpose. Good talkers entertain their listeners through the colorful and descriptive words they use and the creative, yet skillful, ways they put ideas together. Good talkers adjust their language choices and presentation styles to the others in the conversation. They also pay attention to the reactions of their listeners to make sure they are being understood. Writers are most successful when they follow these same principles: writing for a purpose, making use of interesting words and phrases, and keeping focused on their audience.

Yet in important ways, writing is different from conversing. To write effectively, you must be sensitive to these differences. Here are some of them:

- When you talk, you build a conversation with others. When you write, you work alone. Others may give you assistance beforehand or afterward, and others may read your words later. However, in the act of writing it is only you. No one else is present inside your head to help you develop your ideas, to contribute thoughts, to contradict you, or to interrupt with questions.

- When you talk, you use your voice, your hands, your facial expressions, and your whole body to help get meaning across. When you write, meaning is carried only by the words you choose and the medium in which they appear (the paper or the computer screen, for example).

- When you talk, you can watch the faces of your listeners to see how they are reacting. Based on their responses, you can modify your presentation. When you write, you have to make assumptions in advance about how your audience will respond.

- When you talk, you draft as you go along. You can correct yourself or start over with such phrases as "what I want to say is" or "in other words" or "no, that's not what I mean—what I mean is this." When you write, readers become impatient if you repeatedly correct yourself. People want to read a finished, well constructed version of your thoughts.

- When you talk, the workings of your brain are obvious to others. When you write, you can present a much more intelligent and articulate self than you are at any one moment. This is because your writing reflects the thinking you have done over time as you worked and reworked your words. It also reflects the wisdom of others who advised you while writing.

- Finally, when you talk you do not have to put in as much effort as when you write. This is because it is harder for listeners to escape a conversation than for readers to abandon a piece of writing. Therefore when you write, you have to be twice as interesting and twice as clear.

Write Now (2)

Where the circles overlap below, list characteristics common to conversation and writing. In the nonoverlapping sections of each circle, list characteristics that are unique to conversation or writing, respectively. Use the points listed above and your own ideas. Examples have been provided.

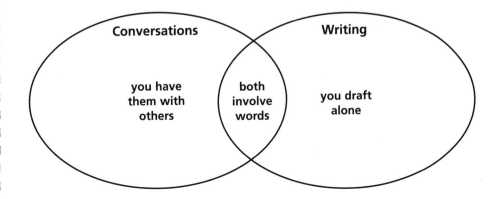

Conversations — you have them with others

both involve words

Writing — you draft alone

Write Now (3)

Move into pairs. Hold out a coin or a dollar bill. For three to four minutes, discuss with your partner what it looks like. Then hold out another coin or bill. This time, working independently, take three to four minutes to write a description of it. Exchange descriptions with your partner to read. As a class, discuss how the two forms of communicating were alike or different.

Writing with a Purpose and for an Audience

According to the dictionary, "effective" means "adequate to accomplish a purpose." A **purpose** is what you intend to make happen. Effective writing, therefore, is writing that realizes your intentions. For example, if you send a get-well note to someone in the hospital and it gives them a moment of cheer, then your writing is effective because it accomplished its purpose. If you write a memo to your supervisor explaining why you should be upgraded to a new position and you receive the upgrade, then your writing is effective because it accomplished its purpose.

When you write, you may have more than one purpose. For example, you may have a writing assignment at school for which the purpose is to summarize the results of an experiment. You also may complete the assignment for the purpose of getting a passing grade in the class, or you may use the assignment as an opportunity to explore an interesting topic. In any event, you should have at least one purpose for each piece of writing, and you should keep that purpose in mind as you write.

If you know your purpose, then you should know what sorts of people will be reading your work. Picturing one of those persons as you write can help you write effectively. Here are one writer's thoughts on why imagining the reader is useful:

Once I was playing the piano and a musician, overhearing it, said to me: "It isn't *going* anywhere. You must always play to *someone*—it may be to the river, or God, or to someone who is dead, or to someone in the room, but it must go somewhere."

This is why it helps often, to have an imaginary listener when you are writing, telling a story, so that you will be interesting and convincing throughout. You know how a listener helps to shape and create the story. Say that you are telling a story to children. You instinctively tell it, change it, adapt it, cut it, expand it, all under their large, listening eyes, so that they will be arrested and held by it throughout.

Do that when writing. You have to hold your audience in writing to the very end—much more than in talking, when people have to be polite and listen to you.

If You Want to Write
Brenda Ueland

Write Now (4)

Work in small groups to identify a possible purpose for each written work listed below. Then state possible results when the written work has been done effectively or ineffectively. An example has been provided.

Written Work	Purpose	Effective	Ineffective
1. *a horror story*	*to entertain a reader*	*the reader is thrilled and chilled*	*the reader tosses it aside without finishing*
2. a classified ad to sell an antique bedroom set			
3. a repair manual for Ford Mustangs			
4. a journal entry			
5. a grocery shopping list			
6. a letter of complaint to an airline			
7. a magazine article about a hot new band			
8. a fan letter to an actor			
9. a research paper for a history class			
10. a Web page for a home business			

Write Now (5)

Pick three of the works mentioned in Write Now (4). Then describe a possible reader. An example has been provided.

Type of Writing
Example: *a horror story*

Description of a Possible Reader
Someone who likes to stay up late at night—likes to be scared—does not mind lots of "blood and guts"—average reading ability—appreciates a good plot—me, for example

1. _____   _____

                                _____

                                _____

                                _____

2. _____   _____

                                _____

                                _____

                                _____

3. _____   _____

                                _____

                                _____

                                _____

Written versus Spoken English

To write effectively, you must choose your language according to your audience. Should you use street language for the eulogy at a funeral service? Profane language for a business memo? Academic language for hip-hop song lyrics? Remembering your purpose and imagining your readers as you write can help you make an appropriate choice.

Many word processing programs allow you to specify British, American, Australian, or Canadian English (and also such options as "formal," "standard," and "casual") for spell-checking and grammar checking functions. If you want to change these specifications, look under the "preferences" menu.

Standard Written English (SWE) is usually the best choice for academic or work-related writing. It is the variety of the English language that is taught for writing in English-language school systems and that is universally accepted and understood by educated people.

Everyone who speaks English has a **dialect**—a particular vocabulary, pronunciation style, and grammar structure shared with others from the same community. If you write in SWE, you can communicate effectively with all other speakers of English who know the rules of SWE, even the ones who do not share your spoken dialect. Using SWE does not mean that you have to "give up" your voice. It means that your original, authentic voice will be understood by the entire community of readers of English.

It is important to remember that no one speaks in perfect SWE. Even television news broadcasters who speak in a standard form of English slur words, drop endings, and use grammatical constructions that do not conform to SWE. It is also important to remember that all languages change over time, including SWE. Some of the forces influencing SWE today are the rising power of different ethnic groups in English-speaking countries, the rule-breaking use of language in advertising, and the rapid style of writing that occurs on the Internet.

SWE is the form of English used in and taught by this textbook. Once you know the rules of SWE, you can decide when to use it and when to break the rules. You can make that choice based on your audience and purpose for writing.

Write Now (6)

As a group, make a list of the communities where class members were raised (mark them on a map if your classroom has one). Discuss the differences in the spoken English of these communities. Collect samples of sentences as they would be spoken in the dialect of these different communities. "Translate" each sample into SWE. Two examples have been done for you.

Community	Sentence in Dialect	Sentence in SWE
Upper Midwest U.S.	How come she's cryin?	Why is she crying?
Suburban Maryland	I got the tickets.	I have the tickets.

Characteristics of Effective Writing

Three characteristics of effective writing are:

1. A **main idea**.

2. A logical organization.

3. An appropriate presentation.

A main idea. You should write so that readers can see what your point is, and this point is your main idea. It is sometimes called a **theme.** It is called a **thesis** if the main idea is an opinion or claim that you are making.

A logical organization. Writing that has a logical organization starts with an attention-grabbing opening that states the main idea. All other ideas contribute to and build upon this main idea. Each idea is supported and then connected to the next idea in a pattern that makes sense. Details needed to flesh out the main idea are included, and details that do not contribute are left out. A logically organized piece of writing ends with a conclusion that reasserts the main idea but in a fresh, powerful way.

An appropriate presentation. Well presented writing contains a minimum of errors. The length fits the purpose. So do the choice of language (as discussed in the previous section) and the style (such as humorous or serious). Formatting details (how the writing is presented on the page) also match the purpose.

Consider these points against what is by all measures a piece of effective writing: the *Gettysburg Address* of United States President Abraham Lincoln. Lincoln gave this speech in November 1863 at the dedication ceremony for a cemetery established on a Civil War battleground. The war would rage for another year and a half, but this great speech of just over 250 words helped sustain the country's morale. To this day it is often quoted:

Four score and seven years ago our fathers brought forth on this continent, a new nation, conceived in Liberty, and dedicated to the proposition that all men are created equal.

Now we are engaged in a great civil war, testing whether that nation, or any nation so conceived and so dedicated, can long endure. We are met on a great battle-field of that war. We have come to dedicate a portion of that field, as a final resting place for those who here gave their lives that that nation might live. It is altogether fitting and proper that we should do this.

But, in a larger sense, we can not dedicate—we can not consecrate—we can not hallow—this ground. The brave men, living and dead, who struggled here, have consecrated it, far above our poor power to add or detract. The world will little note, nor long remember what we say here, but it can never forget what they did here. It is for us the living, rather, to be dedicated here to the unfinished work which they who fought here have thus far so nobly advanced. It is rather for us to be here dedicated to the great task remaining before us—that from these honored dead we take increased devotion to that cause for which they gave the last full measure of devotion—that we here highly resolve that these dead shall not have died in vain—that this nation, under God, shall have a new birth of freedom—and that government of the people, by the people, for the people, shall not perish from the earth.

Lincoln's speech is effective for these three reasons:

1. He presents a clear *main idea,* which is: We dedicate this cemetery by dedicating ourselves to the continuing battle.

2. He *logically organizes* his speech: First, Lincoln speaks of the past (the birth of the nation), then he speaks of the present (the war that may destroy the nation), and finally he speaks of the future (the resolution of the war that may bring forth a new, greater nation). The first two paragraphs reveal his purpose: to dedicate the battlefield-turned-cemetery. The last paragraph twists this idea around: Lincoln says the soldiers themselves already dedicated the field; therefore, those who survive must instead dedicate themselves to the war. His concluding sentence restates, in four increasingly powerful ways, why citizens should continue the war effort.

3. He uses an *appropriate presentation:* Lincoln uses solemn, formal language that matches the seriousness of the occasion. The speech is modest and short, in line with his stated belief (in the third sentence of the last paragraph) that actions are more important than words.

Write Now (7)

Listen to Lincoln's speech read aloud. (You, the instructor, or a classmate will need to volunteer for this task.) Underline one phrase, sentence, or section of the speech that you find especially effective. Explain why you find it effective:

_____

_____

_____

Share your opinion with the rest of the class.

The Effective Essay

Lincoln's speech at Gettysburg is an **essay**, presented in spoken form. Because you are in a writing class, you will soon be called upon to write essays. An essay is a composition on a theme or subject. Essays take many forms. They can be short or long. They can be formal or informal. They can describe, inform, or persuade. They can explore an idea. They can simply entertain. They can be on any topic, trivial or significant. Today you find essays in many places. Opinion columns in newspapers or magazines are essays. Commentaries on the radio are essays. Web pages are stocked with essays. Advertisements often contain essays. A letter, unless it is just a series of anecdotes, is an essay.

A writer who specializes in the essay describes what happens when an essay is effective:

[The essay] co-opts agreement; it courts agreement; it seduces agreement. For the brief hour we give to it, we are sure to fall into surrender and conviction. And this will occur even if we are intrinsically roused to resistance.

The Best American Essays 1998
Cynthia Ozick

A well written essay persuades its audience to see things the way the writer sees things. Whether you are a student composing an answer to a test, a consumer writing a letter to the editor, or a President addressing war-weary citizens, your purpose is to sway the audience to your point of view.

Subsequent chapters of this book go into more detail about how to write essays and the various strategies you can use to write them effectively. However, if you can speak a language, you already know a lot about communicating. You already know much of what you need to know to write effectively. The rest is details.

Write Now (8)

Practice writing an essay by composing one in the form of a letter of advice or opinion to the President of the United States. Keep the President in mind as you write. Also keep the letter focused on your main idea: one piece of advice or one opinion. Organize the contents of the letter to support and build on this main idea. Decide on an appropriate presentation for submitting a letter to the President. Create a final copy of the letter. (Although you may have to share this letter with your instructor, you are not obliged to send it to the President.)

Summing Up

1. Name one important way that writing is like talking, and one important way that the two are different.

   _____

   _____

2. What are the two key things to remember in order to write effectively?

   _____

   _____

3. Consider the characteristics of effective writing: a main idea, a logical organization, and an appropriate presentation. Underline the characteristic that is usually easiest for you to achieve in your writing. What makes this easy for you to do?

   _____

   _____

Second Thoughts

Review the illustration that opened this chapter; then think about or discuss the following questions:

1. Of the people you know, which ones are good conversationalists?

2. What makes them good talkers?

3. What form of English (or other language) do they speak?

4. As far as you know, are they also effective writers? Why or why not?

   Based on what you have learned in this chapter about effective communication, what new thoughts do you have about the people in this picture? Write your reaction in the *Responses* section of your journal.

4. Circle the characteristic that presents the greatest challenge to you. What is one thing you can do to make your writing better in this regard?

   _____

   _____

5. Name one situation outside of school where it is appropriate for you to use your community dialect and one situation where it would be more appropriate to use Standard Written English.

   _____

   _____

6. As a result of completing this chapter, what is one change you will make to become a more effective writer? Write your resolution in the *Habits for Life* section of your journal.

Write Now: Describing an Effective Communicator

Write a description of a good conversationalist. You may want to make use of the writing you did in Write Now (1) or the responses you had to the chapter's opening illustration. The readers of your description will be your instructor and classmates: keep them in mind as you write. Focus on a main idea, such as one conversation you remember, one characteristic that stands out, or one impression that person made on you. Organize the rest of your description to support and build on this main idea. Write the description in Standard Written English, although if you quote your subject you may want to use his/her particular dialect for the quotations.

The Soul of the Game
Images and Voices of Street Basketball

by Pee Wee Kirkland

Richard "PeeWee" Kirkland is a hoops legend from the Harlem neighborhood of New York City. He now coaches youth basketball at a school in Manhattan, teaches the philosophy of basketball coaching at Long Island University, and runs the School of SkillZ, a children's basketball camp.

The following essay comes from an oversized book filled with rap, hip-hop poetry, interviews, and gorgeously produced black-and-white photographs, all about the players and playgrounds of street basketball. In his essay Kirkland communicates his passion for the game by comparing it to professional basketball and by describing the action.

Kirkland wrote for an audience he assumed would be familiar with his topic. However, you don't have to know or even care much about the sport to be swayed by his enthusiasm. As you read this essay, imagine it is Kirkland talking to you on the sidelines of a game.

What does Kirkland say is being invented today and by whom?

The best things you see in pro ball today were invented 25 years ago in the schoolyards of Harlem. And that's still where it's done best.

All the best moves of tomorrow are being invented today by some unknown kid in Philly, Chicago, Atlanta or you name it. Razzle and dazzle, creation and devastation—these are what the street brings to the game. When a player does a sandlot move in a pro game situation, you know he's for real, not the other way around. It's on the street that players earn their places in the hearts of the people. Where Earl Monroe became Black Jesus. Where Joe Hammond became the Destroyer.

What does Kirkland say happens when you see a legend?

I've seen the game played on playgrounds in ways I'll never forget. In ways that took my mind somewhere it had never been before. On the playground, legends are born, and you'll never forget what you see a legend do because you will never see anybody repeat it in quite the same way.

A finger roll by Connie Hawkins after he floats in from the foul line?

How about Jackie Jackson, New York's greatest leaper? This man had incredible springs. His hang time was unbelievable—don't check your watch, check your beeper. Imagine yourself trying to score points when you're laying up against a human astronaut. How're you not going to get your shot blocked? I remember first seeing him play at 129th Street and Seventh Avenue. I was a high school freshman, watching through the fence. He was playing on his Brooklyn team with Connie Hawkins against Wilt Chamberlain, the 7-foot-1 Big Dipper, whom many consider the best big man ever to play the game. Wilt was shooting hooks that day. And Jackie would go up with him and block them. Not just block them, but catch them in midair. Jackie cuffed the ball under his arm and took it away. The impact and intensity from the crowd—you wouldn't believe it.

After the game was over, the crowd wouldn't leave. People started shouting, "Take it off the top, Jackie! Take it off the top!" I had no idea what they were talking about. Somebody brought out a ladder and put a 50-cent piece on top of the backboard. And Jackie jumped into the air and took the coin down. It shocked me. Here was a man who would spend 13 years with the Harlem Globetrotters and never play a minute in the NBA.

I guess that's what being a legend is: creating an indelible, lifelong impression in the minds of the crowd, like Jackie did to me. Excelling as a professional basketball player, even being in the Hall of Fame, don't make you a street legend. The difference is that a guy on the street will not be considered a legend unless he has something about his game that's phenomenal. If he's a scorer, that means he cannot be stopped. If he's a jump shooter, he has to shoot 90 percent under pressure. If he can trick people, then that means he gotta have a bag of tricks, like St. Nick. If he's a rebounder, then he can't win and have thin skin. He gotta be tough.

When you see a guy playing in the NBA, everybody knows it's sort of restricted. A guy may come down the court, put the ball behind his back and pass, and everybody goes crazy. That's not acceptable in street basketball. When a guy come down the court, he has to go behind his back twice, flip it through his legs and throw a blind pass for an alley-oop yoke. Then the crowd is in an uproar.

What things did Jackie Jackson do that were so legendary?

How does Kirkland define "legend"?

What is the significance of the Rucker Pro Tournament?

In my days, the Rucker Pro Tournament in Harlem was the proving ground. I played at Rucker against teams with two or three NBA players. I played against some of the all-time greats, Wilt, Pearl, Julius. The pros played in the NBA for salary; they played in Rucker to prove they were for real. You could talk about it all year long, but it didn't mean anything until you had done it at Rucker. The streets were crowded for five blocks. People would watch from the highway overpass; people would hang from trees. Some would use binoculars to watch from the projects.

In the fourth quarter, when we was putting that showtime down so heavy, the crowd would be sitting in the stands trying to avoid going to the bathroom. Addicts be sittin' there, forget they had habits. When the game was over, people didn't know where they parked their cars. And the most amazing thing was, there were no police. There were never any problems, because people had too much respect for the game.

That's the legacy of the playground, where heart, hustle and pride rule the day. For some it's a place of refuge. For others, a place of challenge. For all, a place of hope. To the sports world, basketball is a multimillion-dollar business. To the kid on the street, it means a lot more. It's his or her identity. It's his or her reputation and, in too many cases, the final determination of his or her future.

What is the one basketball statistic Kirkland says is not kept?

The game of basketball is more loved today than ever. Courtside seats cost thousands of dollars. We have all-defensive teams, the top 50 players ever; every kind of statistic is kept, every outstanding accomplishment recorded. Except one: where the game came from, the playground. The real school of skillZ, where every crossover, head fake, three-sixty and reverse crossover is practiced. Where talents are first noticed and success first achieved. It's the arena of goodwill, where the game is played from the heart and the love is there from the start.

THINK AND RESPOND

1. In what way is this essay like or not like a conversation?

   _____

   _____

2. What are three assumptions Kirkland makes about his audience?

   _____

   _____

3. What is Kirkland's main idea?

   _____

   _____

4. How does Kirkland organize his essay to support this main idea?

   _____

   _____

5. Kirkland's essay is written primarily in Standard Written English, with occasional use of dialect. Why do you think he chose this presentation style?

   _____

   _____

6. Provide synonyms or definitions for these words from the essay, and add at least two of the words to the *Words Worth Remembering* section of your journal:

   devastation _____

   legend _____

   hang time _____

   cuffed _____

   indelible _____

phenomenal _____

rebounder _____

hustle _____

refuge _____

arena _____

7. If you liked this reading, make a record of it in the *Readings Worth Remembering* section of your journal.

COMPARING VIEWS

How does Pee Wee Kirkland's description of street basketball remind you of pick-up games (in basketball or any other sport) that you have watched or played in yourself? What were the rules of play? Who were the greats of the game, and what made them so? What was it like as a spectator? After discussing this topic with others, continue to explore it on your own, in your journal—if it interests you. You may be able to use material from the discussion and your journal in a future writing activity.

APPLIED WRITING

Pee Wee Kirkland wrote his essay as a tribute to an under-appreciated sport. What else do you think is under-appreciated? It might be a sport or it might be a person, an organization, a thing of nature, or something else entirely. Write a tribute to it. As Kirkland did, decide on one main idea, then develop details and examples in support of this main idea. Develop a logical organization for your idea. Make the presentation appropriate for your purpose, which is to convince your instructor and classmates to have a greater appreciation for your subject.

Underground
Harvey Dinnerstein

CHAPTER 3

How Writing Happens

These are the **key ideas** of this chapter:

- Writing is a series of actions—a process.

- The process of writing is similar to the process that underlies almost everything you do.

- By being conscious of the writing process, you can become a more effective writer.

Picturing Meaning

Examine the picture on the opposite page; then think about or discuss these questions:

1. What are the different individuals doing in this picture?

   _____

   _____

2. What do you think each individual might have been doing before this moment?

   _____

   _____

3. What do you think each individual might do next?

   _____

   _____

   In the *Responses* section of your journal, write down your thoughts about this picture.

Write Now (1)

What do *you* do when you have to wait? How do you spend your time in subways, elevators, lines, and waiting rooms? Write down your responses to these questions. Keep this work because you may use it in a later activity.

Writing as a Process

A writing task can often seem overwhelming. It helps, however, to recognize that writing is a process: it involves a series of actions. Looking at your work this way, you can break it into smaller steps. As you accomplish each step, the next one actually becomes easier. You are able to do the work, and do it well.

Most skills and activities that you do repeatedly involve a process. You may not always be conscious of the process, but it is there. This process is a series of learned behaviors. As an example, consider this description of golfing professional Tiger Woods's short putt (a putt is a gentle stroke of the ball to send it into the cup):

Once arriving on the green, Tiger stalks the putt, carefully analyzing the slopes from all angles to determine which way the ball will break. . . . Tiger and other top pros know only too well that it's not enough to be able to correctly judge the line of a putt. Like Johnny Miller, who was a great putter in his heyday, Tiger pays close attention to the grain, or the direction in which the blades of grass grow, since it affects the roll of the ball. . . .

Tiger's last look is from behind the ball, usually in the company of his caddie. Once they agree on the line, Tiger starts to swing his putter back and forth, sometimes with just his right hand, to get a feel for how hard to stroke the putt. Finally, he stares intently down the line, giving his confidence level a positive lift by envisioning the ball rolling toward the hole and dropping into the cup.

The Short Game Magic of Tiger Woods
John Andrisani

The preceding description only covers Woods's "preswing routine." His grip on the putter, his body positioning, and the stroke itself take up another eight pages. The putt may take only a few moments, but it involves a series of actions—a process. Writing, too, involves a process of planning, doing, and refining. You already are expert at many processes in life. With practice, you can become expert at the writing process, too.

Write Now (2)

1. **Think of something that you love to do. Write it here:**
   I love to _____
   Example: *I love to have guests over for meals.*

2. **Now list three things you do *before*, three things you do *during*, and three things you do *after* doing this thing that you love to do.**

   BEFORE • _____

   • _____

   • _____

   DURING • _____

   • _____

   • _____

   AFTER • _____

   • _____

   • _____

   Example: *(before) get groceries, clean, cook.*

3. **Pick one of the items you just wrote. Describe the action in greater detail:**

   • _____

   • _____

   • _____

   Example: *(cook) assemble casserole, put in oven, remember to take out of oven.*

Steps in the Writing Process

Writing is no different from making a short putt, entertaining guests, or any other activity in life. The difference is that with writing, the process leads to words on paper that you keep secret or publish for others to see. Thus, one might illustrate the process like this:

write ⟶ finish writing ⟶ share/don't share

This may be how you picture the writing process, if you think about it at all. But people who teach writing—and people who write—say it does not happen like this. They say the process is not so much like a straight line and not so simple, either. They say writing happens more like this:

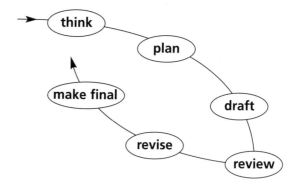

Think. In terms of the writing process, to think means getting your mind ready for writing. It also involves "working the brain" to determine your purpose for writing and to consider who your readers will be. In the initial thinking stage, you also explore ideas to find a topic.

Plan. To plan means to do formal thinking in your mind and on paper. When you plan, you develop ideas of what to say about your topic. You consider the research you must do and how you will do it. You also start to make decisions about how to organize and present your ideas.

Draft. To **draft** means to draw up in written form. This is the stage where you work with your purpose and your plan to shape your ideas into sentences and paragraphs. A draft is a work-in-progress. As you draft, you will find that some of your initial planning decisions work and some do not. You therefore may have to rethink, replan, and redraft until you have a working draft.

Review. To review is to read over your working draft with a critical eye. You do this for several reasons: to see if your writing makes sense; to decide if it says what you really want it to say; to make sure that the writing fulfills your purpose; to make sure that it is organized well; and to find errors. It helps to keep your readers in mind as you review, to get a sense of how they will receive it. At this stage you also may ask for feedback from others.

Revise. To **revise** is to make improvements to your working draft based on what you discovered in the review stage. When you revise, you make specific changes to meaning, structure, and style. Revising can be quite dramatic—practically a redrafting—or rather minor—just a few edits—depending on what you have determined is needed.

Make final. To make final means to prepare a clean, error-free version of the writing in a format that suits your purpose and audience. The completion of the writing process for one project often leads into the next. This is when you ask yourself questions such as:

- How successfully did I handle the writing process?

- What did I learn?

- What new ideas have come out of this effort?

As movie director Spike Lee says:

When I'm putting the finishing touches on one film,
I'm thinking about the next Spike Lee joint. . . . then wham,
presto, change-o! It's time to start writing again.

> *Do the Right Thing*
> (companion book to movie)

Write Now (3)

Working in pairs, think of synonyms to describe each stage of the writing process. An example for each has been provided.

Think   *chew over* _____

Plan   *strategize* _____

Draft   *type up* _____

Review   *look over* _____

Revise   *make changes* _____

Make final   *put in finished form* _____

Keep this work because you may use it in a later activity.

Writing as a Messy Process

Take another look at the model of the writing process:

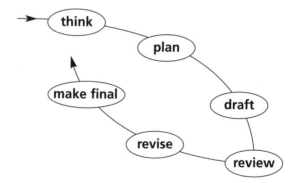

This model is still too simple to be an accurate picture of how you write. For example, sometimes you might review and revise over and over again:

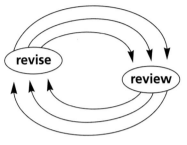

Your review stage might involve several people:

Sometimes you may skip steps altogether, such as when you are just dashing off a quick note to a friend:

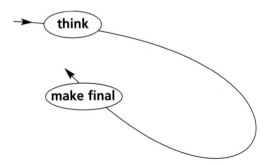

Sometimes your topic just does not work or your approach to the topic fails. In such instances, you have to set that draft aside and rethink your approach:

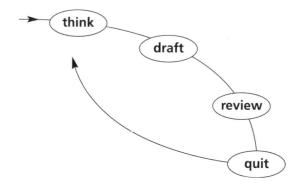

Making a final copy often involves a series of steps:

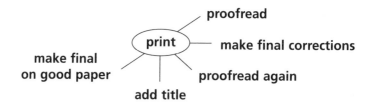

In many writing projects, certain stages of the writing process are revisited again and again:

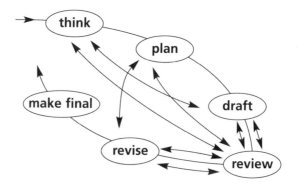

This model of the writing process is not an exact representation of the process that *you* use to write. Nor does it represent every writing task. Nonetheless, it can help you think about what you need to do to write effectively.

Being conscious of your writing process can improve your writing. Imagine that it is Monday and you have a writing assignment due Friday. Do you stay up until 4 a.m. Thursday night to write it? Perhaps. On the other hand, you could mull over topic ideas on Monday, sketch an outline on Tuesday, do the bulk of the drafting Wednesday, and finally revise and make a final copy on Thursday. You may not put in any more time on the assignment than if you pulled an all-nighter, but you probably will turn out a better product.

Write Now (4)

Think about a recent work of writing you have done—for this class, on the job, or elsewhere. Then move into pairs. Describe the process you went through to write and, with your partner's help, sketch it using the diagrams above as models. Your partner should also describe a recent writing project and, with your help, sketch the process. Share your sketches with the class. Keep this work because you may use it in a later activity.

Computers are a great tool when writing because they make it so much easier, *physically,* to move back and forth between the different stages of the writing process. It is also easier to be objective about your work (and the work of others) when looking at typed-up copy instead of a handwritten manuscript.

Write Now (5)

Being conscious of the writing process, create a short statement expressing your philosophy of life. As a starting place, consider your responses to Write Now (1) and (2) and other writings in your journal. Proceed as follows:

Think: Consider these questions: What do you believe in? How do these beliefs affect your conduct? How have they influenced the direction of your life? How can you express your beliefs in just a few words? What thoughts are you willing to share with your instructor and classmates (your audience)?

Plan: Consider various ways to summarize and present your philosophy. Possible ideas include: making a list of "rules for living," quoting famous sayings, or relating an anecdote that reflects your philosophy.

Draft: Choose the words to express your philosophy of life. Work at this until you have created a statement expressing your ideas clearly and specifically.

Review: Wait a day or more before reviewing your draft. Does it say what you think? Show your draft to others for their comments.

Revise: Use the input from the review stage to make changes.

Make final: Decide how to present your statement. Possible ideas include: creating the statement as a poster, including an illustration, or hand writing it using calligraphy.

Keep this work because you may use it in a later activity.

A Poet Talks about the Writing Process

The concept of a writing process becomes less abstract when you hear how other writers actually experience it. An editor once sent letters to more than a hundred poets asking them how they came to write a particular poem. She made a book out of the replies from fifty of them. One of those poets was Phil Hey, who had written a poem called "Old Men Working in Concrete." Here is how Hey responded to the question, "How did the poem start?"

I hadn't written in a long time, and despaired of ever writing again. But the concern at the moment was not writing. My friend Bill needed help with his garage floor. He'd had a heart attack, so his friends helped out: George, Al, and me (the only one under sixty). All retired but me; all working with their hands all life long, but me. We did it, we finished more than Bill hoped we would. He was proud of the floor, deeply moved by friends happy to do so much for him. So was I. So the poem was not begun, in a sense: it was there complete in the experience, needing not so much invention as transcription.

Here is how he answered a second question, "What changes did it go through from start to finish?"

The poem did not write itself. It demanded a kind of faithfulness to the experience, a sense of working in language somehow like the sense of working with concrete. Only enough to make it firm and level; unspectacular: strong, without decoration. From first word to completion, perhaps twenty lines of description were eliminated; the poem ended up less colorful and less narrative than when it began (which was by a rapid dumping onto the page of all associative materials, images, names, etc., roughly in the order in which they had been noticed).

"Phil Hey"
Fifty Contemporary Poets:
The Creative Process
Alberta T. Turner, ed.

Here is the poem:

Old Men Working Concrete

won't be rushed; will take
their own sweet time.
Now and then, will stop
for snuff (reaching in
the pocket where the circle
of can has worn a circle
in the cloth); and then
get back to work, mix mud
and fill and walk that barrow
back and back and back.
Soon enough the slab end
takes shape. The one man
on his knees with a float
checks it with his eye
stopping time and again
to run his striker saw-wise
and level across the top.
Soon enough it gets long;
smooth with broad swings
of trowel it gets long.
Finally they stop the mixer.
One trowels out the last space,
one works the edger.
Done, they stand back.
They look one more time.
It's good. Yes sir, it's good.
They talk. They dip snuff.
They are happy.

Phil Hey

Write Now (6)

Review Phil Hey's comments on writing "Old Men Working Concrete" and review the poem to answer the following questions:

1. What part can mood and experience play in getting started writing? _____

   _____

   _____

2. Hey says that he "transcribed" the experience to create his first draft. How does this compare to the way you draft? _____

   _____

   _____

3. Hey says he used the image of making concrete to help him revise his poem. How does this match the way you revise? _____

   _____

   _____

4. How do you think Hey knew when his poem was in final form?

   _____

   _____

Write Now (7)

Using the poem by Phil Hey as a starting point, write a brief statement responding to this saying: "You have to work hard to make something read easily." To gather ideas, think about successful examples of your own writing or the writings of authors you admire. As you write your statement, be sure to involve each step in the writing process: think, plan, draft, review, revise, and make final. Keep this work because you may use it in a later activity.

Summing Up

1. Consider once more the components of the writing process: think, plan, draft, review, revise, and make final. Underline the stage of the process you do best. What makes this stage easy for you?

   _____

   _____

2. Circle the stage you tend to skip over. What is one thing you can do to give more effort to this stage of the process?

   _____

   _____

3. Name one activity in life (not including writing) that you do so well or so easily that you do not have to think about the process involved.

   _____

   _____

Second Thoughts

Review the picture that opened this chapter; then think about or discuss the following questions:

1. How is a subway journey a process?

2. In what ways is the writing process like a journey?

3. How is the process like life itself?

   Based on what you have learned in this chapter about the writing process, what new thoughts do you have about the picture as a whole or about any individuals in the picture? Write your thoughts in the *Responses* section of your journal.

4. Name another activity (not including writing) in which you must carefully think through every step in order to do it right.

   _____

   _____

5. As a result of reading this chapter, what is one thing you will do differently to be more attentive to the process involved as you write? Write your resolution in the *Habits for Life* section of your journal.

Write Now: Personalizing the Writing Process

Create a personalized model of the writing process. Draw from the model of the writing process presented in this chapter as well as from the synonyms and sketches you created in Write Now (3) and (4) and the process you went through to complete Write Now (5) and (7). Make a final copy of this model as a small poster that you can paste into your journal or display where you do your writing.

Consider putting the personalized model of the writing process onto computer as your screen saver.

Weathering the Storms

by Stephon Gray

Stephon Gray is a person who is intrigued yet challenged by writing. Although he graduated from high school, he was such a poor writer that he attended community-based writing classes for several years to improve his skills. Eventually he had the confidence to try coursework at a community college.

Gray now works in the Literacy Resources Division of the public library in the District of Columbia. His job involves helping others with reading and writing difficulties find tutors, programs, and reading materials. For himself, Gray's biggest challenge remains writer's block: getting words on the page. He has continued, therefore, to work with a writing tutor. When the library sponsored an essay contest for adult learners, Gray decided to enter. The contest was in honor of Women's History Month, so the topic was: "Tell us about a woman (living or dead) you look up to or a woman who has been a role model for you." Gray's essay was selected as one of two winning entries. "Weathering the Storms" is reprinted below and is followed by an interview with Gray. As you read, consider how his writing skills, and the process he uses to write, compare with yours.

This here is to my role model who knows how to make things happen.

> **What exactly is Gray referring to when he says "this here"?**

I could have written about anyone from Rosa Parks, who refused to give up her seat on the bus and move to a seat in the back of the bus, to Althea Gibson, who fought so hard to play tennis.

But actually seeing and working with a person who believes in many of the same things that Rosa and Althea believe in is inspiring to me.

> **Who are Rosa Parks and Althea Gibson?**

This person works hard for humanity. She is out there fighting for many causes, such as literacy, people with AIDS, and women's issues.

Sometimes just watching her do all that she does amazes me. I wonder how she fits all of the things she cares about into her schedule.

She is my supervisor at work, and also my teacher. Her way of teaching is very fulfilling to me. It reminds me of a good meal my mother would give me, but instead of food, it's a big serving of math, science, geography, and reading. And I have to say, it's delicious.

> **What is delicious to Gray?**

So just having her as my teacher and supervisor gives me the inspiration to go out and make a difference.

This person is Marcia Harrington.

That's why I chose her as my role model—a woman who has the strength to weather the storms. So don't stop with those meals yet Marcia!

What does Gray mean by "weather the storms"?

Why did you decide to enter the essay contest?

It was an opportunity to do some writing. I wanted to write, to see if I had improved.

How did you get started?

First I had to read the topic over several times, to get me in the mood. I had to build my confidence. Once I did that, I did some reading. I wasn't sure who I should write about.

What did you read?

I read different short stories that we have here in our collection about women who have made a contribution to society. Once I did that, I thought about several people to write about. One in particular was the woman I wrote about. That motivated me to write.

Are you saying that once you fixed on your subject, you became excited about writing?

Yes, I wanted to show Marcia that I have come a long way. I wanted to show my appreciation for the work she has done and the time she took with me.

How long did the draft stage take?

Two weeks. I wrote several pages, and I didn't like it. It didn't fit. I wasn't expressing myself. After I read several pages that I didn't agree with, I removed parts that I liked and put them on a blank sheet of paper. From there I just worked with it, trying to put it together.

You say you wrote several pages with your first draft. Was that difficult?

Yes, I struggled with it. I had to convince myself that even though my writing is not going to be as good as I want it to be, I was going to write this anyway.

How many drafts did you go through?

It took awhile for me to get the ball rolling. I tore up about eight or ten sheets of paper. Then I had to get some help from a friend to tie it all together. I think that person probably tore it up once and had me bring it back. We worked on it together from there.

How did you know when you were done?

Getting the approval of someone else.

Did you agree with your friend that the piece was done?

Yes, slightly. The reason I say "slightly" is because I didn't want to believe that I am at a level where I can write something and have someone else read it and say it was okay.

When your essay won the prize, how did you react?

I was more thrilled about the whole process of writing. The prize to me was just writing it on the paper. I kind of enjoyed that.

How has writing that essay affected you?

It was a big help. It let me know that people liked my idea and that I can write, I can do this, this is not something I can't obtain. I'm still struggling with myself, trying to convince myself that I can write. Because for so long—if you tell yourself that you can't do something, you begin to believe it. So now I've got to convince myself, saying that I can write, or I can enjoy writing. It's another process I have to go through.

THINK AND RESPOND

1. What do you think are the strengths or weaknesses of Gray's essay?

   _____

   _____

2. How did the process Gray used to write his essay compare to this model of the writing process: think, plan, draft, review, revise, and make final?

   _____

   _____

3. Gray indicates that he lacks confidence as a writer. How can an awareness of the writing process help writers like him gain confidence?

   _____

   _____

4. Provide synonyms or definitions for these words from the essay, and add at least one of the words to the *Words Worth Remembering* section of your journal:

   role model _____

   humanity _____

   literacy _____

   supervisor _____

   motivate _____

5. If you liked this reading, make a record of it in the *Readings Worth Remembering* section of your journal.

COMPARING VIEWS

Gray says that he still has to go through "the process" of convincing himself that he can enjoy writing. Why do some people naturally like to write, while others find it so painful? By what process can Gray and others like him discover pleasure in writing? After discussing this topic with others, continue to explore it on your own, in your journal—if it is important to you. You may be able to use material from the discussion and your journal in a future writing activity.

APPLIED WRITING

Gray begins his essay like a salute or a drinking toast: "This here is to . . ." Who has been an important influence in your life? Write a salute to that person. Think of all the people you know and focus on one who has made a difference in your life. Gray compared his supervisor's help to a "good meal." As you plan your essay, try to include a similar imaginative comparison as well as specific examples of significant things this person has done. Draft the essay and then set it aside for an hour or more. Review it, revise it, and show it to someone you trust for another review. When you are satisfied that the essay fulfills your purpose, prepare a final error-free copy. Use your personalized model of the writing process to guide you in this project.

UNIT 2

GETTING INSIDE THE WRITING PROCESS

This unit explores in greater detail the different activities involved in writing: thinking, planning, drafting, reviewing, revising, and making final. Goals of the unit are to help you:

- Familiarize yourself with a variety of planning and outlining strategies.

- Understand the function and form of paragraphs.

- Learn about essay structure.

- Create coherence and unity when drafting through careful word selection, sentence construction, and paragraph development.

- Begin reviewing and applying grammar principles.

- Recognize the importance of the revision stage.

- Learn how to evaluate your own and others' works.

Activities in this unit will build toward the development of completed essays.

Haverstraw, New York
Lee Friedlander
Courtesy Fraenkel Gallery, San Francisco

CHAPTER 4

Thinking and Planning Creatively

These are the **key ideas** of this chapter:

- Starting to write involves getting your mind ready and thinking through ideas.

- Writers use many different strategies to think through and plan a piece of writing.

- By using these strategies, you will find it easier to begin writing.

Picturing Meaning

Examine the photograph on the opposite page; then think about or discuss these questions:

1. What do you see the person doing in this photograph?

   _____

   _____

2. What might he be thinking?

   _____

   _____

3. Why is the car a good place to think?

   _____

   _____

   In the *Responses* section of your journal, write down your thoughts about this photograph.

Write Now (1)

Where do *you* do your best thinking? Is it behind the wheel of a car, in the shower, or while on a walk with your dog? Write a description of this place and explain how it helps you think. Keep this work because you may use it in another activity.

Getting in the Mood to Write

It is far easier to do something you want to do than something you do *not* want to do. It follows, then, that to write well you need to be in a mood to write.

Sometimes you will be in the proper mood for writing when you need to be. Other times you must create the proper mood. Experienced writers have discovered many different ways to prepare their minds for writing. You can borrow from them or you can invent your own methods.

One way that many writers put themselves in the mood to write is by giving their bodies a workout first. A brisk walk, a run, or some stretching exercises relax the muscles so that you are able to sit calmly to write. Movement also gets the blood flowing through your brain to clear and energize the mind.

Another way that writers put themselves in a writing mood is by beginning each effort with a **writing ritual.** Many writers begin with a prayer or meditation, with several deep breaths, or by reading a favorite author. Jack Kerouac would light a candle when starting to write and blow it out when finished. Julia Alvarez places a bowl of water on her desk each morning. In her essay collection *Something to Declare,* she explains that she does this to "contain my dread and affirm my joy and celebrate the mystery and excitement of the calling to be a writer."

Write Now (2)

What can you do to put yourself in the mood to write? In small groups, make a list of ideas for writing rituals. Share them with the class. Jot down some of the best ideas. Then try one next time you begin to write.

Rituals to try for getting in the mood to write:

* _____

  _____

* _____

  _____

* _____

  _____

Getting Ready to Write by Freewriting

Many experienced writers do not sit down and immediately jump into their primary writing project. Instead, they start with a warm-up exercise: they write without any purpose in mind. This is called **random freewriting.** It simply means to write freely on anything at all—the kind of writing you may like to do in your journal.

Random freewriting allows you to limber up your writing muscles and to begin tapping into the creative side of your mind. It allows you to begin writing without worrying about quality. Because it is like writing without trying, freewriting can get you started even if you are feeling listless and dull.

Peter Elbow, one of the foremost instructors of the freewriting process, explains it this way:

If you freewrite using word processing, create a file named "freewriting" that you store in your Writing Folder. Add to it each time you freewrite, so that all of your freewriting is in one place to scroll through when searching for writing ideas. If you find good ideas, copy and paste them into a new file to work on them. If you prefer not to look back at old freewrites, just open a new file to freewrite and close it without saving when you are done.

Freewriting is the easiest way to get words on paper and the best all-around practice in writing that I know. To do a freewriting exercise, simply force yourself to write without stopping for ten minutes. Sometimes you will produce good writing, but that's not the goal. Sometimes you will produce garbage, but that's not the goal either. You may stay on one topic, you may flip repeatedly from one to another: it doesn't matter. Sometimes you will produce a good record of your stream of consciousness, but often you can't keep up. Speed is not the goal, though sometimes the process revs you up. If you can't think of anything to write, write about how that feels or repeat over and over, "I have nothing to write" or "Nonsense" or "No." If you get stuck in the middle of a sentence or thought, just repeat the last word or phrase till something comes along. The only point is to keep writing.

Or rather, that's the first point. For there are lots of goals of freewriting, but they are best served if, while you are doing it, you accept this single, simple, mechanical goal of simply not stopping. When you produce an exciting piece of writing, it doesn't mean you did it better than the time before when you wrote one sentence over and over for ten minutes. Both times you freewrote perfectly. The goal of freewriting is in the process, not the product.

Writing with Power: Techniques for
Mastering the Writing Process

Some writers save their freewriting to look through afterward for good ideas or well turned phrases that might find a useful home in a writing project. Other writers throw their freewriting in the trash without ever looking at it. It is up to you to decide what to do with your freewriting once it has served its main purpose, which is to get you ready to write.

Write Now (3)

Freewrite for ten minutes about *anything at all.* Write fast and without conscious thought. If you need help getting started, begin by writing the phrase, "I am thinking about . . ." over and over until you discover what you are thinking about. Do not share what you produce with others unless you feel comfortable doing so.

Afterward, discuss with your classmates the following questions:

1. How did it feel to write for ten minutes straight?

2. How difficult was it to start writing?

3. How difficult was it to continue?

4. What do you think of freewriting as a warm-up exercise for doing more focused writing?

Write Now (4)

Experiment with paired freewriting. With a partner, conduct a conversation on paper by passing a sheet of paper back and forth. Do this for ten minutes. As with solo freewriting, write fast and without conscious thought. Then, as a class, discuss the questions in Write Now (3).

You can do your paired freewriting on computer if you have networked computers or if you have Internet access and your service provider allows instant messaging.

Discovering What to Say about a Topic

Sometimes you may have a hard time focusing on a topic because you are afraid of getting locked into a bad idea. You may wonder, "What if I have nothing to say about this?" The best way to overcome such fear is to remind yourself that you are just exploring the idea, not committing yourself to it.

The way to explore is to **brainstorm.** To brainstorm means to have a storm in the brain—to let ideas "rain down" without worrying about whether they are good or bad. The best brainstorming happens in the places where you do your best thinking, for example, while out for a drive, in the shower, or on a walk. Train yourself to take advantage of these moments to think about current writing projects. Alternatively, if you get stuck when trying to think through a writing idea, go take a shower or a walk or a drive—it might help! Jot down notes during or right after your brainstorming session, so that when you begin writing you can remember your ideas.

Good writing is often preceded by good discussion. Therefore, another very useful way to explore a subject is to talk it through with someone who is willing to listen. A discussion can help you think beyond a general idea to a more focused topic and particular details. It can help you generate specific words and phrases that you might be able to use when writing. As with brainstorming, take notes during or right after your conversation to save important ideas.

If you cannot find someone to discuss your subject with, be your own listener. Ask yourself questions and answer them. Use the who-what-when-where-why-how formula to generate a list of questions. For example, if you are considering writing something about trains, you might ask yourself:

- Who takes trains these days?

- What makes train travel different from traveling by plane or car?

- When was the golden age of railroads?

- Where is the best rail journey in the world?

- Why aren't trains as great as they used to be—or are they?

- How much does it cost to travel by train across the United States?

As you write questions about trains and think over possible answers, you will pull to the forefront of your consciousness what you feel about trains, what you already know about them, and what you would like to know. This is material you can sift through and select from as you write. You also may discover that a single question is the one that really interests you because it is something you know a lot about or care a lot about.

Another strategy for exploring a topic is **focused freewriting.** This is to write freely and without conscious effort on whatever topic you are considering. Alternatively, spend that time drawing a detailed, labeled picture of your subject. A variation on focused freewriting is focused list making: making a list of everything you know or want to know about your topic.

Each of these strategies can help you focus on the aspect of your topic that is of most interest to you. Each also can help you pull together an abundance of facts, ideas, impressions, and questions related to your topic that you can use in your writing.

Write Now (5)

As a class, brainstorm on the topic of weekend trips. Talk together about good close-by destinations. Make a list of words associated with recreational travel. Share ideas on specific themes fitting this topic that could be covered adequately in a short essay. Take notes of this discussion because you may use them in a later activity.

Write Now (6)

In small groups, make a list of questions related to the topic of pets. Create questions that begin with the words *who, what, when, where, why,* and *how.* Next, reread each question and exchange answers. Keep a copy of this list because you may use it in a later activity.

Write Now (7)

Freewrite for ten minutes on the topic of exercise. Freewrite by writing without stopping, by making a long list of statements about the topic, or by working out a detailed diagram inspired by the topic. Keep this work because you may use it in a later activity.

Clustering to Explore What to Say

One of the most effective methods for developing ideas on a topic is called **clustering.** It also has been called diagramming or mapping.

Gabriele Lusser Rico, who introduced clustering in her book *Writing the Natural Way,* defines this technique as "a nonlinear brainstorming process akin to free association." Rico says that clustering is a way to do the "wondering" that is essential to creative work. To cluster, put your key word or phrase in a circle at the center of a blank page like this:

Then write the first words that come to mind in circles connected to the main circle, like this:

As more words come to you, draw them in, too. Some may be attached to your main circle and others to your outer circles, depending on how they flow:

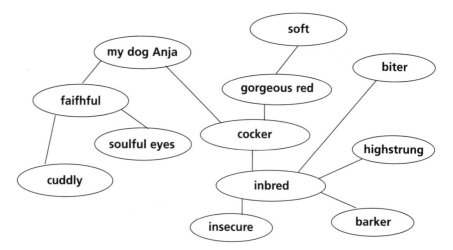

Some routes may end and others may keep unfolding. If you get stuck, draw empty circles and see if any words arrive in your mind to fill them. The key is to be open and nonjudgmental. Rico says clustering involves "a certain playfulness." There is no right or wrong way to cluster.

According to Rico, clustering usually leads to a "sudden, strong urge to write." The writing that follows may incorporate a little or a lot of the words from the cluster. What is important is that through clustering you free up the creative side of your mind so that images, ideas, and words become available to you.

Write Now (8)

Move into groups of three to try clustering. Have one person select a color as the key word for the cluster. Have another person serve as the recorder. Working together for several minutes, free-associate ideas related to your color. Then write, separately, for about ten minutes on the topic of that color. Afterward, share your efforts. How did the same cluster take each writer in different directions? Keep this work because you may use it in a later activity.

Write Now (9)

Try clustering on your own. Pick another color as your topic. Cluster ideas about this color for several minutes, then switch to writing. Afterward, reflect on the process. How did clustering affect your ability to begin writing? Keep this work because you may use it in a later activity.

Summing Up

1. Describe an instance when your mood affected your ability to write.

   _____

   _____

2. What is the difference between brainstorming and daydreaming?

   _____

   _____

3. Methods for discovering what to say about a topic include brainstorming on the topic, talking your ideas over with someone, asking and answering questions about the topic, doing focused freewriting, and clustering. Underline the method you think will be most useful to you. Why do you think so?

   _____

   _____

Second Thoughts

Review the photograph that opened this chapter; then think about or discuss the following questions:

1. What features make a place useful for thinking through writing ideas?

2. What features make a place not useful for thinking through writing ideas?

   Based on what you have learned in this chapter about creative thinking, what new thoughts do you have about how this man is spending his time behind the wheel? Write your reactions in the *Responses* section of your journal.

4. What is the difference between discovering what to say about a topic (such as through focused freewriting) and drafting?

   _____

   _____

5. Think of one time in your regular schedule that might be good for thinking through writing ideas and one person who might be willing to talk with you about them.

   _____

   _____

6. As a result of completing this chapter, what is one change you will make in your writing-related thinking and planning? Write your resolution in the *Habits for Life* section of your journal.

Write Now: Thinking and Planning Creatively

Select a topic that interests you. To find a topic, look through the writing you did for Write Now (1), (5), (6), (7), and (8). Also look through your random freewriting (if you kept it) from Write Now (3) or (4) and your journal. Explore the topic you have selected in greater depth using at least two additional methods: brainstorming on the topic, talking about the topic with someone (remember to make notes during or after your discussion), asking and answering questions about the topic, doing focused freewriting, or clustering. Keep this work because you may use it in a later activity.

Developing Good Computer Habits

The start of a writing project is a good time to get into good habits. Here is a collection of tips for effective use of computers and the Internet.

Using computers

1. Make sure you are sitting **ergonomically**. This means with a posture that is correct for your body. Refer to the diagram below. When working at the computer, remember to blink to avoid eye fatigue and to give your muscles a stretch every fifteen minutes or so.

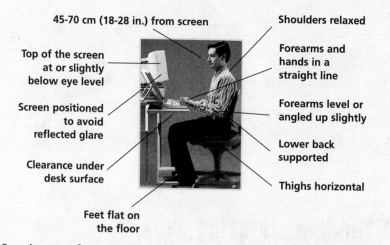

45-70 cm (18-28 in.) from screen

Shoulders relaxed

Top of the screen at or slightly below eye level

Forearms and hands in a straight line

Screen positioned to avoid reflected glare

Forearms level or angled up slightly

Clearance under desk surface

Lower back supported

Thighs horizontal

Feet flat on the floor

2. Arrange for your most important folders (and your most important files) to appear near the top of the desktop window by naming them starting with "1" or "2" such as *1—Writing Folder*.

3. When drafting, use a typeface, size, and leading (space between lines) that are easy for you to read, such as 12 point Geneva double-spaced. You can change the formatting before printing out your final copy.

4. Use the "header and footer" function of your word processing program to label each draft with a topic name, date, and page number, such as *Description Draft 1 — 3/7/01 — Page 1*. This will help you keep track of different documents and different versions of documents.

5. Take maximum advantage of the capabilities of your word processing program. When you have extra time, look at every menu choice and experiment with it so that you become an efficient user of the program.

6. Save your work on the hard drive at regular intervals. Hit the save key every ten minutes or so. Better yet, program your computer to save automatically at ten-minute intervals.

7. Make a backup copy of important folders and files onto a removable diskette at frequent intervals, such as after each draft or every few days.

8. When you have a problem, go first to your computer manual's index to find the pages that address the issue (it is more detailed than the table of contents). Also, you can fix many problems simply by restarting your computer (*after* saving your file).

9. If you have lost a document in your computer, it may not be gone forever—perhaps you saved it into the wrong folder by mistake. Use your computer's "find" function to locate it. Many computers can search by file name and by the key words inside the file.

Using the Internet

1. Be disciplined. It is easy to get sidetracked by the Internet's vast network of information. When you go on the Internet, have a goal and a time limit and stick to them.

2. Remember that correspondence on the Internet is less likely to stay private than mail or hand-delivered messages. This is because forwarding e-mail takes only a few keystrokes. Correspondents may be tempted to pass on your message without reflecting on whether it is appropriate to do so. Also, it is relatively easy to mistakenly send an e-mail to the wrong address or to multiple addresses.

3. Treat e-mail messages like any letter: draft and revise them before sending.

4. Remember also that Internet use leaves a trail. Internet correspondence is stored for long periods of time in several locations—on the computer you are using, on recipients' computers, and on the computer servers that transmit messages, among other places. Web sites also may keep records of your visits. Hackers, investigators, and nosy people can find their way into your correspondence and may be able to obtain personal information about you.

5. Do not believe everything you read on the World Wide Web. Anyone can put up a Web page with information that may or may not be true. People can assume disguises, too, pretending to be someone they are not.

6. Do not use any information off the Web in your writing unless you are very sure the author and the material are credible.

7. Remember that writing is more than cutting and pasting. While it is easy to take information off the Internet, as a writer you need to synthesize information (sort through it, organize it with your own insights and conclusions, and present it in your own words). You also need to credit your sources. More on how to do this appears in Chapter 15.

8. When you find a good location on the Internet, remember to bookmark it. That way you can return to it quickly. Follow your Internet software instructions for organizing bookmarks.

9. Learn the properties of the different search engines, such as AltaVista, Yahoo!, Excite, and Lycos. Most of the major search engines provide information on their home pages explaining how to use their services efficiently.

Exercise

Take the following quiz.

Are you a savvy computer user?

1. I (have, have not) checked to make sure my posture at the computer is ergonomically correct.

2. When working on an important document, I save (at frequent intervals, when I quit, if I remember).

3. My habit of making a hard-copy backup of important folders and files is (good, weak, nonexistent).

4. I know (most, some, few) of the features of my word processing program.

5. When I am on the Internet, I (usually, sometimes, never) have a goal and time limit.

6. When I am sending e-mail, I am (very, somewhat, not at all) conscious of the Internet's privacy limitations.

7. When I visit a Web page, I (usually, sometimes, never) try to determine if the source is credible.

8. When I type an e-mail, I (usually, sometimes, never) review it before sending.

9. I know (a lot, some, a little) about using search engines efficiently.

If you selected the first response for six or more items, you are a savvy computer user. If you didn't, review the advice above and get savvy!

Writing as a Practice

by Natalie Goldberg

Check out Natalie
Goldberg's Web site at
www.nataliegoldberg.com

Natalie Goldberg has published one novel, Banana Rose, *but is most known for her several books on writing, particularly* Writing Down the Bones. *She lives in Taos, New Mexico.*

 Goldberg does Zen meditation, a spiritual practice to gain wisdom and enlightenment. She likes to emphasize the personal, meditative benefits of writing. She sees writing as a way to unleash the creative spirit and also to discover meaning in life.

 In the following essay from Writing Down the Bones, *Goldberg asserts that writers need to allow time for themselves to practice. What she essentially describes is random freewriting. As you read, think of how what she recommends might apply to how you use your journal.*

How does
Goldberg
define
"practice"?

This is the practice school of writing. Like running, the more you do it, the better you get at it. Some days you don't want to run and you resist every step of the three miles, but you do it anyway. You practice whether you want to or not. You don't wait around for inspiration and a deep desire to run. It'll never happen, especially if you are out of shape and have been avoiding it. But if you run regularly, you train your mind to cut through or ignore your resistance. You just do it. And in the middle of the run, you love it. When you come to the end, you never want to stop. And you stop, hungry for the next time.

 That's how writing is, too. Once you're deep into it, you wonder what took you so long to finally settle down at the desk. Through practice you actually do get better. You learn to trust your deep self more and not give in to your voice that wants to avoid writing. It is odd that we never question the feasibility of a football team practicing long hours for one game; yet in writing we rarely give ourselves the space for practice.

 When you write, don't say, "I'm going to write a poem." That attitude will freeze you right away. Sit down with the least expectation of yourself; say, "I am free to write the worst junk in the world." You have to give yourself the space to write a lot without a destination. I've had students who said they decided they were going to write the great

American novel and haven't written a line since. If every time you sat down, you expected something great, writing would always be a great disappointment. Plus that expectation would also keep you from writing.

My rule is to finish a notebook a month. (I'm always making up writing guidelines for myself.) Simply to fill it. That is the practice. My ideal is to write every day. I say it is my ideal. I am careful not to pass judgment or create anxiety if I don't do that. No one lives up to his ideal.

In my notebooks I don't bother with the side margin or the one at the top: I fill the whole page. I am not writing anymore for a teacher or for school. I am writing for myself first and I don't have to stay within my limits, not even margins. This gives me a psychological freedom and permission. And when my writing is on and I'm really cooking, I usually forget about punctuation, spelling, etc. I also notice that my handwriting changes. It becomes larger and looser.

Often I can look around the room at my students as they write and can tell which ones are really on and present at a given time in their writing. They are more intensely involved and their bodies are hanging loose. Again, it is like running. There's little resistance when the run is good. All of you is moving; there's no you separate from the runner. In writing, when you are truly on, there's no writer, no paper, no pen, no thoughts. Only writing does writing—everything else is gone.

One of the main aims in writing practice is to learn to trust your own mind and body; to grow patient and nonaggressive. Art lives in the Big World. One poem or story doesn't matter one way or the other. It's the process of writing and life that matters. Too many writers have written great books and gone insane or alcoholic or killed themselves. This process teaches about sanity. We are trying to become sane along with our poems and stories.

Chögyam Trungpa, Rinpoche, a Tibetan Buddhist master, said, "We must continue to open in the face of tremendous opposition. No one is encouraging us to open and still we must peel away the layers of the heart." It is the same with this way of practice writing: We must continue to open and trust in our own voice and process. Ultimately, if the process is good, the end will be good. You will get good writing.

What does Goldberg mean by "Only writing does writing"?

What does Goldberg mean by "Art lives in the Big World"?

What attitude does Goldberg say you should have when you practice writing?

What does
Goldberg say
happens if
you truly
practice writing?

A friend once said that when she had a good black-and-white drawing that she was going to add color to, she always practiced first on a few drawings she didn't care about in order to warm up. This writing practice is also a warmup for anything else you might want to write. It is the bottom line, the most primitive, essential beginning of writing. The trust you learn in your own voice can be directed then into a business letter, a novel, a Ph.D. dissertation, a play, a memoir. But it is something you must come back to again and again. Don't think, "I got it! I know how to write. I trust my voice. I'm off to write the great American novel." It's good to go off and write a novel, but don't stop doing writing practice. It is what keeps you in tune, like a dancer who does warmups before dancing or a runner who does stretches before running. Runners don't say, "Oh, I ran yesterday. I'm limber." Each day they warm up and stretch.

Writing practice embraces your whole life and doesn't demand any logical form: no Chapter 19 following the action in Chapter 18. It's a place that you can come to wild and unbridled, mixing the dream of your grandmother's soup with the astounding clouds outside your window. It is undirected and has to do with all of you right in your present moment. Think of writing practice as loving arms you come to illogically and incoherently. It's our wild forest where we gather energy before going to prune our garden, write our fine books and novels. It's a continual practice.

Sit down right now. Give me this moment. Write whatever's running through you. You might start with "this moment" and end up writing about the gardenia you wore at your wedding seven years ago. That's fine. Don't try to control it. Stay present with whatever comes up, and keep your hand moving.

What images does
Goldberg use
to describe
writing practice?

THINK AND RESPOND

1. How can the kind of writing Goldberg recommends put you in the proper mood to write?

    _____

    _____

    _____

    _____

2. Name one specific way that writing practice makes you a better writer.

    _____

    _____

    _____

    _____

3. What other exercises besides freewriting can you do to train for writing?

    _____

    _____

    _____

    _____

4. What does Goldberg suggest is the true purpose of writing practice, and do you agree?

    _____

    _____

    _____

    _____

5. Provide synonyms or definitions for these words from the essay, and add at least two of the words to the *Words Worth Remembering* section of your journal:

feasibility _____

psychological _____

nonaggressive _____

dissertation _____

memoir _____

limber _____

unbridled _____

astounding _____

incoherently _____

prune _____

6. If you liked this reading, make a record of it in the *Readings Worth Remembering* section of your journal.

COMPARING VIEWS

Based on her own experience, Goldberg advises writers to practice writing. What is something you do that you would recommend to others? Like Goldberg, give reasons for your advice. Give examples of how you or other persons practice the behavior you recommend. After discussing this topic with others, continue to explore it on your own, in your journal—if it interests you. You may be able to use material from the discussion and your journal in a future writing activity.

APPLIED WRITING

Open your journal and do what Natalie Goldberg instructs: "Sit down right now. Give me this moment. Write whatever's running through you."

History

Ocean Surface Woodcut, 1992. Vija Celmins. 19¼ x 15½ inches. Edition of 50.
Courtesy McKee Gallery, New York

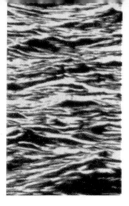

CHAPTER 5

Drafting Your Thoughts

These are the **key ideas** of this chapter:

- Drafting is the creative process of developing ideas into an organized structure of words.

- Drafting begins with a review of your purpose, audience, and ideas and the construction of an outline.

- Drafting then consists of shaping paragraphs until you have a version complete enough to review yourself or to share with others for feedback.

Picturing Meaning

Examine the woodcut on the opposite page; then think about or discuss these questions:

1. What do you see in this woodcut?

   _____

   _____

2. What do you *not* see that you might expect to be here?

   _____

   _____

3. What process do you think the artist went through to compose this scene?

   _____

   _____

   In the *Responses* section of your journal, write down your thoughts about this woodcut.

Write Now (1)

When *you* picture the ocean or some other significant body of water, what do you see? What meaning does it hold for you? What role does it play in your life? Write down your responses to these questions. Keep this work because you may use it in a later activity.

Moving from Planning to Drafting

Drafting begins after you have identified your purpose for writing, determined what to write about, and done some planning on your topic. It is the stage where you begin to shape ideas into an organized structure of words. As with any activity, drafting is done differently by each person. For most people, however, drafting involves these four steps:

1. Remind yourself of your purpose and audience.

2. Review your ideas.

3. Sketch an outline.

4. Begin at the beginning (or somewhere else).

   Remind yourself of your purpose and audience. If you have not done so already, summarize your purpose into a single statement. Put it on a small piece of paper to keep before you at all times. Or, write it at the top of each draft. A sample purpose statement is: "Describe what it is like to be in the military reserves." Beneath your purpose statement, write a brief description of your audience. Even if, in reality, your only reader will be your instructor, it still helps to identify an ideal audience. A sample audience description for the purpose statement given above might be: "People who have never served in the military." As you draft, the purpose statement and audience description will help you keep in mind such things as the background information you will have to include (or can leave out), whether you will have to explain any special terms, and which points you must cover to achieve your purpose.

Review your ideas. To begin drafting, set out in front of you all of the brainstorming materials you created in the thinking and planning stages. This includes any freewritings, drawings, lists, clusters, and so forth. In order to read with attention, involve yourself physically. Circle or highlight important points or good words, add fresh ideas, or draw arrows connecting related thoughts. The idea is not to memorize all the points you want to make but rather to refresh your mind so that you can recall the points easily as you work. Tape your brainstorming materials up on the wall where you work or spread them out so that you can refer to them easily.

If your brainstorming materials are on computer, keep those files open underneath your draft file. Alternatively, print them out to set in front of you.

Sketch an outline. As you review your brainstorming materials, develop an outline. An outline is a brief sketch of the points you want to make. It may be as simple as a list of three to five key points. Add to this simple outline by jotting details beneath each point, for example:

> *The problem of spam*
> *1. What it is*
>   *e-mail*
>   *junk mail*
> *2. Why it is a problem*
>   *clutters in-box*
>   *waste of time to open and read*
>   *can't get to important messages*
>   *some carry viruses*
> *3. Examples*
>   *get-rich-quick schemes*
>   *ads for pornographic Web sites*

A "quick and dirty" way to outline is to number ideas on your brainstorming materials. For more thoughtful planning, recopy the points you want to make onto a new sheet of paper, or draw a fresh cluster. (Clustering is described in detail in Chapter 4.) To make a cluster outline, put your topic in the center circle, with supporting ideas in outer circles linked by lines to the topic. Then number the circles in the order you think you might use them in your essay. For example:

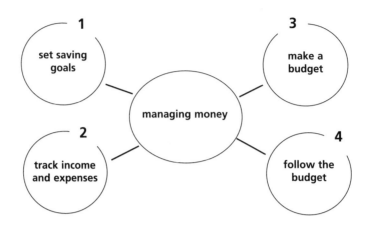

Begin at the beginning (or somewhere else). A Native American proverb says, "The way to cross a river is to cross a river." In terms of drafting, this means start anywhere so long as you start. Some writers work best by beginning at the beginning and moving steadily forward. Others prefer to start with the ideas that most interest them or that are clearest in their minds. They backtrack later to draft the opening or to flesh out other points. Occasionally, writers will begin with their closing thoughts and then figure out what to say first in order to lead there.

If you write with a word processor, it is easy to cut, paste, delete, and add. This makes it tempting to skip the outline stage, on the theory that you can organize as you go. This usually does not work very well. You will be more efficient if you start a draft with a carefully considered plan.

Write Now (2)

Complete each of the sentences below.

1. The first thing I should do when drafting is to _____

   _____

2. A good way to stay reminded of my ideas as I work is to _____

   _____

3. I can sketch an outline by _____

   _____

4. I can begin drafting by _____

   _____

Write Now (3)

Select a topic to outline. To find a topic, look through your writing folder, particularly at the brainstorming and planning you did for the activities in Chapter 4. (Alternatively, use the thinking strategies suggested in Chapter 4 to explore a new topic.) Determine a purpose for writing about this topic and visualize your audience. Describe both in writing. Then create an outline on this topic by drawing up a list of key points or by creating a cluster and numbering the points into a logical order. Save this work because you may use it in a later activity.

Drafting in Paragraphs

Your finished work will consist of **paragraphs**—organized sets of sentences—so it makes sense to draft using them. The function of paragraphs is to help readers understand meaning. Dividing your writing into paragraphs is much like cutting a steak into small bites. It makes it easier to digest. Paragraphs divide the text into meaningful chunks that readers can absorb one section at a time.

Usually each separate paragraph presents and develops a single idea, or **topic.** The topic may be very different or just a little different from the paragraphs that come before or after, but it should be different in some way. Usually, one sentence in the paragraph states the topic, and other sentences add meaning, evidence, or detail. The sentence stating what the paragraph is about is sometimes called the **topic sentence.** It can appear anywhere within a paragraph. Most often, however, it comes at the beginning.

The following passage, from a book about the brain, explains how smoking delivers a brain-altering substance to the body. Notice how each paragraph develops one idea:

> **If you don't smoke, you probably wonder why anyone would bother with such a filthy, expensive habit!** On the other hand, there must be a reason why millions of people smoke cigarettes.
>
> **That reason is nicotine.** It is a mood-altering drug found in tobacco. Most people take nicotine by smoking cigarettes. Pipe tobacco, cigars, chewing tobacco, and snuff all have nicotine in them, too.

Each paragraph begins with a topic sentence (which is in bold type here but not in the original).

One cigarette contains about 10 milligrams of nicotine. For every cigarette smoked, about one or two milligrams of nicotine end up in the lungs. From there, the nicotine gets right into the bloodstream.

Nicotine collects in the body and stays there even after the last cigarette of the day. This means that if you smoke, you are exposed to nicotine round the clock, even when you are sleeping. This is just one of the reasons why nicotine is so addictive and why quitting smoking is so hard. Your body isn't used to having nicotine just when you light up. It's used to having it all the time!

Nicotine affects the body and mind in many ways. It increases your heart rate. It tightens up your blood vessels, which means there is less room for the blood to pass through. Because of the faster heartbeat and tighter blood vessels, your blood pressure increases, too. If you are not used to it, nicotine can also make you sick to your stomach.

Brain and Behavior: Mental Disorders and Substance Abuse
American Association for the Advancement of Science

Sometimes a paragraph does not have one topic sentence. Instead, two or more sentences work together to develop the paragraph's main idea. In the following excerpt from a magazine article about health-privacy laws, neither of the two paragraphs has a single obvious topic sentence:

The topic of each paragraph is expressed by two sentences working together. (They are in bold type here but not in the original)

When medical records existed mainly on paper, your personal information couldn't go too far. But computer databases and managed care have changed things.
In many ways, these changes are for the better. They enable health plans to better track whether patients are getting the correct treatment for a condition and whether treatment regimens are working. **But they also raise privacy issues.** Who has access to this information? Can they use it against you?

"Rx for Medical Privacy"
Consumer Reports

Use your outline to help you write in paragraphs. Start a new paragraph for each major point in your outline. Summarize the point in the first sentence of the paragraph, then add supporting thoughts and details to that paragraph in additional sentences. Start a new paragraph for the next major point in your outline. Indicate where each paragraph begins by indenting the first line. Alternatively, indicate each paragraph by separating it with an extra line of space from the next paragraph (this is called "block paragraph" style).

While it is not necessary to have one obvious topic sentence per paragraph, it is best to begin drafting that way. As you work, you may choose to alter the position of the topic sentence or reword it. Sometimes you will end up with a paragraph that has no single topic sentence. The important thing to remember is this: whether stated in a single sentence or not, the topic of the paragraph must be clear to readers.

Pull up your outline on-screen, save it with a new name, such as "Draft v.1," and begin to draft right in your outline. For example, draft your first paragraph right underneath your first outline point. Delete that part of the outline when you are done. Then start a new paragraph underneath the next point on your outline. Working this way puts your plan and your draft in front of you at the same time. Save this file back into the same folder where the original outline is stored.

Write Now (4)

Review the two preceding passages; then summarize the topic of each paragraph.

Nicotine

Paragraph 1 _____

Paragraph 2 _____

Paragraph 3 _____

Paragraph 4 _____

Paragraph 5 _____

Health privacy

Paragraph 1 _____

Paragraph 2 _____

Write Now (5)

Draw horizontal lines to divide the following two passages into three paragraphs each. Underline the topic sentence of each paragraph. Then summarize each paragraph's main idea.

Depression

Everybody feels depressed now and then. Some people, however, feel sad and worthless for long periods without any particular reason for feeling that way. They may have little energy and either sleep too much or have trouble sleeping. They may have a hard time focusing on decisions. They may feel as though life is hopeless, leading to thoughts of suicide. Such people may suffer from a mental illness called depression, caused by chemical imbalances in the brain. Depression affects many people. In fact, it is so common that it is called the "common cold" of mental illness. One form of depression is manic depression. Another name for it is bipolar disorder. "Bipolar" means two poles, and people with bipolar disorder swing between depression and another very different, "manic" state. People in the manic state feel very upbeat and energetic. They do not require much sleep. They get excited quickly—and they get annoyed quickly, too. They may become unusually talkative. They may feel so powerful and confident that their decision-making skills are affected. They may do rash things, such as spend too much money. Their creativity may be exceptionally strong, though they may be too excitable to stick to any one project. This manic mood can last from days to months until it suddenly or slowly swings back into depression. Lithium is often prescribed to treat bipolar disorder. This drug helps moderate the flow of brain chemicals called neurotransmitters, so that nerve cells are not too active (causing the mania) or inactive (causing the depression). Lithium must be prescribed in just the right amount, which varies from person to person. It also has a number of side effects. However, for many people who suffer from manic depression, the side effects are easier to live with than the severe mood swings.

Paragraph 1: _____

Paragraph 2: _____

Paragraph 3: _____

Tattoos

The popularity of tattoos is at an all-time high. A long time ago, tattoos were the mark of a sailor or a rebel. Nowadays, you see tattoos on just about everybody. Many of the new tattoos carry on the old traditions: a dragon, a rose, or a skull. Today's tattoos, however, have a wider vocabulary. Nothing is too mainstream for tattoos now. You even see cartoon-character tattoos. There is one big reason why so many people wear tattoos now: stickers. While a lot of adults and older teens are getting real tattoos, the younger set is getting tattoos from the neighborhood convenience store. These tattoos are not at all painful to put on, but they look realistic. Even more important, sticker tattoos are not permanent. Myself, I don't like tattoos. I don't like strangers knowing my thoughts. I won't even wear T-shirts with slogans, so why should I wear a heart around the word "mom" or an anchor or a motorcycle logo? I enjoy seeing all the tattoos on other people, but you won't find one on

Paragraph 1: _____

Paragraph 2: _____

Paragraph 3: _____

Drafting Essays

When drafting an essay, it is useful to keep its structure in mind. Essay structure is actually quite simple, consisting of three sections:

1. Introduction
2. Body
3. Conclusion

Introduction. The first section of the essay is where the main idea is presented. It may be one or more paragraphs. The **introduction** often uses a "hook" to lure readers into the subject. An interesting anecdote, a colorful description, a startling observation, or a frank opinion are four possible ways to begin an essay. Here, for example, is a question used to open an essay:

Out of the corner of my eye I see my ninetieth birthday approaching. It is one year and six months away. How long after that will I be the person I am now?

"Nearing Ninety," William Maxwell
The New York Times Magazine

Whatever hook is used, it should lead to the main idea. In Maxwell's essay, the reader can infer from this opening paragraph that the essay is going to be about the author's thoughts on approaching the end of his life.

Body. The middle section of the essay is usually much longer than the introduction. It contains the paragraphs in which the main idea of the essay is explored from different angles or with accumulating detail. Here is one paragraph from the **body** of Maxwell's essay:

> I am not—I think I am not—afraid of dying. When I was seventeen I worked on a farm in southern Wisconsin, near Portage. It was no ordinary farm and not much serious farming was done there, but it had the look of a place that has been lived in, and loved, for a good long time. I was no more energetic than most adolescents, but the family forgave my failures and shortcomings and simply took me in, let me be one of them. The farm had come down in the family through several generations, from the man who had pioneered it to a woman who was so alive that everything and everybody seemed to revolve around her personality. She lived well into her nineties and then one day told her oldest daughter that she didn't want to live anymore, that she was tired. Though I was not present but only heard about it in a letter, this remark reconciled me to my own inevitable extinction.

Other paragraphs in the body of the essay reveal Maxwell's thoughts on different matters: how he feels about the way the world has changed in his lifetime (he tries not to complain about it); what he hopes to accomplish before dying (to reread everything he has ever read); what he does with memories (he enjoys them immensely, though sometimes they keep him awake all night long); and whether he still works as a writer (not a lot).

Conclusion. The end of an essay ties together everything that has been said to complete the purpose of the essay. Often the **conclusion** refers in some way back to the opening. For example, the closing may be a restatement of the opening but with special insight. Alternatively, the closing may be a question that arises from the essay's exploration of the issue. Maxwell's essay ends with a very short paragraph describing how his behavior has changed as he approaches ninety:

Every now and then, in my waking moments, and especially when I am in the country, I stand and look hard at everything.

This concluding image is of an old man staring—a man who knows that whatever he looks at, he may be seeing it for the last time. This image echoes the opening question of how much longer the author will remain vital. The stark, one-sentence conclusion reveals the intensity of the author's awareness that time is short. This conclusion fulfills the purpose of the essay, which is to show readers what it is like to approach ninety.

Use your purpose for writing as a guide when drafting the opening of an essay. Use your outline as a guide when drafting the body. The conclusion should emerge through the act of drafting, but it also helps to remind yourself of your purpose.

Write Now (6)

As a class, review an essay you have read together. For example, you may choose one of the Read and Reflect essays that follow Chapters 2, 3, or 4. Put the title of the essay here:

_____

Then answer the following questions.

1. In paragraphs, how long are the opening, the body, and the closing?
   opening _____ body _____ closing _____

2. What is the main idea expressed in the opening? _____

   _____

3. What makes the opening interesting so that readers are drawn in?_____

   _____

4. What points are covered in the body of the essay? _____

   _____

5. How does the conclusion differ from the opening? _____

   _____

Aiming for a Working Draft

When drafting, use your outline as a guide but feel free to make changes. If you think of new ideas or better ways to organize your ideas, by all means use them. Remember also that when drafting, your first mission is to get your thoughts down in a somewhat organized manner. Do not, therefore, concern yourself with getting each sentence correct or fixing minor errors. Once you have your ideas down, you can go back to make improvements.

When you begin drafting, the goal is to complete a rough form of the whole piece. To avoid stoppages, allow yourself the freedom to skip through troublesome sections. When you are stumbling on an idea but want to keep moving forward, insert a reminder to yourself, such as ADD MORE HERE or FIX THIS LATER. Use dashes (-------) as placeholders for words or phrases you can't pin down. Circle words that are not quite right and will need attention later. Early drafts do not have to be neat. In fact, some people call this the "sloppy copy" stage. Just remember that drafts have to be neat enough for your own eyes, so you can read back what you have written.

As was illustrated in Chapter 3, writing is a messy process. You may not move smoothly from brainstorming to outlining and drafting. You may bounce back and forth between these three stages. For example, if you are drafting and you come to an idea that needs developing, you may need to stop and brainstorm. Put that undeveloped idea in a circle and cluster from it. For example, here is a new cluster that develops a single point from the cluster presented earlier on managing money:

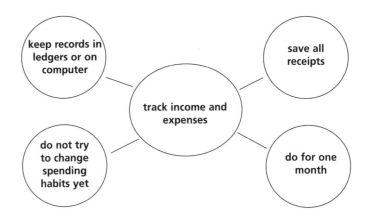

Sometimes you will have the energy to work through an entire draft in one attempt. Other times you will hit a wall and not know what to do next. In such cases, you may need to take a break—a break in which you direct your mind to work on your dilemma. Good break activities are stretching and walking or some other physical activity. Another option when you are stumped is to do more brainstorming, such as clustering, sketching, or list making.

If you draft by hand, use double-spacing and wide margins. This gives you room for making changes and corrections. Recopy your draft to incorporate changes you decide to make. Recopying may seem like extra work, but the act of copying often helps you think through changes. Date each draft and add page numbers, so if you drop your sheets you can put them back in order with no trouble. Staple or paperclip each draft, and do not throw any draft away until you are completely done with the project. Save them in case there is something from an early version you later decide to put back in.

Whatever drafting process you use, keep working (in one or more sittings) until you have a good first draft. A "good first draft" is a **working draft**. It is a legible version of your piece with all the basic elements present. Think of it as the rough cut of a movie. It is a best attempt at pulling together all the elements, with the final product in clear sight. It is something you can look at to decide whether it succeeds or does not yet succeed. This working draft is *not* your first attempt to put words on paper. It is your first working through of those words. Set your standards of production high by thinking of your first draft as your first effort at a final draft.

If you word process your drafts, you can revise on-screen without ever generating a hard copy. However, many writers find it useful to print out a double-spaced copy at some point to mark up by hand. This allows them to see the entire document at once (as opposed to screen by screen). Be sure to date your draft and to add page numbers before printing it out. On many word-processing programs, such actions can be done with simple mouse-click commands.

Write Now (7)

In the preceding discussion, the comparison was made between a first draft and "the rough cut of a movie." A director uses this rough cut to decide what edits to make. In small groups, think of other comparisons to a first draft of writing. An example has been provided.

Example: A first draft is like the pattern pieces pinned to a dressmaker's dummy used by a tailor to decide where to hem, where to take in or let out.

A first draft is like _____

_____

_____

used by _____

_____

_____

to _____

_____

_____

A first draft is like _____

_____

_____

used by _____

_____

_____

to _____

_____

_____

Write Now (8)

Select a topic to draft into an essay. You may use the topic you explored in Write Now (1) or the topic you outlined in Write Now (3), or you may select, plan, and outline another topic. Be sure to determine your purpose and audience. As you draft, keep in mind the structure of an essay, with its opening, body, and closing. Draft in paragraphs, using your purpose and outline as guides. Produce a working draft. Keep this work because you may use it in a later activity. Use the space below to begin planning and/or drafting.

_____

_____

_____

_____

_____

_____

_____

_____

_____

_____

_____

_____

_____

_____

_____

_____

_____

_____

Summing Up

1. Consider the four drafting steps described in this chapter: remind yourself of your purpose and audience, review your ideas, sketch an outline, and begin at the beginning (or somewhere else). Underline the step you usually do best. What makes this step easiest for you?

   _____

   _____

2. Circle the step you tend to skip over. What is one thing you can do to give more effort to this step in the drafting process?

   _____

   _____

3. Consider the three parts of an essay: the introduction, the body, and the conclusion. Underline the part that you think is generally easiest to write. What makes it easiest?

   _____

   _____

Second Thoughts

Review the woodcut that opened this chapter; then think about or discuss the following questions:

1. What do you think the author's purpose might have been?

2. Whom do you think she visualized as her audience?

3. With that purpose and audience in mind, how do you think she might have planned this work?

Based on what you have learned in this chapter about the process of drafting, what new thoughts do you have about the effort that lies behind a work of art such as this one? Write your thoughts in the *Responses* section of your journal.

4. Circle the part that you think is hardest to write. What can you do to be more successful drafting that part?

_____

_____

5. Name a situation in your life (not including writing) where you "draft," that is, work through rough versions of something before completing it in final form.

_____

_____

6. As a result of reading this chapter, what is one change you can make to improve your approach to drafting? Write your resolution in the *Habits for Life* section of your journal.

Write Now: Creating a Working Draft

Using the excerpts from the essay about approaching age ninety by William Maxwell as your example, draft an essay describing your outlook on life as you approach the next decade in life. First think about and plan your essay by brainstorming on the topic. Next, create a statement that summarizes your purpose and another statement that describes your audience. Sketch an outline. Then develop a draft, keeping in mind the structure of the essay with its introduction, body, and conclusion. Complete a working draft of this essay. Keep this work because you may use it in a later activity.

Using the Dictionary and the Thesaurus When Drafting

Two handy tools to keep by your side when drafting are the **dictionary** and the **thesaurus.** The dictionary's main function is to define words. It also indicates the category to which each word belongs (such as **noun** or **verb**) and how to spell the word, pronounce it, and break it into syllables. Some dictionaries also offer information on the word's origins. The thesaurus (which means "treasury") groups words according to meaning, but it does not define words. While the dictionary lists every word, the thesaurus only lists synonyms—words and phrases that are related in meaning to other words. The thesaurus also may list **antonyms**—words and phrases of opposite meaning. Here are the dictionary and thesaurus listings for the same word:

diverting (di vûr′tiñg, dī-), *adj.* serving to divert; entertaining; amusing. [divert + -ing²]—di-vert′-ing-ly, *adv.*
Webster's New Universal Unabridged Dictionary

diverting *adj.* amusing, entertaining, enjoyable, pleasant, humorous, playful, whimsical, sportive, beguiling, festive, fun. *ant.* serious, earnest, solemn, intense, profound.
The Doubleday Roget's Thesaurus in Dictionary Form (Revised Edition)

The dictionary and the dictionary-style thesaurus both list words in alphabetical order (a traditional thesaurus lists words according to established categories). Both have **guide words** in the upper left and right margins of each page. These guide words are the first and last word listed on that page. They can help you quickly locate the page of the word for which you are searching. If your word falls alphabetically between the two guide words, you are on the right page. The following abbreviations will help you use your dictionary and thesaurus:

adj.	**adjective**		*interj.*	**interjection**
adv.	**adverb**		*n.*	**noun**
ant.	**antonym**		*pron.*	**pronoun**
colloq.	**colloquial (informal speech)**		*prep.*	**preposition**
conj.	**conjunction**		*v.*	**verb**
dial.	**dialect**			

(If you do not know what the above words mean, use a dictionary or the glossary in this textbook to find out!)

USEFUL WEB SITES

www.infoplease.com Multiple almanacs (books of facts) as well as a 125,000-entry dictionary and a 57,000-article encyclopedia.

www.m-w.com The interconnected dictionary and thesaurus let you look up a word in both places simultaneously.

www.dictionary.com Another interconnected dictionary and thesaurus—with the added bonus of encyclopedia links.

When you are drafting, a dictionary can help you decide if you are using a word properly and spelling it correctly. A thesaurus can help you hunt down exactly the right word for your purpose. A thesaurus also can be useful for drafting, because for any one word you may find a whole list of other words useful for your topic. For example, if you are writing about thunder, looking up the word in the thesaurus would suggest these useful words: *peal, boom, roar,* and *crash.*

When using a thesaurus, remember that related words are just that—related. They do not always substitute well for each other because there may be subtle or significant differences in meaning. For example, if you are trying to find new ways to describe a sweet and loving kitten, you can look up *loving* in the thesaurus. There you will find several synonyms, but not all of them will do. *Adoring, devoted,* and *affectionate* may work, but *romantic* or *sentimental* probably will not. For this reason, you may want to check words you have picked out of a thesaurus or a dictionary to make sure their meaning is appropriate for your purpose.

Exercise

Use a dictionary to write one definition for each word (a word may have several different meanings). Then use a thesaurus to find one synonym for that particular meaning of the word and, if the word has any, one antonym. The first item has been done as an example.

Word	Definition	Synonym	Antonym
1. *smirk*	*an affected or knowing smile*	*simper*	*glower*
2. hamper	_____	_____	_____
3. paucity	_____	_____	_____
4. billow	_____	_____	_____
5. defunct	_____	_____	_____
6. authentic	_____	_____	_____
7. shackle	_____	_____	_____
8. tenuous	_____	_____	_____
9. mediocre	_____	_____	_____
10. mélange	_____	_____	_____

The Jigsaw Puzzle in the Wrong Box

by Renee Hawkley

Check out
the Mothers at
Home Web page at
www.mah.org

Welcome Home is a small magazine published by a national nonprofit organization called Mothers at Home. Each month's issue is filled with short essays, articles, poems, illustrations, and photographs about one subject: motherhood. Contributors to Welcome Home are mothers and occasionally fathers. They are not paid for their submissions and most are not professional writers. They contribute because they have something to share with others in similar circumstances.

Renee Hawkley is one such contributor. She has been married more than thirty years and is a mother and grandmother living in Boise, Idaho. As you read her essay from Welcome Home, pay attention to its structure: how the introduction, body, and conclusion are connected to each other.

There's something I've noticed about wise people. Their wisdom didn't sprinkle out of the heaven like cool, summer rain. They got it by taking crash courses they didn't sign up for.

Take my wise young friend, Diane. She qualifies as being young in my book because she isn't yet a veteran of teenagers. She qualifies as being wise (in anybody's book) because she's been mining some pretty big nuggets of wisdom out of the deep and scary minefields of adversity with some old-fashioned tools: faith, sweat, and dedication.

What is meant
here by "special
needs"?

Nearly three years ago, her fifth child, a boy named Logan, was born with special needs, and the family has made many life-altering adaptations with love and devotion. I see Diane often, and I marvel at how she continues to balance all the aspects of being a "regular" mother with the on-going and constant needs of little Logan. When I asked her how she manages, she told me her "puzzle" story, which helps to shape many of her days and gives her strength.

Diane loves jigsaw puzzles. However, since jigsaw puzzles and being the mother of preschoolers don't exactly mesh, she has disciplined herself to do only one puzzle a year. One year, after carefully shopping for the puzzle with the most pieces and the most captivating picture, she brought it home, set up the card table, and began working on it, using the picture on the box as a frequent point of reference.

As jigsaw puzzles go, this one got off to a slow start. The normal strategies didn't seem to work, and in time, it became apparent that the puzzle pieces didn't match the picture on the box. Frustrated that the puzzle company couldn't perform the seemingly simple task of matching puzzle pieces with boxes, she considered returning it and requesting a puzzle that wasn't flawed.

However, having already worked hard at assembling bits and pieces of the puzzle, she noticed hints of a beautiful scene had begun to reveal themselves. She wondered what the final picture would look like.

It isn't hard to guess the end of the story. She decided to finish the puzzle. Even though the process was much harder and the final product much different from her initial expectation, her satisfaction at finishing it surpassed that of any previous puzzle she had worked on. The picture turned out to be even more beautiful than the one she had selected.

Watching Diane's family is reminiscent of her puzzle story. They didn't choose their challenges, but when presented with them, they have chosen not to buckle or blame. Each family member, regardless of age, has grown in compassion and understanding. Their "impossible" puzzle is now taking shape, and the beauty of how it is turning out could not have been predicted.

Adversity is an unyielding taskmaster. Most of us, no matter how careful we are in making life's choices, find that we are, in one way or other, working on puzzles and challenges with no "picture on the box." We can consider returning our "puzzles" and demanding a refund or at least an explanation, but unfortunately many of life's puzzles are nonrefundable and cannot be explained. We can either pick up the next piece and work with study, diligence, and heart to discover how and where it fits, or we can pick a convenient scapegoat to blame, throw up our hands in frustration, and quit.

The choice is ours.

Why was Diane having trouble putting this particular puzzle together?

Why did Diane decide to keep working on the puzzle?

What is the family's " 'impossible' puzzle"?

What kind of puzzles is the author talking about here?

THINK AND RESPOND

1. What is the value of the "puzzle story" to Diane and to the author?

   _____

   _____

2. Summarize the author's purpose and audience.

   _____

   _____

3. How many paragraphs make up the introduction, body, and conclusion?

   Introduction _____ Body _____ Conclusion _____

4. How is the introduction of the essay like or different from its conclusion?

   _____

   _____

5. How does the theme of wisdom appear in the introduction, body, and conclusion?

   _____

   _____

6. Provide synonyms or definitions for these words from the essay, and add at least two of the words to the *Words Worth Remembering* section of your journal:

   crash courses _____

   adversity _____

   adaptations _____

   mesh _____

   captivating _____

reminiscent _____

unyielding _____

taskmaster _____

diligence _____

scapegoat _____

7. If you liked this reading, make a record of it in the *Readings Worth Remembering* section of your journal.

COMPARING VIEWS

How is raising a child—any child—similar to drafting? List the ways the two activities are alike. Make another list of the ways the two activities differ. After discussing this topic with others, continue to explore it on your own, in your journal—if it interests you. You may be able to use material from the discussion and your journal in a future writing activity.

APPLIED WRITING

In this essay Hawkley describes a wise person. She then offers a piece of wisdom. What is something you have learned from facing a challenge? Use brainstorming strategies to think through the topic and plan an essay. Write statements describing your purpose and your audience. Then use the guidelines in this chapter to develop an outline. Finally, draft the essay, taking care to write an introduction, body, and conclusion. It may help to develop your draft as a letter to a specific person who could benefit from your experience. Complete a working draft of this essay. Keep this work because you may use it in a later activity.

Lois on the Bench
Andre Cypriano

CHAPTER 6

Selecting Words and Constructing Sentences

These are the **key ideas** of this chapter:

- Drafting allows you to experiment with words to find the ones that best express what you want to say.

- Drafting also allows you to experiment with sentence structure.

- To write effectively, give yourself the time and freedom to experiment with words and sentences.

Picturing Meaning

Examine the photograph on the opposite page; then think about or discuss these questions:

1. What different elements do you see in this photograph?

   _____

   _____

2. Do you think this photograph was random or composed, and why?

   _____

   _____

3. What effort do you think the photographer went through to capture this image?

   _____

   _____

In the *Responses* section of your journal, write down your thoughts about this photograph.

Write Now (1)

When *you* take a photograph, how do you decide what elements to put into the picture and how to arrange them? Think about a favorite picture you have taken or a photograph that you really like that was taken by someone else. What is effective about the way the photograph is arranged and the images it captures? Write down your responses to these questions. Keep this work because you may use it in a later activity.

Selecting Words

When drafting, one of your objectives is to find those words that best express what you want to say. This can be difficult because there are an infinite number of ways to say almost anything. You have to put effort into finding the right words because some will be better for your purposes than others. Some will be more accurate, more interesting, more to the point, or more appropriate for your audience. For example, if you want to write an essay describing a memorable job, your first draft might include this sentence: I sold shoes.

The sentence may be true, but it contains a bare minimum of information. Drafting allows you to experiment with words to create more specific and vivid pictures in the minds of your readers. Here are some ways you might redraft "I sold shoes":

I worked at a shoe shop.

I labored at a shoe outlet.

I peddled foot products at a shoe warehouse.

I was employed in the shoe section of a department store.

I earned a living at a shoe boutique.

The above sentences provide a little more detail compared with the original. For example, the word *warehouse* offers a picture of a specific place where shoes are sold. The word *labored* suggests hard work, while *peddled* suggests some skill at selling. Words like these not only add detail, they help to create **tone.** Tone is the reflection in your writing of your attitude toward your subject. When you speak, your voice helps set the tone. When you write, tone is conveyed through the words you choose and how you arrange them.

When you write, five categories of words (called **parts of speech**) do most of the work to carry information and create tone. You use these parts of speech all the time, even if you do not already know what they are called:

1. Nouns.

2. Verbs.

3. Adjectives.

4. Adverbs.

5. Prepositional phrases.

Nouns. The words or phrases that stand for persons, places, objects, or concepts are called nouns. Here are the same five sentences about selling shoes, with the nouns underlined:

I worked at a shoe <u>shop</u>.

I labored at a shoe <u>outlet</u>.

I peddled foot <u>products</u> at a shoe <u>boutique</u>.

I was employed in the shoe <u>section</u> of a department <u>store</u>.

I earned a <u>living</u> at a shoe <u>warehouse</u>.

In the sentences above, *I* is the **subject** of the sentence. The subject is whoever or whatever the sentence is about. *I* stands for a person, but it is not a noun. It is a **pronoun,** a word used as a substitute for a noun. Note also that the words *shoe, department,* and *foot* usually function as nouns, but in these sentences they are functioning as adjectives (see below).

Verbs. Verbs are the words or phrases that express the action, condition, or relationship involving the subject of a sentence. In the sentences below, the verbs are underlined:

I <u>worked</u> at a shoe shop.

I <u>labored</u> at a shoe outlet.

I <u>earned</u> a living at a shoe warehouse.

I <u>was employed</u> in the shoe section of a department store.

I <u>peddled</u> foot products at a shoe boutique.

Adjectives. Words or phrases that add description to nouns are called adjectives. An adjective is said to modify a noun because it changes the meaning of the noun by making it more specific. In the sentences below, the adjectives are underlined:

I worked at a little shoe shop.

I labored at a factory-sized shoe outlet.

I earned a living at a low-priced shoe warehouse.

I was employed in the shoe section of a discount department store.

I peddled foot products in commissioned sales at a fancy shoe boutique.

Adverbs. Adverbs are the words or phrases that add description to verbs. An adverb modifies the meaning of a verb by making it more specific. Adverbs also modify adjectives and other adverbs. In the sentences below, the adverbs are underlined:

I worked hard at a little shoe shop.
(The adverb *hard* modifies the verb *worked*.)

I labored mightily at a shoe outlet.
(The adverb *mightily* modifies the verb *labored*.)

I barely earned a living at a discount shoe warehouse.
(The adverb *barely* modifies the verb *earned*.)

I was employed in a very swank shoe section of a department store.
(The adverb *very* modifies the adjective *swank*.)

Most enjoyably, I peddled foot products at a shoe boutique.
(The adverb *most* modifies the adverb *enjoyably*, which in turn modifies the verb *peddled*.)

Prepositional phrases. Prepositional phrases add extra information to a sentence. They begin with words called prepositions;

these are listed in Figure 6–1. In the sentences below, the prepositional phrases are underlined and the prepositions are in bold:

I worked hard **at** <u>a little shoe shop</u> **near** <u>my school</u>.

I labored **for** <u>low wages</u> **at** <u>a shoe outlet</u>.

Before <u>the job I have now</u>, I earned a living **at** <u>a shoe warehouse</u>.

I was employed **in** <u>the shoe section</u> **of** <u>a discount department store</u>.

I peddled foot products **at** <u>a shoe boutique</u> **inside** <u>the city</u>.

For most people, it is fairly easy to remember what nouns and verbs are. The other parts of speech are more difficult to keep straight. The important thing to remember when writing is not the category to which a particular word belongs. The important thing to remember is simply that you have whole categories of words at your disposal. For any noun or verb, you can find other nouns or verbs that might work as well or better. And for any noun or verb, you can tag on extra, descriptive words—adjectives, adverbs, or prepositional phrases—that can sharpen the meaning even more.

Also remember that you do not have to have talent or a huge vocabulary to use words well in writing. You just have to give yourself the time to rove over possibilities and get precise. Give yourself the freedom to experiment as you draft. If a word or phrase strikes you as inexact, inauthentic, inconsistent, out of place, awkward, or just not right for any reason, try something else.

Figure 6–1: Common Prepositions

about	at	during	of	to
above	before	except	off	toward
across	behind	for	on	under
after	below	from	out	until
against	beneath	in	outside	up
along	beside	inside	over	upon
amid	between	into	past	with
among	beyond	like	since	within
around	by	near	through	without
as	down	next	throughout	

Write Now (2)

Work in pairs to write five sentences about jobs. Then place the words you used into the categories below. A sentence has been done as an example.
Example: *I worked hard at a great job.*

Nouns	Verbs	Adjectives	Adverbs	Prepositions	Other Words
job	*worked*	*great*	*hard*	*at*	*I, a*
___	___	___	___	___	___
___	___	___	___	___	___
___	___	___	___	___	___
___	___	___	___	___	___
___	___	___	___	___	___
___	___	___	___	___	___
___	___	___	___	___	___

Your five sentences:

1. _____

   _____

2. _____

   _____

3. _____

   _____

4. _____

   _____

5. _____

   _____

Write Now (3)

Rewrite each sentence below at least three ways, each time adding more information. Do this by using different nouns or verbs or by adding descriptive words such as adjectives, adverbs, or prepositional phrases. Summarize the tone of your longest sentence. The first item has been done as an example.

1. I like this bread.
   I am fond of this bread.
   I am a big fan of this rye loaf.
   I like nothing better than a hot slice of fresh rye from the corner bakery.

   Tone: *enthusiastic*

2. You feel bad when you have the flu. _____

   _____

   _____

   Tone: _____

3. The movie was good. _____

   _____

   _____

   Tone: _____

4. The stock market fell today. _____

   _____

   _____

   Tone: _____

5. Mahmoud smiled. _____

   _____

   _____

   Tone: _____

Write Now (4)

Practice experimenting with word selection by writing a cinquain.
Cinque is the French word for five, and a cinquain is a five-line poem.
It follows this form:
Line 1: One word that states the subject (often a noun).
Line 2: Two words that describe the subject.
Line 3: Three words about the subject.
Line 4: Four words about the subject.
Line 5: One word that restates the subject (usually a noun).

Since there are so few words in a cinquain, each one is valuable and must be chosen wisely. A subject for your cinquain could be a person, place, object, or condition, for example:

mother	home	animal	dawn
stranger	ocean	cactus	pregnancy

Draft your cinquain on a separate sheet of paper, then recopy it on the lines below. After finishing, share your cinquain with the class. Discuss whether being limited to just eleven words helped you focus on word selection. Two examples of cinquains are provided.

Examples:

Squirrels	
Furry creatures	*Coffee*
Scampering, climbing, swinging	*Bitter hot*
Chasing through the garden	*Daily caffeine load*
Yardpets	*Gives me the jitters*
	Vice

Your cinquain:

_____

_____   _____

_____   _____   _____

_____   _____   _____   _____

_____

Constructing Sentences

Sentence drafting is a task that goes hand-in-hand with picking the right words. This task can go more easily if you are aware of what makes a sentence and the different options you have for putting them together. A sentence expresses a complete thought and describes an action, a condition, or a relationship:

> Elephants are hunted for their ivory tusks. *(sentence expressing an action)*

> Elephants are endangered. *(sentence revealing a condition)*

> The elephant's greatest enemy is the human. *(sentence showing a relationship)*

Of course, sentences vary in length because some ideas take more words to express than others:

> Protect elephants! *(short sentence)*

> The international ban on ivory is not supported by all African countries, and even in the countries where it is enforced, poachers continue to hunt elephants. *(long sentence)*

Four important sentence forms are:

1. The simple sentence.

2. The compound sentence.

3. The complex sentence.

4. The compound-complex sentence.

Simple sentence. The simple sentence expresses a single complete thought. At a minimum, the **simple sentence** contains a noun operating as the subject of the sentence (who or what the sentence is about) and the verb (the word or phrase that expresses the action, condition, or relationship involving the subject). Another term for the simple sentence is **independent clause.** An independent clause can stand independently—the thought it expresses is complete by itself. Below are examples of simple sentences. In each, the subject is underlined and the verb is in italics:

> The <u>steak</u> *is served.*

> The <u>customer</u> *eats.*

> <u>He</u> *begins to cough.*

A simple sentence may have more than one subject, more than one verb, or both:

The <u>steak</u> and <u>potatoes</u> are served. *(two subjects)*

The customer <u>eats</u> and <u>drinks</u>. *(two verbs)*

The <u>waitress</u> and the <u>cook</u> <u>talk</u> and <u>laugh</u>. *(two subjects and two verbs)*

A simple sentence also may contain adjectives, adverbs, and prepositional phrases:

The <u>well</u> <u>dressed</u> customer <u>at</u> <u>the</u> <u>bar</u> <u>eats</u> <u>rapidly</u>. *(adverbs, adjective, prepositional phrase, and adverb, respectively)*

Compound sentence. A compound sentence is two or more simple sentences joined together into one sentence. The compound sentence, therefore, contains two or more complete thoughts. Compound sentences are constructed with the use of connecting words. Commonly used connecting words appear in Figure 6–2. Usually, a comma is placed before the connecting word. In the following compound sentences, the connecting words are underlined:

The steak is served, <u>so</u> the customer eats.

He begins to cough, <u>and</u> he turns red.

Is he choking, <u>or</u> is he okay?

The other customers stare, <u>but</u> no one moves.

They do nothing, <u>yet</u> they are concerned.

Figure 6–2: Connecting Words

and	but	or	so	not	yet	for

Complex sentence. A complex sentence is a simple sentence to which a **dependent clause** has been added. A dependent clause contains a subject and a verb and usually begins with one of the words listed in Figure 6–3. It is called dependent because it depends on an independent clause to complete its meaning. In other words, a dependent clause cannot stand alone as a sentence. In the following examples of complex sentences, the dependent clauses are underlined:

The steak is served <u>although the customer has not finished his salad</u>.

The customer eats <u>while he talks to the bartender</u>.

<u>After he takes a really big bite</u>, he begins to cough.

Is he okay <u>if he is gagging and wheezing like that</u>?

No one moves <u>until the waitress runs up to him</u>.

Compound–complex sentence. The compound-complex sentence is a sentence that is compound (two or more simple sentences connected together) and complex (contains one or more dependent clauses). In the following examples of compound-complex sentences, the connecting words are italicized and the dependent clauses are underlined:

The steak is served, *and* the customer eats <u>while he talks to the bartender</u>.

He begins to cough, *but* no one moves <u>until the waitress runs up to him</u>.

Is he okay <u>if he is gagging and wheezing like that</u>, *or* is he choking?

The most important thing to remember when writing is not the names for the different kinds of sentences. Rather, remember that you have several options for putting any sentence together. You can keep it simple, or you can combine thoughts into longer sentences. Variety in sentence length and structure creates pleasing rhythm, which makes your writing more interesting. Just as with choosing the right words, drafting effective sentences is a matter of giving yourself the time and opportunity to experiment.

Figure 6–3: Words That Begin Dependent Clauses

after	if	what	whichever
although	in order to	whatever	while
as	since	when	who
because	so that	whenever	whoever
before	that	where	whose
even if	though	wherever	
even though	unless	whether	
how	until	which	

Write Now (5)

Pairs of simple sentences are provided below. Combine each pair into a compound sentence using a connecting word from Figure 6–2. Include a comma before the connecting word. Try to use a variety of connecting words for this exercise. The first item has been done as an example.

, and he
1. The man raises his hands. He grabs his neck.

2. He turns blue. He cannot breathe.

3. The bartender shouts for a doctor. No one answers.

4. Should we try to help? Should we call 911?

5. The waitress stands behind the man. She clasps him around the waist.

6. She squeezes him. Nothing happens.

7. She squeezes hard. He spits out some meat.

8. He is embarrassed. He turns red again.

9. He thanks the waitress. He sits back down.

10. He resumes eating. He does not look happy.

Write Now (6)

There are ten complex sentences in the following paragraph. Each word beginning a dependent clause is in italics. Underline the rest of the dependent clause (the phrase in each sentence that cannot stand independently from the rest of the sentence).

When someone is coughing strongly, [he/she is] not choking. [She] may be choking *if* [she is] gagging but cannot cough. *When* that is the case, you need to perform the Heimlich maneuver. The Heimlich maneuver is named after the doctor *who* invented it. *In order* to do the maneuver, stand behind the victim. Wrap one fist around the other. Place the thumbs against the victim's abdomen. Thrust hard into the abdomen *so that* the object in the airway is pushed out. *Even if* it does not work at first, try again. Each thrust will force more air upward from the lungs *so that* eventually the object may be pushed out. There is another reason to try again. *As* the victim loses oxygen, muscles will relax. New attempts may be successful *where* previous attempts were not.

Text adapted from
Textbook of Pediatric Basic Life Support

Write Now (7)

Write several sentences about a health situation, for example:

going in for a check-up	**being in a car accident**
using insulin	**having an illness**

Use at least one compound sentence (two sentences joined by a connecting word). Also use at least one complex sentence (a sentence containing a dependent clause). See if you can also create at least one compound-complex sentence.

Example: *When my brother was a child, he had asthma. He used an inhaler, and he had to take pills. Because he had asthma, we had to get rid of our cats, and I was angry about that. After I grew up, I understood why we had to do that. My brother is twenty now, but he still has asthma.*

_____

_____

_____

_____

_____

Keep this work because you may use it in another activity.

Common Errors in Sentence Construction

There are four common errors in sentence construction. The following sentences display each of these errors:

1. my neighbors grow tulips

2. My neighbors grow tulips they also grow roses.

3. My neighbors grow tulips, they also grow roses.

4. My neighbors grow tulips. Also grow roses.

In Example 1, the sentence does not begin with a capital letter and end with punctuation. Mistakes in capitalization and punctuation are called **mechanical errors.** In Example 2, two sentences are run together without punctuation separating them. This error is known as a **run-on.** In Example 3, the two sentences are separated, but by a **comma** instead of a period. This error is known as the **comma splice** because the comma is incorrectly used to splice, or stitch together, the two sentences. In Example 4, a complete sentence is followed by only part of a sentence—its subject is missing. A sentence that is incomplete is called a **sentence fragment**.

When people speak, they often run sentences together or leave words out, creating what sound like sentence run-ons, comma splices, or fragments. (Of course, no one uses capital letters or punctuation when speaking.) Deliberate sentence errors can be found in music, poetry, advertising, and creative writing. Sometimes professional writers will make these sentence errors on purpose, for special emphasis. For example, the comma splice and the fragment can be spotted often in informal essays and "style" articles published in magazines and newspapers. When you write for school, official business, or any other formal purpose, however, avoid these errors. They are not part of Standard Written English, and so they are not generally acceptable for serious writing. They also can easily confuse your readers and give the impression that you are not in command of your writing.

If your word processing program offers grammar and spelling assistance, you may be able to have it highlight any sentences that have questionable structure. Check out your options under the "preferences" menu.

Write Now (8)

Identify the type of error in each sentence.

a. mechanical error
b. run-on

c. comma splice
d. fragment

____ 1. Like to eat but need to learn to cook.

____ 2. it would be nice to be able to cook well enough to entertain

____ 3. In particular I would like to learn how to barbeque, I also would like to learn how to do stir-fry.

____ 4. At the Bridge Street Cooking School you can learn how to cook more nutritious cuisine you can learn how to cook food that has taste without extra calories.

____ 5. My sister is taking a class at that school however it is not about cooking it is about preparing attractive food baskets they make beautiful and unique gifts.

____ 6. Recently I bought two cookbooks, I bought *The Yellow Farmhouse Cookbook* and *The Cake Bible*.

____ 7. it is hard to learn cooking from a book

____ 8. Fifty ways to cook potatoes.

Write Now (9)

From the following notes, write up a description for each flower. Feel free to embellish each description, but use only complete, error-free sentences. Try to use a variety of sentences: simple, compound, complex, and compound-complex. The first has been done as an example.

1. hydrangea "Snow Queen" the number-one shrub for American gardens. It is truly a remarkable plant it is for the most distinguished gardens. Hardy in Zones 5–9

   The "Snow Queen" hydrangea has become the number-one shrub for American gardens. It is truly a remarkable plant, and it is worthy of being included in the most distinguished gardens! Snow Queen is hardy in Zones 5–9.

2. peony "Plena" extremely rare, double-flowered red form of the Fern Leaf peony. It is a treasure seldom offered, it is beloved by peony connoisseurs.

   _____

   _____

   _____

   _____

3. narcissus "The True Pheasant's Eye" truly one of the all-time great Narcissus. Delicious fragrance, charmingly reflexed outer petals of purest white, lemon-yellow cup fringed in deep scarlet. The stuff of legend. It is one of the last of the daffodils to bloom, best in a little shade, in moisture-retentive soil

   _____

   _____

   _____

   _____

4. tulip "Angelique" gracefully incurved, ruffled, and fluttered petals form the large, fully double flowers, deep dawn pink on the inside, lighter pink and cream on the outside, Angelique is truly outstanding, it has late blooms on 20-inch stems.

_____

_____

_____

_____

5. camellia "Mrs. Charles Cobb" intense red, anemone-like blooms, 2 to 3 inches wide, blooms appear midseason. spectacular. Long-lasting flowers are a lovely choice for arrangements reaches 6 to 8 feet high in 5 years

_____

_____

_____

_____

**Text adapted from the
Wayside Gardens *Complete Garden Catalog***

Summing Up

1. What is the most important thing to remember about nouns, verbs, adjectives, adverbs, and prepositional phrases?

    _____

    _____

2. What is the most important thing to remember about the different sentence forms, such as simple, compound, complex, and compound-complex?

    _____

    _____

3. Give an example of these common errors in sentence construction:

    Mechanical error: _____

    _____

    Run-on: _____

    _____

Second Thoughts

Review the photograph that opened this chapter; then think about or discuss the following questions:

1. What makes a snapshot different from a work of art?

2. What artistic values are involved in selecting elements to photograph and organizing those elements in the frame?

3. What errors are important to avoid when taking pictures?

   Based on what you have learned in this chapter about the decisions that go into drafting, what new insights do you have about the decisions the artist may have made when setting up this photograph? Write your thoughts in the *Responses* section of your journal.

Comma splice: _____

_____

Fragment: _____

_____

4. Name one situation in life where it would be acceptable to submit something in writing that contained the above kinds of sentence errors, and name one situation where it would not be acceptable.

_____

_____

5. As a result of reading this chapter, what one change will you make to the way that you draft? Write your resolution in the *Habits for Life* section of your journal.

Write Now: Drafting with Attention to Words and Sentences

Develop an essay based on the photograph you described in Write Now (1). Alternatively, develop an essay having to do with the health situation you described in Write Now (7). Think about and plan your topic. Decide what your purpose for writing is and who your audience will be. Develop an outline; then write a draft. Make an effort to select words and construct sentences that create clear, specific pictures in readers' minds. Be sure to give yourself time to review and experiment as you draft. Complete a working draft of this essay. Keep this work because you may use it in a later activity.

Punctuating Compound and Complex Sentences

Compound and complex sentences require special punctuation. When you connect two independent clauses together, insert a comma before the connecting word.

> The steak is served, and the customer eats.
>
> Add a comma before the connecting word

When you place a dependent clause at the beginning of a sentence, separate it by a comma from the rest of the sentence:

> After he eats a really big bite, he begins to cough.
>
> Use a comma

Do not use a comma before a dependent clause that comes at the end of a sentence:

> No one moves until the waitress runs up to him.
>
> No comma

Exercise

Add commas where two independent clauses are joined by a connecting
word or where a dependent clause precedes an independent clause.
If the sentence does not need a comma, put "okay" next to it.

1. It appears that many Americans are turning to "green" gardening.

2. Another word for "green" is "organic."

3. Organic means natural so organic gardening means gardening
   without artificial chemicals.

4. Overuse of pesticides can kill plants and it also can poison the soil.

5. Because fertilizers can seep into the water table overuse of such
   products can affect far-away lakes and bays.

6. Fertilizer chemicals cause algae to flourish and this affects the
   natural balance of water habitats.

7. Gardeners are turning to native plants for they often do well in the
   soil without chemical additives.

8. If you replace your grass lawn with wildflowers a side benefit is that
   you won't have to mow.

9. If you do mow your lawn leave the clippings on the yard to
   decompose.

10. Prepare to work hard whatever kind of gardening you plan to do.

How to Poach an Egg

by Elaine Corn

Check out
Cooks Illustrated
magazine at
www.cooksillustrated.com

Cooks Illustrated *is a magazine for amateurs. Its articles address the down-to-earth dilemmas of the humble kitchen chef. Typical subjects are how to make a good soup broth, how to cut a green pepper, and how to make excellent brownies.* Cooks Illustrated *is also a magazine for people who simply like to read about cooking. To be published in* Cooks Illustrated, *you have to be an entertaining writer as well as a clever cook.*

The following article from Cooks Illustrated *was written by Elaine Corn, the author of a book called* 365 Ways to Cook Eggs. *As you read her instructions on how to poach an egg, notice how her word choices and construction of sentences rise above such an ordinary topic.*

What is a bad
way to cook
an egg?

Poaching is the nicest way to treat an egg, provided you know the nicest way to poach. Eggs don't respond well to random acts of culinary violence. Cast them about like a raft at sea in water that's too hot and too rough, and they will get revenge by tightening, toughening, getting stringy, and falling apart.

A poached egg should be something quite different than that: a lovely, tender white pouch cooked evenly all the way through. The top of the egg yolk should look a little pink, and when cut, the yolk should run just a little. The whites that surround it should glisten and jiggle a little like baked custard, and the cooking liquid should be left with no stray strands of egg white.

By trial and error, I have found a foolproof method that consistently produces poached eggs that live up to these expectations every time.

My first fix was to ditch the standard saucepot. In its place, I now own an eight-inch-diameter nonstick skillet, with flared sides two inches high, that I reserve just for poaching eggs.

When poaching eggs, I first fill the skillet nearly to the rim with water. The first advantage of the skillet quickly becomes clear: The shallower water comes to a boil more quickly, making poached eggs a speedy proposition. Second, an egg meets the bottom of a skillet sooner than it does the bottom of a pot just a few inches taller.

This gives the egg an early floor on which to land gently, before velocity builds. The sooner the egg is on solid ground, the quicker the whites hold. Hence an egg will not stick to this shallow skillet.

What are the two advantages to poaching eggs in a shallow frying pan?

The highest heat possible upon impact sets egg whites most quickly. Because water is the cooking medium, that means 212 degrees Fahrenheit. This high heat also gooses the yolks to hurry up and cook. I also perform a corrective measure to prevent those feathering whites; I add vinegar to lower the pH of the water. This lowers the temperature at which the whites and yolks set, which means that after the initial dunk into boiling water, the egg can cook in water that's slightly cooler and, hence, calmer.

Why is vinegar added to the water?

It is here that I depart completely from any concept of water held at a "poach." Yes, my poaching liquid is at a boil when the eggs go in. But for the actual cooking time, I've concluded that absolutely still water, as long as it's very hot, will poach an egg just the same.

So I turn off the heat and cover the skillet.

During the three and one-half to four minutes that it takes the captured heat to cook the eggs, the temperature of the covered water drops only about twenty degrees. This means that poaching eggs in residual heat eliminates the need to simmer, which can create rough waters that cause the egg to partially disintegrate. It also outwits home stoves that run "hot" and can't hold a simmer.

What are two reasons for turning off the heat after the eggs are in the water?

Now that my eggs have safe haven, how will they taste? Heavily salted water, I found, makes the eggs taste more mellow than lightly salted water. I use at least one full teaspoon in the filled skillet; otherwise the eggs are bland.

What does "safe haven" mean here?

The next question is how to get the eggs into the boiling water without breaking them apart. Cracking the egg onto a saucer is often mentioned in old recipes, but you lose a lot of control as the slithery egg and gravity derail your aim. Cracked into a small cup, the egg stays in one piece through its entire descent into purgatory. *Each* egg is cracked into its *own* cup before the water boils. Working two-handed and using cups with handles for easy grasping, I can dump four eggs into the water in two motions. Refilling the same little cup with a freshly cracked egg just so I don't have to wash four of them throws off the timing. If the eggs aren't in the water within seconds of each other, I lose track of which egg went in when, making it impossible to time them separately.

How does Corn put four eggs into the water at once?

When time's up, I use an oval-bowled slotted spoon to get the eggs out of the poaching liquid. The spoon mimics the shape of the egg so it can nestle comfortably. A skimmer picks the egg up nicely, but I find the shape too flat to pick up something that's fragile and, uh, egg-shaped, so that it rolls about.

I let the egg "drip-dry" by holding it aloft briefly over the skillet. For really dry eggs a paper towel blots to the last drop. I actually like a little of the cooking water to come with my poached eggs, the better to taste the vinegar. Pass the salt and pepper and give me a bottle of Tabasco, and I'm ready to eat poached eggs.

Master Recipe for Poached Eggs
Serves 2, two eggs each

Poached eggs take well to any number of accompaniments. Try serving them on a bed of grated mild cheddar or Monterey Jack cheese or creamed spinach; in a pool of salsa; on a thick slice of tomato topped with a slice of Bermuda onion; on a potato pancake; or simply with plain buttered toast.

- 4 large eggs, each cracked into a small handled cup
- 1 teaspoon salt, plus more to taste
- 2 tablespoons distilled white vinegar
- Ground black pepper

1. Fill 8- to 10-inch nonstick skillet nearly to rim with water, add 1 teaspoon salt and the vinegar, and bring mixture to boil over high heat.

2. Lower the lips of each cup just into water at once; tip eggs into boiling water, cover, and remove from heat. Poach until yolks are medium-firm, exactly 4 minutes. For firmer yolks (or for extra large or jumbo eggs), poach $4^{1}/_{2}$ minutes; for looser yolks (or for medium eggs), poach 3 minutes.

3. With slotted spoon, carefully lift and drain each egg over skillet. (Can drop into ice water and refrigerate up to 3 days . . . .) Season to taste with salt and pepper and serve immediately.

THINK AND RESPOND

1. How is Corn's essay like or different from the actual recipe for poached eggs?

   _____

   _____

   _____

2. What are some of the words and phrases the author selected to use that make the essay livelier than the recipe instructions?

   _____

   _____

   _____

3. What kinds of sentences does Corn use (check all that apply)?

   _____ simple   _____ complex

   _____ compound   _____ compound–complex

4. What process do you think the author went through to come up with this master recipe for poaching eggs?

   _____

   _____

   _____

5. How is Corn's description of the process of poaching eggs similar to the process you go through when you write something important?

   _____

   _____

   _____

6. Provide synonyms or definitions for these words from the essay, and add at least two of the words to the *Words Worth Remembering* section of your journal:

culinary _____

ditch _____

velocity _____

gooses _____

hence _____

bland _____

derail _____

purgatory _____

nestle _____

aloft _____

7. If you liked this reading, make a record of it in the *Readings Worth Remembering* section of your journal.

COMPARING VIEWS

Elaine Corn obviously likes to work with eggs. In order to produce this essay, she certainly had to poach a lot of them. To do research for her book *365 Ways to Cook Eggs,* she probably cooked more eggs than most people do in a lifetime. What is something you have done hundreds of times? Were you trying for the same result or different results each time? What sort of expertise did you develop? After discussing this topic with others, continue to explore it on your own, in your journal—if you like. You may be able to use the material from the discussion and your journal in a future writing activity.

APPLIED WRITING

Expand the word list below with additional vocabulary from Corn's essay. Then write several sentences that have nothing to do with eggs. Try to write at least one compound, complex, or compound-complex sentence. An example has been provided.

Nouns	Verbs	Adjectives	Adverbs	Prepositions	Other Words
raft	cast	nicest	quite	with	the
sea	ditch	hot	consistently	to	and
heat	depart	tender	evenly	of	I
liquid	crack	foolproof	quickly	into	they
____	____	____	____	____	____
____	____	____	____	____	____
____	____	____	____	____	____
____	____	____	____	____	____
____	____	____	____	____	____
____	____	____	____	____	____
____	____	____	____	____	____
____	____	____	____	____	____
____	____	____	____	____	____
____	____	____	____	____	____

Example: *I quickly ditched the hot liquid into the sea, and the waters glistened.*

Your five sentences:

1. _____

2. _____

3. _____

4. _____

5. _____

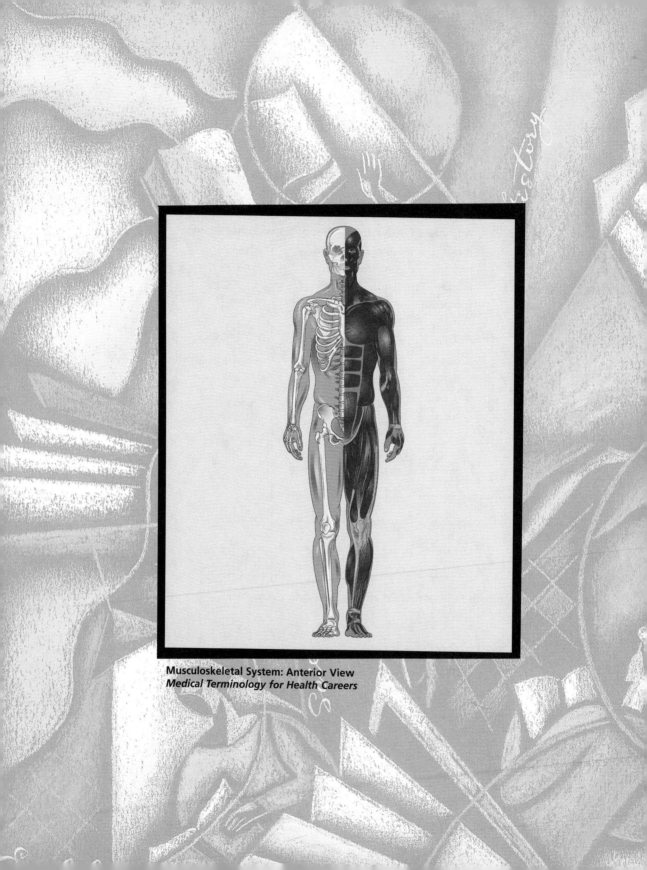

Musculoskeletal System: Anterior View
Medical Terminology for Health Careers

CHAPTER 7

Connecting Sentences and Paragraphs

These are the **key ideas** of this chapter:

- Writing is coherent when readers can easily follow meaning.
- Key words, pronouns, synonyms, and transition words help provide coherence.
- Unity in writing is achieved when each sentence contributes to its paragraph's topic and when each paragraph contributes to the main idea.

Picturing Meaning

Examine the illustration on the opposite page; then think about or discuss these questions:

1. What do you see in this illustration?

   _____

   _____

2. What are the functions of the different parts?

   _____

   _____

3. How do the different parts function together?

   _____

   _____

   In the *Responses* section of your journal, write down your thoughts about this illustration.

Write Now (1)

What parts of *your* body are involved when you decide to pick up a pen and write? Make a sketch or write some notes on how your body moves in the physical act of writing. Keep this work because you may use it in a later activity.

Creating Coherence

A goal when writing is for readers to be able to follow your thoughts within a sentence and from one sentence to the next. This goal is called **coherence.** To "cohere" means to stick together. The opposite of coherence is disjointedness, which means to be disconnected, with parts separated. A simple way to describe coherent writing is to say that it "hangs together." Strategies that help create coherence are:

1. Repeating key words

2. Using synonyms

3. Using pronouns

4. Using transition words

Key words. Key words are those words that are central to the idea being addressed. The repetition of key words helps readers stay focused. In the following short chapter from a book about the Dakota region of the United States, the key word is "rain":

In seven paragraphs, the key word "rain" appears eight times (it is underlined here but not in the original).

Until I moved to western South Dakota, I did not know about <u>rain</u>, that it could come too hard, too soft, too hot, too cold, too early, too late. That there could be too little at the right time, too much at the wrong time, and vice versa.

I did not know that a light <u>rain</u> coming at the end of a hot afternoon, with the temperature at 100 degrees or more, can literally burn wheat, steaming it on the stalk so it's not worth harvesting.

I had not seen a long, slow <u>rain</u> come at harvest, making grain lying in the swath begin to sprout again, ruining it as a cash crop.

Until I had seen a few violent hailstorms and replaced the shingles on our roof twice in five years, I had forgotten why my grandmother had screens made of chicken wire for all the windows on the west side of her house.

I had not seen the whimsy of wind, <u>rain</u>, and hail: a path in a wheatfield as if a drunken giant had stumbled through, leaving footprints here and there. I had not seen hail fall from a clear blue sky. I had not tasted horizontal <u>rain</u>, flung by powerful winds.

I had not realized that a long soaking <u>rain</u> in spring or fall, a straight-down-falling <u>rain</u>, a gentle splashing <u>rain</u> is more than a blessing. It's a miracle.

An old farmer once asked my husband and me how long we'd been in the country. "Five years," we answered. "Well, then," he said, "you've seen <u>rain</u>."

Dakota: A Spiritual Geography
Kathleen Norris

Synonyms. Synonyms are words or phrases that can be substituted for each other because they mean essentially the same thing. Examples of synonyms are *house, home, abode, dwelling place, homestead,* and *residence.* Synonyms allow you to avoid repeating a word too many times, too close together. They also can add depth, color, and tone. In the following text about a Universal Studios amusement center attraction called "The Amazing Adventures of Spider-Man," synonyms help describe the attraction's exciting features:

In the parlance of the thrill biz, it's a "<u>dark ride</u>," <u>the roller coaster's indoor cousin</u>—<u>a Tunnel of Love gone mad</u>, playing out at an amphetamine clip. It's also a <u>$100 million investment</u> in "The Theme Park of the 21st Century," at the center of Universal's full-frontal assault on Disney's entertainment stronghold in Florida...

Making it all work requires serious hardware. Once <u>Spider-Man</u> is operational, more than 70 networked computers—costing more than $15 million—will be deployed to integrate the <u>ride's</u> every element to within 5 milliseconds. "When it's finished, there'll be nothing else on the planet like it," says Peter Jelf, a control systems engineer Universal pulled in to build its one-of-a-kind systems. "Disney had better be afraid."

"Scream Machine"
Wired

Six synonyms are used to stand in for "The Amazing Adventures of Spider-Man." (They are underlined here but not in the original.)

Pronouns. Pronouns are words that stand in place of nouns. By substituting a pronoun for a noun, you can avoid too-frequent repetition of the noun, which can be dull and cumbersome. For example, in the following sentences, the pronouns *they* and *them* are used in place of the noun *neighbors*:

> "My neighbors are pleasant. *They* are friendly and I enjoy talking to *them*."

This reads much more smoothly than:

> "My neighbors are pleasant. My neighbors are friendly and I enjoy talking to my neighbors."

The use of pronouns also makes it clear that the *same* neighbors are being referred to each time. A list of pronouns appears in Figure 7–1.

Figure 7–1: Pronoun Forms

Pronouns that change form:

Subject	Object	Possessive
I	me	mine
you	your	yours
she	her	hers
he	him	his
it	it	its
we	us	our, ours
they	them	their, theirs
who	who or whom	whose

Pronouns that do not change form:
another, any, anybody, anyone, both, each, either, everybody, everyone, everything, few, many, much, neither, nobody, none, no one, nothing, one, several, somebody, someone, something, this, there, what

In the following passage from a book-length memoir by a Japanese American, the author relies extensively on pronouns to explain why he was not particularly excited about his first trip to Japan:

Japan? That was where <u>my</u> grandparents came from. <u>It</u> didn't have much to do with <u>my</u> present life.

But then Japan had never seemed that important to <u>me</u>, even in childhood. On holidays when <u>we</u> would get together with relatives, <u>I</u> didn't notice that the faces around <u>me</u> looked different from most of the faces at school. <u>I</u> didn't notice that <u>my</u> grandfathers were in Japan, <u>my</u> grandmothers dead. <u>No one</u> spoke about <u>them</u>, just as <u>no one</u> spoke about Japan. <u>We</u> were American. <u>It</u> was the Fourth of July, Labor Day, Christmas. All <u>I</u> noticed was that the food <u>we</u> ate—futomaki, mazegohan, teriyaki, kamaboko—was different from what <u>I</u> liked best—McDonald's, pizza, hot dogs, tuna-fish salad.

Turning Japanese: Memoirs of a Sansei
David Mura

> Eighteen pronouns are used to stand in for Japan, the author, his relatives, and the holidays they spent together. (The pronouns are underlined here but not in the original.)

Transition words. Transition words help readers move smoothly from one idea to the next. "Transition" means a change of position. In writing, transition words indicate a change of thought. Connecting words such as *and* and *but* help to indicate transition. Other frequently used transition words appear in Figure 7–2.

Figure 7–2: Frequently Used Transition Words

> **Words indicating order:** first, second, third (and so on), afterward, before, consequently, during, finally, in conclusion, last, meanwhile, next, then
>
> **Words indicating contrast:** actually, but, besides, however, in fact, instead, nevertheless, nonetheless, on the other hand, still, yet
>
> **Words indicating location:** above, behind, below, beside, following, in front of
>
> **Words indicating consequences:** also, as a result, consequently, if, in fact, indeed, likewise, moreover, therefore, similarly, whatever, whenever, wherever
>
> **Words indicating detail:** for example, for instance, once, specifically
>
> **Words indicating extension:** also, furthermore, in addition, likewise, moreover

In the following passages describing why English has become the dominant language of the world, the authors use transition words and phrases to connect one idea (the advantages English does *not* have over other languages) to another (the advantages English does have):

Nine transition words or phrases are used to indicate order, contrast, and consequence (they are underlined here but not in the original).

<u>First</u>, we must dispose of some myths. English is not intrinsically easier to learn than French or Russian, nor is it more lyrical, more beautiful, mellifluous or more eloquent than any other language. Such judgements are almost meaningless. Lyrical for whom? English is, <u>moreover</u>, highly idiomatic. How does one begin to explain phrases like "put up with" and "get on with it"....

<u>On the other hand</u>, the English language has three characteristics that can be counted as assets in its world state. <u>First of all</u>, unlike all other European languages, the gender of every noun in modern English is determined by meaning, and does not require a masculine, feminine or neuter article. In French, <u>by contrast</u>, the moon is *la lune* (feminine) while the sun, for no obvious reason, is *le soleil* (masculine). <u>Worse</u>, in the Germanic languages, is the addition of the neuter gender. In German the moon is *der Mond* (masculine), the sun is *die Sonne* (feminine), while child, girl, and woman, are *das Kind, das Mädchen* and *das Weib,* all neuter. As Mark Twain put it, "In German, a young lady has no sex, but a turnip has."

<u>The second</u> practical quality of English is that is has a grammar of great simplicity and flexibility. Nouns and adjectives have highly simplified word-endings. This flexibility extends to the parts of speech themselves. Nouns can become verbs and verbs nouns in a way that is impossible in other languages. We can *dog* someone's footsteps. We can *foot* it to the bus. We can *bus* children to school and then *school* them in English ... .

<u>Above all</u>, the great quality of English is its teeming vocabulary, 80 percent of which is foreign-born. Precisely because its roots are so varied—Celtic, Germanic (German, Scandinavian and Dutch) and Romance (Latin, French and Spanish)—it has words in common with virtually every language in Europe: German, Yiddish, Dutch, Flemish, Danish, Swedish, French, Italian, Portuguese, and Spanish. <u>In addition</u>, almost any page of the Oxford English Dictionary or Webster's Third will turn up borrowings from Hebrew and Arabic, Hindi-Urdu, Bengali, Malay, Chinese, the languages of Java, Australia, Tahiti, Polynesia, West Africa and even from one of the aboriginal languages of Brazil. It is the enormous range and varied source of this vocabulary, as much as the sheer numbers and geographical spread of its speakers, that makes English a language of such unique vitality.

The Story of English
Robert McCrum, William Cran, and Robert MacNeil

Write Now (2)

Review the four passages to answer the questions below.

Rain

1. What one synonym is used for rain in the fourth paragraph?

   _____

2. The pronoun *it* is used as a substitute for what three different nouns?

   in paragraph 1 _____

   in paragraph 2 _____

   in paragraph 3 _____

3. What transition words are used? _____

   _____

Amusement park ride

1. What pronoun is used as a key word in the first paragraph?

   _____

2. What transition words are used? _____

   _____

Japanese heritage

1. What key word appears three times? _____

2. "The faces around me" is used as a synonym for what word?

   _____

The English language

1. What key word is used? _____

2. What is a synonym for "borrowings"? _____

   _____

Write Now (3)

Circle one transition word in each numbered paragraph. Also, underline the synonyms in each paragraph. The first synonym in each paragraph is underlined, and the total number of synonyms in each paragraph is indicated in parentheses. The first has been done as an example.

1. Thousands of Americans are flocking to <u>Cuba</u>, and this <u>Caribbean island</u> has become a darling of the travel media. Travel by U.S. tourists to this <u>Communist enclave</u>, (however,) has been restricted by the U.S. Department of the Treasury. (3)

2. The <u>goat lookalike</u> oreotragus oreotragus is actually a dwarf antelope. These hoofed creatures go by the name klipspringer (which means "rock-springer"). They can be found in Africa south of the Sahara and also, of course, in some zoos. (6)

3. For some people, a <u>garden</u> is a necessity, not a luxury. They must have a patch of summer beauty to tend themselves. If they live in a modest bungalow, they will have a grand flowerbed. If their town home has only a small patch of lawn, nonetheless they will have a border of bright annuals along their walkway. Even confinement to a small apartment does not stop serious gardeners, for they will have a well tended window box or a nursery of potted plants on the balcony. (6)

4. My coworker is out sick today. Apparently, he has been struck by that <u>mysterious malady</u>, that unnamed illness, that not-unpleasant ailment brought about by the sudden onset of warm weather on a Friday after an unusually cold spring. (3)

5. Some people think that if they are not <u>drunk</u> every day, then they are not alcoholics. That is not necessarily true. Getting flat-out smashed once a week actually can be just as much a problem as getting a little tight every night. (3)

6. <u>Bimota SB8R</u> is a stunning Italian motorcycle. Indeed, one reviewer calls this metal model "rolling artwork—at once eye candy and serious sporting machine." Unfortunately, this handsome hunk of bike is as expensive as it is stylish—it costs a cool $23,000. (7)

7. <u>The personal Web page</u> is the twenty-first century equivalent of the old-fashioned calling card. It is one's introduction to computer-savvy society. Some people feel that an online presence is practically required. They seem to think that if you don't have a site in cyberspace staked out, then you are not really real. (5)

8. *Citizen Kane* is one of the greatest films ever made. This black-and-white cinematic masterpiece was directed and starred in by Orson Welles. Made more than fifty years ago, it is in fact a thinly veiled documentary of newspaper tycoon William R. Hearst. It was recently ranked the number-one movie of all time by the American Film Institute. (5)

9. The <u>epidemic of 1918</u> was one of the worst medical disasters of the twentieth century. It was called the Spanish flu because Spain was especially hard hit, but actually the disease may have first appeared in Kansas and then spread to Europe as U.S. soldiers were shipped overseas for the war then going on. The virus claimed 20 million lives from all over the world in less than a year. (5)

10. Despite being legal for decades in the United States, <u>abortion</u> remains extremely controversial. Some people support what they call a "woman's right to choose" and consider this outpatient medical treatment as nothing more than a last-resort form of contraception. Others, on the other hand, consider it baby killing. (5)

Write Now (4)

Working in pairs, substitute into each paragraph at least one synonym and one pronoun to avoid excessive repetition of the same noun. Read each revision aloud to decide if it sounds smoother (less choppy) than the original. The first has been done as an example.

1.   George and my half-sister recently married. ~~George and my half-sister~~ are expecting a child. ~~George and my half-sister~~ both work days and go to school nights.

     The newlyweds (above first sentence)
     They (after "child.")

2.   Blueberry bushes grow several feet high. It is easy to gather the berries from blueberry bushes. Just comb your hand through the blueberry bush and ripe berries will fall right off the blueberry bush.

3.   Having a garbage disposal in the kitchen sink is a great convenience. A garbage disposal can be purchased from a plumbing supply store or a home improvement store. A garbage disposal is not too difficult to install.

4.   Mosquitoes can be a problem in summer. Mosquitoes can ruin a picnic or barbeque. To keep mosquitoes from bothering you and your guests, try citronella candles.

5.   "Bark" is the word for the outside cover of a tree. "Bark" also means a kind of ship that has three or more masts. "Bark" also can mean the sharp cry of a dog.

Write Now (5)

Write four or five sentences about one of these four things: a kind of weather, an amusement park ride, an important element in your family heritage, or a language. Use the writings in this chapter (about rain, Spider-Man, being Japanese, and the English language) as models. Include key words, synonyms, pronouns, and transition words. An example is provided. Keep this work because you may use it in a later activity.

Example: *Some people love snow. It only snows, however, when the temperature is cold. For example, today we have light flurries and it is ten degrees. I do not like the cold. Therefore, I do not like snow.*

Your sentences:

_____

_____

_____

_____

_____

_____

_____

_____

_____

_____

To identify synonyms for a word, highlight it and then use the "thesaurus" function of your word processor.

To identify how often a key word appears in a piece of writing, highlight it and then use the "find" function of your word processor.

Creating Unity

A paragraph is said to have unity if all of its sentences contribute to the same topic. Any sentence that addresses a different point upsets that unity. In the following paragraph, written by a surgeon, every sentence contributes toward a description of a knife. Almost every sentence makes a direct reference to this important surgical tool:

The author describes how the knife is held.

The author describes how to cut with the knife.

The author describes how he feels about the knife.

One holds the knife as one holds the bow of a cello or a tulip—by the stem. Not palmed nor gripped nor grasped, but lightly, with the tips of the fingers. The knife is not for pressing. It is for drawing across the field of skin. Like a slender fish, it waits, at the ready, then, go! It darts, followed by a fine wake of red. Even now, after so many times, I still marvel at its power—cold, gleaming, silent. More, I am still struck with a kind of dread that it is I in whose hand the blade travels, that my hand is its vehicle, that yet again this terrible steel-bellied thing and I have conspired for a most unnatural purpose, the laying open of the body of a human being.

"The Knife"
Richard Selzer

An essay is said to have unity if all of its paragraphs contribute to the same main idea. Think of an essay as a necklace made of several strands of multicolored beads:

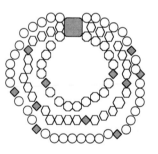

Beads = words
Segments = sentences
Strands = paragraphs
Necklace = essay

Words are linked together into sentences, each of which expresses a complete thought. Sentences are linked together into paragraphs, each of which is an elaboration of an idea. Finally, paragraphs are linked together into the essay, which is the complete, satisfying exploration of a theme. A necklace looks good when the beads are strung in a pleasing combination. In the same way, an essay is effective when the separate elements are connected harmoniously.

Write Now (6)

In the discussion above, essay unity was explained by comparing it to a necklace in which the parts are unified into a whole. Work in small groups to think of other ways to picture essay unity. Two examples are provided.

Words:
Units of meaning   *ingredients*   *soldier*   _____   _____

Sentences:
Complete thoughts   *dishes*   *brigades*   _____   _____

Paragraphs:
Expressions of ideas   *courses*   *battalions*   _____   _____

Essay:
Explorations of themes   *meal*   *army*   _____   _____

Write Now (7)

For each paragraph below, cross out the one sentence that does not contribute to paragraph unity. Then identify the topic of each paragraph in the margin and summarize the essay's main idea.

     Like much of modern technology, two lawn care tools bring both blessings and problems. They are the weed whacker and the leaf blower. Lawn mowers have been around a long time. Once the domain of professionals, these gardening gadgets are now owned by every suburbanite with a credit card from Home Depot.

     The two tools have raised our expectations of the well manicured lawn. They permit a perfection that is clearly absurd. For example, there are big lawns at my apartment complex, but not many trees. If you are equipped with a blower, it becomes hard to tolerate even a single dead leaf tangled deep inside a hedge. Once armed with a weed whacker, you feel compelled to cut off at the knees every last stray wisp of weed.

     You can end up spending a lot of money on lawn care equipment. These powerful tools are fun to use, if you like to play with weapons. Using a leaf blower is like aiming a bazooka. A weed whacker mows down the enemy like machine gun fire. But for the innocent bystanders to this battle, the noise is really bothersome. The lawn-mower's whine is now joined by the *bzzzz* of the weed whacker and the *vroom* of the leaf blower. Like Genghis Khan and Attila the Hun, this brawny pair has invaded the neighborhood and forever destroyed the quiet of Saturday mornings.

Essay main idea: _____

Summing Up

1. Define coherence.

   _____

   _____

2. Consider these four writing strategies that help create coherence: repeating key words; using synonyms; using pronouns; and using transition words. Underline the one you handle most easily in your writing. What makes it easiest for you?

   _____

   _____

3. Circle the strategy you tend not to employ. What is one thing you can do to make better use of this strategy in your writing?

   _____

   _____

Second Thoughts

Review the illustration that opened this chapter; then think about or discuss the following questions:

1. What are the names of the different muscles and bones of the body?

2. What happens when any one part is not present or functioning?

3. When you use your leg, how conscious are you of the different parts working together?

Based on what you have learned in this chapter about how coherence and unity are created in writing, what new insights do you have about the functioning of the human body? Write your thoughts in the *Responses* section of your journal.

4. Define unity.

   _____

   _____

5. Name a situation in your life (that does not involve writing) where coherence and unity are important.

   _____

   _____

6. As a result of reading this chapter, what one change will you make to bring more coherence and unity to your writing? Write your resolution in the *Habits for Life* section of your journal.

Write Now: Cohesive and Unified Working Draft

Using the paragraph about the surgeon's knife as a model, draft an essay describing a tool, such as

a Swiss army knife	a pair of knitting needles
a spatula	a compass

For ideas on how your hand works when it uses this tool, you may want to review your responses to the opening illustration of this chapter or to Write Now (1). If you choose not to write about a tool, you can expand on the subject you wrote about in Write Now (5). Write cohesively by repeating key words and by using synonyms, pronouns, and transition words. Also aim for unity by making sure that every sentence contributes to its paragraph's topic, and that every paragraph contributes to the main idea of the essay. Complete a working draft of this essay. Keep this work because you may use it in a later activity.

Using Pronouns Properly

Using pronouns can make writing smoother (see the list in Figure 7–1). You must take care, however, with the following pronouns: *I, you, he, she, it, we, they,* and *who.* These pronouns are used to replace nouns operating as the subjects of sentences. But they change form when they are used to replace nouns that operate as objects (receiving the action of the verb) or when indicating ownership (possession):

Juanita put on Dion's hat.

The hat belongs to Dion.

<u>She</u> borrowed <u>it</u>.   ← object pronouns

<u>He</u> loaned it to <u>her</u>.

<u>She</u> had given it to <u>him</u>.

subject pronouns

The hat is no longer <u>hers</u>.

It is <u>his</u>. ← possessive pronouns

<u>They</u> own a dog.

It is <u>their</u> dog.

The cat is <u>theirs</u>, too.

The cat belongs to both of <u>them</u>.

pronoun changes form only when used possessively

All other pronouns that can be used possessively add an apostrophe and *s*:

<u>Nobody</u> can play poker as successfully as I do.

I lose to <u>nobody</u>.

It's <u>nobody's</u> business how I always manage to win.

Another important key when using pronouns is to make sure that the references are clear:

The groomer clipped my dog, and <u>she</u> was very good.

who, the groomer or the dog?

<u>They</u> say a hurricane is likely in the next few days.

who? TV weather reporters, co-workers, people on the street?

Note: Another important issue in pronoun usage is making sure there is agreement in number and gender. This is discussed in Chapter 12.

Exercise 1

Fill in the blanks with the proper pronoun. Your choices are provided after each sentence.

1. Oh true love of _____, you can make _____ happy by saying, "_____ do." (I, me, mine)

2. The job was _____ for the asking, but _____ had to sleep through the alarm and miss the interview! There goes _____ future! (you, your, yours)

3. Carol is my sister. This little girl is _____ daughter. I have two nephews that are _____ also. _____ has another child on the way. (she, her, hers)

4. Jocko plays the saxophone. You should hear _____ play. _____ is really good. _____ band will be at the club tomorrow night. (he, him, his)

5. The party after a wedding is fun, but _____ ends. The exchange of vows is _____ lasting gift. What you get out of a marriage depends on what you put into _____. (it, its)

6. _____ should win the tennis match today. I don't think any of the other pairs can beat _____. They can't match _____ incredible teamwork. By the end of the day, the trophy will be _____! (we, us, our, ours)

7. Cissie's great grandparents came from Lebanon. _____ moved to New York with _____ children in 1927. The furniture in her house was once _____. She knows a lot of stories about _____. (they, them, their, theirs)

8. The carpenter _____ tools were left at my house is not the man _____ repaired our backdoor. The carpenter is the one _____ I would recommend for the work you need done. (who, whom, whose)

9. Did _____ see Vivian? She did not leave with _____. It's _____ guess when she will return. (anybody, anybody's)

10. I hear _____._____ steps are coming closer. _____ is coming this way. (someone, someone's)

Exercise 2

Rewrite each sentence to eliminate unclear pronoun use.

1. Mary and Martha are partners, but she owns a larger share of the business.

   _____

   _____

   _____

2. In this book they have a lot of good biographical sketches.

   _____

   _____

   _____

3. I was in Phoenix and Seattle. It is beautiful there.

   _____

   _____

   _____

4. They do not have a lot of crime in my neighborhood.

   _____

   _____

   _____

5. Corinne told Isabel how to fix the window, but she did it wrong.

   _____

   _____

   _____

Useful Web Sites

• **Guide to Grammar and Writing**

http://webster.commnet.edu/HP/pages/darling
Prepared by Professor Charles Darling of the Capital Community-
Technical College in Hartford, Connecticut, this site is well organized
and offers good information on such matters as constructing sentences,
sentence variety, and writing at the paragraph and essay level.

• **OWL Handouts Indexed by Topic**

http://owl.english.purdue.edu
Purdue University claims to have "one of the foremost OWL [Online
Writing Labs] in the world." This page from its Web site offers
information sheets and exercises, each specific to one writing-related
topic such as sentence construction, punctuation, and parts of speech.

• **Grammar Hotline Directory**

www.tc.cc.va.us/WRITCENT/gh/hotlinol.htm
This location contains a directory of grammar staffed by real people to
answer your questions by phone and e-mail. The directory is put
together by Tidewater Community College, Virginia Beach, and is
organized by state (plus Canada).

Vietnam
Reflexes and Reflections
by Douglas Clifford

American military involvement in Vietnam ended more than twenty-five years ago, but it remains alive in the art of those who experienced it. Back in 1981, a group of veterans formed a collective to exhibit their artwork. That eventually led to the creation of the National Vietnam Veterans Art Museum in Chicago. To celebrate its opening, the museum published a book called Vietnam: Reflexes and Reflections. *The book features paintings, drawings, photographs, sculptures, and other works from ninety-five artists, most American but some Vietnamese.*

Douglas Clifford is one of the featured artists. He served a tour in Vietnam beginning in 1968, working as a film-lab technician at Phu Cat Air Base in the Central Highlands. On the side, he took his own photographs. Two of those photographs appear in the book, along with the following "artist's statement" describing why he took the kinds of photographs he did. As you read this statement, think about the importance of the topic to the author. Think about how carefully Clifford must have worked to choose his words and shape his sentences.

What is an "effort not without purpose"?

As they were for millions of Americans, images of Vietnam were a significant part of my life for several years before I went there. I watched along with my family as the nightly news showed story after story of the war, American GIs, in or out of action, and Vietnamese soldiers and civilians, along with related statistics. The newspapers, weekly news magazines, and other purveyors of images were all involved in this effort to show us that war in a land so far away from us. It was an effort not without purpose, for to support the war it was necessary to see it in a certain way: to see how destructive war can be, how terrible is the unleashed strength of a military superpower, how we could identify with American GIs, and how without substance or context were the Vietnamese. It is that last point that struck me so forcefully when I got there in late 1968, about eight months after the Tet offensive, which began the change in the war that led to its conclusion.

Having been trained as a photographer by the Air Force, by the time I went to Vietnam, twenty-three years old and with more than two years of service already completed, I was capable of forming my own images. What I found there, from my first day in the country, was in sharp contrast to what I had previously been exposed to: not that war wasn't terrible, because signs of the war's destruction were all around. And the American GI's experience was, after all, now my own. It was the Vietnamese who surprised me. I saw people doing things that everybody does, or at least tries to do—kids selling cold orange soda and Coca-Cola at the roadside, kids chasing chickens, farmers knee-deep in lush green fields tending their rice, women washing and hanging out laundry, and old people doing very little. These were the images we had not previously seen.

It was not, as I had expected, the war for which I was most unprepared. For that I had, in some fashion, been trained. My older brother had spent thirteen months in I Corps in 1967 and come home wounded. Two cousins had gone and come back. There were friends, guys I was stationed with, acquaintances, schoolmates, and others who had gone, and some of them had not come back. There were lots of images to go with that reality.

The other reality, the one that lacked images, was the reality of Vietnam—the country, the place. That reality included the shoreline of the South China Sea, the cordillera of the Central Highlands, where I was stationed, and between the highlands and the sea the rice paddies, rich green in the rainy season and tawny brown when it was dry. The people in this reality were not just soldiers, VC and ARVN, but schoolchildren, farmers, merchants, and the countless others who worked at the bases, providing services, both legitimate and illegitimate, to the United States military. That was the reality to which I had to supply my own images.

I was not a combat soldier as my brother has been. Those guys had a different existence, for which I had a profound respect, but which I had few illusions of trying to depict in photographs. Not only was combat not my own experience, but it was an experience that was being extensively documented.

What surprised Clifford when he arrived in Vietnam?

What does Clifford mean by a "reality" that "lacked images"?

Why did Clifford feel he should not try to show combat in his photographs?

166

When did Clifford take his photographs?

What was surprising to people who saw his photographs?

To what two stories is Clifford referring?

My photographs, then, are from my environment at the time and show something about Vietnam as a country and the Vietnamese as people. I did not ignore that other reality, that world of GIs and what we were doing there, but I wanted to show it from a different perspective. There was so much to reveal about where we were, what we were doing, who we were doing it with and to and for that the endeavor became a serious avocation for me. As any veteran can tell you, whether in war or nearly war or peace, military life contains stretches of time that are devoted to being ready and standing down after something happens, or just after being ready. I used the time I had to photograph as much as I could.

I tried to present Vietnam as a place where people lived, worked, went to school, and struggled with their lives, in spite of the war. People seem surprised by this and by how the American military presence looked in that context. I wanted to take pictures of little children looking like children; I wanted the landscape to be shown for its beauty: the tropical sunsets were spectacular and with the monsoon came every shade of green, from rice stalks to the grass on the hills; and on some days the Central Highlands rose up through the low cloud cover like a panorama in a Chinese screen painting. The military airplanes were beautiful but terrible, and noisier than can be imagined. Their grace and fluidity were aspects of their capacity for destruction. The resources devoted to the airplanes were overwhelming and the relationship of these machines to the surrounding environment of water buffalo in rice fields and fishing boats trailing nets was absurd. So there were two stories to be told.

I have found that most of us picture soldiers overseas in terms of what they leave at home and what they are doing without. To see a war from the perspective of the land where the war is—the perspective of its people—is an experience not to be underestimated.

My pictures are artifacts of the war. They were shot, processed, printed, and mounted in Vietnam. They owe their existence to Vietnam.

THINK AND RESPOND

1. How many times do the following key words appear in this essay?

   war _____

   Vietnam (or Vietnamese) _____

   images _____

   reality _____

2. What synonyms does Clifford use for the following words?

   Soldiers (paragraph 1) _____

   _____

   _____

   The people of Vietnam (paragraph 4) _____

   _____

   _____

3. The pronoun *I* stands for the author, but who does the pronoun *we* in paragraph six stand for?

   _____

   _____

4. Name at least four transition words used in this essay.

   _____

   _____

5. The word *then* in the first line of paragraph 6 is a major transition point separating the two halves of the essay. What is each half about?

   _____

   _____

6. Provide synonyms or definitions for these words from the essay, and add at least two of the words to the *Words Worth Remembering* section of your journal:

purveyors _____

cordillera _____

rice paddies _____

tawny _____

endeavor _____

avocation _____

standing down _____

monsoon _____

panorama _____

artifacts _____

7. If you liked this reading, make a record of it in the *Readings Worth Remembering* section of your journal.

COMPARING VIEWS

How do the images you see on TV and through other media differ from what you have found to be real? Think of this question in terms of any social disturbance you have experienced (for example, a war, riot, protest, or public controversy). After discussing this topic with others, continue to explore it on your own, in your journal—if it interests you. You may be able to use material from the discussion and your journal in a future writing activity.

APPLIED WRITING

Clifford says that his attempt to see Vietnam from the perspective of the Vietnamese was "an experience not to be underestimated." Draft an essay about an experience that has affected you in important ways. For example, write about an important journey or task. Like Clifford, think about how you were affected and how you responded. Develop an outline and then make an effort to draft the essay cohesively, using key words, synonyms, pronouns, and transition words. As you draft, set paragraph and essay unity as a goal. Complete a working draft of this essay. Keep this work because you may use it in a later activity.

The Building of a Custom Home
Eager Web Page Design

CHAPTER 8

Revising and Evaluating

These are the **key ideas** of this chapter:

- Revision is the process of making improvements to a draft to turn it into a polished piece of writing.
- Checklists, feedback from others, and scoring guides can be useful in the revising process.
- With any draft, keep revising until you feel the writing accomplishes its purpose.

Picturing Meaning

Examine the series of photographs on the opposite page; then think about or discuss these questions.

1. What do you see happening in these photographs?

   _____

   _____

2. How do the workers check their work?

   _____

   _____

3. What role do inspectors play in the construction of a house?

   _____

   _____

4. Why is all this checking important?

   _____

   _____

   In the *Responses* section of your journal, write down your thoughts about this series of photographs.

Write Now (1)

Think of something you have done—such as a job assignment, a hobby task, or a physical activity—that required a high level of performance and had consequences if you did poorly. As you did this work, how did you check yourself to make sure you were doing it effectively? Who else monitored or evaluated your efforts? Write down your recollections of the process. Keep this work because you may use it in a later activity.

Making Major Revisions

When you have completed a working draft, what do you do next? What many writers do next is . . . nothing. They put the draft aside and let it sit.

There are two reasons for giving your draft a rest. First, when you have just written something, you are probably still emotionally caught up in it. You may find it hard to be critical. Second, when you have just written something, you are usually worn out. The last thing you want to do is look for changes to make. For these reasons, it is a good idea to let an hour, a day, or even more go by before doing anything with your draft. Writers call this period "letting it cool."

When you *are* ready to turn back to your draft, the next stage is revising. This is the stage where you make changes to your work to turn it into a polished piece of writing. What many writers learn through experience is that revision often takes longer to complete than the first draft. The benefit of this effort, however, is that it can make the difference between an adequate and an excellent piece of writing.

A good way to begin the process of revision is to reread your draft all the way through to get an overall impression. As you read, ask yourself these types of questions:

- Does the writing fulfill its purpose?

- Is it appropriate for the intended audience?

- Is it coherent?

- Does it have unity?

- Is it interesting?

Before you begin making changes to a word-processed draft, save it under a slightly different name. For example, add "v.2" to the file name to indicate that it is version number two. Then move your original file into a folder called "Old Drafts." This allows you to keep the original draft (in case you dislike the revisions) while preventing you from getting mixed up about which file is the most current.

If your answer to any of the above questions is no, then you may have to make major revisions. For example, you may have to reorganize the material, delete unnecessary sentences, or create better transitions. You may even need to do some more brainstorming to come up with additional ideas and details. Tackle these major issues first before focusing on details such as sentence-level editing.

When revising, create a subhead at the end of your file called "Out-takes." Paste large chunks of cut material here. The cut material can be easily retrieved if you decide you want to use it after all. Delete this section when you are finished drafting.

A good method for reviewing your own work is to read it aloud. This forces you to pay attention to every word. As you read, notice if you hesitate or find yourself reading twice to figure out meaning. If you stumble as you read, readers will stumble, too, so put an "X" near these spots to remind yourself to work on them. When you have finished reading, go back over the work to mark it up. For example, you can number sentences into a new order, draw lines through words you want to take out, insert new language, or indicate where you want to break one paragraph into two. If your changes are extensive, produce another draft.

A writing checklist appears in Figure 8–1. Use this checklist to review any draft of writing. Use your notes on this checklist and the draft itself as a guide for creating a second draft.

If you want to make major changes to a paragraph, copy it and paste the copy below the original. Make your changes to the copy. Delete the original only when you are satisfied with your changes.

Write Now (2)

Go through your writing folder. Find a draft that you like, such as one you created for the final Write Now activities in Chapter 5, 6, or 7. Reread the draft and mark it up. Also, review the draft using the Writing Checklist in Figure 8–1. Then produce a second draft.

Figure 8-1: Writing Checklist   **Name of Work:**_____

1. Purpose
   _____ The purpose is very clear.
   _____ The essay sticks to the purpose.

2. Introduction
   _____ The introduction clearly expresses the main idea.
   _____ It catches readers' attention.

3. Body
   _____ The main idea is supported with major points and details.
   _____ The body is logically organized.

4. Conclusion
   _____ The conclusion summarizes the main idea.
   _____ It completes the purpose of the essay.

5. Paragraphs
   _____ The essay is divided into meaningful chunks.
   _____ Each paragraph presents and develops a topic.

6. Transitions
   _____ Each idea and each paragraph is clearly connected to the next.
   _____ Transitions are smooth and not obtrusive.

7. Title
   _____ The title summarizes the main idea.
   _____ It catches readers' attention.

8. Language
   _____ Words are interesting and correctly used.
   _____ Sentences are complete and varied, with a balance between simple and complex.

9. Mechanics
   _____ Spelling is correct.
   _____ Punctuation marks are used appropriately.

Comments: _____

_____

_____

_____

_____

_____

_____

_____

Making Minor Revisions

Once you have a draft that works as a whole, reread it again for the details. Ask yourself such questions as:

- Are words used and spelled correctly?
- Are the sentences complete and grammatical?
- Is the punctuation correct?

Make these sentence-level corrections as you read through the draft. You may want to once again read out loud, so that you focus on each word. If your changes are extensive, produce another draft.

How many times should you revise your work? Ernest Hemingway, a journalist and novelist celebrated for his spare writing style, once answered that question in an interview:

Interviewer: How much rewriting do you do?

Hemingway: It depends. I rewrote the ending of *Farewell to Arms,* the last page of it, thirty-nine times before I was satisfied.

Interviewer: Was there some technical problem there? What was it that had stumped you?

Hemingway: Getting the words right.

Writers at Work: The "Paris Review" Interviews
George Plimpton

Few writers have revised anything thirty-nine times, but it is not at all unusual to revise more than once. The number of revisions you should make to a piece of writing depends on its importance, how much time you have, and how much better you want to make it. For an illustration of the revision process, see Figure 8–2.

Figure 8–2: Illustration of the Revision Process

Compare the drafts below with the final version which appears, of course, on the first page of this chapter.

Draft 1

CHAPTER 8: REVIEWING AND REVISING

Introduction

These are the key ideas of this chapter:

1.

2.

3.

Draft 2

CHAPTER 8: REVISING

Introduction

These are the key ideas of this chapter

1. *Revision is the process of making improvements to a draft to turn it into a polished piece of writing.*

2. *Revising can be done 1 or more times.*

3. *You, as the author, make the final decision on what changes to make. Outside reviewers, checklists, and scoring guides can* ~~*help you improve your draft.*~~ *give valuable feedback*

Draft 3

CHAPTER 8: REVISING

Introduction

These are the key ideas of this chapter:

1. Revision is the process of making improvements to a draft to turn it into a polished piece of writing.

2. Checklists, reviewers, and scoring guides can be ∧useful in the drafting process. *and feedback from others*

3. *With any draft,* You should keep revising ~~a draft~~ until you feel ~~the piece~~ accomplishes its purpose. *it*

Draft 4

CHAPTER 8: REVISING

Introduction

These are the key ideas of this chapter:

1. Revision is the process of making improvements to a draft to turn it into a polished piece of writing.

2. Checklists, feedback from others, and scoring guides can be useful in the ~~drafting~~ process. *revising*

3. With any draft, keep revising until you feel i̶t̶ accomplishes its purpose. *the writing*

Write Now (3)

Revise your draft from Write Now (2) to check for sentence-level details. Check your revised draft against the Writing Checklist in Figure 8–1.

Selecting a Title

If you did not come up with a title for your work in the drafting stage, now is the time. Usually a title summarizes the topic, such as these titles of writings that appear in this textbook:

How to Poach an Egg
Music Education: A Much Needed and Important Discipline
A Lighthouse Keeper's Wife

Sometimes a title does not explicitly say what a piece is about. Rather, it serves to pique readers' interest. For example:

The Jigsaw Puzzle in the Wrong Box
Pick Your Part

Some titles are full sentences:

The Great Cities Have Lost Their Night Skies

Questions also can be used as titles:

Why Should Government Be Concerned About Light Pollution?

Titles can use alliteration (repetition of sound) or rhyme:

How to Talk to Anyone, Anytime, Anywhere
Scream Machine

Titles can involve word play:

Tent Revival (a "tent revival" is a type of outdoor religious gathering, but this is the title of an essay about a good place to go camping)
The Undertaking: Life Studies in the Dismal Trade (an "undertaking" is a project, but this is the title of a collection of essays by a funeral director—an undertaker)

Ideally, a title helps readers focus on your topic and catches their attention. If your piece is serious and has a formal function, the title needs to be more serious. Less formal pieces can have more creative and whimsical titles. You may want to think of several titles and get feedback from others before making a final decision.

Write Now (4)

In small groups, think of possible titles for an essay on each of the following subjects. Be as creative as you can. The first item has been started as an example.

1. Childhood memories

    Childhood on Chadwick Court
    Life with Father
    Marbles and Mudpies

    _____

    _____

    _____

    _____

2. Climbing a volcano

    _____

    _____

    _____

3. Baseball

    _____

    _____

    _____

    _____

4. Investing in the stock market

    _____

    _____

    _____

5. Commercial transactions
    on the Internet

    _____

    _____

    _____

Write Now (5)

If you did not have a title for the draft essay you worked on in Write Now (2) and (3), create a list of possible titles now. Select one and add it to your draft.

Getting Feedback

It is always a good idea to have someone else review a draft. Choose your reviewer carefully—someone who will not be too hard or too soft, and who will do a careful job of reading to give you useful comments. Ask for specific feedback. General statements such as "this is good" or "this is bad" are much less helpful than focused comments such as "your first sentence really caught my attention" or "this sentence is repetitive." (The same, of course, applies when you review the work of others. Give specific, useful advice in a friendly and encouraging tone.)

When you ask someone to review your draft, be clear about whether you want written comments. If you do, ask your reviewer to write comments on the draft itself, to use the Writing Checklist in Figure 8–1, or to do both. If you will be discussing the draft with your reviewer, use the Peer Conference Form in Figure 8–3 to make notes of your conversation.

What you do with the feedback you get from others is up to you. Take each recommended change and decide whether it will make your piece stronger. Perhaps some other change is needed than the one recommended by your reviewer, or perhaps you feel strongly that you should not make that change. Those are decisions that you, as the author, must make alone.

Based on reviewers' comments, you may need to produce yet another draft. Once you feel you have the best possible work you can produce and have selected a good title, all that is left to do is to produce a final copy. Proofread your final draft. This means to look it over carefully for minor mistakes such as typographical errors, misspellings, or commas in the wrong places. If you find any errors, make the corrections and create another copy. Know what standards are expected, for example, what kinds of margins and line spacing you should use and whether you need a cover sheet listing your name, the course number, and the date. Produce a final version that meets those standards.

You can send your drafts by e-mail to a reviewer. Copy the draft and paste it into the body of the e-mail letter or send it as an attached file. Indicate to the reviewer how you want comments to be made (for example, by return e-mail or by phone, in the body of the essay or following the essay) and the deadline by which you need comments.

Write Now (6)

Move into pairs. Have your partner review the draft you revised in Write Now (3), making notes on your draft and also using the Writing Checklist in Figure 8–1. Then discuss the draft with your partner. Use the Peer Conference Form in Figure 8–3 to take notes. Do the same for your partner, reading his or her revised draft and offering feedback. Use this feedback to revise your essay. Produce a final copy, proofreading it carefully.

Figure 8–3: Peer Conference

Reviewer _____

Title of Work Being Reviewed _____

Date _____

My reviewer liked these things:

My reviewer had these questions:

My reviewer thinks I should add or change these things:

From the discussion with my reviewer, I think I should make these changes to my draft:

Working with a Scoring Guide

How do you know if a finished piece of writing is successful? Many instructors use a **scoring guide** (also sometimes called a rubric) to measure your writing against expectations for college-level students. A scoring guide uses a scale, such as from 5 to 1 (with 5 being excellent and 1 being poor), and describes the features of essays that fit each score. Usually, scoring guides are accompanied by **benchmarks,** which are samples of writing. For example, a scoring guide that ranks essays from 5 to 1 should have attached to it a benchmark 5 essay and a benchmark 1 essay, along with benchmark essays for the other scores in between.

Instructors can use a scoring guide to give you specific feedback on works-in-progress or to grade final versions. Classmates also can use a scoring guide to do peer evaluations on drafts and final versions. For you as a writer, the value of a scoring guide is that it lets you know what you will be judged against, even before you begin writing.

An Essay Scoring Guide appears in Figure 8–4. Use this scoring guide for evaluating your work and that of your classmates. Another option is to work with your instructor and classmates to custom-design a scoring guide. You also may, as a group, decide to modify any scoring guide you use to match different writing assignments.

Figure 8-4: Essay Scoring Guide

Instructions: Evaluate the essay against the features described below, and give it a score from 5 to 1.

5 — Excellent

The main idea is clearly expressed.

The essay is focused on the main idea.

Several different points are made in support of the main idea.

There are specific and interesting details that support each point.

Transitions from one point to the next are smooth and logical.

The essay has a clear introduction, body, and conclusion.

The essay has a logical yet interesting title.

Mechanical errors are few and minor.

3 — Adequate

The main idea can be figured out but could be more clearly stated.

For the most part, the essay is focused on the main idea although it wanders in some places.

Some points are made in support of the main idea.

There are some details to support each point, but they tend to be vague and superficial.

Transitions from one point to the next are present, but sometimes awkward.

The essay does not have a distinct introduction, body, and conclusion, or at least one section is underdeveloped.

The essay title is appropriate but uninteresting.

Mechanical errors are frequent but for the most part are not significant.

1 — Poor

The main idea is not clearly expressed; therefore, the essay is difficult to understand.

The essay moves off the main idea in major areas.

Very few points are made in support of the main idea.

There are few or no details to support any point.

Transitions from one point to the next are weak or nonexistent.

The essay structure of an introduction, body, and conclusion is incomplete or not apparent.

The essay has a dull, unhelpful title or no title at all.

Mechanical errors are frequent and significant and impede the reading of the essay.

Note: A score of 2 or 4 may also be given to essays that fall between scores 1, 3, and 5.

Write Now (7)

The student essays below were produced as first drafts in a writing class. Working in small groups, practice using the Essay Scoring Guide in Figure 8–4 to evaluate each essay.

Essay #1: My Neighborhood   Score: _____

I like my nieghborhood for several reasons.

I like my nieghborhood, because the people are very friendly and nice.

They will watch out for your property if and when you are out of town. And it is quiet. Most of the people are middle age.

We have a little shopping center across the street and over there you will find a commuity store, a cleaners, and a barber shop.

Also my church is one block up on Stanton Rd and most of my nieghbors attentin the same church.

One orther reason why I like my nieghborhood is that it is conviniet, to public tranportion. There is a bus route on both sides, of my house. One is on Stanton Rd. which is on the front of my house, and right out the back of my house on Morris Rd. is anther bus stop.

There is also a school in the next block for people with young children.

But most of all I like my nieghborhood, because the people are nice and friendly.

Jean Shade

Essay #2: Army Training   Score: _____

When I think of the U.S. Army, one of the things that come to mind is the basic training that I had to go through.

First, that early to rise stuff didn't sit to well with me. I mean, come on, 3:30 in the morning just to get up and start the day with morning exercise. It's bad enough that I was not and still and not an early riser. Oh, I almost forgot to mention, that the drill sergeants were the barracks alarm clocks with all that yelling and screaming.

It's a lot of hard training preparing for fighting wars in basic training with weapons training, first aid, and a lot of mental stuff, but, it can be very amusing at times when recruits mess up and the drill seargent gets after the recruit while training. I've kept a lot more of those memories then the rough parts of the training that I went through.

After basic training comes advance individual training (A.I.T.). A.I.T. is basicly where a soldier goes to school to learn how to do the primary job that he or she picks when entering the Army. I also have to mention, that people who reenlist and decides to choose a different job in the Army have to go to A.I.T. (school) again to learn how to do whatever job that they chose. A.I.T. training is located in different U.S. cities. Mine was at the U.S. Army Communication School located in Augusta, Georgia.

Just like basic training, advance training has its rah rah moments as well. Even though a soldier spends most of his time in class, the soldier still has to do certain drills like marching, or drills with weapons, and what nots, and have to hear the instructors (usually sergeants) yell and scream. But, you know what? After going through basics already, the soldier pretty much gets use to it.

The Army's "my way or the highway" approach to things are good I believe, because it saves lives. An undisciplined, hard-headed soldier can go out to war and get his squad, or worse, his whole plattoon wiped out from being undiscplined. I must mention one important thing that I almost forgot. Sometimes when a soldier has a hard time being a soldier from the disiplined part of it, sometimes the misfit can in up being jailed for such.

Kevin Summers

Essay #3: How Are Mother Influenced Our Family Lives   Score: _____

our mother made sure that all her children knew that if we were doing something possitive, and benefitual for us in our daily challege, that we have her support in it.

Our mother did not have to demand respect we all knew what was expected from us, because we know how hard our mother had to worked to take care of eight girls, and five boys on a regular bases while our father was at work.

In having eight girls, and five boys, it takes a lot of time for loving and caring for us, and making sure that all children received the some amount of love and caring.

Thomas K. Wynn

Write Now (8)

As a class, discuss the strengths and weaknesses of the Essay Scoring Guide in Figure 8–4. Is it an appropriate guide for your class? If it is, work in small groups to find benchmark essays for each score. Use the student essays by Shade, Summers, and Wynn and essays produced in your class. Your instructor also may have essays from previous classes that can be used as benchmarks. After you have selected your benchmark essays, compare your selections with those of the other small groups. As a class, make final decisions on the essay that will represent each benchmark.

Benchmark 5 essay: _____

Benchmark 4 essay: _____

Benchmark 3 essay: _____

Benchmark 2 essay: _____

Benchmark 1 essay: _____

Write Now (9)

If you decide as a class to custom-design a scoring guide, follow these procedures:

1. Brainstorm two lists: one describing the features of an excellent essay and one describing the features of a poor essay (you may choose other descriptive words besides "excellent" and "poor").

2. Next, read and discuss several student essays, such as those by Shade, Summers, and Wynn. Based on the discussion, add to or modify the lists above.

3. Create another list of features for essays that fall between the two categories.

4. Use these descriptive lists to create a scoring guide. The guide should be no more than one page, and the descriptions of each score should be clear and specific.

5. Working alone, test out the scoring guide by evaluating Student Essay #4, which follows. Compare your score with your classmates'. If there is great variation in scores, revise the guide to create clearer descriptions of essay features.

6. Repeat this testing process until you have devised a scoring guide that produces relatively consistent scores from different classmates for the same work.

7. Identify benchmark essays for each score in the guide.

Essay #4: My Neighborhood   Score: _____

My neighborhood is a very quite place to live. Everyone basically
plants flowers and cut grass during the summer month. All of my
neighbors has a very busy schedule. We don't get to see each others
until the weekends. Every first Thursdays of each month we have a
community meeting to talked about the neighborhood and, what's
going on in the community. Most of the children's on my block will
graduates next weeks. This be will a joyful occasion for the
community. Children's will be going off to college this summer and
will be missed. Most of the children looks out for each other in my
neighborhood. This fall our neighborhood will be lonely, because we
don't have anyone left to tell us, who stop pass our house and what
kind of car they were driving. I guess now it's up to the parent's to
keep each other informed about about the community.

Queen Brown

Write Now (10)

**Divide into pairs. Exchange the essays you completed in Write
Now (6). Use the Essay Scoring Guide in Figure 8–4, or the scoring
guide created by your class, to evaluate your own essay and your
partner's essay. Discuss the scores you each gave, pointing to
specific strengths or weaknesses in the essays.**

Summing Up

1. What is the purpose of revision?

   _____

   _____

2. What is the difference between major revisions and minor revisions?

   _____

   _____

3. What are three qualities of a good reviewer?

   _____

   _____

Second Thoughts

Review the series of photographs that opened this chapter; then think about or discuss the following questions:

1. Do you think a construction worker ever has to redo a job more than once? What makes you think so?
2. How do home builders know ahead of time what they will be checked against?
3. What is the role of home buyers in making sure a house is built to their satisfaction?

   Based on what you have learned in this chapter about revising, how would you compare the review process you go through as a writer with that which occurs in home building? Record your thoughts in the *Responses* section of your journal.

4. Name one function of a checklist or scoring guide.

    _____

    _____

5. Name one possible situation outside of school where you could be called upon to review and revise something you have *done* and one possible situation where you could be called upon to review and revise something you have *written*.

    _____

    _____

6. As a result of completing this chapter, what one change will you make to improve the way you approach the revision stage? Write your resolution in the *Habits for Life* section of your journal.

Write Now: Revising and Evaluating Your Draft

Select another draft essay from your writing folder, such as a draft you created for the final Write Now activities in Chapter 5, 6, or 7. Alternatively, create a new draft based on your response to the photographs that open this chapter, the topic you identified in Write Now (1), or any other topic. Review your draft and revise it as many times as you feel are necessary, using the Writing Checklist in Figure 8–1 to measure the success of each draft. Obtain feedback on a near-final draft from one or more reviewers. Make any last revisions, and produce a final, proofread copy. Evaluate your finished essay using the scoring guide your class has selected to use.

Using Editing Marks

Editing marks are quick ways to indicate sentence-level changes that need to be made to writing. Use them when you review your own work in the drafting and proofreading stages. You also can use them to comment on the drafts of classmates. Your writing instructor will probably use editing marks like these. Since these marks are universally known, learning them prepares you for situations outside the writing classroom in which others review your work.

—	or	ℯ	delete (take out)
∧	or	∨	insert (a word or a letter or a punctuation mark)
≡			capitalize
/			make lowercase
∼			transpose (reverse order)
¶			create new paragraph
⌒			close up (remove space)
#			insert space
—			italicize or underline

agr	agreement error (in person, tense, or number)
awk	awkward wording
frag	sentence fragment
rs	run-on sentence
cs	comma splice
sp	incorrect spelling
ww	wrong word

If you just want to make a quick note about something that needs fixing, you can circle the problem word or words and make a note in the margin, such as:

?	not sure of meaning
fix	fix this

Finally, you can create your own quick remarks, such as:

tighten up

zzzzz

wow!

nice!

Exercise

The student essay below was produced as a first draft in a writing class. Use editing marks to make corrections on it. Some marks have already been indicated as examples.

My Neighborhood

My neighborhood is located in Southeast Washington, on Central Ave.   *spell out*

Its the only apartment building that runs ^a long that street. A place where at   *frag*

first my heart and mind feel like, being here was a big misstate by moving   *sp*

there. The one thing I didn't take in cunsideration was the diversity   *sp*

between people, and the personality. ❡ If you would ^bring a camera and recorded   *agr*

the neighborhood. you would see the neighbors showing their true colors.   *tr*

I notice in the area, there are some low income people and a good number

of unemployed soul. Its not unusual for them to be out on the frond kicking

it being cool, but it seem their answer to it all is bowing smoke, cigartts and

wash it down with a cold beer, or any kind of strong drink, oh lets not forget

about the drugs that coming with it. You know the neighborhood, it's kind

of funny, a whole block with just one apartment on it. I would say its like any

other neighborhod but its not, peeple come from who knows to visit with

their family or their back-stabbing firends. They are wrong, loud, uneducated,

educated, and some are worker and noneworkers, drug users, drug dealers,

bums, freed loaders, and some are just studpit or like. There children with

home tranin and children without any training. Parents who curst their

children out and make them feel dum as dirt where unemploy woman on

welfare set and hang out of there windows just check out the type of beer

that come pass their noses. Where at any giving time cars take their liberty

to race up and down the small back street, just for the fun of it. That my

neighborhooded.

Andre Lyles

SIGN WRITING

by Calvin Trillin

Check out Calvin Trillin's
light verse on current
political events, appearing
in his column in
The Nation, at
www.thenation.com

*Calvin Trillin has written a lot. He has authored twenty books, is a staff writer
for* The New Yorker, *and also works as a columnist for* The Nation *and*
TIME. *Trillin has a very large following because he has an absurd sense of
humor and because his observations are usually, in the words of one reviewer,
"right on the mark."*

*Though Trillin is an experienced writer, he struggles like anyone else to get
his words right. This struggle is the topic of the essay reprinted below from a
collection of essays called* Too Soon to Tell. *As you read Trillin's essay, think
about this question: can humorous writing be produced spontaneously, or does it
require a careful revising of drafts?*

November 21, 1994

For people who make their living as writers, the routine messages of
everyday life have to be put together with some care. You don't want to
leave rough drafts lying around. I've known novelists for whom the
prospect of composing a note asking that a son or daughter be excused
from gym that day can bring on a serious case of writer's block.

**Whom might
Trillin be
describing here?**

I was reminded of that recently when our car had to be left on city
streets for a few days, and I, attempting to benefit from the experience of
a couple of trips in the past to AAAA Aardvark Auto-Glass Repair, took
on the task of composing a sign to inform potential pillagers that it
contained nothing of value. Hours later, my wife happened to ask me to
do some little chore around the house and I heard myself saying, "I can't
right now. I'm on the fourth draft of this car sign."

**Why has Trillin
made trips before
to AAAA Aardvark
Auto-Glass Repair?**

There was no reason for her to be surprised. She has seen me stuck
badly on an RSVP. In fact, routine social communication can be
particularly knotty for writers, since they habitually try to express
themselves in ways that are not overused. This is why a biographer who
seems capable of producing a 1,200-page volume in fairly short order
can often be inexcusably late with, say, a simple thank-you note.

**Whom might
Trillin be
describing here?**

Reading over what he's put on paper, he'll say to himself, "I can't
believe that I wrote anything as lame as 'Thanks for a wonderful
weekend.'" Then he'll put aside the entire project until a more original
phrase comes to him. A few weeks later, while the draft is still marinating
on the writer's desk, the weekend's hostess feels confirmed in her

impression—an impression that began to surface with the wine-spilling incident on Saturday night—that the biographer is a boor or a yahoo.

What my fourth draft of the car sign said was "No Radio." I thought that was spare and to the point, without extraneous language. I came to it from "No Radio or Any Other Valuables," which I decided, after some reflection, protested too much.

"What do you think?" I asked my wife, handing her the sign.

"It's O.K.," my wife said. "I saw some ready-made signs for car windows at the hardware store, and that's what one of them said, so I guess it's what people think is effective."

"You saw the same sign, worded in just that way?"

"I'm not saying you plagiarized it from the hardware store."

"Actually, I haven't been in there in some time," I said.

"It's really O.K.," my wife said. "'No Radio' is fine."

It's fine if you're satisfied to be writing at the same level as some gorilla at the sign factory. Thinking I needed some fresh ideas, I phoned my older daughter, who lives just around the corner. "What would be a good sign to put in the car to discourage crackheads from smashing the window so they can get at six cents in change on the floor and the spare fan belt and an old pair of pliers?" I asked.

My daughter, a survivor of one of those earnest and progressive nursery schools in Greenwich Village, said, "How about 'Use Words Not Hands'?"

This was a reference to what the teachers at her nursery school were constantly saying as the little monsters attacked one another with any weapon at hand. At one point we all began to wonder exactly what the words for sneaking up behind another kid and pulling her hair might be.

It wouldn't surprise me at all if that hair-puller had turned to a life of petty crime. As much as I enjoyed contemplating the look on his face when he spotted his nursery-school slogan on a car he was about to break into, I decided that the impact of "Use Words Not Hands" rested on the sort of allusion that an editor would criticize as "too inside."

What does it mean to say his draft of the sign "protested too much"?

What does his question reveal about Trillin's car?

What does "too inside" mean?

The next draft was a complete departure—more of a new approach, really, than another draft. It said, "There Is Nothing of Value Here." Upon reflection, I decided that it sounded too philosophical. I could picture a car thief who came upon it turning to his partner in crime and saying, "Talk about pretentious!"

So now I'm sort of stuck. Meanwhile, the car's on the street. It is not completely without protection. An old shirt cardboard taped onto the backseat window bears the words "Sign in Preparation."

THINK AND RESPOND

1. How many drafts does Trillin make of his sign?

   _____

   _____

   _____

2. From whom does he seek advice as he drafts the sign?

   _____

   _____

   _____

3. Where in this essay is Trillin's humor "right on the mark"?

   _____

   _____

   _____

4. In what ways are Trillin's drafting difficulties absurd, and in what ways are they realistic?

   _____

   _____

   _____

5. Using the Essay Scoring Guide in Figure 8–4 (or the scoring guide created by your class), decide what score you would give this essay and explain why.

_____

_____

_____

6. Provide synonyms or definitions for these words from the essay, and add at least two of the words to the *Words Worth Remembering* section of your journal:

pillagers_____

knotty _____

marinating _____

boor _____

yahoo _____

extraneous_____

plagiarized_____

petty _____

allusion _____

pretentious _____

7. If you liked this reading, make a record of it in the *Readings Worth Remembering* section of your journal.

COMPARING VIEWS

What makes something funny? Why do people like to read funny essays? What is the role of humor in communicating ideas? After discussing the topic of humor with others, continue to explore it on your own, in your journal—if it interests you. You may be able to use material from the discussion and your journal in a future writing activity.

APPLIED WRITING

Using the Trillin piece as a model, draft a humorous essay. Review your draft and revise it. Continue to revise your draft as many times as you feel are necessary, using the Writing Checklist in Figure 8–1 to measure the success of each draft. Obtain feedback from several reviewers—not only for cohesion, unity, and correctness, but to see if they find it funny. Use the Peer Conference Form in Figure 8–2 to take notes on the feedback you receive from reviewers. Evaluate your finished essay using the scoring guide your class has selected to use, except add these qualifications: a benchmark 5 essay makes readers laugh out loud; a benchmark 3 essay is mildly amusing in places; and a benchmark 1 essay is not funny at all.

UNIT 3

METHODS OF ESSAY DEVELOPMENT

This unit focuses on six different methods—named in the chapter titles—that you can use to think through and organize an essay topic. Goals of the unit are to help you:

- Become familiar with these various methods as they are used in writing.

- Understand their different purposes.

- Practice strategies for applying these methods in your writing.

- Practice using a combination of strategies.

- Continue to review and apply grammar principles.

This unit contains many examples of writings that you can use as models for your own work. Activities in each chapter help you identify a variety of topics to write about, using the method that chapter explores. At the end of each chapter, you will be directed to select a single topic that most interests you and to develop that topic into a completed essay.

Earth Garden
Francisco Malespin

CHAPTER 9

Describing

These are the **key ideas** of this chapter:

- Description lets readers know what is unique and particular about your subject.

- Description can include information about how the subject affects the senses and emotions, as well as any images the subject brings to mind.

- Description needs to be presented in some logical order, so that readers can put the details together into a clear picture.

Picturing Meaning

Examine the artwork on the opposite page; then think about or discuss these questions:

1. What kind of place do you see in this painting?

   _____

   _____

2. What physical features does this place have?

   _____

   _____

3. What kind of atmosphere do you think this place has?

   _____

   _____

   In the *Responses* section of your journal, write down your thoughts about this painting.

Write Now (1)

Think of a place that *you* love. Describe it. Explain what it looks like and how it feels to be there. In words on paper, create a picture of this place. Keep this work because you may use it in a later activity.

Describing an Object

A **description** is a picture drawn in words. It is a full and detailed representation of an object, place, person, or event. When you describe something, your purpose is usually to let readers know what is unique and particular about your subject. Your purpose also is to make readers feel as though they can actually see what you are describing.

Descriptive writing is relatively easy to do, since everyone does a lot of describing in day-to-day conversation. The main requirements for description are focused attention, creative thinking, and a willingness to work hard to get the words right. Here are six ways to describe something in writing:

1. Describe what you see.

2. Describe how your other senses are affected.

3. Describe what you do *not* see or feel.

4. Describe how your emotions are affected.

5. Describe the images that come to mind.

6. Combine some or all of these techniques.

Each of these strategies is explained below in terms of describing an object. However, they also apply to describing persons or places.

Describe what you see. Note the physical features of your object such as its size, shape, color, or texture. Note the environment in which it sits: the objects around it as well as the general setting. Observe the functioning of the object, any activity connected with the object, or any changes that the object is undergoing.

Describe how your other senses are affected. Observe the object not only by looking at it but also through the other senses. As appropriate, describe how it sounds, tastes, feels to the touch, or smells.

Describe what you do not see or feel. Opposites are an important element of description. Notice what the object is *not*. Notice how it does *not* affect you. Consider what is *not* present that could be, should be, might be, or used to be. If the object has a function but is not in use, explain how it could be used.

Describe how your emotions are affected. Note your personal feelings, opinions, and impressions about the object. Note also the emotions of others in relation to it.

Describe the images that come to mind. Allow your mind to free-associate. Note what you are reminded of as you observe the object. Note any similarities between the object and other things.

Combine some or all of these techniques. To see how these five strategies might be used together in a description, take as an example the object "sofa." You can look at the sofa, then write exactly what you see:

It was an old leather couch with stuffing hanging out between torn seams.

You can describe how the couch affects your other senses.

It smelled of basement mildew and spilled drinks and old popcorn kernels under the cushions.

You can describe what the couch does not look like or what is not happening with the couch.

This was no fashionably antique sofa. No one would pay money for it.

You can describe how the couch affects your emotions.

I always feel at home on that couch.

Finally, you can describe something that the couch resembles.

It was worn soft like the inside of a much-used baseball mitt.

Once you have described the sofa in several ways, you can pick and choose what to keep. You can combine your statements together and, with a little tweaking, create a specific description of the sofa:

This was no fashionably antique sofa. No one would pay money for it. It was just an old leather couch with stuffing hanging out between torn seams. It smelled of basement mildew and spilled drinks and old popcorn kernels under the cushions. Yet it was worn soft like the inside of a much-used baseball mitt, and I always felt at home on that couch.

Consider the following description of sofas from a furniture store's mail-order catalog. In just a few sentences, this advertising copy uses all of the descriptive strategies discussed above. The purpose of this advertising copy is to sell the couches, of course, and the audience is prospective customers:

Visual description: "dark brown leather."

Emotional description: "sophisticated."

Image description: "a sofa for your children to play on."

Sensory description: "comfy."

Opposite description: "not just [for] looking at."

The authentic buffalo leather on this HALLAND sofa creates a genuinely natural look and feel. Each HALLAND sofa in "Struktur" dark brown leather has a unique character that only gets more beautiful with age. . . .
With its sophisticated design and durable leather, BYA is just what you're looking for in a sofa. Shapely ash legs lend a tailored look, while "Modern" red leather adds the glamour. . . .
SANDÖ is a sofa for your children to play on and your guests to party in. The green "Modern" leather is easy to care for and wears well. And you won't have to worry about this sofa losing its shape—a fixed back will keep it looking sharp for years to come. . . .
With a high, 37-inch back, this BALA sofa is a comfy place for long chats with a friend. It's shown here in "Bas" black leather with a child-friendly, easy-care surface. . . .
ÖSTERUND sofa has a durable, green "Bonus" leather that's made for living in, not just looking at.

IKEA Catalog

One of the hardest things about describing is getting beyond the obvious. When working on a description, make a list. Challenge yourself to come up with five, ten, or fifteen different observations. Take the time to consider the object using each of the strategies discussed above. If the object you want to describe is not in front of you, then shut your eyes and recall the object. Find a picture of it if you can. It may help to sketch a picture as you think. A Description Outline appears in Figure 9–1. Study the example of the completed form (Figure 9–2) to see how it was used to plan a description of a pair of clogs. Then use it to help plan your own written descriptions.

Figure 9–1: Description Outline

Photocopy this form before using.

Part A. The subject for description is: _____

Describe what you see:

_____

_____

Describe how your other senses are affected:

Smell _____

Taste _____

Touch _____

Hearing _____

Describe what you do not see or feel:

_____

_____

Describe how it affects your emotions:

_____

_____

Describe the images it brings to mind:

_____

_____

Part B (for descriptions of persons). Describe character traits as demonstrated through specific actions or behaviors:

Character trait   Action or behavior revealing that trait

_____ _____

_____ _____

Describe what this person has often said or has said in a particular situation:

"_____"

"_____"

Describe any facts you know or could find out about this person:

_____

_____

Part C (for descriptions of places). Pick two specific objects within the setting and describe them:

(Object 1) _____

(Object 2) _____

Identify time frames you could use to describe this place:

_____ Present day (when?) _____

_____ In the past (when?) _____

_____ In the future (when?) _____

Describe any people or other living things in the setting and their responses to it:

_____

_____

Part D (for all descriptions). Pick an organizing strategy.

_____ Physical order _____ Order of importance

_____ Special order (what is it?) _____

Figure 9–2: Example Description Outline

Part A. The subject for description is: <u>the clogs I'm wearing</u>

Describe what you see:

<u>black leather clunky-looking plain wooden soles blue socks falling</u>

<u>down   tarnished buckles   upturned buckle flaps</u>

Describe how your other senses are affected:

Smell _____

Taste _____

Touch <u>feel great on my feet</u>

Hearing <u>"clop clop clop" when I walk   I like the sound</u>

Describe what you do not see or feel:

<u>these are not dress up shoes</u>

<u>these are not light as slippers</u>

<u>these are not for sneaking up on people</u>

Describe how it affects your emotions:

<u>I feel taller when I wear them   "above the mud"</u>

Describe the images it brings to mind:

<u>Dutch   '60s fashions   Guindon cartoon characters</u>

Part D (for all descriptions). Pick an organizing strategy.

_____ Physical order _____ Order of importance

_x_ Special order (what is it?) <u>how they look/feel/sound/make me feel</u>

Write Now (2)

The phrases below are from the IKEA furniture catalog description of sofas. Connect each phrase with the type of description it is.

1. Phrases that describe how the couches look

2. Phrases that describe how the couches feel

3. Phrases that describe what won't happen

4. Phrases that appeal to your emotions

5. Phrases that bring images to mind

a) A natural ... feel

b) Red leather

c) Wears well

d) Shapely

e) Worry

f) Child-friendly

g) Durable

h) Just what you're looking for in a sofa

i) A comfy place for long chats with a friend

j) Authentic

Write Now (3)

Working in pairs, find a sofa or some other object to describe, such as:

a backpack   a chair   the floor
a window   a wallet   a jacket

Look closely at your object or at a picture of that object. Plan a description of the object, using Part A of the Description Outline (Figure 9-1). Just work on the outline—you do not need to draft an essay at this time. Keep this work because you may use it in another activity.

Describing a Person

A description of a person is called a **profile** or a **characterization**.
Describing a person can be done in the same way as describing an
object. You might begin by describing what the person looks like or
wears or is doing. You might describe the sound of the person's voice,
the scent of the cologne being worn, or the feel of a handshake. You
might describe what this person does *not* look like or wear or do. You
might describe your own or other people's physical and emotional
responses to this person. Finally, you might describe the images this
person brings to mind.

People also have personalities. A description of a person is not
complete without some capturing of character. This can be challenging,
because a person's character is not always consistent. For example, a
person may be honest in some ways but not in others. General
statements such as "he is exceptionally honest" are less telling than
observations of specific behaviors such as "he always counted his change
to make sure he did not receive too much."

When people speak, they reveal a great deal about themselves. The
words they say can be an important element in a description. Most
people use the same phrases over and over, which then become a mark
of their character. Spontaneous remarks made in response to a situation
also shed light on someone's personality or beliefs. Recalling and
recording these quotations can enrich a characterization.

In the following description, a Tennessee woman uses both specific observations and quotations to describe her mother. The audience for this story was a group of women like herself, from the South, attending a conference on women and work. Her purpose was to share some of her personal history:

Observation: how the mother entertained her children with stories.

Observation: how she provided amusements for her children.

My mother was artistic. We didn't have money to buy toys; but she was a great storyteller. Even when we was in the field, she made work a pleasure. I mean she told so many stories and she would say, "Don't you want to hear...?" And we just loved it. We would say, "Tell us more, tell us more!" And that was a way to get us to work, picking the cotton, chopping the cotton, or whatever. And at Christmas time, she would make us toys. We always had something for pleasure, some kind of games or something. We would sit beside the stove and sing and she would tell us all these stories and scare us half to death. But she always kept some kind of fun in our lives. I guess it took our minds off of what we thought was hard work, because she put a little pleasure in it. My mother was good on games. She was real active, played with us out in the yard, playing hide-and-go-seek, playing ball with us. Even when we was in high school, my mother was still in the yard playing; and she could turn cartwheels and I couldn't. I don't think there was a generation gap between us and our mother. You know people say that they are old and they can't understand the younger generation. But she did. She really did.

Rosemary Derrick, Cedar Grove, Tennessee
Quoted in *Picking Up the Pieces:*
Women In and Out of Work in the Rural South

Factual details also contribute to a description of a person. An accumulation of facts is crammed into the following short profile of stock-car driver Richard Petty. It comes from the "Heroes" section of *The Illustrated History of Stock Car Racing*:

Simply put, [Richard Petty was] the most successful racer in NASCAR [National Association for Stock Car Auto Racing] history. But more important than that, he was stock car racing's most popular and enduring star, a humble and gracious man who never let the success of 200 victories, seven championships, and tens of millions of fans go to his head. He drove his first race in 1958 and his last in 1992, and made a record 1,177 starts in the intervening 35 years. In addition to 200 victories, 127 poles, and several titles, he was 1959 Rookie of the Year, won eight Most Popular Driver awards, three American Driver of the Year awards, and was top-10 in points 18 times in addition to his seven titles. On super speedways, he won 11 times at Rockingham, 10 times at Daytona Beach, seven at Dover, six at Atlanta, five each at Texas and Riverside, four each at Charlotte and Michigan, three at Darlington, and two times at Pocono and Talladega. And just for good measure, he won 145 short-track races.

> Factual description: numbers of victories, championships, fans, starts, poles, and titles.

The Illustrated History of Stock Car Racing
Don Hunter and Al Pearce

Since people are so complicated, the real task when describing them is picking and choosing among the many things to say. It may help to focus on the person in one moment in time or on one aspect of that person's life. Remember your purpose for writing and your audience. This will help you to focus on those details that are most important.

Write Now (4)

Review the two descriptions to answer the following questions:

Rosemary Derrick's mother

1. How would you summarize this description?

    _____

2. What other personality traits do think this mother might have had?

    _____

3. Do you think you would have liked Rosemary Derrick's mother? Why or why not?

    _____

4. What person in your life does this mother remind you of, either by similarity or contrast?

    _____

Richard Petty

5. How would you summarize this description?

    _____

6. What else do you think Petty might have accomplished in his career?

    _____

7. Are you impressed by Petty's achievements? Why or why not?

    _____

8. What person in your life does he remind you of, either by similarity or contrast?

    _____

Keep this work because you may use it in a later activity.

Write Now (5)

Select one of the two persons you mentioned in questions 4 and 8 of Write Now (4). Alternatively, select another person who interests you. Describe that person using Parts A and B of the Description Outline (Figure 9–1). Just work on the outline—you do not need to turn your outline into an essay at this time. Keep this work because you may use it in a later activity.

Describing a Place

An outdoor landscape, a room inside a house, or some other significant setting can be described using the same strategies used to describe objects. Place descriptions, however, have an extra dimension. A place is like an object yet it contains many objects, each of which could be described. Focusing on and selecting details becomes more difficult yet more important. The details to use are the ones that make the place unique and particular. The following description of Las Vegas focuses on the gambling capital's super-intense sights and sounds. It comes from a travel guidebook, and its purpose is to advise potential visitors of what to expect:

As often as you might have seen it on TV or in a movie, there is nothing that prepares you for that first sight of Las Vegas. The skyline is hyperreality, a mélange of the Statue of Liberty, a giant lion, a pyramid and a Sphinx, and preternaturally glittering buildings. At night, it's so bright, you can actually get disoriented— and also get a sensory overload that can reduce you to hapless tears or fits of giggles. And that's without setting foot inside a casino, where the shouts from the craps tables, the crash of coins from the slots, and general roar combine into either the greatest adrenaline rush of your life or the eleventh pit of hell.

Detail:
unique skyline.

Detail:
unusual brightness.

Detail:
extreme noisiness.

Frommer's 98 *Las Vegas*

Except for the mention of the "Statue of Liberty" and other relatively new casino constructions, this description would fit Las Vegas twenty years ago. It probably will still fit twenty years from now. The time frame of this description is nonspecific. Nevertheless, places do change over time—over time of day and from day to day or year to year. When describing a place, therefore, you need to decide whether to use a specific or a nonspecific time frame. In the following example, N. Scott Momaday uses a specific time frame. He describes what a New Mexico village was like when he first arrived there as a child in 1946. His purpose is to establish in his readers' minds the setting for a story he will tell:

The village is described in terms of the few modern conveniences it had back in 1946.

The village is described in terms of the many traditional features it had back then.

The village is described in terms of the landscape and atmosphere it once had.

I was a boy of twelve when my parents and I moved to Jemez Pueblo, New Mexico, in 1946. There was a village of a thousand people, three telephones, two windmills, three or four pickups and no automobiles. But there were horses and wagons. There were cornfields and orchards, there were beehive ovens and brilliant strings of chilies, and there was an ancient architecture that proceeded immediately from the earth. There was an immense and incomparable landscape, full of light and color. And there were people of great dignity and good will and generosity of spirit. It was a place of singular beauty and wonder and delight.

"Native American Christmas Story"
Circle of Wonder
N. Scott Momaday

When people are in a setting, their responses to it can become part of the description, as shown in the following example where two people and a dog sit by an ocean in South America. This description comes from a book by Ernesto "Che" Guevera (who later became a leader of the revolution in Cuba), based on his original travel journals. His purpose was to share with others the adventures that helped shape his politics:

The full moon, silhouetted over the sea, showers the waves with silvery sparks. Sitting on a dune, watching the continuous ebb and flow, we each think our different thoughts. For me, the sea has always been a confidant, a friend which absorbs all you tell it without betraying your secrets, and always gives the best advice—a sound you can interpret as you wish. For Alberto, it is a new, oddly perturbing spectacle, reflected in the intensity with which his gaze follows every wave swelling then dying on the beach. At almost thirty, Alberto is seeing the Atlantic for the first time and is overwhelmed by a discovery which opens up infinite routes to all points of the globe. The fresh breeze fills the sense with the power of the sea, it transforms all it touches; even Come-back gazes, his funny little snout aloft, at the silver ribbon unfurling before him several times a minute.

The Motorcycle Diaries: A Journey around South America
Ernesto "Che" Guevera
Ann Wright, Trans.

Description: author's own response to the ocean.

Description: his friend's response to the ocean.

Description: his dog's response to the ocean.

Write Now (6)

Review the three descriptions to answer the following questions.

Las Vegas

1. How would you summarize this description?

   _____

   _____

2. What other unusual characteristics do you think Las Vegas might have?

   _____

   _____

3. Do you think you would like Las Vegas? Why or why not?

   _____

   _____

4. What city does it remind you of, either by similarity or contrast?

   _____

   _____

Jemez Pueblo, New Mexico

5. How would you summarize this description?

   _____

   _____

6. What other features do you think distinguished the Jemez Pueblo of 1946?

   _____

   _____

7. Do you think you would have liked Jemez Pueblo as it was in 1946? Why or why not?

   _____

   _____

8. What place (now or in the past) does it remind you of, either by similarity or contrast?

_____

_____

Ocean

9. How would you summarize this description?

_____

_____

10. What other feelings do you think observers at this ocean scene might have experienced?

_____

_____

11. Do you think you would have liked to be sitting beside this ocean? Why or why not?

_____

_____

12. What natural setting does it remind you of, either by similarity or contrast?

_____

_____

Keep this work because you may use it in a later activity.

Write Now (7)

Select one of the places you identified in question 4, 8, or 12 of Write Now (6). Alternatively, select the place you described in Write Now (1) or some other place that interests you. Describe that place using Parts A and C of the Description Outline (Figure 9–1). Just work on the outline—you do not need to turn it into an essay at this time. Keep this work because you may use it in a later activity.

Using Figurative Language

Anything you are trying to describe can become more alive to your readers through the use of **figurative language**. Figurative language is language that creates figures, or pictures, in the mind. Another word for figurative language is **imagery**. Three kinds of figurative language are:

1. **Simile**

2. **Metaphor**

3. **Analogy**

   Simile. A simile is a comparison between two items constructed with the words *like, as, as if,* or *as though*. Four similes (beginning with *like* and *as if*) are used in the following description of a woman who has just realized her cat was run over. It comes from an autobiographical comic novel. The unflattering similes help create a ridiculous picture out of a usually sorrowful situation:

Simile: lips are like large slugs.

Simile: lips slide down as if they are fainting.

Simile: face is like pale, spreading pancake batter.

Simile: hair is like a cheerleading pompom.

I saw her do a classic double take: Her eyelids peeled so far off her eyes, there was nowhere else for them to go, the corners of her purple lips stretched across her face like banana slugs and slid down as if they were passing out. Then she got whiter than cheap supermarket flour and her face spread out like a brand-new pancake. I realized it was *her* dead cat when she put her fists on the side of her head and started screaming. The black ponytail on top of her head covered her hands and face like a giant pom-pom sadly rooting for the Panthers.

Flaming Iguanas:
An Illustrated All-Girl Road Novel Thing
Erika Lopez

Metaphor. Like a simile, a metaphor is a comparison of two items, but it does not rely on connecting words such as *as* and *like*. A metaphor is a statement that one item is the other (a direct comparison) or a statement in which the word for one item is used in place of the other (an implied comparison). In the example on the opposite page, a metaphor is used to describe how the woman's eyes widen in shock: "Her eyelids peeled so far off her eyes, there was nowhere else for them to go." Metaphor is used extensively in the following excerpt from a funeral speech given by the Reverend Martin Luther King, Jr., a leader of the civil rights movement. It was delivered at the funeral of little girls killed in a bomb attack on their church in 1963. His purpose in this section of the speech is specifically to console the families of the little girls, and he does so by offering a positive description of death:

May I now say a word to you, the members of the bereaved families. It is almost impossible to say anything that can console you at this difficult hour and remove the deep clouds of disappointment which are floating in your mental skies. But I hope you can find a little consolation from the universality of this experience. Death comes to every individual. There is an amazing democracy about death. It is not aristocracy for some of the people, but a democracy for all of the people. Kings die and beggars die; rich men die and poor men die; old people die and young people die; death comes to the innocent and it comes to the guilty. Death is the irreducible common denominator of all men.

> Metaphors:
> disappointment = deep clouds, thoughts = skies.

> Metaphor:
> death = democracy.

I hope you can find some consolation from Christianity's affirmation that death is not the end. Death is not a period that ends the great sentence of life, but a comma that punctuates it to more lofty significance. Death is not a blind alley that leads the human race into a state of nothingness, but an open door which leads men into life eternal. Let this daring faith, this great invincible surmise, be your sustaining power during these trying days.

> Metaphor:
> death = comma.

"Eulogy for the Martyred Children"
compiled in *A Testament of Hope*
Martin Luther King, Jr.

Analogy. An analogy compares things that are very different, making a difficult or unfamiliar idea understandable by matching it with something familiar. Analogies are usually extended, going on for several sentences or paragraphs. The following analogy comes from a magazine column in which the author compares herself with her sister. The purpose is to show how she and her sister have different relationships to their clothes:

Analogy: clothes = true and loyal friends.

Cindy's closet is full of close friends who have nurtured her and supported her. She pats her handbags, folds her scarves respectfully, gazes approvingly at her dresses before zipping them back into their plastic bags. These are not clothes, but a rack of loyal allies ready to do continued service.

Analogy continued: clothes = unreliable and undependable companions.

By contrast, my closet is full of brief infatuations that have let me down—skirts, blouses, and suits that didn't change my life and now hang, neglected, upon a sagging rod like orphans in a badly run asylum. Belts could be anywhere. Shoes lie pigeon-toed and unpaired upon the floor.

"Closet Lovers"
Phyllis Theroux
House Beautiful

Write Now (8)

Review the three descriptions, underlining the similes, metaphors, and analogies. Then answer the following questions:

Shocked and unhappy woman

1. How would you summarize the woman's appearance?

    _____

    _____

2. What is another simile that would describe such a face?

    _____

    _____

Funeral speech

3. How would you summarize King's description of death?

    _____

    _____

4. What is another metaphor that would fit with King's description of death?

    _____

    _____

Clothes closets

5. How would you summarize the appearance of these two closets?

    _____

    _____

6. What analogy describes your clothes closet?

    _____

    _____

Write Now (9)

Working in pairs, draft sentences that employ a simile, metaphor, or analogy for each word below. The first item has been done as an example.

1. Milk *I was so thirsty, the milk tasted like champagne. (or) To the dairy farmer, milk is white money.*

2. Cell phones _____

   _____

   _____

3. Tornadoes _____

   _____

   _____

4. Insomnia _____

   _____

   _____

5. The moon _____

   _____

   _____

Write Now (10)

Select one of the description outlines you created in Write Now (3), (5), or (7). As you reread the outline, think of at least one simile, metaphor, or analogy that fits your subject. Jot each of these down on the outline. Keep this work because you may use it in another activity.

Organizing Descriptive Detail

Any description needs to be presented in some sort of logical order. Otherwise, readers will have to work too hard to put the different details together into one clear picture. Here are three options for organizing material:

1. Organize by physical location.
2. Organize by order of importance.
3. Organize using some other suitable order.

Organize by physical location. When you have a lot of visual details, you can present them as they appear from left to right, top to bottom, inside to outside, or the reverse of any of these. By doing this, you take your readers in a logical sweep across your subject. The guidebook description of Las Vegas uses a physical ordering of details. It begins with an overhead view of the town and then moves inside the casinos.

Organize by order of importance. The most significant or obvious details can be presented first, followed by other details in descending order of importance. The profile of driver Richard Petty first summarizes his main career achievements. Other subsets of facts also are listed by order of importance. For example, his super speedway records are given in order starting with the track where he won the most.

Organize using some other suitable order. Consistency is key when customizing the organization of descriptive details. Rosemary Derrick's description of her mother first presents examples of her entertaining nature (telling stories, making toys, singing) and then of her playful nature (engaging in games with the children, turning cartwheels). Scott Momaday's description of Jemez Pueblo in 1946 presents the village first in terms of its few modern conveniences (telephones and pickup trucks) and then in terms of its many traditional features (horses and cornfields). Che Guevera alternates description of the ocean with the responses of those observing it. Martin Luther King describes death first in terms of who is affected by it and then in terms of what death is (for more on definition, see Chapter 12). Erika Lopez organizes her description of a shocked woman's face by the order in which her appearance changes. Phyllis Theroux's description of each closet moves from a general statement to specific details about particular items of clothing.

Write Now (11)

Review the description outline you worked on in Write Now (10). Determine a good way to organize your description. Select an organizing strategy in Part D on the outline. Then, number your descriptive statements in the order you would include them in a draft. Do not write an essay at this time, but keep this work because you may use it in a later activity.

Summing Up

1. Consider the five strategies for creating description presented in this chapter: describe what you see, describe how your other senses are affected, describe what you do *not* see or feel, describe how your emotions are affected, and describe the images that come to mind. Underline the type of description you do best. What makes this type of description easiest for you?

    _____

    _____

2. Circle the type of description you tend not to include in your writing. What is one thing you can do to give more effort to this kind of description?

    _____

    _____

Second Thoughts

Review the picture that opened this chapter; then think about or discuss the following questions:

1. How do you think this place would affect the senses or emotions?

2. What other place is it like or not like?

3. What metaphor, simile, or analogy could you use to describe this place?

4. If you were to describe this place in writing, how would you organize that description?

Based on what you have learned in this chapter about description, in what new ways can you describe this picture? Write your thoughts in the *Responses* section of your journal.

3. Give an example of each:

   • simile _____

   • metaphor _____

   • analogy _____

   _____

   _____

4. Name two situations outside of school where you might be called upon to describe something in writing.

   _____

   _____

5. As a result of reading this chapter, what one change will you make to enhance your descriptive writing? Write your resolution in the *Habits for Life* section of your journal.

Write Now: Composing an Essay That Describes

Select the description you finished outlining in Write Now (11). Turn it into a full-length essay. Alternatively, select another description from the outlines you created in Write Now (3), (5), or (7), but be sure to consider how you might use simile, metaphor, and analogy. Also pick an organizing strategy. Before drafting the essay, consider what your purpose will be and who your audience is. Use both the Writing Checklist and the Essay Scoring Guide from Chapter 8 to help you revise. Prepare a final copy of the essay.

Using Adjectives in a Series

When using two or more adjectives together to describe something, you need to consider what order to place them in. If you are a fluent speaker of English, you do not have to think about this order because it will come naturally to you. If English is not your first or best language, however, you may have to make a conscious effort to learn how to arrange adjectives appropriately.

Adjectives go before the noun:
new house

[unless the adjective is connected by a verb, as in the sentence: "The house is new."]

Nouns used as adjectives go directly in front of the noun:
new *brick* house

Subjective adjectives (those that reflect an opinion) usually go before objective adjectives (those that reflect a fact):
attractive new house

Adjectives of size usually go before other objective adjectives, while adjectives of color usually go near the end of a list of adjectives (but before any noun used as adjectives):
the attractive, *little, red* brick house

If you have more than one adjective describing the same characteristic, separate them by commas:
the *attractive, well constructed* house (both adjectives are subjective)
the *split-level, shingle-roofed* house (both adjectives are objective)

Note that when words are combined to create an adjective, they often (but not always) are hyphenated:
the *split-level* house
the *glass-walled* house

As a general practice, you do not want to use too many adjectives together in a sentence. More than three in a row can weigh down a sentence. It can give your writing a plodding sound, for example:
She lives in an attractive, old, well constructed, little, Colonial-style, red brick house.

Such a sentence would be better broken into two, or rewritten to balance the adjectives with other kinds of description, as in
She lives in an attractive, little, Colonial-style house that is old but well constructed of red brick.

Exercise

Write a sentence using the noun and adjectives provided. Put the adjectives in an appropriate order. Use commas to separate adjectives of the same type.

1. noun: staircase

   adjectives: circular / unlit / creaking

   _____

   _____

2. noun: pineapple

   adjectives: ripe / Hawaiian / fresh

   _____

   _____

3. noun: window

   adjectives: leaded glass / original / unbroken

   _____

   _____

4. noun: tiger

   adjectives: tamed / white / beautiful / Bengal

   _____

   _____

5. noun: doctor

   adjectives: foot / wise / old

   _____

   _____

Gale's Pot

by Sue Bender

Sue Bender was a woman deeply entrenched in a consumerist lifestyle who found herself enchanted by the simple beauty of Amish crafts. The Amish are people whose religion requires them to keep a simple lifestyle: no cars, no radios, not even buttons on their clothing. Curious about what they had that she did not, Bender decided to observe two Amish communities. She described their way of life and its effects on her as an observer in the 1989 book Plain and Simple: A Woman's Journey to the Amish. *It became a bestseller.*

Bender followed Plain and Simple *with another book called* Everyday Sacred: A Woman's Journey Home. *This second book contains suggestions for enjoying life by living simply and by noticing the special in everyday experience. "Gale's Pot" is one essay from this book. As you read it, think about this idea: observing something in order to describe it to others can help you see it better.*

One evening, needing a ride to see a friend who was in town from Japan, I was given the name of a woman named Gale who was also planning to go. I called and she offered me a ride. As Gale said goodnight to her six-month-old twin sons, I looked at the drawings on her wall: round, fat, voluptuous, sensuous, luscious-looking pots, in pastels that burst with vitality and joy.

It was in fact the same pot, done each time in different, intense colors and combinations.

"How did this pot find its way into your life?" I asked Gale several days later.

"It was just around, part of the surroundings in a studio I rented," she said, "always in the corner of my eye. Just the kind of shape I liked, fat and simple." A white metallic enamel pot, fourteen inches wide and nine inches high.

Gale had been in the studio seven years when a fire destroyed nine-tenths of her work. Cleaning up afterwards she had trouble parting with the most unlikely things—an old wood stool she used to stand on and the pot! She asked the owner of the studio if she could have the pot. "Sure, take it. It has no magic for me!" The pot went with her to a new studio in Berkeley and became the receptacle for cleaning utensils.

> How was Bender first introduced to Gale and the story of the pot?

Gale was also teaching a graduate art class called *The 100 Drawings Project*. The task of the class was to find and draw one hundred times, one simple, familiar object, portable enough to bring to class each time. It had to be neutral in content, not religious, not a family heirloom, nor an object that held any sentimental attachment. After hearing Gale describe the assignment to the first class, one of her students asked if she had done this project herself. She hadn't, and decided to join the class in the homework.

Looking around her environment Gale spotted the pot! She stared at it and felt the pot observing her. "Take me off the shelf," it seemed to say. "It tells you, rather than you telling it," was her description of the transaction. Her first four black-and-white drawings were made easily, quickly, with little attachment to the outcome. Then, with ninety-six more to do, and later with fifty more, Gale had exhausted all known possibilities and didn't know what to do.

Why did Gale start drawing pictures of the pot?

Knowing nothing about photography, she began taking pictures of the pot in different circumstances. She noticed that its white enamel surface could reflect anything; it acted as a *mirror,* taking on the qualities of its surroundings. She experimented. At midnight she went out to photograph the pot using the car's headlights to illuminate it. The headlights created a dramatic black-and-white contrast; brake lights turned the pot red; hazard lights produced a yellow pot. Sitting next to the TV, the pot turned blue.

What did Gale do to come up with new ways to draw the pot?

As Gale experimented, she became more and more interested in color. She thought about the pot's original function. She put the pot on the stove and boiled water in it. Silhouetted against other dark pots, a golden glow in the background produced the quality of a seventeenth-century Chardin painting. Over time her drawings became very real, intensely photorealistic.

She took the pot with her in a knapsack on a European vacation. Wanting to capture the colors of Italian cities, she photographed the pot in Florence where the stones reflected ochre and mustard and beige on the pot's surface. Rome produced a deeper, dark yellow and ochre, and a pink cast found its way onto the pot in Bologna. Reflections of the many tiny colored lights at night by the water's edge at Piazza San Marco were captured on the pot's surface. The pot visited and had its picture taken underneath Michelangelo's tomb in Santa Croce, in Florence, and on a niche outside the cathedral in Chartres.

What did Gale do with the pot while on vacation in Europe?

"Sometimes I'd find the simple, unassuming little place would be more remarkable than the remarkable place," Gale told me.

Sitting down at a fountain to rest and think about where to photograph next, she'd turn around and there—just where the pot was sitting, resting—was the perfect place to photograph it. "Chance settings were often the magic settings."

Making one hundred drawings of the same object forced Gale to find new techniques, materials, and ways to work. The goal here was to take risks and exceed limits. Hopefully, along the way, a personal style would emerge.

I spent a lot of time daydreaming about Gale's pot.

The pot led many lives: utilitarian object, icon, travel companion, and mirror. There's something universal about a simple pot. Gale's pot didn't have any innate drama or significance. Working for hours, day after day, she was able to take this most ordinary object and imbue it with meaning.

What struck me was that if you can take a white enamel household pot and begin seeing it brand new each time, *you can do it with anything*. If there are one hundred ways to see an ordinary white pot, imagine all the possibilities for viewing with fresh eyes an "average" child, an "average" marriage.

Gale was telling me a story about relationships.

Each time, the pot was just being the pot, but at the same time it reflected everything that was around it. It was Gale's ability to be present to see, really see—to recognize the sacred in this seemingly mundane pot—that made the difference.

"I don't look at objects the same way anymore," Gale said.

"Objects have begun to look back at me. Any object can have a magical quality. When I'm drawing I don't want to be anywhere else but right there, doing that drawing in that moment."

One day I asked Gale, "Were there any surprises?"

"Yes," she said. "When the project was finished, I realized that it didn't matter where I was drawing or what I was drawing—whether it was a landscape or still life or an object—the same quality came through. Everything I drew conveyed a quality—a feeling of waiting—expectation. Something about to happen."

Eventually Gale realized the choice to draw her pot wasn't all that neutral. This pot, a survivor of the fire, was also a metaphor for her body, her belly. The pot was always drawn empty—waiting to be filled. For some time she had been longing to have children. Each one of those one hundred drawings was a self-portrait.

"Now look what's happened," she added. "Twins!"

What does the pot have to do with "relationships"?

What does Bender mean by "the sacred in this seemingly mundane pot"?

THINK AND RESPOND

1. How would you describe Gale's pot in terms of how it affects the senses and emotions?

   _____

   _____

2. What is Gale's pot like or not like?

   _____

   _____

3. What metaphor, simile, or analogy could you use to describe Gale's pot?

   _____

   _____

4. How does Bender organize her description of Gale's pot?

   _____

   _____

5. What benefits came to Gale from drawing the pot 100 times?

   _____

   _____

6. Provide synonyms or definitions of these words from the essay, and add at least two of the words to the *Words Worth Remembering* section of your journal:

voluptuous _____

luscious _____

pastels _____

receptacle _____

heirloom_____

ochre _____

utilitarian _____

icon _____

innate _____

mundane_____

7. If you liked this reading, make a record of it in the *Readings Worth Remembering* section of your journal.

COMPARING VIEWS

Bender makes the point that simple objects can have great significance. Think of an object, person, or place that is not of special importance to anyone except you. How would you describe it to others? After discussing the topic of things "insignificant yet significant," continue to explore it on your own, in your journal—if you want. You may be able to use material from the discussion and your journal in a future writing activity.

APPLIED WRITING

Bender writes about a friend who learned how to really see an object by drawing it 100 times. Try a short experiment along this line. Select an object and describe it in words 10 times. Observe the object in different settings, in use by different people, or at different times of day. Consider whether the process gives you any insight into yourself, the way Gale's pot did for her. Then write an essay about this object. To do so, organize your observations into an outline. Use the outline as a guide while you draft. Use both the Writing Checklist and the Scoring Guide from Chapter 8 to help you revise. Prepare a final copy of the essay.

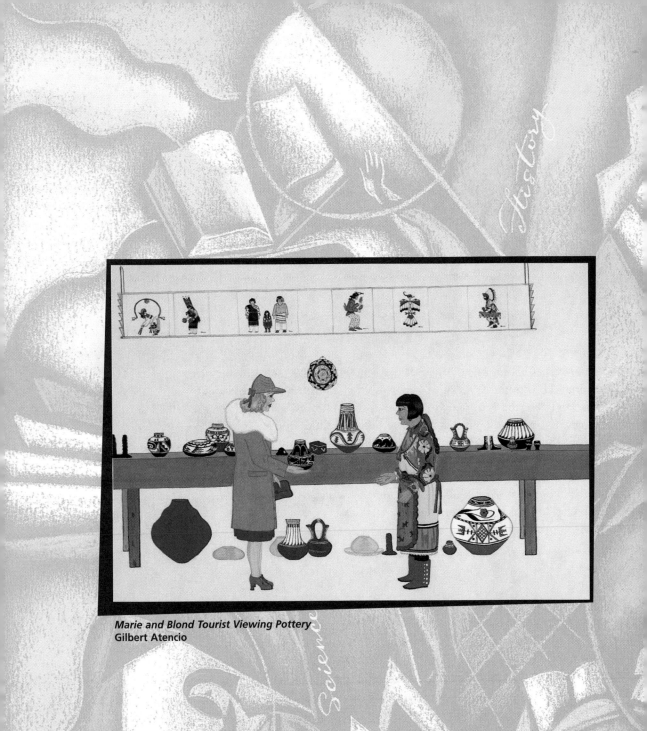

Marie and Blond Tourist Viewing Pottery
Gilbert Atencio

CHAPTER 10

Narrating

These are the **key ideas** of this chapter:

- Narrative writing tells a story.

- Narrative writing can be used to entertain, to make a point, or to introduce a topic.

- Narrative writing can be enhanced through descriptive detail and dialogue.

Picturing Meaning

Examine the illustration on the opposite page; then think about or discuss the following questions:

1. What transaction is taking place in this picture?

_____

_____

2. When do you think this occurred?

_____

_____

3. Where do you think it is taking place?

_____

_____

4. Why do you think the artist recorded this scene?

_____

_____

In the *Responses* section of your journal, write down your thoughts about this picture.

Write Now (1)

Think about a time that *you* bought or sold something important. What happened? Where did it happen? What words were exchanged? How do you feel about the way the transaction turned out? Write down your thoughts about this incident. Keep this work because you may use it in a later activity.

Purposes of Narrative Writing

Describing an event, or narrating, involves the dimension of action over time. It requires you to observe carefully, or recall carefully, a series of moments. **Narrative writing** answers these questions: *Who* was involved? *What* happened? *When* did it occur? *Where* did it take place? *Why* and *how* did the events unfold the way they did?

Narrative writing is much like telling stories out loud. It requires you to give your readers enough information to understand what is happening—but not so much that they cannot follow the story. You decide which details to include based on your purpose and your audience.

Narratives are often used in essays, reports, and other nonfiction forms. This is because stories are entertaining and fun to read. Just as important, they are a good way to make a point. The following narrative is from a newspaper column called "News of the Weird," under the heading "Unclear on the Concept." The purpose of this and other items under the same heading is to demonstrate how events sometimes turn out absurdly when people lose sight of their goals:

The first sentence answers the questions of when and where the event happened, who did it, what they did, and why.

The last two sentences answer the question of how it worked out.

In August at several mink farms in England, animal rights activists surreptitiously "liberated" 6,000 of the aggressive, unruly animals. In the following weeks came dozens of reports of minks killing pets (dogs, cats, hamsters), chickens, birds in a sanctuary, and endangered water voles. Many minks themselves were killed, either by people protecting their own animals or in fights with other minks, and some minks were said to have died of the stress of being released into the wild.

NEWS OF THE WEIRD © by Chuck Shepard. Reprinted with permission of UNIVERSAL PRESS SYNDICATE. All rights reserved

Narratives also are useful devices for introducing a topic and for making a point. The following anecdote does both. It opens a book-length biography of U.S. president Franklin Roosevelt. During his presidency (from 1933 to 1945), Roosevelt could not walk because his legs had been weakened by polio. The story underscores Roosevelt's remarkable willpower:

On nights filled with tension and concern, Franklin Roosevelt performed a ritual that helped him to fall asleep. He would close his eyes and imagine himself at Hyde Park as a boy, standing with his sled in the snow atop the steep hill that stretched far below. As he accelerated down the hill, he maneuvered each familiar curve with perfect skill until he reached the bottom, whereupon, pulling his sled behind him, he started slowly back until he replayed this remembered scene in his mind, obliterating his awareness of the shrunken legs inert beneath the sheets, undoing the knowledge that he would never climb a hill or even walk on his own power again. Thus liberating himself from his paralysis through an act of imaginative will, the president of the United States would fall asleep.

No Ordinary Time: Franklin and Eleanor Roosevelt:
The Home Front in World War II
Doris Kearns Goodwin

The first sentence answers the questions of what happened, when, by whom, and why.

The last sentence answers the question of how it worked.

Write Now (2)

Review the two stories to answer the following questions.

Mink release

1. **How would you summarize this narrative?** _____

_____

_____

2. **What else do you think might have happened when the minks were released?** _____

_____

_____

3. Do you think the activists did the right thing? Why or why not?

_____

_____

4. What incident in your life had unintended consequences like this one?

_____

_____

Falling asleep

5. How would you summarize this narrative?

_____

_____

6. What other details of that childhood memory do you think Roosevelt might have recalled?

_____

_____

7. Do you think Roosevelt's method for falling asleep might work for you? Why or why not?

_____

_____

8. What sleep ritual do you have?

_____

_____

Write Now (3)

Select an anecdote (a brief story) from the ones you identified in questions 4 and 8 of Write Now (2). Alternatively, select the anecdote you reflected on in Write Now (1). Write six questions about this anecdote, each starting with one of these words: *who, what, when, where, why,* and *how.* Answer each question in terms of that anecdote. Keep this work because you may use it in a later activity.

Organizing Narrative Writing

Usually you organize narrative writing by presenting events in the order in which they occur. This is called **chronological order.** The "News of the Weird" incident is reported in chronological detail: the release of the minks followed by the unintended consequences. The Roosevelt story also is organized chronologically: first Roosevelt is trying to fall asleep, then he is recalling a childhood experience (which itself is told in chronological order), then he falls asleep.

The following narrative also is told in chronological order. It is from a travel magazine, and the author's purpose is to introduce readers to the James River in Virginia:

I cock my fishing rod and cast a little topwater plug toward a promising stretch of slick water behind a boulder. Twitching the rod makes the lure chug across the surface, and within moments there's a small explosion where the lure was. The rod arcs and the line comes alive, tracing shaky fish handwriting in the water for a few seconds before a smallmouth bass leaps a foot into the air, three-quarters of a pound of pure ferocity.

> 1: He tosses out the fishing line.
>
> 2: The fish goes for the bait.

In just 30 seconds I have him up to our canoe. He's maybe 12 inches long, a beautiful mottled olive color, possessed of a wild eye. After I unhook him, he rests in my hands for a few seconds, stunned and impossibly vivid, like a traveler from another dimension waking to the world of air and sunlight. I move him back and forth through the water until he revives, suddenly snaps his body and darts back into the depths.

> 3: The fish is hauled into the canoe.
>
> 4: The fish is unhooked.
>
> 5: The fish returns to the water.

My wife, Jane, and I float on, past riffles and rock ledges, giant sycamores that overlean the water and blue herons stalking the shallows. It's so scenic I can hardly believe we began the day slugging it out in Saturday traffic on I–66.

Tent Revival
Bill Heavey

The last sentence of this description refers to a difficult highway drive that occurred earlier in the day. A reference like this to something that happened earlier is called a **flashback.** Flashbacks can be placed before or after a chronological ordering of events to add emphasis. In this case, the flashback emphasizes the calmness of the James River compared with the hectic traffic of the highway.

The opposite of flashing back is flashing forward, called **foreshadowing.** In foreshadowing you refer to something that happens after or at the end of the event you are describing. Like flashback, foreshadowing heightens the contrast between two events. It adds drama by hinting at what is going to happen. Foreshadowing is used in the following narrative about a man dancing. It is from a memoir about the final conversations a journalist had with his former professor, who is dying. This passage is from an early chapter in the book and describes what the professor was like before he learned he had Lou Gehrig's disease. Notice how the chronological order of actual events is altered in the narrative through foreshadowing:

4: Morrie learns he has terminal illness.

3: Morrie realizes something is wrong with his health.

1: Morrie likes to dance.

His death sentence came in the summer of 1994. Looking back, Morrie knew something bad was coming long before that. He knew it the day he gave up dancing.

He had always been a dancer, my old professor. The music didn't matter. Rock and roll, big band, the blues. He loved them all. He would close his eyes and with a blissful smile begin to move to his own sense of rhythm. It wasn't always pretty. But then, he didn't worry about a partner. Morrie danced by himself.

He used to go to this church in Harvard Square every Wednesday night for something called "Dance Free." They had flashing lights and booming speakers and Morrie would wander in among the mostly student crowd, wearing a white T-shirt and black sweatpants and a towel around his neck, and whatever music was playing, that's the music to which he danced. He'd do the lindy to Jimi Hendrix. He twisted and twirled, he waved his arms like a conductor on amphetamines, until sweat was dripping down the middle of his back. No one there knew he was a prominent doctor of sociology, with years of experience as a college professor and several well-respected books. They just thought he was some old nut.

Once, he brought a tango tape and got them to play it over the speakers. Then he commandeered the floor, shooting back and forth like some hot Latin lover. When he finished, everyone applauded. He could have stayed in that moment forever.

But then the dancing stopped.

2: Morrie stops dancing.

Tuesdays with Morrie: An Old Man, Young Man, and Life's Greatest Lessons
Mitch Albom

To plan an anecdote or longer story, use the Narrative Outline in Figure 10–1. This outline is a cross between a cluster map and a brainstorming list. It reminds you to consider *who, what, when, where, why,* and *how.* It also helps you outline the event in time order. After outlining the event, you can decide whether to use flashback, foreshadowing, or a strict chronological order. Study the example of a completed outline (Figure 10–2) to see how it was used to plan a narrative about a purse snatching. Then try using it when writing your own narratives.

Figure 10–1: Narrative Outline

Photocopy this form before using.

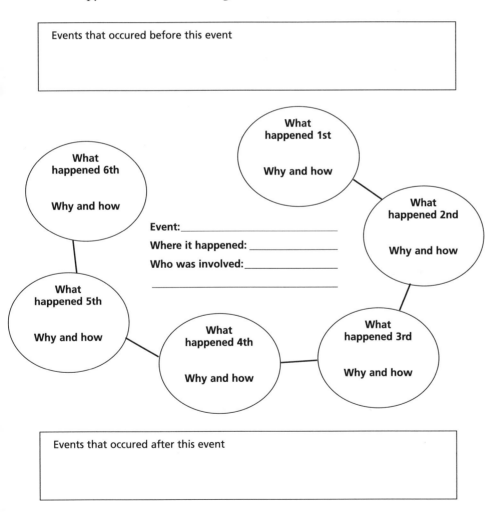

Figure 10–2: Example Narrative Outline

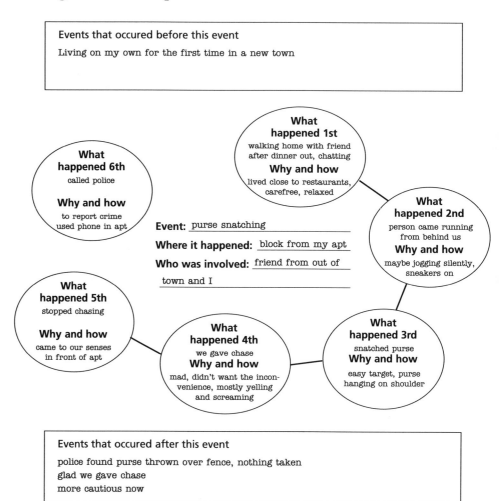

Events that occured before this event

Living on my own for the first time in a new town

What happened 1st
walking home with friend after dinner out, chatting
Why and how
lived close to restaurants, carefree, relaxed

What happened 6th
called police
Why and how
to report crime used phone in apt

What happened 2nd
person came running from behind us
Why and how
maybe jogging silently, sneakers on

Event: purse snatching

Where it happened: block from my apt

Who was involved: friend from out of town and I

What happened 5th
stopped chasing
Why and how
came to our senses in front of apt

What happened 4th
we gave chase
Why and how
mad, didn't want the inconvenience, mostly yelling and screaming

What happened 3rd
snatched purse
Why and how
easy target, purse hanging on shoulder

Events that occured after this event

police found purse thrown over fence, nothing taken
glad we gave chase
more cautious now

Write Now (4)

Review the two stories to answer the following questions.

Fishing

1. **How would you summarize this narrative?**

_____

_____

2. What else might have happened before, during, or after the moment described?

_____

_____

3. Do you think it was an experience you would have enjoyed? Why or why not?

_____

_____

4. What memorable day—wonderful or disastrous—do you recall?

_____

_____

Morrie

5. How would you summarize this narrative?

_____

_____

6. What else might have happened before, during, or after the moment Morrie realized he was terminally ill?

_____

_____

7. Do you think you would have liked to know Morrie? Why or why not?

_____

_____

8. What discovery of change—pleasant or unpleasant—has happened to you?

_____

_____

Write Now (5)

Select an anecdote from the ones you identified in questions 4 and 8 of Write Now (4). Develop the story using the Narrative Outline in Figure 10–1. Just work on the outline—you do not need to turn it into an essay at this time. Keep this work because you may use it in a later activity.

Adding Descriptive Detail

Descriptive detail enhances narrative. As covered in Chapter 9, description makes use of visual and other sensual details, emotional responses, and imagery. In Heavey's narrative about catching a fish, he offers a physical description of the setting ("riffles and rock ledges, giant sycamores that overlean the water and blue herons stalking the shallows"). He reveals his feelings about the setting (the water is "promising"). He uses simile (the fish was "like a traveler from another dimension") and metaphor (it was "three-quarters of a pound of pure ferocity"). Albom's description of his former professor also includes physical details ("sweat was dripping down the middle of his back"), simile (he "waved his arms like a conductor on amphetamines"), and metaphor ("they just thought he was some old nut"). The following anecdote uses descriptive detail to set the scene for a strange incident. Notice in particular the use of vivid verbs and adverbs. It is from a memoir by an American who spent a year in China. His purpose was to explain why he decided to purchase a bicycle:

Descriptive verbs: squeezed, crushed, grab, screamed, crashed.

Descriptive adverbs: terribly, desperately, cheerfully.

I did not like riding the buses in Changsha; they were always terribly crowded, sometimes with passengers squeezed partway out of the doors and windows. I once rode a bus which stopped at a particularly crowded streetcorner. Women were holding their children above their heads so they would not be crushed in the shoving, and I saw a man desperately grab onto something inside the bus while most of his body was not yet on board. The bus attendant screamed at him to let go, but he would not, so she pressed the button operating the doors and they crashed shut on him, fixing him exactly half inside and half out. The bus proceeded to its destination, whereupon the doors opened and the man stepped down, cheerfully paid the attendant half the usual fare, and went on his way.

Iron and Silk
Mark Salzman

Descriptive language not only helps to set the scene, it can carry the story. In the following passage from an essay about creativity, the author uses metaphor, simile, and analogy to help readers understand what the act of writing is like for her:

Living in a state of psychic unrest, in a Borderland, is what makes poets write and artists create. It is like a cactus needle embedded in the flesh. It worries itself deeper and deeper, and I keep aggravating it by poking at it. When it begins to fester I have to do something to put an end to the aggravation and to figure out why I have it. I get deep down into the place where it's rooted in my skin and pluck away at it, playing it like a musical instrument—the fingers pressing, making the pain worse before it can get better. Then out it comes. No more discomfort, no more ambivalence. Until another needle pierces the skin. That's what writing is for me, an endless cycle of making it worse, making it better, but always making meaning out of the experience, whatever it may be.

Tlilli, Tlapalli:
The Path of the Red and Black Ink
Gloria Anzaldúa

> Metaphor: life for artists = a disturbed state.
>
> Analogy: a creative idea is like a festering needle in the skin.
>
> Simile: artists play with ideas the way musicians play on musical instruments.
>
> Metaphor: writing = endless cycle.

Write Now (6)

Review the two stories to answer the following questions.

Bus ride in China

1. How would you summarize this narrative?

_____

_____

2. What other verbs or adverbs might be used to describe what happened on the bus?

_____

_____

3. Do you think you would enjoy traveling by bus in China? Why or why not?

_____

_____

4. What travel incident does it remind you of from your life?

_____

_____

Cactus needle

5. How would you summarize this narrative?

_____

_____

6. What other simile, metaphor, or analogy might you use to describe how artists create?

_____

_____

7. Do you agree that creativity can be a painful process? Why or why not?

_____

_____

8. What "endless cycle" do you experience in life?

_____

_____

Write Now (7)

Select an anecdote from the ones you identified in questions 4 and 8 of Write Now (6). Consider this event in terms of descriptive details. To help you do this, you may want to sketch a picture or fill in the Description Outline from Chapter 9. Just work on your descriptive notes—you do not need to turn them into an essay at this time. Keep this work because you may use it in a later activity.

Adding Dialogue

Conversations help tell a story. Conversations in writing are called **dialogue**. The following dialogue shows what it is like to try to talk to a sleep-deprived parent of a baby. In this dialogue, the tired new father is speaking to his wife:

"Honey, when you go to the uh . . ."

Reiser speaks.

"To the what?"

His wife speaks (and so on, back and forth).

"To the . . . whad'ya call it . . . the place? With the things . . . they have things that you can buy . . ."

"To the store?"

"Yes, thank you. To the store . . . Make sure we pick up some . . . some, uh . . ."

"What?"

"Little . . . um . . ."

"What do you want?"

"You know. They're small, you stick them in your ears . . ."

"Earrings?"

"No. Fuzzy things."

"Q-Tips?"

"Yes, exactly. Q-Tips."

Babyhood
Paul Reiser

Reiser's dialogue is presented like a play. He makes a statement and then his wife makes a statement, with no narration inbetween. That is one way to present dialogue. Another way to use dialogue is to weave it into the narrative. This is how dialogue is used in the following story about a garage operator's experience with a "comeback" customer. Comeback customers are people who return with complaints about repairs. The purpose of the story is to show readers why they should not take advantage of their auto repairer:

A customer blustered into my shop an hour or so before closing time on a busy afternoon. He was the kind of comeback who could give comebacks a bad name. Positioning himself to be heard by customers in the crowded waiting room, he began to berate my lead mechanic, who had performed a tuneup on his car earlier in the day. "Come out and look at the old spark plugs you left in my car," he demanded. "I paid you for a tuneup, you charged me for eight brand new spark plugs, and the ones in my engine are old, used junk!"

The customer is quoted.

I checked with the lead mechanic who showed me the customer's old plugs in our trash bin. We both realized what happened. Our customer had swapped his new plugs with a friend, or removed them to store for future use, and was "working" us for a free set. I directed the customer to drive his car into a service bay, then closed and locked the bay door behind it. We installed the eight new plugs. I prepared a "no charge" service order, written in the form of a receipt for the plugs, and presented it to the customer for his signature. Abrasively, he refused. "In that case," I told him, "we won't be able to open the bay doors and release your car to you. And we leave for the night in fifteen minutes." He signed and left.

The author quotes himself.

"Pretty clever," my lead mechanic said. "He conned us out of eight free spark plugs." "True," I admitted, "but he can never be a comeback of ours again. He's conned himself out of a darned good shop—forever."

The author quotes himself in conversation with the mechanic.

The Armchair Mechanic:
A Non-Mechanic's Guide to Understanding
Your Car and Getting Good Repairs
Jack Gillis and Tom Kelly

Write Now (8)

Review the two stories to answer the following questions.

Tired parent

1. **How would you summarize this narrative?**

_____

_____

2. What else do you think Reiser and his wife might have said to each other?

_____

_____

3. Does this conversation seem realistic to you? Why or why not?

_____

_____

4. What conversation does it remind you of from your life?

_____

_____

Comeback customer

5. How would you summarize this narrative?

_____

_____

6. What else do you think the customer, the garage operator, or the mechanic might have said?

_____

_____

7. Do you think the mechanic handled the customer appropriately? Why or why not?

_____

_____

8. What incident does this remind you of from your experience being or serving a customer?

_____

_____

Write Now (9)

Select an anecdote from the ones you identified in questions 4 and 8 of Write Now (8). Consider this event in terms of the dialogue that occurred. Write down your recollection of this conversation. Just work on recording the dialogue—you do not need to turn it into an essay at this time. Keep this work because you may use it in a later activity.

Accuracy in Dialogue

Readers of Paul Reiser's book know that the dialogue with his wife did not happen word for word the way he reports. They know he is just making fun of what he sounds like when he is tired. Readers of the book on car repair also know that the conversation between the mechanic and the customer probably did not happen exactly the way it is presented. They know that the mechanic is recalling a story and could not possibly remember exactly what he and the customer said. In both cases, the exact words are not essential because these are informal, personal stories. Readers will assume that the conversations have been tailored to fit the purpose of the story. When you use dialogue in informal essays like the two you just read, you can **paraphrase.** This means to approximate what was said using your own words. The paraphrase may not be exact, but it should be authentic—true to the essence of what you are describing.

Paraphrasing is not acceptable when you write for formal purposes, such as a business memorandum, research paper, newspaper article, or formal essay. In such cases, use *only* exact quotes. In these kinds of writings, readers will assume that all information you present is true, exact, and can be confirmed. Do *not* use quotation marks around any statements if you cannot recall them exactly or if you do not have a documented record of the conversation. Getting a documented record requires careful note taking or the use of a tape recorder. When quoting, you may leave out the "ums," "ahs," "you knows," and other verbal repetitions. You also may make very minor changes, for example, to standardize grammar. However, such changes should only be done for the purpose of helping readers comprehend the statements. They should not affect the speaker's original meaning.

Write Now (10)

Move into groups of three. Two of you hold a short conversation about what you plan to have for your next meal. Then work as a team to turn the notes into a written dialogue. Afterward, discuss how the written dialogue differs from the actual conversation. Discuss the challenges of capturing dialogue in writing. Use the form in Figure 10–3 to develop the dialogue.

Figure 10–3: Writing Dialogue

Conversation: _____

_____

_____

_____

_____

_____

_____

Dialogue: _____

_____

_____

_____

_____

_____

_____

_____

_____

Summing Up

1. What are three purposes of narrative writing?

   _____

   _____

   _____

2. Define these three ways to organize narrative writing:

   Chronological order: _____

   Flashback: _____

   Foreshadowing: _____

3. Consider these two important elements to narrative writing: descriptive details and dialogue. Of the two, underline the element you tend to include more in your narrative writing. What makes this element easier for you?

   _____

   _____

Second Thoughts

Review the picture that opened this chapter; then think about or discuss the following questions:

1. How would you describe the women, the objects in the room, and the room itself?

2. What do you think the women might be saying to each other?

3. If you were to write a narrative based on this picture, what kind of order would you use to tell the story?

Based on what you have learned in this chapter about narrative writing, what new insights do you have about the story told in this picture? Write your thoughts in the *Responses* section of your journal.

4. Circle the element of narrative writing that you tend to include less. What is one thing you can do to give more effort to this element in narrative writing?

   _____

   _____

5. Name two situations outside of school where you might be called upon to tell a story in writing.

   _____

   _____

6. As a result of reading this chapter, what one change will you make to enhance your narrative writing? Write your resolution in the *Habits for Life* section of your journal.

Write Now: Composing an Essay That Tells a Story

Select one of the anecdotes you worked on in Write Now (3), (5), (7), and (9). Turn it into a full-length story. Plan your essay using each of these three methods:

- Organizing a narrative (use the Narrative Outline in Figure 10–1).
- Developing descriptive details (use the Description Outline in Figure 9–1 of Chapter 9).
- Recalling any dialogue that occurred during the incident (make notes of it).

   Use both the Writing Checklist and the Essay Scoring Guide from Chapter 8 to help you revise your draft. Prepare a final copy of the essay.

Using Quotation Marks

To show that a person is speaking, frame what he or she says inside a pair of quotation marks. Each mark should turn toward the quotation. If the quoted statement stands alone, without a reference to whoever is speaking, enclose all sentence punctuation inside the quotation marks:

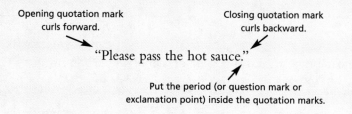

Opening quotation mark
curls forward.

Closing quotation mark
curls backward.

"Please pass the hot sauce."

Put the period (or question mark or
exclamation point) inside the quotation marks.

When you indicate who is speaking after a quotation, use a comma at the end of the quoted sentence and put the period after the reference to the person:

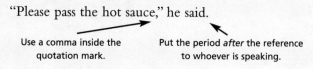

"Please pass the hot sauce," he said.

Use a comma inside the
quotation mark.

Put the period *after* the reference
to whoever is speaking.

When you indicate who is speaking before the quotation, use a comma after the reference to the person, outside the quotation mark:

He said, "Please pass the hot sauce."

Use a comma outside
the quotation mark.

When you interrupt a quoted sentence to indicate who is speaking, use a comma after the reference to the person and do not capitalize the continued sentence:

"Please pass the hot sauce," he said, "because this is too mild."

Use a comma outside
the quotation mark.

Do not capitalize.

If the interruption follows a complete sentence, any new quotation should start with a capital letter:

"Please pass the hot sauce," he said. "It tastes good on everything."

Capitalize.

If you do not have the exact words, you can indicate what was said without quotation marks:

> He asked her to please pass the hot sauce because he uses
>   it on everything.

"To" and "that" introduce what was said.

> He requested that she pass the hot sauce, please, because he uses
>   it on everything.

To indicate that a quotation is approximate, use qualifying words:

Qualifying words

> I think he said something like, "Pass that there hot sauce,
>   darlin', cuz I douse just about everythin' with it."

Exercise

Add quotation marks and other punctuation where needed to the following sentences. Some sentences do not require any.

1. Give me back my money the customer said hotly.

2. The woman explained to the admitting nurse I think my daughter broke her collar bone.

3. People don't seem to use ma'am or sir anymore when they address their elders.

4. Give me a back rub Victor groaned from the couch where he had tossed himself because my muscles are killing me.

5. This is not the exit the guard said. The exit is over there.

6. The policeman told her to stand facing her car with her hands on the hood.

7. The waitress responded to our complaint about the long wait for our food with some smart-aleck remark along the lines of If you don't like the service, take your business elsewhere.

8. The dentist told her she needed a root canal.

9. Watch out for that falling rock!

10. Just wait until you have children of your own my mother used to say to me.

Pick Your Part

by Ian Frazier

"Pick Your Part" is an essay that first appeared in the magazine Atlantic Monthly. *Journalist Ian Frazier opens the essay with the statement, "Man, I love L.A." He proceeds to explain that most of what he knows about the city of Los Angeles, California, comes from TV and the movies. Next, he describes his first visit after a twenty-year absence. On that visit, he enthusiastically prowled the streets of the city for hours, finding them to be amazingly familiar. Later, he accompanied his brother-in-law on a search for a used auto part: a rearview mirror for an '83 Ford pickup truck.*

The original essay is about one-third longer than what is reprinted here. As you read this excerpt, consider how Frazier's narrative of activity at the used-parts lot contributes to a description of that place as well as of L.A. itself.

Who is "we"?

We went from one used-parts store to another, farther and farther into the unendingness of greater L.A. Finally we got to a place he had heard about but had never been to before. The sign above the sheet-iron fence along the road said PICK YOUR PART, with a subheading, "The world's largest self-service auto recycler." A smiling octopus on the sign held various automotive tools in its legs. My brother-in-law comes from Louisiana, and has a connoisseur's appreciation of L.A. He told me that Pick Your Part is famous among people who fix cars in L.A.

How does Pick Your Part differ from a retail store?

Pick Your Part is a fifty-four acre lot containing junk cars of all makes and models. For a small admission fee people seeking car parts can go into the lot and explore; if they find the part they're looking for, they remove it themselves, present it at a window by the exit, pay a price usually less than a fifth of what a regular parts place would charge, and take it home. They can't try the part out in the parking lot, however; signs all over say you're not allowed to work on cars there.

Where is Pick Your Part?

Pick Your Part is in Sun Valley, in the northwestern reaches of the city. Some miles beyond it is Pacoima and the site on Foothill Boulevard where the police beat Rodney King. On the horizon to the east are low mountains covered with scrubby greenery that blooms yellow in the spring. To the west and south are the grayish silhouettes of the gravel heaps and towers and conveyors of a concrete company. We got in a long line of guys with hopeful expressions on their faces and socket wrenches in their hands, paid our one dollar apiece at the gate, and went in.

Before us the vast acreage of junk cars stretched on beneath a sky that was the hazy bluish-gray of a blank video screen. Pillars here and there indicated the kind of vehicle to be found in that particular district— Ford, GMC, Toyota, and so forth. My brother-in-law headed off in the direction of the Ford pillar. I proceeded by the principle of the random walk, following aisles and rows vertically and horizontally until I was deep in the middle of the lot. I stopped by a car of a make I couldn't identify, which had a single bright-yellow cowboy boot sitting on its roof. Here in the middle of all these silent machines that had once made so much noise and smoke seemed to me the most peaceful place I had been in L.A. From where I stood I could see no other people. The occasional clinking of feet kicking parts on the concrete pavement was the only nearby sound. The cars, none with tires, sat on small steel pedestals supporting the axles at each corner. On the ground around each car was an arrested explosion of its parts, scattered on glistening stains of oil. The cars had been placed in rows facing each other, all with their hoods raised, like soldiers in a raggedy crossed-swords salute.

What makes Pick Your Part a peaceful place?

None of the cars were really old. They seemed to be of the age of cultural artifacts that we had just recently forgotten, like the rock group Toto. Many had once had bright paint jobs, but now they were all the basic color of cars, which is the color of oil. As I stood there daydreaming, suddenly a guy popped out from somewhere. He had on a muscle shirt and a U.S. Post Office baseball cap. "I need a clutch fan on a three-oh-one engine," he said. "Have you seen any three-oh-ones around?" I didn't know what he was talking about, but I said I hadn't. Then, to account for myself, I said I was looking for a rearview mirror from an '83 Ford. "Fords are over there," he said, gesturing vaguely. I began walking in that direction. Farther along the row I came upon a guy standing legs astraddle in a car's engine cavity, pushing down with all his weight on the handle of a big pipe wrench.

Unexpectedly, I emerged into a wider aisle, a kind of thoroughfare where forklift trucks came and went. Some of the forklifts were carrying cars that had been so long in the lot that almost nothing remained of them but body and frame; the empty shells of their sides wobbled and shivered as they passed by. I followed the aisle to an open piece of

How does the
Aljon work?

ground at the edge of the lot where the forklifts were taking the cars. Here an even bigger forklift (a machine called an Aljon, I later learned) awaited them. Beneath the tines of its fork the Aljon had two pincers making a claw about four feet long. When a car was deposited before it, the Aljon grabbed a bumper with the pincers, yanked it off, and tossed it onto a pile of bumpers. Then it did the same to the other bumper. Next the Aljon flipped the hood from the engine (if there still was a hood) with its fork, opened the pincer claw wide, and lowered it into the engine housing as the fork smashed and flattened the windshield and roof. Then the claw seized the engine block and lifted, shaking and worrying it until with a grinding, giving way it came free, trailing cables and wires. The Aljon then tossed the engine block onto a small mountain of engine blocks nearby, and a smaller forklift took the car's last remains to a crusher across the way.

Through the cracked and blue-tinted window of the Aljon I could see its operator—sunglasses, baseball cap, straggly blond hair, mouth in a plumb-bob horizontal line. With several control levers at the fingers of each hand he made the Aljon move without lurch or stutter, taking out the engine blocks as casually as if he were shucking peanuts. In a telepathic moment I realized that the Aljon operator was having a wonderful time.

I watched him, mesmerized. When you watch like that, often other people will show up to watch with you; soon I noticed that a stocky guy in sunglasses and a baggy blue T-shirt was next to me. He and I got to talking. He told me that his name was Ernesto and that he was looking for a rearview mirror too—a leftside mirror from an '86 Toyota. On the only '86 Toyota he had found so far, the left-side mirror was already gone, but he had taken a long, narrow piece of curved plastic with holes in it, which he said went to a door molding.

He said, "I came to L.A. from El Salvador in 1989, and when I was first here I bought a '71 Toyota Celica. It was a good car but after three or four years it didn't have enough power to go on the freeway. I was living in East L.A., and I left it on the street until I got money to fix it. I got one ticket. I got another ticket, and my brother-in-law told me if I want to fix it, pay the tickets—otherwise the city will tow the car away. So I left it and didn't pay the tickets and the city took it. A few months after that I was in this lot with my brother-in-law looking for a part, and my brother-in-law called to me, 'Ernesto! Come here!' There was my car—I recognized it because it had a hole in the side where we had fixed it and I had put my initials on the patch. I was very sad to see my car here. I had a lot of memories in that car, and now it was so destroyed. When we got home, my brother-in-law was making fun of me, telling everybody how sad I was about my car."

Ernesto stood watching the Aljon for a while in silence. Then he said, "You love your car, you take care of him, you wash him, you wax him. Then you see him in the jaws of a monster like that . . ."

Probably everyone here was with his brother-in-law. I said good-bye to Ernesto and went looking for mine, again proceeding randomly, dawdling through the rows of cars... . Finally, at the distant end of a wider aisle I saw my brother-in-law... . He had not found the rearview mirror but didn't seem to mind. He had come across a tire tool that he thought he could use. We got in a line of oily guys at a window by the exit to pay for it. The guy in front of us was wheeling an assortment of parts in a baby stroller. The guy behind us had the sides of his head shaved bare and his top hair in a long ponytail flowing down his back, and studs and rings in different parts of his body. His arms were oil past the elbows, and he cradled a power-steering pump and hose (I asked) in his hands. He and a studded companion were beaming in satisfaction. My brother-in-law and I paid for the tire tool, and then drove on various freeways and other roads to an open-air stand where we got Mexican food so hot it tanned my tongue like boot leather. I considered this an excellent day in L.A.

Why does Ernesto refer to the Aljon as a "monster"?

What did Frazier ask, and why?

THINK AND RESPOND

1. Give short answers to these questions:

   Whom did Frazier accompany to Pick Your Part? _____

   _____

   What were they searching for? _____

   _____

   When did they go to Pick Your Part? _____

   _____

   Where in L.A. was Pick Your Part? _____

   _____

   Why did Frazier wander the lot by himself? _____

   _____

   How do you find the part you want at Pick Your Part? _____

   _____

2. What time order did Frazier use to organize the story of his visit to Pick Your Part?

   _____

   _____

3. Frazier includes a great deal of description in his essay. What two descriptive details stood out in particular?

   _____

   _____

   _____

4. Frazier includes a long quote from a man named Ernesto. How does this quotation contribute to Frazier's narrative about his trip to Pick Your Part?

_____

_____

5. If Frazier's purpose is to show why he loves L.A., why do you suppose he chose to describe his visit to Pick Your Part?

_____

_____

6. Provide synonyms or definitions for these words from the essay, and add at least two of the words to the *Words Worth Remembering* section of your journal:

connoisseur _____

conveyors _____

hazy _____

astraddle _____

thoroughfare _____

tines _____

pincers _____

plumb-bob _____

telepathic _____

mesmerized _____

7. If you liked this reading, make a record of it in the *Readings Worth Remembering* section of your journal.

COMPARING VIEWS

Frazier's essay suggests that when he visited the used parts lot, he was simply enjoying himself, not acting as a writer or reporter. Yet he later wrote this detailed narrative. What observation skills might he have used? What kind of note taking do you suppose he did during or after his visit? What strategies can *you* use to be a good observer and recorder of events? After discussing this topic with others, continue to explore it on your own, in your journal—if it interests you. You may be able to use material from the discussion and your journal in a future writing activity.

APPLIED WRITING

Frazier begins his essay by declaring his love for L.A. He then shows why, through a description of his activities in the city. Think of a place you feel strongly about. Then, write an essay about that place. Use narrative writing to show what happens in that place and to reveal how you feel about it. Make use of the Narrative Outline (Figure 10–1) to get started. Include descriptive detail in your draft. Also include dialogue, if relevant to your narrative. Use both the Writing Checklist and the Scoring Guide from Chapter 8 to help you revise. Prepare a final copy of the essay.

Ozone, Tennessee photograph

CHAPTER 11

Defining

These are the **key ideas** of this chapter:

- A definition can be used to clarify the meaning of an essential term or a term that will be unfamiliar to readers.

- A definition can communicate the general meaning of a term, the particular sense in which it is being used, or an interpretation of the term's meaning.

- A variety of information can be included in any definition; what to include depends on your purpose and how much readers already know about the term.

Picturing Meaning

Examine the photograph on the opposite page; then think about or discuss these questions:

1. What do you see in this photopgraph?

   _____

   _____

2. How do you know what it is?

   _____

   _____

3. How is it like others of its kind?

   _____

   _____

4. How is it unique?

   _____

   _____

In the *Responses* section of your journal, write down your thoughts about this photograph.

Write Now (1)

When you see something you have never seen before, how do *you* figure out what it is? Answer this question in terms of a particular example, such as when you were served an unfamiliar food or when you saw something unusual in a place you had never been before. In writing, describe the thinking your mind goes through to identify the object. Keep this work because you may use it in a later activity.

Purposes of Definition

Description is a way of explaining what something *is like*—what it looks like, feels like, or calls to mind. (See Chapter 9 for more about describing.) By contrast, a definition is a form of description that explains what something *is*. A definition provides the meaning of the thing and its essential qualities. This sentence describes what something is like:

A coupe is trim and sporty-looking.

This sentence defines what it *is:*

A coupe is a closed automobile (not a convertible) with two doors and a shorter body compared to a four-door car.

One set of choices you must make as a writer is when to define terms and how substantial to make those definitions. Such decisions should always be made based on your purpose and the background knowledge of your readers. No definition is necessary if the term is not essential or if your audience is familiar with it. A definition may be necessary if the term is key to understanding the rest of the text or if some part of your audience will not be familiar with it. For example, assume you work for a financial services company and are writing promotional materials about 401(k) plans. In a brochure for investment counselors, you may not need to define "401(k)" or you may need to define it only briefly. In a brochure for consumers, you may need to include a detailed definition.

Definitions introduce readers to a term you use, but they do more. They also direct readers to the particular meaning of the term. Here is a sentence where one term is used twice, each time carrying a different meaning:

Apollo 13 was a near disaster, but *Apollo 13* was a clear success.

As written, the sentence is confusing because it suggests that the same thing was both a disaster and a success. The two different meanings for the same term, *Apollo 13*, become apparent when definitions are added:

The space mission *Apollo 13* was a near disaster, but the movie *Apollo 13* was a clear success.

A third function of definitions is to present your interpretation of a term's meaning. Here is a paragraph defining the word "quilt." It is the very first paragraph in a book about making quilts:

A quilt is more than fabric, batting and stitches. It is a rare and wonderful creation of the soul which expresses our personal statements, our likes and dislikes, feelings, thoughts and loves. It is a bridge that encourages friendships. It supports our need for recognition, as we display it proudly to the applause of its admirers. And it links us with those who've stitched before and those who will follow, as it gives a wordless but meaningful description of who we are and what we feel. A quilt is all these—and more: it is the embodiment of love.

Quilts! Quilts!! Quilts!!!
The Complete Guide to Quiltmaking
Diana McClun and Laura Nownes

> Quilt = more than a physical object.

> Quilt = a connection to others.

This definition places more emphasis on the significance of quilts— what the authors believe to be their essential purpose—than on the quilts' physical properties. Definitions are often subjective like this: they convey the writer's personal opinion. They reveal tone. When a term you are using is subject to different interpretations (and many terms are), you can express your point of view in the definition.

Write Now (2)

In each of the following sentences, circle the term being defined and underline the definition. Then add a checkmark beside each type of definition that applies: general meaning of the term, particular meaning of the term, or author's opinion about the term.

1. Block busting is a despicable practice by which some realtors create panic in homeowners so that they will sell their properties.
    _____ general meaning of the term
    _____ particular meaning of the term
    _____ author's opinion about the term

2. Höder, the Scandinavian god of darkness, is called the blind old god.
    _____ general meaning of the term
    _____ particular meaning of the term
    _____ author's opinion about the term

3. Queen Elizabeth—the one who ruled England from 1558 to 1603, not the twentieth century monarch—was called the Virgin Queen.
    _____ general meaning of the term
    _____ particular meaning of the term
    _____ author's opinion about the term

4. The *Mayflower*, a ship of 180 tons, sailed in 1620 from Southhampton, England, to Plymouth Rock in what is now the United States.
    _____ general meaning of the term
    _____ particular meaning of the term
    _____ author's opinion about the term

5. "Terminate with extreme prejudice" is chilling jargon that hides what it means: to kill.
    _____ general meaning of the term
    _____ particular meaning of the term
    _____ author's opinion about the term

6. Nashville, the capital of the state of Tennessee, is home to the Grand Ole Opry.
    _____ general meaning of the term
    _____ particular meaning of the term
    _____ author's opinion about the term

7. My mother's cream cheese pie is the best dessert in the world.
    _____ general meaning of the term
    _____ particular meaning of the term
    _____ author's opinion about the term

8. The Robert Kennedy I am talking about was not John Kennedy's brother.

_____ general meaning of the term

_____ particular meaning of the term

_____ author's opinion about the term

9. *Ex utero* genetic testing is a procedure used in the early stages of a pregnancy to provide security and relief to many and wretched choices to the rest.

_____ general meaning of the term

_____ particular meaning of the term

_____ author's opinion about the term

10. Evolution, the process by which species change trait by trait over time, was the discovery of Charles Darwin.

_____ general meaning of the term

_____ particular meaning of the term

_____ author's opinion about the term

Ways to Define

Here are five strategies for defining something in writing:

1. State the **category** to which it belongs.

2. State what sets it apart within that category.

3. Provide synonyms for it.

4. Give examples and nonexamples.

5. Explain its origins.

Each of these strategies is discussed below in terms of defining an object, but they also apply to defining concepts, persons, places, or events.

State the category to which it belongs. A category is a group of things that have similarities and share features. Another term for category is **class**.

State what sets it apart within that category. An object within a category has features that set it apart from others in that category. Mentioning these distinct features can help readers develop a specific, accurate understanding of the term.

Provide synonyms for it. Synonyms are words or phrases that can be substituted for each other without substantial change in meaning. While readers may not know a certain word, they may know some of its synonyms, which can be a quick clue to a term's meaning.

Give examples and nonexamples. Examples help readers understand the range of the term you are defining, while nonexamples help them understand the limits and boundaries. Examples and nonexamples have features in common, but only examples have the specific features of the term being defined. Examples and nonexamples also may describe how the object is used or not used or how it operates or does not operate.

Explain its origins. Information about where the object comes from, about how it came to be, or about how it came to be named can help readers develop a fuller sense of the term being described.

The term "water," for example, falls into the category of beverage. Within that category, it is distinguished as being natural, healthful, and refreshing. A synonym for water is "thirst quencher." Examples of water within the category of beverage include club soda, spring water, and mineral water. Nonexamples include beer, soda pop, and coffee. The word water stems from the Old English word "wæter," and it is related to the German word "wasser" and the Icelandic word "vatl." These different ways of specifying the word water can be combined to create a brief but detailed picture of the substance:

> "Water is nature's own beverage. It is healthful and refreshing. Whether plain as spring water or dressed up as mineral water, water is a superior thirst quencher compared with beer, soda pop, or coffee. Throughout time people have used different names for it— *wæter, wasser, vatl*, to name a few—but whatever you call it, water is the most essential drink of all.

Like any other form of description, defining involves a careful selection of detail. Context is key. A definition that is appropriate in one writing situation may not work in another. Here is another definition of water from an encyclopedia. It uses a different category, mentions different features, and presents different examples. This definition is unlike the previous one, but it is equally valid:

Water [is the] common name applied to the liquid form (state) of the hydrogen and oxygen compound H_2O. Pure water is an odorless, tasteless, clear liquid. . . . Water is the only substance that occurs at ordinary temperatures in all three states of matter: solid, liquid, and gas. As a solid, ice, it forms glaciers, frozen lakes and rivers, snow, hail and frost. It is liquid as rain and dew, and it covers three-quarters of the earth's surface in swamps, lakes, rivers, and oceans. Water also occurs in the soil and beneath the earth's surface as a vast groundwater reservoir. As gas, or water vapor, it occurs as fog, steam, and clouds.

"Water"
Encarta Online Concise Encyclopedia

Category: chemical compound.

Synonym: H_2O.

Features: odorless, tasteless, clear.

Examples: ice, rain, dew, groundwater, fog, steam, clouds.

Origins: earth's surface, in soil, beneath surface, in atmosphere.

If a term is essential to meaning or is the subject of your writing, you may choose to use all of the strategies described above to define it. If readers know something about the term, you may want to use just one or two of the strategies. The kind of information to include, and how much, depends on your purpose and audience. When writing any definition, ask yourself:

• What do readers already know?

• What do readers need to know?

• What do you want them to learn?

• How much detail is appropriate for the context?

To plan a written definition, you can use the Definition Outline in Figure 11–1. When using the outline, do not feel as though you must fill out the whole form or that you must use everything you put on the outline in your writing. The outline is intended simply to be a guide for generating ideas. Study the example of a completed outline (Figure 11–2) to see how it was used to plan a definition for the term "sewing." Then try using it when writing your own definitions.

Figure 11–1: Definition Outline
Photocopy this form before using.

Part A

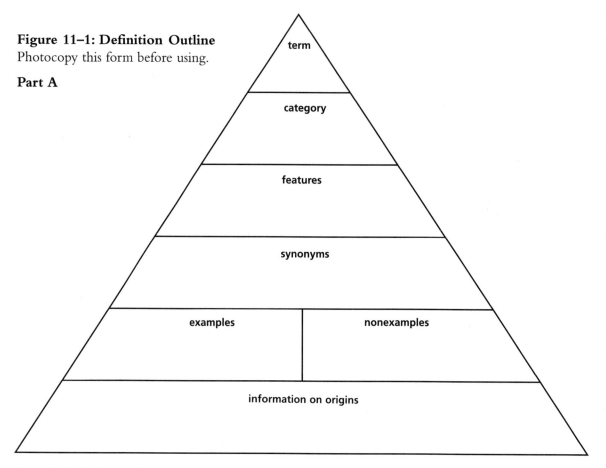

Part B: Definitions also may answer questions that begin with the words below. To continue
outlining your definition, phrase a question with each word, then answer it:

(Who)   Question: _____
         Answer: _____

(What)   Question: _____
         Answer: _____

(When)   Question: _____
         Answer: _____

(Where) Question: _____
         Answer: _____

(Why)   Question: _____
         Answer: _____

(How)   Question: _____
         Answer: _____

**Figure 11–2: Example
Definition Outline**

Part A

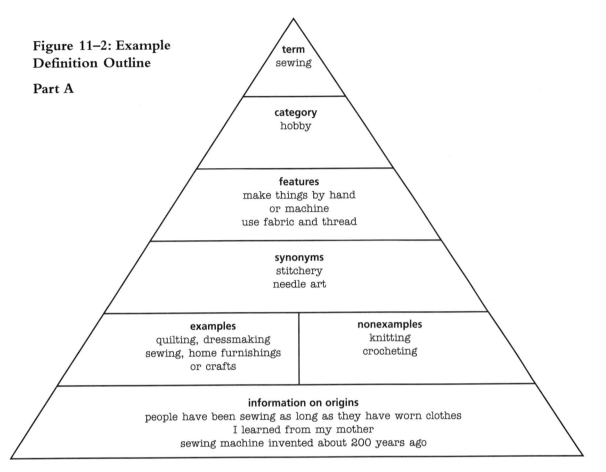

term
sewing

category
hobby

features
make things by hand
or machine
use fabric and thread

synonyms
stitchery
needle art

examples
quilting, dressmaking
sewing, home furnishings
or crafts

nonexamples
knitting
crocheting

information on origins
people have been sewing as long as they have worn clothes
I learned from my mother
sewing machine invented about 200 years ago

Part B: Definitions also may answer questions that begin with the words below. To continue outlining your definition, phrase a question with each word, then answer it:

(Who)   Question: Who sews?

Answer: I do, lots of women do, some men

(What) Question: What equipment is needed to sew?

Answer: Needles, good scissors, machine, iron

(When) Question: When do hobbyists find time to sew?

Answer: Can do it anytime, for short or long periods

(Where) Question: Where do I set up my sewing corner?

Answer: Have a sewing closet, use a desk

(Why)   Question: Why do I sew?

Answer: Fun, let's me be creative, relaxing (sometimes frustrating)

(How)   Question: How good are home-sewn projects?

Answer: Not always better than store-bought, but more meaningful

Write Now (3)

Two dog breeds are described below. Each description uses some of the defining strategies discussed above. Read each one and answer the questions that follow.

Basenji: When people in central Africa brought gifts to the Egyptian pharaohs, the offerings often included Basenji dogs. Carvings of these dogs have even been found in Egyptian tombs. The name Basenji descends from the African Bantu word meaning "native." Over the years, basenjis have worked as pointers, retrievers and hunters (even dispatching toothy, twenty pound rats).

Midsized dogs with a silky copper coat, they do not bark but yodel when happy. For many people, their alert, playful, gentle and obedient temperaments make them ideal pets. Basenjis even clean themselves by licking their coats.

Caucasian Mountain Dog: In its native region, the Caucasus Mountains near the Georgian Republic, the Caucasian Mountain Dog is known as the Ovcharka, meaning something like shepherd dog. These large, strong dogs with a bearlike appearance have lived with human companions for hundreds of years, though their original ancestry may date back several thousand years to a Mastiff-Spitz dog cross.

Whatever the direct origins, the dogs lived in relative isolation for many centuries under challenging environmental conditions. The result of this situation is a natural, healthy, instinctive breed. Once used as Soviet government guard dogs, they often have reputations as aggressive animals. While discipline and proper socialization is needed to produce a compatible dog, many owners find them to be excellent pets and companions.

Better Care Makes Better Pets
Inroads Interactive (CD-ROM)

Basenji

1. Name one or more categories of dog to which Basenjis belong.

   _____

2. What is an unusual feature of Basenji dogs?

   _____

3. Name one or more examples of how humans have used Basenji dogs.

   _____

4. Where did Basenjis originate?

   _____

5. What is the meaning of the word "Basenji"?

   _____

Caucasian Mountain Dog

6. Name a category to which the Caucasian Mountain Dog belongs.

   _____

7. What is a synonym for Caucasian Mountain Dog?

   _____

8. What example is provided of how humans have used the Caucasian Mountain Dog?

   _____

9. From which two kinds of dogs might the Caucasian Mountain Dog be descended?

   _____

10. What is the native region of these dogs?

   _____

Write Now (4)

Select a subject to define. You may select the subject you described in Write Now (1), or something suggested by the writings in this chapter, such as:

a physical compound; for example, diamonds
an animal breed; for example, laboratory mice

Then plan an in-depth definition of the term using Part A of the Definition Outline (Figure 11–1). Just work on Part A of the outline— you do not need to draft the definition at this time. Keep this work because you may use it in a later activity.

Crafting Short Definitions

Use a short definition when you do not want readers to pause too long over a term. Also use a short definition when only a few readers may not know what a particular term means. One way to construct a short definition is to insert one or more defining words into the sentence where the term appears. Here is an example of a sentence without any definition:

On their walk they saw several curlews.

If some of your readers may not know what curlews are, insert some defining words:

On their walk they saw several *shorebirds called* curlews.

Short, in-sentence definitions also can be used to direct readers to the specific meaning of a term. Here is another sentence where meaning could be clarified:

Chu Vang was in an accident.

Readers may recognize that Chu Vang is a person, but they may not have any idea who he is. Or, they may know more than one Chu Vang. Defining words can explain exactly who is being talked about:

My neighbor, Chu Vang, was in an accident.

Another way to quickly define terms is to do so indirectly. Readers can use the text surrounding a term (its context) to guess at meaning. Words that indirectly define are called **context clues**, and the guesses readers make from context clues are called **inferences**. Here is an example of a sentence in which context clues help readers infer the meaning of the word "hoofed":

Ricky hoofed it to the store so fast he got there before anybody on wheels.

Readers can pick up that "hoofed" is a way of moving fast and that it is *not* a way of moving by wheel. From these two clues, readers can infer that "hoofed" means "ran."

Sometimes you will need to add a sentence or two to define a word you are using. Here is an example:

My friend Marta does improv. "Improv" is short for improvisation, a kind of theater where there is no script.

When you need to create a definition, the dictionary, the thesaurus, and the encyclopedia can be quite useful. Even when you already know what a term means, these resources can help you find the right words to explain it to your readers. For example, if you look up "improvise" in the dictionary, you will find the definition, "make or do hastily or without previous preparation." In the thesaurus, you will find as a synonym for "improv" the phrase "ad lib." A current encyclopedia will have an entry on "improvisation" giving detailed information about how it is used in theater. Making use of ideas from reference works can help you draft the best definition for your purpose and your readers.

Write Now (5)

Add definitions for the underlined words in the sentences below. Create definitions in one of three ways: add defining words to the sentence, rewrite the sentence to provide context clues, or write additional defining sentences. The first item has been rewritten in each of these three ways as an example. Use a dictionary, thesaurus, or encyclopedia as needed.

1. Donita is good at hip-hop.
   Donita is good at the dance form known as hip-hop.(defining words added) Donita dances well to the hip-hop beat.(context clues provided) Donita is good at hip-hop. That's the name for a kind of dancing that originated among Black and Puerto Rican youth in the South Bronx of New York in the mid-1970s. (defining sentences added)

2. Sean broke his leg <u>snowboarding</u>.

   _____

   _____

3. The <u>kaffiyeh</u> is often black and white.

   _____

   _____

4. The man in front of the crowd held a <u>hurdy-gurdy</u>.

   _____

   _____

5. The <u>IRS</u> deadline is April 15.

   _____

   _____

6. They are from <u>Kwuangtung</u>.

   _____

   _____

7. Shinetta is <u>besotted</u> with that band.

   _____

   _____

8. Stop <u>cavorting about</u>.

_____

_____

9. I am not afraid of any <u>rottweiler</u>.

_____

_____

Write Now (6)

Working in pairs, choose a word from the dictionary that your classmates probably will not know. Work together to draft a sentence using the word. Then add a definition for the word in one of three ways: by adding defining words to the sentence, by rewriting the sentence to provide context clues, or by writing one or more extra sentences that define the word. Then, in turn with the other pairs, present your word to the class. Do this by first stating the word and then reading aloud the sentence or sentences containing the word. Classmates should try to infer the word's meaning from the sentences. Those who guess the proper meaning should explain how they were able to figure it out. Keep this work because you may use it in a later activity.

Developing Longer Definitions

When a term is central to the subject you are writing about, you may want to provide readers with an in-depth definition. For example, if you are writing about what it is like to be a single parent, you may want to spend one or more paragraphs defining what you mean by "single parent." In some cases, your whole paper might consist of definition. An in-depth definition answers questions that begin with _who, what, when, where, why,_ and _how._ The following paragraphs from a fact sheet by the National Organization for Rare Disorders (NORD)® on a sleep disorder known as narcolepsy answer several of these kinds of questions:

What it is.

Why it occurs.

How symptoms
are exhibited.

Who suffers from it.

When (at what age)
it shows up.

Narcolepsy is a rare disorder characterized by chronic, excessive drowsiness during the day, sudden extreme muscle weakness (cataplexy), hallucinations, paralysis while sleeping, and disrupted sleep during the night. Although the exact cause of Narcolepsy is not known, many researchers suspect that the disorder is inherited... .

Exaggerated daytime drowsiness is usually the first symptom of Narcolepsy. People with Narcolepsy usually experience periods of sleepiness, tiredness, lack of energy, an irresistible urge to sleep ("sleep attack"), and/or an inability to resist sleep. This susceptibility to unending drowsiness and/or falling asleep may occur every day but the severity varies throughout each day. The total sleep time for people with Narcolepsy in every 24 hour period is generally normal because they sleep repeatedly for short periods during the day and night... .

The exact number of people with Narcolepsy in the United States is unknown. The American Narcolepsy Association has estimated that Narcolepsy affects approximately 200,000 Americans but other estimates are lower. Approximately 5 percent of people with Narcolepsy experience symptoms by the age of 10 years; 5 percent of patients have symptoms after the age of 20 years, and 18 percent of people with Narcolepsy develop symptoms after the age of 30 years. Symptoms rarely begin after the age 40. Narcolepsy tends to remain a lifelong condition. Slightly more males are affected by this disorder than females.

Narcolepsy
National Organization for Rare Disorders, Inc.
Rare Disease Database <www.rarediseases.org>

Other questions answered by the rest of the fact sheet on narcolepsy include: What causes narcolepsy? What other disorders are related to narcolepsy? How is narcolepsy treated? What research is being undertaken on narcolepsy? Where can one obtain more information on narcolepsy?

Write Now (7)

Read the following definition of National TV-Turnoff Week. Then write a list of questions that are answered by this definition.

National TV-Turnoff Week

This April 22–28, 1999, millions of individuals in thousands of homes, schools, libraries, churches and community groups will voluntarily turn off their TV sets and rediscover that life can be more constructive, rewarding, healthy—even informed—with more time and less TV. Since 1995, more than 12 million people have experimented (and flourished!) with a TV-less lifestyle.

National TV-Turnoff Week is part of a broadly supported effort to reduce the amount of television Americans watch. The annual event, which takes place during the last week of April, helps move beyond the usual discussions about program content and instead focuses on what TV-viewing displaces: creativity, productivity, healthy physical activity, civic engagement, reading, thinking and doing.

National TV-Turnoff Week is sponsored by TV-Free America, a national nonprofit, nonpartisan organization that encourages Americans to reduce, voluntarily and dramatically, the amount of television they watch in order to promote richer, healthier and more connected lives, families and communities.

Organizer's Kit
1999 National TV-Turnoff Week

Questions answered by the definition:

Who _____

What _____

When _____

Why _____

How _____

Write Now (8)

Select a subject to define. You may continue to work with the subject you selected for Write Now (4), or you can use another subject suggested by the writings in this chapter, such as

a medical condition; for example, insomnia
a national event; for example, Take Your Daughter to Work Day

Then plan an in-depth definition of the term using Part B of the Definition Outline (Figure 11–1). Just work on the outline—you do not need to draft the definition at this time. Keep this work because you may use it in a later activity.

Summing Up

1. What are three purposes for defining a term in your writing?

   • _____

   • _____

   • _____

2. Consider the five strategies for defining: state the category to which the term belongs, state what sets it apart within that category, provide synonyms for it, give examples and nonexamples, and explain its origins. Underline the strategy you tend to use most in your writing. What makes this easiest for you?

   _____

   _____

3. Circle the defining strategy that you tend to include less often. What is one thing you can do to make better use of this strategy when defining a term?

   _____

   _____

Second Thoughts

Review the photograph that opened this chapter, then think about or discuss the following questions:

1. To which category does this object belong?

2. What sets it apart within that category?

3. What synonyms can be used for this object?

4. Give examples and nonexamples.

5. Explain this object's origins.

Based on what you have learned in this chapter about defining, what new insights do you have about the object in this photograph? Write your thoughts in the *Responses* section of your journal.

4. How do you decide what and how much to include in any definition?

_____

_____

5. Name two situations outside of school where you might be called upon to define something in writing.

_____

_____

6. As a result of reading this chapter, what one change will you make to improve the way you define essential terms for your readers? Write your resolution in the *Habits for Life* section of your journal.

Write Now: Composing an Essay That Defines

Select a subject from the ones you worked on in Write Now (4), (5), (6), and (8). Turn it into a full-length essay defining that term. Plan your essay using the Definition Outline in Figure 11–1. Before beginning the draft, reflect on your purpose and your audience. Use both the Writing Checklist and the Essay Scoring Guide from Chapter 8 to help you revise. Prepare a final copy of the essay.

Punctuating Within-Sentence Definitions

A word or phrase that identifies a term in a sentence, or adds defining information to it, is called an **appositive**. Use commas to separate an appositive from the rest of the sentence, as in these examples:

The meeting was ably run by the committee chair, the venerable Mrs. Hamilton.

Separate the defining phrase (appositive) from the rest of the sentence with commas.

The stuffed body of Jumbo, the famous circus elephant, is displayed at the Natural History Museum in Washington, D.C.

Defining phrases also can be enclosed in parentheses:

Parentheses are acceptable in place of commas.

My husband (the epitome of the absent-minded professor) drove off with his bookbag on top of the car.

Do not separate with commas any words or phrases that are essential to the meaning of the sentence:

The woman holding the flag is Rhonda.

The phrase "holding the flag" is necessary to identify *which* woman is Rhonda. Therefore, no commas are used.

The man, seeing the thunderclouds, hurried home.

The phrase "seeing the thunderclouds" is not necessary. Therefore, commas are used.

If you are using a quotation that contains a term you want to define for readers, insert the defining words or phrases inside brackets:

> The senator stated, "Supporters of my legislation [S. 1215, regarding mandatory seat belt use] will be glad to know that it has reached the full committee."

Add clarification in brackets.

> "Felicitationes [congratulations]," she said.

Exercise

Add commas or parentheses to separate appositives (defining or clarifying phrases) as needed. Remember that if information is essential to the meaning of the sentence, it should not be set off by commas. Place a checkmark next to any sentence that does not need correction.

1. Sheila my younger sister graduates from high school next year.

2. My friend is a devotee of body piercing the adornment of the body with rings attached through the skin.

3. Some people believe that Shakespeare the great writer of the Elizabethan Era did not actually exist and that his works were written by someone else who assumed the name.

4. The Native American sweat lodge which is rather like a sauna with spiritual significance has assumed new importance in the rehabilitation of those addicted to alcohol and drugs.

5. The Oscars are movie awards and the Emmys are television awards.

6. I am very close to Santos my second cousin once removed.

7. Coffee that is shade-grown tastes better than coffee grown in full sun.

8. I prefer the work of Lorca the great Spanish poet to that of Rilke the great German poet.

9. Early records called 78s got their nickname from their rotation of 78 times per minute, and later records called LPs got their nickname from the fact that they were "long-playing."

10. Eighteen karat gold is of a finer quality than fourteen karat gold.

FARMWORKERS: I EARNED THAT NAME

by Daniel Rothenberg

Daniel Rothenberg first came into personal contact with migrant farmworkers when he had a job in outreach for a legal services program. He was surprised by how little he knew about people upon whom he was so dependent. He decided to document their conditions, and the result was a book called With These Hands: The Hidden World of Migrant Farmworkers Today. *The book is based on more than 250 interviews conducted throughout North America with farmworkers, contractors, and growers. Throughout the book, Rothenberg alternates his own reporting with remarks of the people he interviewed—what he refers to as "oral portraits."*

The first chapter of the book defines the term "migrant farmworker." An excerpt from this chapter, including part of an oral portrait, appears below. As you read, pay attention to how the author and his interview subject use very different techniques to define the same term.

What different kinds of work do migrant farmworkers do?

Each year over 1 million migrant farmworkers and their families labor in America's fields and orchards. They stoop among long rows of vegetables, filling buckets with produce under the stark heat of the summer sun and the bitter cold of late autumn. They climb ladders in orchards, piling fruit into sacks slung across their shoulders. They prune vines, tie plants, remove weeds, sort, pack, spray, clean, and irrigate. They travel across the nation, drifting from one field to another, crossing state lines and international borders. Farmworkers labor in every region of the country, wherever there are fields to be planted, tended, or harvested—in isolated rural communities, within the shadows of great cities, scattered among suburban tracts.

In what different kinds of places do they work?

Few Americans know much about the world of farmworkers—their struggles, their travels, the key role they play in our lives. Farmworkers provide the hand labor necessary to produce and harvest the fruits and vegetables we eat, and in this sense, they are bound to every consumer in a direct, almost visceral manner. Every orange, peach, tomato, or watermelon we purchase was handpicked by a farmworker. Every pepper, apple, head of lettuce, or bunch of grapes—pulled from the earth,

What is the connection between the farmworker and the consumer?

plucked from a bush, or picked from a tree—was harvested by a farm laborer, a member of the poorest and most disadvantaged class of American workers.

Every year, migrant farmworkers fan out across the nation, traveling the country in a collection of old cars, buses, vans, and trucks. They pass through thousands of communities, finding temporary homes in labor camps, trailers, or cheap motels, sometimes sleeping by the side of the road, under bridges, or in the fields and orchards where they work. Every year, the $28 billion fruit-and-vegetable industry spurs the mass movement of workers and their families. They arrive where they're needed, guided to the fields by intermediaries and informal networks, by necessity and, at times, desperation.

There are currently over 1.5 million seasonal farmworkers in the United States, laborers whose employment shifts with the changing demands of planting, tending, and harvesting our nation's crops. These workers have over 2 million dependents, most of whom are children, bringing the nation's total population of seasonal farmworkers and their families to over 3.5 million. Migrant farmworkers are those seasonal farm laborers who travel from one place to another to earn a living in agriculture. There are 700,000 migrant farmworkers in the United States, who are accompanied by 300,000 children and 100,000 adult dependents, bringing the country's total population of migrant farmworkers and their families to over 1 million.

Seasonal farm labor draws workers from a variety of backgrounds and ethnic groups. Currently, three out of every ten seasonal farmworkers were born in the United States, a diverse mix of Latinos, African Americans, whites, and Native Americans. The remaining 70 percent of the nation's farmworkers are immigrants. The vast majority of immigrant farmworkers—over 90 percent—are from Mexico. Other immigrants come from Central America, particularly Guatemala or El Salvador, or Caribbean nations such as Haiti or Jamaica. A small percentage of farmworkers are from Asian countries such as the Philippines, Laos, and Vietnam.

Exactly how would "desperation" guide farmworkers to the fields where they are needed?

How many seasonal farmworkers are there, and of these, how many are migrants?

From the oral portrait of James "Shorty" Spencer Jr.:

Around here, when I'm stripping tobacco, they call me the Bear. I stick my hand in the bush, and *whap*, I got all these leaves. Say you got twenty-seven stalks of tobacco on this bush. Twenty-seven stalks. A little bitty hand like this won't get it all, will it? Can't hold it. Ain't no way. Well, I go down about eight here—*ktch, ktch*—eight here—*ktch, ktch*— *ktch, ktch*—get all three out the top; I got twenty-seven. With the move I show, you get all of 'em in one wipe. I got all these leaves in my hand and I am proud to step back from the stalk—because I am a real migrant worker.

Suppose I wasn't no migrant worker? I'd be tired. I'd be bushed out. I'd be blowing out my breath. With the move I showed you—when you hit it rushin'—your arms be full of tobacco. See what I'm saying?

I bet you not an exercise person you know could sand lug all day. Sand lugging is when you get the four leaves off the bottom of the tobacco plant. You don't touch no more leaves, just the four off the bottom. If you can do that there for eight or ten hours, then you's a good one.

Potatoes? If you can run to that truck every fifteen minutes with about seventy-five pounds of potatoes, then you's a good one. Cutting cabbages? If you can pick that cabbage up and sling it at that truck while the wagon's moving, I tell you, you's a good one. Orange picker? You reach out there and snatch your orange, grab the limb and shake it down to the ground, and fill that bag up in fifteen minutes, you's a good one. That's when you could name yourself a real migrant worker.

What does this "ktch, ktch" sound stand for?

What is "an exercise person"?

THINK AND RESPOND

1. How does Rothenberg categorize "farm laborer"?

   _____

   _____

2. What distinguishes migrant farmworkers from others in that category?

   _____

   _____

3. Where do migrant farmworkers come from?

   _____

   _____

4. What examples does Rothenberg provide to help define migrant farmworkers, and what examples and nonexamples does Spencer provide?

   _____

   _____

5. What is different in how Rothenberg and Spencer define the same term?

   _____

   _____

6. Why do you think Rothenberg chose to include the actual words of a migrant farmworker, James Spencer, in the chapter of his book that defines the term?

   _____

   _____

7. Provide synonyms or definitions for these words from the essay, and add at least two of the words to the *Words Worth Remembering* section of your journal:

stark _____

irrigate _____

tracts _____

visceral _____

spurs _____

intermediaries _____

dependents _____

agriculture _____

stalk _____

lug _____

8. If you liked this reading, make a record of it in the *Readings Worth Remembering* section of your journal.

COMPARING VIEWS

"Migrant farmworkers" is a category of people. As a class, select a category of people to which one or all of you belong. Possible categories of people include:

community activists	union members	low-wage workers
night students	volunteers	first generation Americans

Discuss how you would define it. Consider whom you could interview to prepare a definition of this category. Generate a list of the questions you would need answered to prepare the definition. For example, for the category of "security officers," useful questions might include:

- How are security officers like and different from other kinds of uniformed officers?

- What need is there for security officers?

- What kind of people become security officers?

- How does a person qualify to be one?

- What are the duties of a security officer?

- What kinds of situations do security officers experience in the course of their work?

After discussing this topic with others, pursue it on your own—if it interests you. Find a person to interview to get an insider's definition of the category. Ask the person for permission to interview and arrange a time to talk (ask for 15 to 20 minutes of their time). Bring a notepad and pen to the interview. Take notes. Write down, word for word, the especially interesting statements. If necessary, ask your subject to restate something that you want to copy down, or read back quotations you have written down, to see if they are correct. When you have finished interviewing, thank your subject.

APPLIED WRITING

Write an essay defining the category you discussed above. Use the Definition Outline (Figure 11–1) to plan your essay. As you draft, include information from your interview. Either present the interview as a separate section of your essay (as Rothenberg does) or incorporate your interview subject's comments into the body of your essay. Use both the Writing Checklist and the Essay Scoring Guide from Chapter 8 to help you revise. Prepare a final copy of the essay.

Levers, Ramps and Pulleys
Walter Wick

Chapter 12

Explaining

These are the **key ideas** of this chapter:

- An explanation leads readers through a process so that they can perform it themselves or understand how it is done or occurs.

- An explanation usually includes an introduction, a logical description of the process, and relevant or useful details.

- Transition words and consistency in writing can make an explanation easier for readers to follow.

Picturing Meaning

Examine the photograph on the opposite page; then think about or discuss these questions.

1. What is pictured in this photograph?

    _____

    _____

2. What must be done to start the process?

    _____

    _____

3. Approximately how many steps are involved in the process from start to finish?

    _____

    _____

   In the *Responses* section of your journal, write down your thoughts about this photograph.

Write Now (1)

Think of an experiment *you* have done that was fun: a practical joke, a crazy stunt, or an attempt to win a bet or break a record. Write up the steps you went through to accomplish your objective. Keep this work because you may use it in a later activity.

Explaining How to Do Something

Writing to explain is called **expository writing.** One function of expository writing is to define, since a definition explains what something is. (See Chapter 11 for more about writing definitions.) Another function of expository writing is to explain how something is done. Instructions fall into this category of writing. Here is a useful pattern for writing instructions:

1. Introduce the subject.

2. Present the necessary or suggested actions in a logical order.

3. Use transition words.

Introduce the subject. For some instructions, the title can serve as introduction. Usually, however, you will want to begin with an opening statement that tells readers what the instructions are for and—equally important—why they are worth reading and following.

Present the necessary or suggested actions in a logical order. When you write instructions, you must take care to include every necessary step, to present them in the order in which they must be followed, and to describe them in such a way that other persons can reproduce the action. You may want to number each separate step. Alternatively, you may present each step in its own paragraph. Remember to define any terms readers will need to know in order to follow any step. If readers are more likely to follow a particular step when they know the reasoning behind it, then be sure to include your reasoning. If a particular step is often done wrong, include a statement on what not to do or what to avoid. When writing instructions that must be strictly followed for the proper results, avoid any distracting commentary. Less critical instructions can safely contain more commentary.

Use transition words. Transition words can help readers distinguish between steps. With numbered instructions, the numbers themselves indicate the transitions. With paragraphs, words such as *first, next, finally, if,* and *when,* among others, are useful transition words. Refer to Figure 7–2 in Chapter 7 for a list of transition words.

Write Now (2)

Below are instructions for two experiments. With a partner, read through the instructions for the first experiment. Cross out the two sentences that are unnecessary and number the rest in logical order. As you reread the instructions in the more logical order, write in helpful transition words. Finally, confirm that you have put the instructions into a good order by working with your partner to follow them. Repeat this procedure for the second experiment.

Experiment 1

_____ Wad the paper into a ball.

_____ Exchange roles and repeat the experiment.

_____ Reflexes are automatic movements that your body makes without your having to think about them.

_____ This experiment does not require elaborate equipment.

_____ The purpose of this experiment is to observe reflexes at work.

_____ Each pair will need a sheet of clear plastic and a piece of paper.

_____ Answer these questions: why did you blink (or not blink)? Why do you suppose your body has this reflex?

_____ Have your partner hold the plastic sheet in front of his or her face.

_____ Throw the paper at your partner.

_____ Observe whether your partner blinks.

_____ Get into pairs.

_____ Even though it is simple and rather silly, it is still an experiment.

Experiment 2

_____ Have your partner sit with the right leg crossed over the left, so that the right leg can swing freely.

_____ Tap the right leg of your partner just below the kneecap.

_____ It requires a ruler.

_____ This is another experiment to demonstrate reflexes.

_____ Experiments can make a scientific principle "come to life."

_____ Another reflex experiment is to shine a flashlight into your partner's eyes.

_____ Observe whether your partner's leg jerks up.

_____ If you don't have a ruler, use the side of your hand.

_____ Answer these questions: Can you think of times that these reflexes have been helpful to you? How is a reflex different from a habit?

_____ Continue to work with your partner.

_____ Repeat the experiment, changing roles.

Some Sample Instructions

In the following instructions, two sentences introduce the subject: how to safely cross a street. The steps for safe street crossing are then presented in an easy-to-follow, numbered order:

The introduction tells *why* steps should be followed.

On average, a pedestrian is killed in a traffic crash every 95 minutes. Please use this successfully tested procedure for safe street crossing and share it with others:

1. Before crossing, always stop at the curb or at the edge of the road if there is no curb.

The transition phrase, "before crossing" is repeated to emphasize *when* these steps should be followed.

2. Before crossing, look left, right, and left again. If crossing at a corner, turn your head over your shoulder to see cars coming from behind you.

3. Before crossing, listen! (Keep the volume down in your headset.)

4. Keep watching for approaching vehicles while you cross.

Safety in Our Neighborhood
Fire and Rescue Services, Montgomery County, Maryland

The following advice for apartment managers on how to deal with problem tenants explains both *what* to do and *why* to do it:

The subject is introduced in the form of a question.

How do you deal with a resident who engages in drug abuse, gambling, or prostitution in the apartment? Most leases state that the use of the apartment for illegal or immoral purposes is grounds for eviction, but eviction is a court procedure that is slow, expensive, and open to question. It's better to meet with the resident, cite the objectionable behavior, and offer to cancel the lease and return the security deposit.

Before you take any action, consider whether you want to act against the offender at all. He or she rented the apartment for personal use. If what is done within the apartment is not offensive to others or damaging to the property, you may be better off ignoring it.

If you decide to take action, confront the resident by going to the apartment or asking him or her to your office. Do not write a letter stating the complaint. If the complaint turns out to be unjustified, the resident might use the letter against you in a court action. When you confront the resident, you can simply say, "I know what's going on here, and I think it would be best for all concerned if you moved."

In most cases, the offending resident will leave, not because of a legal requirement but because most people will do what they're asked to do. Have the departing resident sign a mutual cancellation agreement, and return any prepaid rent or security deposit money you may be holding when the apartment is vacated. If the resident is suspicious that you won't refund the money once he or she leaves, offer to put it in escrow.

Practical Apartment Management
Edward N. Kelley

Each possible step is presented in its own paragraph.

The above instructions actually present two paths to follow: ignoring problem tenants or asking them to leave. Often there is more than one way to do something, so explanations sometimes cover multiple possibilities. Instructions that present more than one way to do something are often referred to as "guidelines." The following guidelines present several different techniques for moving out of a conversation at a party:

The subject is introduced in colorful terms.

If you find yourself stuck with a real bore, or simply feel it's time to end a long conversation and move on, there's always one guaranteed way to get out of the conversation: "Excuse me. I have to visit the restroom." If you make it sound urgent enough, no one will take offense at your departure. When you come back, you start another conversation, only this time with someone else.

Another option is presented in another paragraph.

Or, if you spot someone you know nearby, you can make your escape with, "Stacey! Have you met Bill?" As Stacey is shaking hands with Bill, you can say, "I'll be back in a minute, but I know you two will have a lot to talk about." At a busy cocktail party they won't be surprised if you don't come back in a minute. Of course, if your first conversation partner is a killing bore, Stacey may never forgive you, so use this technique with caution.

Interchangeable exit lines are presented in a list.

Other good exit lines:

1. "This food is delicious. I'm going to go help myself to seconds."
2. "Would you excuse me? I'm going to go say hello to our host." (Or ". . . to a friend I haven't seen in a while.")
3. "Well, I guess I'd better go and mingle some more."

Tips are provided on what *not* to do.

It's important not to make too much of your exit. Don't spend the minute beforehand glancing around the room desperately or be too apologetic. Just wait for a slight pause, say something polite, and move on as if it's a natural thing to do. Simply saying, "It was nice talking to you" and turning away can be graceful enough, as long as you sound as though you actually did enjoy the conversation.

How to Talk to Anyone, Anytime, Anywhere:
The Secrets of Good Communication
Larry King

Write Now (3)

Review the instructions to answer the following questions.

Safe street-crossing instructions

1. What could you add to these instructions?

   _____

2. Do you think these instructions are useful? Why or why not?

   _____

3. What safety instructions for a potentially dangerous procedure do you follow (or not follow)?

   _____

Advice for dealing with problem tenants

4. What could you add to this advice?

   _____

5. Do you think this advice is useful? Why or why not?

   _____

6. Who else besides landlords needs advice for dealing with problem people?

   _____

Getting out of a conversation

7. What other tips for exit-making can you add?

   _____

8. Do you think these guidelines are useful?

   _____

9. What other social situations would be good subjects for guidelines?

   _____

Outlining and Drafting Instructions

To plan written instructions, draw up a list of all the steps that occur to you, leaving white space between each item. Review the steps, and insert any others that you think are important. Cross out any steps that are not really part of the process. Next to each step, jot down notes about the reasons behind them, actions to avoid, and critical details that demonstrate the step's logic or importance. Here is an outline for how to safely climb a ladder:

It is easy to plan instructions on computer. Type up a list of steps, then cut and paste to adjust the order. Add extra steps by positioning the curser where you want them. You also may want to make use of your word processing program's capacity for automatic numbering of list items.

Inspect ladder for weaknesses

Set ladder on even ground

Position upper ladder solidly against side of wall or roof ← Check that ladder is steady. Ladder should tilt slightly.

Have helper stand by

Climb using both hands

~~Keep top on the paint can as you climb~~

Add somewhere: Do not use aluminum ladder near power lines

Do not climb onto top rungs

Find out: Ladder safety statistics?

If what you plan to write falls into the category of guidelines, clustering can be a useful planning tool. Here is a cluster outline for the topic of preventing falls in the home:

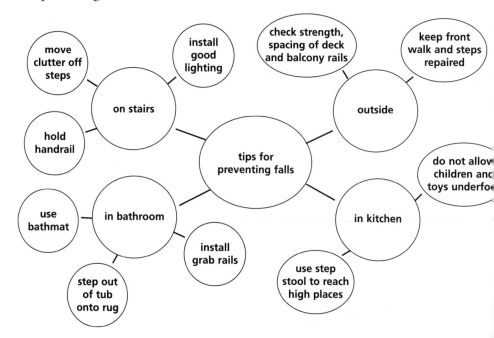

One way to make sure you have remembered everything is to perform the process or participate in the activity while paying attention to the steps involved. Alternatively, shut your eyes and visualize the process. Another option is to observe others performing the procedure and talk with them about the steps or guidelines they use. Depending on your purpose, you also may want to research the topic for pertinent facts or for recommendations from experts.

When drafting, start a new paragraph for each step or for each set of closely related steps. Remember to use transition words to indicate how one step relates to another. Then test your draft by having someone else with expertise in the subject review it. Even more important, have someone who is not an expert on the subject read your instructions and try to follow them. This can be a good test of what you need to clarify, add, or leave out.

Most word processing programs allow you to draw clusters on-screen. If, however, you spend more time trying to manipulate the drawing tools than thinking about the process you want to describe, work up your cluster by hand.

Write Now (4)

Select a set of instructions to outline from the topics you identified in questions 3, 6, and 9 of Write Now (3). Outline the process using a list or a cluster. Just work on the outline—you do not need to turn it into an essay at this time. Keep this work because you may use it in a later activity.

Explaining How Something Occurs

Sometimes your purpose for writing may be to help readers understand a process rather than do it themselves. This may be the case when describing, for example, a medical process, a natural process, a manufacturing process, or a biological process. In such cases, the big picture is more important than a careful explanation of each individual step. Here is a list of what to do when explaining a process:

1. Define essential terms.

2. Answer questions readers are likely to ask.

3. Include examples and interesting or important facts.

Define essential terms. Usually when you explain a process, your readers are not too familiar with the subject—otherwise, why bother explaining? If readers are not familiar with the subject, then it follows that they will not be familiar with any of the special vocabulary. Essential terms need to be defined, in clear language. Also avoid using too much specialized language. (See Chapter 11 for more about providing definitions.)

Answer questions readers are likely to ask. People prefer to read information that is relevant to them or that fills gaps in their knowledge. When explaining a process, think in terms of what questions would occur to your readers and the order in which those questions would arise. In your explanation, answer those questions in that order.

Include examples and interesting or important facts. Illustrations and facts can help readers grasp a complex or difficult explanation. They also can add color and interest to an otherwise weighty or dry subject.

As an example, consider the situation of a doctor trying to persuade a reluctant patient to undergo a hernia operation. The doctor may start by defining "hernia." The doctor may answer questions the patient is likely to ask, such as, "what does a hernia do?" or "why is it giving me such pain?" or "what happens if we don't do the surgery?" The doctor also may give examples of other patients who have had positive results from the operation. Finally, at the end of the discussion, the doctor may explain in a few steps how the surgical repair is done. By giving this kind of full explanation, the doctor does *not* equip the patient to perform the operation. However, the doctor does make the patient more knowledgeable about the operation and therefore more comfortable with the idea of having it done.

Write Now (5)

Working in small groups, decide on useful information to include when explaining each process listed below. The first item has been done as an example.

1. **What it is like to serve on a jury.**
   Essential terms: *"jury of one's peers," plea, verdict, defense, prosecution, foreman/forewoman, voir dire*

   Questions readers are likely to ask: *How do you get picked to be on a jury? How long do you usually have to serve? What if you can't tell if someone is guilty or innocent?*

   Examples or interesting facts: *my jury experience last year*

2. **How a bone fracture is repaired.**
   Essential terms: _____

Questions readers are likely to ask: _____

_____

Examples or interesting facts: _____

_____

_____

3. **How online gaming works.**
   Essential terms: _____

   Questions readers are likely to ask: _____

   _____

   Examples or interesting facts: _____

   _____

   _____

4. **How plants reproduce.**
   Essential terms: _____

   Questions readers are likely to ask: _____

   _____

   Examples or interesting facts: _____

   _____

   _____

5. **How meat is butchered.**
   Essential terms: _____

   Questions readers are likely to ask: _____

   _____

   Examples or interesting facts: _____

   _____

   _____

A Sample Explanation

The following paragraphs introduce an explanation of how autopsies are performed. The author's intention is *not* to teach anyone how to perform this procedure. Rather, it is to make familiar a common practice that most people know very little about. The explanation, therefore, begins with a definition of terms. It sets the context by answering questions readers are likely to have and by providing interesting examples and facts. The step-by-step description of the actual autopsy—how scalpels are used to pull back the skin, how saws are used to open the skull, and so forth—does not begin until after these introductory paragraphs (and several more not reprinted below):

A definition of "autopsy" introduces the subject and sets the context.

A question readers are likely to ask is answered: why are autopsies performed? A personal example and hospital statistic are used to answer the question.

Autopsy means "see for yourself." It is a special surgical operation, performed by specially-trained physicians, on a dead body. Its purpose is to learn the truth about the person's health during life, and how the person really died.

There are many advantages to getting an autopsy. Even when the law does not require it, there is always something interesting for the family to know. In doing around 700 autopsies, I have always found something worth knowing that wasn't known during life. Even at major hospitals, in about one case in four we find major disease which was unknown in life. Giving families the explanations they want is one of the most satisfying things that I do.

A pathologist is a physician with a specialty in the scientific study of body parts. This always includes a year or more learning to do autopsies.

Under the laws of most states, autopsy can be ordered by the government. A coroner is a political position, while a medical examiner is a physician, usually a pathologist. Exactly who makes the decisions, and who just gives advice, depends on the jurisdiction. Autopsies can be ordered in every state when there is suspicion of foul play. In most states, autopsy can be ordered when there is some public health concern, i.e., a mysterious disease or a worry about the quality of health care. In most states, an autopsy may be ordered if someone dies unattended by a physician (or attended for less than 24 hours), or if the attending physician is uncomfortable signing the death certificate.

When a loved one dies, a family can ask the hospital to perform an autopsy. The hospital pathologists are supposed to be independent, and often there's no affection between them and the clinicians who treated the patient. This service is free.

If the family prefers, a private pathologist can do the autopsy in the funeral home. It does not matter much whether the body has been embalmed first.

Whoever does the autopsy, there should not be a problem with an open-casket funeral afterwards. This is true even if the brain has been removed and the dead person is bald. The pillow will conceal the marks.

Autopsy
Ed "The Pathology Guy" Friedlander
www.pathguy.com/autopsy.htm

"Pathologist" is defined.

A question readers are likely to ask is answered: who orders autopsies?

A likely follow-up question is answered: can families order autopsies?

Yet another likely question is answered: does autopsy leave visible scars?

Write Now (6)

Review the previous writing to answer the following questions:

Autopsy

1. What other terms do you think may have to be defined in an explanation of the autopsy process?

    _____

    _____

    _____

    _____

2. Do you think this explanation is helpful? Why or why not?

    _____

    _____

    _____

    _____

3. What other questions about autopsies would you like answered?

    _____

    _____

    _____

    _____

4. What examples or facts about autopsies can you share?

    _____

    _____

    _____

    _____

5. What other procedure, performed on the body, would you like to know more about?

    _____

    _____

    _____

    _____

Outlining and Drafting a Process Explanation

When planning a description of a process, you need to be clear about it in your own mind. Reflect and make a list or cluster of what you know. You may have to supplement what you know about the process with research—consulting reference materials or interviewing experts. Next, consider your purpose and audience: what do you want readers to learn, what do they already know, and what do you think most interests them. Your answers will help you decide how much background information to provide, which steps to describe, and how detailed to make those steps. Add to your initial list or cluster, or draw up a new outline, and use it as a guideline for your draft.

To test your draft, ask one or more persons who are unfamiliar with the process to read it. Can they follow your explanation? Do they have any unanswered questions? Their feedback can help you decide on necessary changes.

Write Now (7)

Select a process to outline. You may want to describe the process you wrote about in Write Now (1) or the process you identified in question 5 of Write Now (6). Alternatively, you may select from the ideas offered in Write Now (5). To begin, make notes of:

Essential terms
Questions readers are likely to ask
Interesting examples or facts

Then outline the process using a list or a cluster. Do additional research as needed to complete the outline. Just work on the outline—you do not need to turn it into an essay at this time. Keep this work because you may use it in a later activity.

Summing Up

1. Consider the three key elements to written instructions: introducing the subject, presenting the necessary or suggested actions in a logical order, and using transition words. Underline the element that is easiest for you to do. What makes it easiest?

    _____

    _____

2. Consider the three key elements to writing process descriptions: defining essential terms, answering questions readers are likely to ask, and including examples and interesting or important facts. Underline the easiest element for you to do. What makes it easiest?

    _____

    _____

Second Thoughts

Review the photograph that opened this chapter; then think about or discuss the following questions:

1. How would you introduce instructions for creating this display?
2. How would you organize the instructions?
3. What transition words might be helpful in those instructions?
4. At what point, if any, would you present options?

   Based on what you have learned in this chapter about explanatory writing, how has the way you look at this photograph changed? Write your thoughts in the *Responses* section of your journal.

3. Circle the element in process descriptions that you tend not to include. What is one thing you can do to give it more emphasis when you describe a process in writing?

   _____

   _____

4. Name one situation outside of school where you could be called upon to write specific instructions, one situation where you might have to write guidelines that present several options, and one situation where you might have to describe a process.

   _____

   _____

5. As a result of reading this chapter, what one change will you make to enhance your writing of instructions, guidelines, or processes? Write your resolution in the *Habits for Life* section of your journal.

Write Now: Composing an Essay That Explains

Select as your subject the instructions you outlined in Write Now (4) or the process you outlined in Write Now (7). Turn that subject into a full set of instructions or a complete essay on the process. Before beginning your draft, reflect on your purpose and your audience. Use the outline you developed to prepare a draft. Get feedback on your draft from someone unfamiliar with the subject. Use both the Writing Checklist and the Essay Scoring Guide from Chapter 8 to help you revise. Prepare a final copy of the essay.

Watching for Errors in Agreement

To be consistent means to follow a predictable pattern. Readers appreciate consistency in writing because it means they do not have to sort through confusing changes in sentence structure. Consistency is important in all writing, but it is especially important for instructions or complex explanations.

The term used for consistency in writing is called **agreement**. When drafting, watch for agreement errors in your use of:

- Tense
- Person
- Number

Tense is the indication of time—past, present, or future. In written sentences, shifts in tense should only be used to indicate actual shifts in time. For example, "I went to the store, I am putting away the groceries, and soon I will make dinner" is correctly written even though each clause is in a different tense. This is because the past tense action in the sentence ("I went to the store") happened before the present tense action ("I am putting away the groceries"). Also, both of those actions will have happened before the future tense action ("soon I will make dinner.") The following sentence is not correctly written, because both actions happen at the same time and therefore needs to be expressed in the same tense rather than in both past and present: "I was tired after dinner, so I fall asleep on the sofa."

Person refers to any of the three distinctive points of view used in writing. Essays about personal experiences often are written in the first person (*I* or *we*)—as if someone is speaking. Instructions, letters, and informal writings usually are written in the second person (*you*)—as if someone is being spoken to. In second person writing, the word *you* is sometimes implied rather than stated; for example: "Open the door. Turn on the light." Instructions frequently use the second person, with the pronoun *you* omitted. More formal writings often are in the third person (*he, she, it, they,* and also *one,* which means "a person")—as if someone or something is being spoken about. The most important thing to remember about person is to be consistent. Do not shift from one to another without reason.

Number. When referring to the same noun more than once in a paragraph or essay, keep it either plural or singular—do not switch back and forth. Also, nouns and any pronouns that substitute for them must always agree in number. For example, "The estimators submitted their bids" is correctly written, because the noun "estimators" is plural and "they" is a plural pronoun. "The project manager has reviewed the bids and they are making a decision today" is not correctly written, because "manager" is singular and "they" is a plural pronoun. When checking for errors in number, look closely at verbs to make sure they are either singular or plural to match the noun. For example:

The project manager has reviewed the bids and ~~they are~~ she is making a decision today.

Exercise

Revise the following sentences so that they are consistent. The number of agreement errors is indicated in parentheses after each item. The first has been done as an example.

1. We constructed the terrace from flagstone. Then we arranged several terra-cotta flower containers around the perimeter. We ~~purchase~~ purchased a glass table with an umbrella and four chairs with comfortable cushions. As soon as it was delivered, we ~~place~~ placed this furniture in the center of the terrace. (2)

2. To jumpstart a dead car battery, pull your car up so that its hood faces the hood of the dead car. The driver should cut off your engine. Attach jumper cables to your battery, connecting the red lead to the positive connection and the black lead to the negative connection. Do the same with the other end of the cables and the dead car battery. Start your engine, then try the ignition of the dead car. Sometimes I need to pump the gas a little to get the jump started. (2)

3. Mercury is the closest planet to the sun, followed by Venus and Earth. Pluto is the farthest planet from the sun, except when its orbit crosses inside the orbit of Neptune. Then for a period of time, Neptune became the farthest planet. (1)

4. In the back of my pocket dictionary there is a list of foreign words and phrases commonly used in English. I like to browse through these pages. From this dictionary one learns to impress one's friends with such *bon mots* (witty sayings) as *de gustibus non est disputandum* (there is no disputing about tastes). (3)

5. Origami is the Japanese art of paper-folding. The crane is a very popular pattern. They take about fourteen steps to make. Other creative folds are the swan, the box, and the fish. The houseboat is particularly amusing because you can actually float them. (3)

6. Do not place plastic cups or trays in your toaster oven. Also, do not use it to heat TV dinners. When operating your toaster oven, monitor them closely. Always unplug this appliance when they are not in use. (3)

7. Both boys and girls play with dolls, but boy dolls are called by a different term than girl dolls. They are called "action figures." Boys and girls played differently with their dolls, too. Girls preoccupied themselves with dressing and undressing their dolls, while boys are more interested in posing and positioning. (2)

8. Hand-held computer devices are increasingly popular. With a small touch pad and pen, you will write data that is transcribed into type, or you can type using a pen tip and a miniature keypad. The data was downloaded to your home or office computer. (2)

9. A piano tuner uses their ears as an instrument. They also have special ratchets that they use to adjust the dampers. Most pianos will stay in tune for a year or more, unlike a guitar that has to be tuned every time you want to play them. (4)

10. The electrician has to pull a permit before they can start her work. My crew will do the drywall after the wires are run. They will do the painting, too. (2)

Clearing the Air: How to Quit Smoking....and Quit for Keeps

The National Cancer Institute

Smoking is a popular habit, but an unhealthy one. According to the World Health Organization (WHO), more than 3 trillion cigarettes are sold a year. At the same time, 3 million people die each year from smoking-related illnesses. Smoking is addictive, which makes kicking the habit very difficult. Clearing the Air: How to Quit Smoking . . . and Quit for Keeps is a booklet published by the National Cancer Institute, a U.S. government health agency. The booklet offers suggestions on how to quit, how to avoid temptation, how to avoid weight gain, and how to overcome withdrawal symptoms. The following excerpt is from a section called "Quitting for Keeps." As you read this excerpt, notice the writing style and the careful organization of the material, both of which are intended to make the recommendations easy to absorb.

Keep Your Guard Up

The key to living as a nonsmoker is to avoid letting your urges or cravings for a cigarette lead you to smoke. Don't kid yourself—even though you have made a commitment not to smoke, you *will* sometimes be tempted. But instead of giving in to the urge, you can use it as a learning experience.

First, remind yourself that you have *quit* and are a *non*smoker. Then look closely at your urge to smoke and ask yourself:

- Where was I when I got the urge?
- What was I doing at the time?
- Who was with me?
- What was I thinking?

The urge to smoke after you've quit often hits at predictable times. The trick is to anticipate those times and find ways to cope with them—without smoking. Naturally, it won't be easy at first. In fact, you may continue to want a cigarette at times. But remember, even if you slip, it doesn't mean an end to the nonsmoking you. It does mean that you should try to identify what triggered your slip, strengthen your commitment to quitting, and try again.

Check out the National Cancer Institute Web site at *http://rex.nci.nih.gov/*

What might be a predictable time for a person to be hit with the urge to smoke?

Look at the following list of typical triggers. Do many of them ring a bell with you? Check off those that might trigger an urge to smoke, and add any others you can think of:

- Working under pressure
- Feeling blue
- Talking on the telephone
- Having a drink
- Watching television
- Driving your car
- Finishing a meal
- Playing cards
- Drinking coffee
- Watching someone else smoke

If you are like many new nonsmokers, the most difficult place to resist the urge to smoke is the most familiar—home. The activities most closely associated with smoking urges are eating, partying, and drinking. And, not surprisingly, most urges occur when a smoker is present.

How to Dampen That Urge

There are seven major coping skills to help you fight the urge to smoke. These tips are designed for you, the new nonsmoker, to help you nurture the nonsmoking habit.

1. Think about why you quit.

Go back to your list of reasons for quitting. Look at this list several times a day, especially when you are hit with the urge to smoke. The best reasons you could have for quitting are very personally yours, and these are also the best reasons to stay a nonsmoker.

2. Know when you are rationalizing.

It is easy to rationalize yourself back into smoking. (See "Common Rationalizations.") Don't talk yourself into smoking again. A new nonsmoker in a tense situation may think, "I'll just have one cigarette to calm myself down." If thoughts like this pop into your head, stop and think again! You know better ways to relax, nonsmokers' ways, such as taking a walk or doing breathing exercises.

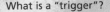

What is a "trigger"?

What situations are most likely to trigger the urge to smoke?

Why does the booklet address the reader as "you, the nonsmoker"?

What might be a personal reason for staying a nonsmoker?

Concern about gaining weight may also lead to rationalizations. Learn to counter thoughts, such as "I'd rather be thin, even if it means smoking." Remember that a slight weight gain is not likely to endanger your health as much as smoking would. (Cigarette smokers have about a 70-percent higher rate of premature death than nonsmokers.) And review the list of healthy, low-calorie snacks that you used when quitting.

3. Anticipate triggers and prepare to avoid them.

By now you know which situations, people, and feelings are likely to tempt you to smoke. Be prepared to meet these triggers head-on and counteract them. Keep using the skills that helped you cope in cutting down and quitting:

- Keep your hands busy—doodle, knit, type a letter.
- Avoid people who smoke; spend more time with nonsmoking friends.
- Find activities that make smoking difficult (gardening, washing the car, taking a shower). Exercise to help knock out the smoking urge; it will help you to feel and look good as well.
- Put something other than a cigarette in your mouth. Chew sugarless gum or nibble on a carrot or celery stick.
- Avoid places where smoking is permitted. Sit in the nonsmoking section of restaurants, trains, and planes.
- Reduce your consumption of alcohol, which often stimulates the desire to smoke. Try to have no more than one or two drinks at a party. Better yet, have a glass of juice, soda, or mineral water.

4. Reward yourself for not smoking.

Congratuations are in order each time you get through a day without smoking. After a week, give yourself a pat on the back or a reward of some kind. Buy a new tape or compact disc. Treat yourself to a movie or concert. No matter how you do it, make sure you reward yourself in some way. It helps to remind yourself that what you are doing is important.

5. Use positive thoughts.

What are "self-defeating thoughts"?

If self-defeating thoughts start to creep in, remind yourself again that you are a nonsmoker, that you do not want to smoke, and that you have good reasons for quitting. Putting yourself down and trying to hold out using willpower alone are not effective coping techniques. Mobilize the power of positive thinking!

6. Use relaxation techniques.

Breathing exercises help to reduce tension. Instead of having a cigarette, take a long deep breath, count to ten, and release it. Repeat this five times. See how much more relaxed you feel?

7. Get social support.

The commitment to remain a nonsmoker can be made easier by talking about it with friends and relatives. They can congratulate you as you check off another day, week, and month as a nonsmoker. Tell the people close to you that you might be tense for a while, so they know what to expect. They'll be sympathetic when you have an urge to smoke and can be counted on to help you resist it. Remember to call on your friends when you are lonely, or you feel an urge to smoke. A buddy system is a great technique.

What is a "buddy system"?

Not Smoking Is Habit-Forming

Good for you! You have made a commitment not to smoke, and by using this booklet, you know what to do if you are tempted to forget that commitment. It is difficult to stay a nonsmoker once you have had a cigarette so do everything possible to avoid it.

If you follow the advice in this booklet and use at least one coping skill whenever you have an urge to smoke, you will have quit for keeps!

Common Rationalizations*

Rationalization	Response
I'm under a lot of stress, and smoking relaxes me.	Your body is used to nicotine, so you naturally feel more relaxed when you give your body a substance upon which it has grown dependent. But nicotine really is a stimulant; it raises your heart rate, blood pressure, and adrenaline level. Most ex-smokers feel much less nervous just a few weeks after quitting.
Smoking makes me more effective in my work.	Trouble concentrating can be a short-term symptom of quitting, but smoking actually deprives your brain of oxygen.

I've already cut down to a safe level.	Cutting down is a good first step, but there's a big difference in the benefits to you between smoking a little and not smoking at all. Besides, smokers who cut back often inhale more often and more deeply, negating many of the benefits of cutting back. After you've cut back to about seven cigarettes a day, it's time to set a quit date.
I smoke only safe, low-tar/ low-nicotine cigarettes.	These cigarettes still contain harmful substances, and many smokers who use them inhale more often and more deeply to maintain their nicotine intake. Also, carbon monoxide intake often increases with a switch to low-tar cigarettes.
It's too hard to quit. I don't have the willpower.	Quitting and staying away from cigarettes is hard, but it's not impossible. More than 3 million Americans quit every year. It's important for you to remember that many people have had to try more than once, and try more than one method, before they became ex-smokers, but they have done it, and so can you.
I don't know what to do with my hands.	That's a common complaint among ex-smokers. You can keep your hands busy in other ways; it's just a matter of getting used to the change of not holding a cigarette. Try holding something else, such as a pencil, paper clip, or marble. Practice simply keeping your hands clasped together. If you're at home, think of all the things you wish you had time to do, make a list, and consult the list for alternatives to smoking whenever your hands feel restless.

*Adapted from *Clinical Opportunities for Smoking Intervention— A Guide for the Busy Physician*. National Heart, Lung, and Blood Institute, NIH Pub. No. 86-2178. August 1986

THINK AND RESPOND

1. How is the subject introduced?

   _____

   _____

2. How is the information organized?

   _____

   _____

3. What transition words are used?

   _____

   _____

4. Is this essay in the first, second, or third person, and why do you think the author made that choice?

   _____

   _____

5. Is this essay written in the past, present, or future tense, and why do you think the author made that choice?

   _____

   _____

6. From the rationalization section, find an example of each:
   • An example used to support a recommendation

   _____

   _____

   • Reasoning used to support a recommendation

   _____

   _____

- A relevant fact used to support a recommendation

  _____

  _____

7. Provide synonyms or definitions for these words from the essay, and add at least two of these words to the *Words Worth Remembering* section of your journal.

   coping _____

   cravings _____

   nurture _____

   rationalization _____

   counter _____

   consumption _____

   stimulant _____

   negating _____

   inevitable _____

   visualize _____

8. If you liked this reading, make a record of it in the *Readings Worth Remembering* section of your journal.

COMPARING VIEWS

Do you agree with the advice on quitting smoking presented here? Why or why not? What different or additional advice would you give? How is the advice here similar to or different from advice for someone who wants to stop drinking or abusing harder drugs? After discussing this topic with others, continue to explore it on your own, in your journal — if it interests you. You may be able to use material from the discussion and your journal in a future writing activity.

APPLIED WRITING

Using the above guidelines as a model, write your own set of guidelines for breaking a bad habit or for developing a good habit. Try to select a topic about which you have some personal experience. Ideas for habit-breaking topics include:

nail-biting or hair-twirling	overeating	overspending
hot-temperedness	gossiping	worrying

Ideas for habit-starting topics include:

studying	exercising	becoming more creative
enjoying life	eating nutritiously	being organized

Make a list or cluster ideas. Ask others with expertise on your topic for their ideas on what works or for examples that can support your recommendations. Use resources such as the library or Internet to obtain relevant facts and ideas. Then develop an outline to guide you as you draft. After drafting, ask someone with an interest in your topic to review your guidelines. Revise it based on their suggestions. Also use both the Writing Checklist and the Essay Scoring Guide from Chapter 8 to help you revise. Prepare a final copy of the essay.

Hunter-Gatherers, North America, Late 20th Century
Sidney Harris

CHAPTER 13

Analyzing

These are the **key ideas** of this chapter:

- An analysis is a close examination of a topic in order to answer questions of how and why.

- Four ways to analyze are: gathering examples, comparing and contrasting, classifying, and showing cause and effect.

- Parallel structure can make writing easier to follow, and it also can strengthen meaning.

Picturing Meaning

Examine the cartoon on the opposite page; then think about or discuss these questions.

1. What do you see happening in this cartoon?

   _____

   _____

2. What is the real meaning of "hunter-gatherer"?

   _____

   _____

3. What point do you think the cartoonist is trying to make?

   _____

   _____

4. Why is the cartoon funny (or why is it not funny)?

   _____

   _____

   In the *Responses* section of your journal, write down your thoughts about this cartoon.

Write Now (1)

In what ways are consumers of Western culture like or different from consumers in other cultures? Jot down your ideas. Focus your comparison on two cultures: the one in which you live and another, different culture about which you know something. Also, focus your comparison on one characteristic such as manner of dress, leisure time activities, or eating habits. Use your own experiences as examples to make your comparison. Speculate on how you would respond if you suddenly moved into that other culture. Keep this work, because you may use it in a later activity.

Gathering Examples

To **analyze** means to examine critically by dissecting a subject into its essential features. A basic way to analyze is to explore *how* something happens, for example, how a process occurs or how a certain procedure should be performed. (See Chapter 12 for more about explaining *how*.) Another way to analyze is to explore *why* something happens, for example, why a certain situation resulted or why a process occurs the way it does. Many other questions of how and why—such as how things compare or why things are the way they are—can be answered by analyzing.

One way to analyze a topic is to gather examples. An example is one item used to represent many items. Writers probably use examples to support an analysis more than any other kind of evidence. There are two reasons for this. First, examples are relatively easy to obtain. Second, people love stories, and most examples are little stories. A good example helps readers see the point as clearly as a picture—this is why they also are called **illustrations**.

An example can be real or hypothetical. A real example shows how something has actually occurred that fits your analysis. Hypothetical examples show how, according to your analysis, something could occur. Some examples are not stories. Single items, facts, statistics, truisms, sayings, and quotations also fit into the category of examples used to support a point. In the following analysis, a variety of examples are used to answer the question, "How have computers affected productivity?"

Most people assume that the widespread use of personal computers in business has increased productivity. Indeed, in the developed countries, productivity rose during the first six years of the 1990s by about 1.5 percent per year. What puzzles economists, however, is that the annual growth of productivity has declined since the 1960s, when it measured about 4.5 percent per year. In other words, productivity growth has slowed since the introduction of personal computers. That fact has led some people to argue that computerization of the workplace has not led to real economic gains.

Statistics are used to support the point.

The problem with such an argument is that much of the value that has been created by computers is not measurable in dollars and cents because that value is aesthetic. That is, it has to do with unquantifiable characteristics such as beauty and elegance. On the whole, computers may not have helped businesses to create more products more quickly, but they have helped to make products look, feel, and sound a lot better. If José the marketing manager takes four-and-a-half hours today to design Powerpoint slides for his presentation to the CEO, whereas his father, who had the same job, took three-and-a-half hours to draw up some charts and graphs on posterboard, there has been no overall gain in productivity. The chances are good, however, that José's slides look much better than his father's posterboards did.

A hypothetical example is used to illustrate the point.

People have a natural tendency to be nostalgic, to imagine a bygone era when everything was simpler and better, but the truth is that if one looks at print media and consumer product design of thirty or forty years ago, the quality is much lower than it is today. The difference in quality is largely due to the use of computers. One might reasonably lament our current culture's overemphasis on style ("More matter, with less art," Hamlet's mother, Queen Gertrude, tells the courtier Polonius), but there is no question that a very real, though unquantifiable, value of personal computers is that they are tools for expressing creativity. Today, individuals working at personal computers can create beautiful graphics, lay out magazines, edit films, design automobiles, or write an eight-part score, print the sheet music, and then listen to the piece with several different orchestrations on different combinations of instruments.

A quotation from Shakespeare is used to support the point.

Real examples of computer applications are used to illustrate the point.

Introduction to Computers and Technology
Robert D. Shepherd

An Outline for Analytical Writing appears in Figure 13–1. Study the example of the completed form (Figure 13–2) to see how it was used to gather examples for an analysis of this question: "Why has the sixties rock group, the Beatles, remained so popular?" Then use the form when planning any writing that explores questions of *why* or *how*.

Figure 13-1: Outline for Analytical Writing

Photocopy this form before using.

Topic: _____

Real life example
Hypothetical example
Facts and statistics
Truisms, sayings, quotations

Figure 13-2: Example Outline for Analytical Writing

Topic: Why has the Sixties rock group, The Beatles, remained so popular?

Real life example

My daughter, born 30 years after their first album came out, likes them.

In 1998 George Martin, former producer of the Beatles, put together a CD with celebrity covers of Beatles tunes.

Hypothetical example

If you step into an elevator, chances are the music you hear is a Beatles tune.

Facts and statistics

Beatles produced dozens of singable tunes: "I Wanna Hold Your Hand," "Hey Jude," "While My Guitar Gently Weeps" (find out how many).

The original recordings are still selling.

Truisms, sayings, quotations

"Now it looks as though they're here to stay" (line from "Yesterday").

"We're more famous than Jesus" (John Lennon's infamous quote – or was it a misquote?).

Write Now (2)

Review the analysis of computers and productivity to answer the following questions.

1. How would you summarize this analysis?

_____

_____

2. What other example can you think of to demonstrate how computers have affected productivity?

_____

_____

3. Do you agree that computers have enhanced productivity? Why or why not?

_____

_____

4. What other effect do you think computers have had on society?

_____

_____

Write Now (3)

Think of a trend that you can analyze. It could be the one you identified in question 4 of Write Now (2), or you may choose another trend, such as:

fashion; for example, the increase or decline in formal wear

food; for example, the restaurants that are in vogue

music; for example, the type of dance music that is popular

Develop examples that could be used in an analysis of this trend. Use the Outline for Analytical Writing (Figure 13–1). Just work on the outline—you do not need to draft anything at this time. Keep this work because you may use it in a later activity.

Comparing and Contrasting

Comparing means to show how two or more things or persons are alike, while **contrasting** means to show how they are different. Almost anything or anyone you choose to examine will have a large range of characteristics shared in common with or distinct from others of a similar nature. Typical points of comparison for objects include physical features, function, how they came into being, and who uses them and how. Typical points of comparison for people include physical features, behavior, personal history, and reactions in a given situation. For some purposes, you may choose to compare *or* to contrast, and for other purposes you may choose to do both. In the following passage, an undertaker-writer uses both comparison and contrast to explain how a casket is different from a coffin:

Coffins are the narrow, octagonal fellows—mostly wooden, nicely corresponding to the shape of the human form before the advent of the junk food era. There are top and bottom, and the screws that fasten the one to the other are often ornamental. Some have handles, some do not, but all can be carried. The lids can be opened and closed at will.

> Physical features are contrasted.

Caskets are more rectangular and the lids are hinged and the body can be both carried and laid out in them. Other than shape, coffins and caskets are pretty much the same. They've been made of wood and metal and glass and ceramics and plastics and cement and the dear knows what else. Both are made in a range of prices.

> Physical features are compared.

But *casket* suggests something beyond basic utility, something about the contents of the box. The implication is that it contains something precious: heirlooms, jewels, old love letters, remnants and icons of something dear.

> Purposes are contrasted.

So casket is to coffin as tomb is to cave, grave is to hole in the ground, pyre is to bonfire. You get the drift? Or as, for example, eulogy is to speech, elegy to poem, home is to house, or husband to man. (I love this part, I get carried away.)

But the point is a *casket* presumes something about what goes in it. It presumes the dead body is important to someone. For some this will seem like stating the obvious. For others, I'm guessing, maybe not.

But when buildings are bombed or planes fall from the sky, or wars are won or lost, the bodies of the dead are really important. We want them back to let them go again—on our terms, at our pace, to say you may not leave without permission, forgiveness, our respects—to say we want our chance to say goodbye.

Purposes are compared.

Both coffins and caskets are boxes for the dead. Both are utterly suitable to the task. Both cost more than most other boxes.

It's because of the bodies we put inside them. The bodies of mothers and fathers and sons, daughters and sisters and brothers and friends, the ones we knew and loved or knew and hated, or hardly knew at all, but know someone who knew them and who is left to grieve.

The Undertaking: Life Studies in the Dismal Trade
Thomas Lynch

A Comparison–Contrast Outline appears in Figure 13–3. Study the example of the completed form (Figure 13–4) to see how it was used to compare and contrast traditional and alternative medicine. Then use the form when planning any writing that explores how things or persons are like or different.

Figure 13–3: Comparison-Contrast Outline

Photocopy this form before using.

Point of comparison/ contrast	How they are different		How they are the same
	Item 1: _____	Item 2: _____	

Figure 13–4: Example Comparison-Contrast Outline

Point of comparison/ contrast	How they are different		How they are the same
	Item 1: _____ traditional medicine	Item 2: _____ alternative medicine	
major aim	cures	prevention	increasing overlap here
orientation	symptom-oriented	holistic (whole body)	ditto
history	dating from Hippocrates	even more ancient	
practitioners	doctors, nurses, specialists	nonWestern doctors, midwives, homeopaths, naturopaths, etc., also nonprofessionals	some doctors apply both forms of medicine
medicines used	chemical compounds	plant-based natural sources such as herbs	
treatments	surgery, medicine	nonsurgical treatments, vitamin therapy, dietary changes, mind-body healing, etc.	some overlap here
effectiveness	established through rigorous clinical research, peer-reviewed	more anecdotal	both rely on research but practitioners may publish in different journals

Write Now (4)

Review the reading on coffins and caskets to answer the following questions.

1. How would you summarize this analysis?

_____

_____

2. How would you compare or contrast the interior of caskets and coffins?

_____

_____

3. Do you agree that caskets have more significance than coffins? Why or why not?

_____

_____

4. What other items used by humans can you think of that are similar to each other yet also distinct?

_____

_____

Write Now (5)

Think of two items to analyze by comparison and contrast. This could be the items you identified in question 4 of Write Now (4) or you may choose another pair of items such as:

manufactured objects; for example, two types of chairs

natural objects; for example, two species of trees

persons; for example, two friends

intangible topics; for example, two states of mind

Analyze your two items using the Comparison-Contrast Outline (Figure 13–3). Just work on the outline—you do not need to draft anything at this time. Keep this work because you may use it in a later activity.

Classifying

A class is a group of objects or persons with common traits. To **classify**, therefore, means to organize into groups of like items. When items are grouped into classes, it is easier to make distinctions between items in one class and another—in other words, to compare and contrast. Food groups, astrological signs, and makes of automobiles are three examples of classification systems. Some classification systems are natural or obvious to everyone, and some are contrived—made up to drive home a point. In the following passage, a home decorator contrives a classification system that divides people into four groups. Her purpose is to help people see how personality affects the ways they prefer to arrange their homes:

Each class is defined by how its members would decorate around the same couch.

There it sits, plumped and perfect, freshly delivered to your living room. Your new sofa. Virginal as its pristine sister on the showroom floor, and just as pretty.

Now comes the challenge: how do you make it your own? Well, that all depends on your personality. If you're a *Visionary*, you'll want to flank it with matching tables, pad it with tapestry pillows, and slip an Oriental rug beneath it. If you're an *Artisan*, you'll think first of comfort: Will an ottoman make the setup cozier? How about an afghan, a reading lamp, a coffee table with a fragrant bowl of flowers? An *Idealist* will think like an architect and keep the setup clean and dramatic. If the sofa's long and low, the Idealist will counterbalance it with a strong vertical element and keep the room open, with no fussy details to distract the eye. The *Adventurer*, on the other hand, will make the sofa into a personal statement. Draped with leopard-print throws or scattered with tiny purple pillows, it will appear to have been created not in a factory but in its owner's imagination.

In the hands of the Visionary, the Artisan, the Idealist, and the Adventurer, one sofa will take on four entirely different looks. It will become a reflection of its owner's yearnings; in fact, it will become an extension of its owner's personality.

The Domain Book of Intuitive Home Design:
How to Decorate Using Your Personality Type
Judy George with Todd Lyon

To classify items, it helps to gather a list of them first and then group them inside circles. Some items may belong to more than one group. If so, create overlapping circles and put these items inside the overlap. If you are not sure where an item belongs, leave it outside the circles. You may decide later to revise your groupings or to create another class for the items that do not fit anywhere. Here is a cluster that classifies food into two classes, nutritious foods and good-tasting foods:

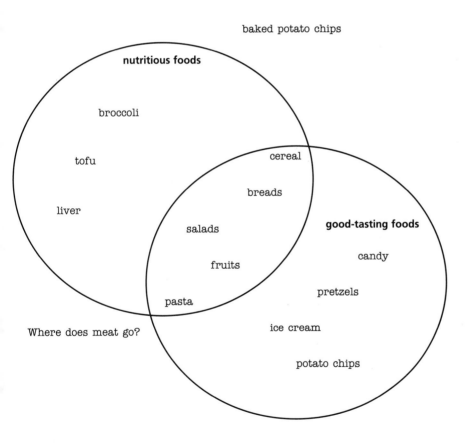

Write Now (6)

Review the reading about different design personalities to answer the following questions.

1. How would you summarize this analysis?

_____

_____

2. Which of the four personality types are you, and why?

_____

_____

3. Do you agree that people have different "design" personalities? Why or why not?

_____

_____

4. How else might you divide people into four groups based on personality types?

_____

_____

When classifying on computer, type your list of items first. Then use the page set-up function to create two or more columns, one for each class. Use the cut and paste functions to sort your items into the different columns. Use a smaller type size, such as 10 point, so you can see most of your lists at one time.

Write Now (7)

Think of a set of objects or persons you could analyze by classifying and then comparing and contrasting. You could classify people based on the personality groupings you identified in question 4 of Write Now (6), or you may choose something else to analyze, such as:

people, on the basis of generations

objects, on the basis of cost

events, on the basis of historical periods

novelists, on the basis of genre (type of novel)

Draw up a list of items that fit your topic and then group them inside circles (overlap the circles if some items fit into more than one class). Then compare and contrast your classes by using the Comparison-Contrast Outline (Figure 13–2). If you have more than two classes, add another column to the form. You do not need to draft anything at this time, but keep this work so you may use it in a later activity.

Showing Cause and Effect

Another way to analyze is to look at the various factors that lead to certain results: this is called **cause and effect**. Sometimes there are many effects from one cause, such as the many individuals who are affected in different ways when one train is delayed. Sometimes there are many causes that lead to one effect, such as the many natural and human-generated processes that cause thinning of the atmosphere's ozone layer. An effect may become the cause of yet another effect, such as when a campfire causes a forest fire that then causes the loss of wildlife. In the following example, many causes lead to one effect. The passage describes how Nike sneakers are made, in order to illustrate the cumulative effect on the environment:

Sneakers make nary a sound on the pavement, but do they tread so lightly on the environment? According to *Stuff: The Secret Lives of Everyday Things*, a report by the Northwest Environmental Watch (NEW) that documents what materials go into various everyday products, the manufacture of sneakers leaves a fairly heavy "footprint" on the ecosystem. For example, consider how much energy is used to ship raw materials to Asia, again to assemble the shoes, and again to ship finished product back to the United States. (NEW reports that shoes were the third-largest source of cargo for container ships going from East Asia to the U.S.)

> The shipment of raw material, the production, and the shipment of finished products (three causes) lead to huge consumption of energy (effect).

Yet sneakers' biggest environmental impact comes from the industries that create the components that go into the shoes, NEW reports. Soles are made from ethylene vinyl acetate (EVA), a synthetic foam made from Saudi Arabian petroleum in Korean refineries. The leather upper is made from cowhides shipped from the United States to Asia, where the leather is tanned. The process once involved natural tannins, but now it's largely a chemical affair involving a solution made of agents such as calcium hydroxide. In Pusan, South Korea, NEW reports, "The tanning plant discharged hair, epidermis, leather scraps, and processing chemicals into the Naktong River." After the component parts of the sneakers make their way to an assembly plant in Indonesia, they are fastened together with a solvent-based toxic glue.

> Various steps in the production process (different causes) create pollution (one effect).

Sneaker production (cause) requires box production (effect) which in turn creates more pollution (secondary effect).

And then there's the box in which the sneakers are sold. The tissue in which they are wrapped, according to NEW, is made from trees that grew in the Sumatran rain forest. There has been some improvement on the box itself, at least for Nike: it's made of unbleached and recycled cardboard and is now held together with tabs and slots rather than petro-chemical-based glue, as it had been for years. The ink on the outside of the box, NEW reports, isn't made from heavy metals. Nike has made one other step to

Environmental problems (cause) have led Nike to make an effort to reduce waste and pollution (effect).

cut down on sneaker waste, NEW reports: its "regrind" program, which takes excess rubber from one production cycle and blends it into the next, has cut down rubber consumption by 40 percent annually. There's yet no word on whether the pressurized-gas "Air" cushioning systems can be similarly recycled.

The Sneaker Book: Anatomy of an Industry and an Icon
Tom Vanderbilt

To plan an analysis using cause and effect, create a cluster on your topic. Inside different circles, write down the steps in the process you are examining. Add details to each step, just as you would in the clusters you have done before. Then, where you can identify one step as leading to another, draw an arrow between them. You may find that you have mostly causes or mostly effects. You also may find that you have some steps that are both. These insights can help you organize your writing. Here is a cluster used to outline the causes of low-birthweight babies:

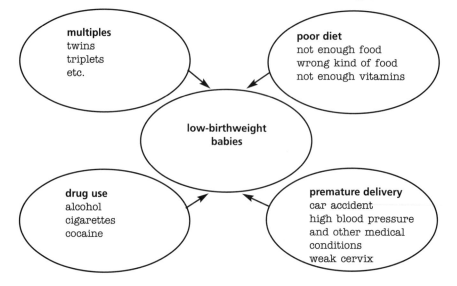

Write Now (8)

Review the reading about sneaker production to answer the following questions.

1. How would you summarize this analysis?

_____

_____

2. What other environmental effect might result from sneaker production?

_____

_____

3. Do you agree that sneaker production has a particularly significant impact on the environment? Why or why not?

_____

_____

4. What other product that you use on a daily basis causes an effect (good or bad) on the environment?

_____

_____

Write Now (9)

Think of a process to analyze for cause and effect. You could choose the process you identified in question 4 of Write Now (8), or you may choose another process such as:

a manufacturing process; for example, how wool cloth is made

a biological process; for example, how germs are spread

a thought process; for example, how memory works

a natural process; for example, how rain happens

Draw up a cluster of the steps in the process; then draw arrows to indicate causes and effects. You do not need to draft anything at this time, but keep this work so you may use it in a later activity.

Combining Analytical Techniques

Writers often combine analytical techniques in order to explore a subject thoroughly. If you look back at the passage from *The Undertaking*, you will see that Lynch is not simply exploring the question of how coffins are different from caskets. The bigger question he answers is, "Why do we use them at all?" Notice how he answers this question not only by comparing and contrasting the two objects, but also by using examples. He presents examples of precious objects to which dead bodies may be compared ("heirlooms, jewels, old love letters"), and he presents examples of situations where coffins and caskets are put to use ("when buildings are bombed or planes fall from the sky"). He classifies objects into two sets: (casket, tomb, grave, elegy, home, and husband in one set; coffin, speech, poem, house, and man in the other). The passage as a whole is a cause-and-effect analysis that may be summarized this way: because we care for people (cause), we put their bodies into special boxes when they die (effect).

The following passage also presents a combination of analytical techniques. This passage is from a book about children's folk practices (the informal ways children educate each other through games, songs, and customs). In it, the authors answer the question of why children cheat when they play tag and other informal games. They claim that cheating in this context is a form of rule testing that helps children internalize right and wrong:

What for lack of a better word is called cheating occurs because in folk games children play *with* as well as *by* the rules, and part of the game is to define what is permissible and to discover what one can get away with.

Examples of cheating are provided.

A girl explained to her mother, "It's against the rules to hide in the house, but it's okay if you don't get caught." Her mother was appalled: "That's cheating." But the issue isn't that simple. Each player in his role as referee is alert for violations committed by others, but a trickster in his role as referee can justify his behavior to himself, and if caught, will try to justify it to others.

Adult cheating is compared with children's cheating.

Cheating in the adult sense occurs when rules are well-defined and impossible to amend. That situation doesn't exist in chasing games. A player caught out-of-bounds can argue like a sophistical lawyer that he understood the boundaries differently or that they need to be revised. Perhaps the green car marking one boundary has been driven away. Obviously, a legal question exists about the line's location, but a clever player who sees the car leave won't mention that it's missing. He will interpret the boundary to his own advantage until another player demands an accounting.

This is not to say that anything goes. Whatever ruins the game, like regularly stepping over the line in dodgeball or running off with the can in Kick the Can, is immediately labeled "No fair!" And if a player continues to break a rule, some children will refuse to play with him. What happens next depends. If the rule-breaker is small or not especially popular, he will have to sit out a few games, until he learns to honor the customs and procedures of the group. But if he has some prestige within the group, there won't be enough of a consensus to exclude him, so some angry players will quit, thereby diminishing the excitement of the game for everyone. At this point, other players will act as honest brokers, putting pressure on the rule-breaker to promise to behave, soothing the feelings of those who have quit, pulling the group together again. They are usually aided in their ministrations by the desire of everyone to keep the game going. But no one wants to lose face. Children on such occasions behave with a kind of "wild civility."

Children are classified into different roles according to how they play.

These experiences of pressuring, compromising, demanding, denying, backing down, confusing the issue, accommodating various temperaments, and so on, are every bit as important as "Two plus two is four" or "Columbus discovered America," but these important experiences cannot be "designed" and presented to children in gradable units. They can occur only when children play together free from the shadow of adult coercion.

Play experiences are sorted into different classes of skills being learned.

In folk games children demystify their ideas of rules and fairness. They learn that rules are not made by God or the teacher, and that fairness is an imperfect balance of competing interests. When an older child breaks a rule, he is defying his comrades, not some authoritarian deity. And his purpose is not exactly to win the game, though that could be the result of his "cheating." His purpose is to test his friends' alertness, to test the rule's strength and clarity, and to test his own cleverness. His "cheating" does not ruin the game; it is part of the game.

A cause-and-effect connection is made between how children play and how they learn to get along with others.

One Potato, Two Potato:
The Folklore of American Children
Mary and Herbert Knapp

The folklorists who wrote about children's cheating spent years in the field observing children at play. Indeed, sorting causes and effects usually requires careful observation, research, or some level of knowledge. If you explore a topic from multiple angles—using example, comparison and contrast, classification, and cause and effect—you will help yourself discover what you know about your topic. At the same time, you will think through what you need to find out and some ideas on where to turn for more information. When you do this kind of thorough analysis, however, you may end up with several different outlines and clusters. To move from planning to drafting, follow these steps:

- Gather any extra information you need to support your analysis through research, interviews, and observations.

- Form your topic into a question beginning with *why* or *how*.

- Organize all of your ideas into one comprehensive outline or cluster.

- Arrange the points on your outline into a logical sequence.

- Write the draft using one paragraph for each point.

- Make use of transition words, such as *however* or *similarly*, to show contrast or connection (see Figure 7–2 in Chapter 7 for a list of transition words).

Finally, as with any essay, review your work, ask others for feedback, and revise it until you are satisfied that the writing accomplishes its purposes.

Write Now (10)

Review *The Folklore of American Children* to answer the following questions:

1. How would you summarize this analysis?

_____

_____

2. What examples of cheating can you recall from your childhood?

_____

_____

3. Do you agree that children's cheating in play has useful purposes? Why or why not?

_____

_____

4. How else might you compare the way children and adults play (or cheat)?

_____

_____

5. What additional roles can you identify for children (or adults) at play?

_____

_____

6. What is another effect that you have seen of children's play?

_____

_____

7. What other behavior pattern in children or adults intrigues you?

_____

_____

Write Now (11)

Select a topic to analyze further from the ones you explored in Write Nows (3), (5), (7), and (9). Alternatively, you may choose to analyze the behavior pattern you identified in question 7 of Write Now (10), but you will need to explore it first using one of the strategies described in this chapter. Move into pairs. Show your partner the outline you created for that topic. Have the partner develop another outline on the same topic, using another analyzing technique. You do the same for your partner. After you have finished, discuss with your partner ideas about who to interview or resources to check for more insight into your topic. Just work on the outlines—you do not need to draft anything at this time. Keep this work, because you may use it in a later activity.

Common Analytical Errors

When you analyze, take care not to make illogical points or draw false conclusions. There are many ways to fall into such errors. Some common pitfalls are described below.

When developing examples:

Irrelevancy—using examples that do not apply: *The houses in my neighborhood are run down. For example, my house is a rental.*

Faulty generalization—assuming one example represents all instances: *Nobody votes anymore. For example, I did not vote in the last election.*

When comparing and contrasting:

Oversimplifying—presenting matters as "either/or" when the truth is shaded and complex: *I was well behaved as a child, but my sister was a terror.*

When classifying:

False logic—creating illogical divisions: *Fruit may be classified as tasty, tropical, or pretty.*

Oversimplifying—dividing into two when more classes may exist: *People are either good or bad.*

Stereotyping—assigning one set of characteristics to a group of distinctive items: *Red-haired people have hot tempers.*

Pigeonholing—trying to fit items into categories that do not fit them or that do not completely describe them: *Dogs can be categorized as very friendly, somewhat friendly, or not friendly, and Doberman pincers are not friendly.*

When drawing cause and effect:

False logic—making a reverse connection between cause and effect: *The car accident damaged the axle* [when the damaged axle caused the car to crash].

False logic—connecting two potentially unconnected events: *Hildy ran away, so she must have been guilty* [Hildy may have run away for other reasons].

Circular reasoning—connecting from a cause or effect back to itself: *I like rodeos because I have always been a fan of them.*

Write Now (12)

Each statement represents an analytical error. Write the letter of the error on the line after the statement.

A. Irrelevancy

B. Faulty generalization

C. Oversimplifying (presenting matters as either/or)

D. False logic (creating illogical divisions)

E. Stereotyping

F. Pigeonholing

G. False logic (making a reverse connection between cause and effect)

H. False logic (connecting two potentially unconnected events)

I. Circular reasoning

J. Oversimplifying (dividing into two when more classes may exist)

1. I broke my leg because it was Friday the thirteenth. _____

2. David was a conscientious objector so he did not believe in fighting the war. _____

3. Homeless people are mentally ill. _____

4. A few sorority sisters were nice to me, but the rest behaved like snobs. _____

5. There are three kinds of cars: inexpensive, family-size, and four-wheel drive. _____

6. Stan is our artistic son, and Josh is our athletic son. _____

7. Women make good lawyers. For example, my friend Cathy earns more than $100,000 a year as a lawyer. _____

8. Young children can quickly become highly skilled players of the violin. I know a child prodigy who gave concerts by age eleven. _____

9. World War II led to Hitler's rise to power. _____

10. Cars are hot, or they're not.

_____

Summing Up

1. What does it mean to analyze something?

   _____

   _____

2. Consider the four analytical strategies explained in this chapter: generating examples, comparing and contrasting, classifying, and showing cause and effect. Underline the strategy that you find easiest to do in your writing. What makes it easiest?

   _____

   _____

3. Circle the strategy that you tend not to do. What is one thing you can do to take greater advantage of this strategy when you analyze?

   _____

   _____

Second Thoughts

Review the cartoon that opened this chapter; then think about or discuss the following questions.

1. Name a person you know who is a good example of a modern-day "hunter-gatherer." Why does this person fit the category?

2. How does your shopping style compare with that of your mother or father?

3. What are four ways to classify shoppers?

4. What are the causes of modern consumption patterns?

5. What are the effects when people purchase so much?

Based on what you have learned in this chapter about analyzing, what new insights do you have from this cartoon? Write your thoughts in the *Responses* section of your journal.

4. Name two situations outside of school where you could be called upon to analyze a question in writing.

_____

_____

5. As a result of reading this chapter, what one change will you make to include better analysis in your writing? Write your resolution in the *Habits for Life* section of your journal.

Write Now: Composing an Essay That Analyzes

Choose a topic to analyze. You may select as your topic one that you looked at in Write Now (1), (3), (5), (7), (9), or (11), or you may choose a new topic. Develop this topic into an analytical essay. To explore your topic, use at least three of the four analyzing techniques described in this chapter: giving examples, comparing and contrasting, classifying, and showing cause and effect. Collect additional information or ideas from other people and resources as necessary. Before beginning your draft, write your topic as a question beginning with *why* or *how*. As you revise, check to see whether you have committed any analytical errors. Use both the Writing Checklist and the Essay Scoring Guide from Chapter 8 to help you revise. Prepare a final copy of the essay.

Enhancing Meaning through Parallel Structure

Two lines are parallel when they are side by side and an equal distance apart at all points. Writing is said to be parallel when words of the same type—such as verbs or descriptive words—are presented in similar form within a sentence or paragraph. Parallelism is important in writing because it helps keeps meaning clear. In the following three examples, each sentence is revised for parallel structure:

Samantha dances, is a writer, and likes running.

↓

Samantha is a <u>dancer</u>, a <u>writer</u>, and a <u>runner</u>.
(parallel—Samantha's traits are all presented as nouns)

They ran through the kitchen. The living room was also where they ran.

↓

They ran <u>through the kitchen</u> and then <u>into the living room</u>.
(parallel—where they ran is presented in two prepositional phrases)

At the craft fair children made goofy hats, a wind chime, pinecone bird feeders, and a melted-wax greeting card

↓

At the craft fair children made goofy <u>hats</u>, wind <u>chimes</u>, pinecone bird <u>feeders</u>, and melted-wax greeting <u>cards</u>.
(parallel—the crafts are all mentioned in the plural form)

Parallelism is important not only to comprehension, but also to writing style. Parallel construction can make a point more quickly, and it can make a stronger connection or a greater contrast. Parallel structure can more clearly or forcefully present an example, compare or contrast, classify, or show cause and effect. When you are writing analytically, it pays to be conscious of parallel structure and to take advantage of it when you can.

In the following four examples, each sentence is rewritten to use parallel structure:

To present examples:
Among other outdoor activities, resort guests can climb mountains. In addition, parasails are available for rent, and so are bicycles.

↓

Among other outdoor activities, resort guests can <u>mountain climb</u>, <u>parasail</u>, or <u>bicycle</u>.

To compare or contrast:
Leo is an experienced and successful salesman. Cyrous has not done much selling before, and he does not make much money at it.

↓

<u>Leo is</u> an experienced and successful salesman. <u>Cyrous</u>, alas, <u>is</u> not.

To classify:
There are two kinds of people. Some like to think of the ways that people can be divided into groups, and some people prefer not to make such distinctions.

↓

People can be <u>sorted into two groups</u>: <u>those who</u> like to <u>sort</u> people <u>into two groups</u>, and <u>those who do not</u>.

To show cause and effect:
The flood destroyed our home. We were homeless and we almost got a divorce from the strain on our marriage.

↓

The flood <u>destroyed our home</u>, and the homelessness almost <u>destroyed our marriage</u>.

Exercise 1

Cross out two items in each list that do not follow the same form as the first item. The first set has been done as an example.

1. **walked to the car**, took out the keys, ~~the ignition started right up~~, backed down the driveway, ~~drives quickly~~

2. **this professor**, that student, people, those men, these ideas, anybody

3. **in time**, before long, at last, soon, after all, we waited and waited

4. **He is my good friend,** he is my kind neighbor, he is my favorite running partner, I like him a lot, we have been best friends a long time

5. **The sun sets,** the sky is darkening, the moon ascends, the stars flicker, nighttime is beautiful

Exercise 2

Make changes to the following sentences to add parallel structure, to reduce wordiness, add clarity, or strengthen meaning. The first has been done as an example.

1. To convert from inches to centimeters, multiply by 2.54.

    To convert   , multiply
    ~~Converting~~ from feet to meters ~~is done by multiplying~~ by .305.

2. The tallest mountain in the world is Everest, on the border between

    Nepal and China. The longest river in the world is the Nile, from

    Burundi up to Egypt. The Pacific is the largest ocean in the world,

    between the western coasts of North and South America and the

    eastern coasts of Asia and Australia.

3. A homicide is the murder of a person, a parricide is the murder of a parent, and an infanticide is to kill an infant.

4. The herbal soaps are made using a natural process blending natural oils, herbs, and we add scented essential oils. The soap is then cut by hand, cured and we wrap them individually.

5. The night comes after each day. Daylight comes again when the night is over. Such is the endless cycle of time.

Bringing Back Baby

by Meredith F. Small

Meredith F. Small is a primatologist—a person who studies primates, the order of animals that includes apes, monkeys, orangutans, and humans. She also is an anthropologist—a person who studies human beings, their culture and customs, and the features that make them distinct from animals. Her most recent book is called Our Babies, Ourselves: How Biology and Culture Shape the Way We Parent.

Small's interests in primates, humans, and parenting combine in the following article, which first appeared in Natural History Magazine. *It opens with the story of an orangutan baby who was kidnapped by an unrelated female. As you read the article, notice how the author uses examples of other "baby borrowings" among primates to explain why this kidnapping may have happened.*

Where is the rehabilitation center?

Near the village of Bukit Lawang, in Sumatra's Gunung Leuser National Park, are a few buildings and cages that once served as a rehabilitation center for captive orangutans being reintroduced to the wild. Among the animals the center successfully released are two females known to park workers as Suma and Edita. In 1997 both gave birth to infants in the surrounding forest, and both infants died. On March 1, 1998, Suma gave birth again, this time to a male that park workers named Forester. But four weeks later, Edita stole Suma's infant and carried it off through the trees as if it were her own.

Which baby was stolen?

Slowly but surely, the baby began to decline. Edita could not have been lactating, so Forester was at risk of starving. Concerned for the infant's survival, park staff used a banana laced with tranquilizers to lure Edita into an old cage left over from the days of rehabilitation. Once she became drowsy, they removed Forester from her lap. Upon waking, Edita broke out of the cage and ambled back into the forest.

How did the park staff get the baby back?

For four days, park staff and volunteers bottle-fed Forester to build up his strength. Then, on April 8, they waited with the revitalized infant near a trail frequented by Suma on her daily rounds of the forest. As she came swinging into view, they quickly placed Forester into the crook of a tree. As soon as mother and baby made eye contact, Forester held up his arms

Why did the park staff put the baby in the tree?

to her, like any infant missing Mom. Pursing her lips in greeting, Suma scooped up Forester and immediately began grooming him. Reunited, they moved back into the forest.

Although this was the first time kidnapping had been reported among wild orangutans, grabbing babies is nothing new for most other primates—and often it's a positive thing. Females of many Asian and African species of leaf-eating monkeys, for example, routinely pull babies from their mothers' chests and pass them around like rag dolls. Researchers believe this system, which they call infant sharing, may benefit mothers (by giving them time off from the demands of baby care) and "aunts" (by giving them mothering experience).

In other primate species, such as macaques, baboons, and chimpanzees, females may develop intense relationships with babies that are not their own. Relatives, in particular, are likely to be in physical proximity to infants and to be tolerated by mothers. In fact, orphaned primate babies have frequently been adopted by kin. Nonrelatives are also attracted to little ones and often look, touch, or try to pull a tiny infant away from its mother.

Primate infants are often the center of attention, and researchers suspect that being in the spotlight provides a social safety net for these vulnerable young. But even experienced females have been known to take infants from their mothers and keep them too long—sometimes for days—thereby putting the babies at risk of starvation. Sometimes abductions seem purposeful, meant to eliminate the competition: high-ranking female Japanese and rhesus macaques have been observed taking newborns from low-ranking troop mates and holding onto the babies until they are dead.

It is not just females that abuse youngsters. Male Barbary macaques steal infants and use them as pawns as they jockey for social status. The infants are held for hours and sometimes caught between these lumbering giants during a fight. In many species of monkey, including the hanuman langur and chacma baboon, males routinely grab unrelated babies and kill them, presumably to end nursing and bring the mothers into estrus again. A rival's offspring is thus eliminated, and an opportunity to spread one's own genes created.

What probably happened at Forester's kidnapping?

Because of these very real threats, most mothers protest when their infant is whisked away. Although no one witnessed Forester's kidnapping, it probably was not pleasant. Suma and Edita had been reintroduced to the wild more than a decade earlier and had been living rather solitary lives around Bukit Lawang ever since. They must have known each other but were neither relatives nor friends. Perhaps Edita was still mourning her previous year's loss. Many primates express grief after infant loss—female monkeys and apes may hold their dead infants for days and weeks or haunt other females with newborns after losing their own.

What is maternal instinct?

While the kidnapping was a desperate move, Edita's behavior reminds us that the roots of longing run deep, and that maternal instinct can be compelling, even without maternity.

THINK AND RESPOND

1. Compare and contrast "infant sharing" and kidnapping.

   _____

   _____

2. Four examples of infant kidnapping among primates are described in paragraphs six and seven. List the different motives involved.

   _____

   _____

3. This article mentions several other types of primates besides orangutans. List as many as you can find, then describe features they all share in common.

   _____

   _____

4. What do you think may have caused Edita to steal Suma's baby?

    _____

    _____

5. What was the effect on Suma when park staff returned her baby, and why do you think she responded the way she did?

    _____

    _____

6. Provide synonyms or definitions for these words from the essay, and add at least two of the words to the *Words Worth Remembering* section of your journal:

    lactating _____

    laced _____

    ambled _____

    crook _____

    pursing _____

    proximity _____

    troop _____

    jockey _____

    lumbering _____

    estrus _____

7. If you liked this reading, make a record of it in the *Readings Worth Remembering* section of your journal.

COMPARING VIEWS

Can animals feel grief and other emotions to the extent that people do? Explore the question using analytical techniques (gathering examples, comparing and contrasting, classifying, and showing cause and effect). After discussing this topic with others, continue to explore it on your own, in your journal—if it interests you. You may be able to use material from the discussion and your journal in a future writing activity.

APPLIED WRITING

This article narrates an incident of baby grabbing by an orangutan. It goes on to describe similar incidents of infant sharing and baby grabbing by other primates. Humans are primates, too. Write an essay exploring how and why instances of infant sharing and baby grabbing occur among humans. Use more than one analytical technique to think through ideas and plan your essay. Use both the Writing Checklist and the Essay Scoring Guide from Chapter 8 to help you revise. Prepare a final copy of the essay.

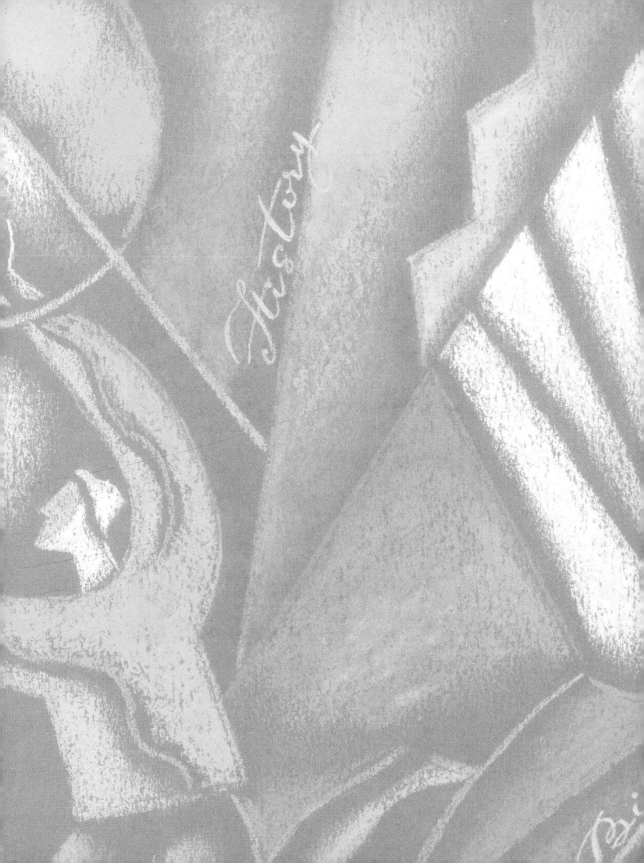
History

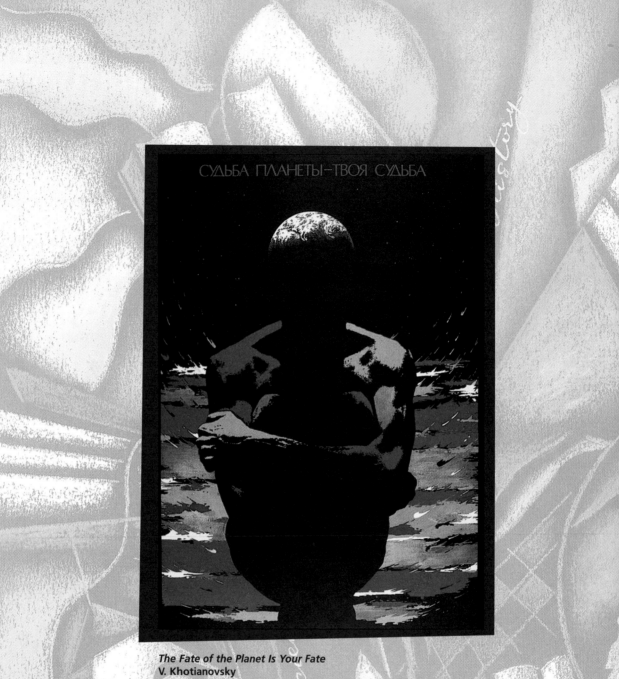

СУДЬБА ПЛАНЕТЫ–ТВОЯ СУДЬБА

The Fate of the Planet Is Your Fate
V. Khotianovsky

CHAPTER 14

Taking a Position

These are the **key ideas** of this chapter:

- The purpose of argument, also called persuasion, is to change how readers think or act.

- Three formats for organizing an argument are problem solving, cause and effect, and point-counterpoint.

- To be persuasive, writing must be well worded and must demonstrate credibility, dynamism, and integrity.

Picturing Meaning

Examine the illustration on the opposite page; then think about or discuss these questions.

1. What do you see in this poster?

   _____

   _____

2. What point is it making?

   _____

   _____

3. How does the poster communicate that point?

   _____

   _____

4. What effect do you think the artist wants this poster to have on you?

   _____

   _____

   In the *Responses* section of your journal, write your thoughts about this poster.

Write Now (1)

What do *you* think is the biggest threat to earth? In your journal or elsewhere, write down your ideas. Explain why it is a threat. Explore how this threat to earth would affect people. Describe what can be done to overcome the threat and who can do it. Keep this work because you may use it in a later activity.

Purposes of Argument

When you analyze, you take a subject apart to understand it (see Chapter 13 for more about analyzing). Once you have fully analyzed a subject, you are ready to form an opinion about it. When you make this opinion known to others, you are taking a position. **Argument** is the name for the kind of writing that takes a position. "Argument" in this sense does not mean "quarrel," but rather "a set of statements that persuades others to agree." Another word for this kind of writing is **persuasion.**

The argument you write can be **explicit**—fully and directly expressed. It can be **implicit**—indirectly stated so that readers must draw their own conclusions about your position. It can appeal to reason, offering evidence that supports your point of view. It can appeal to emotions, arousing readers to feelings of pleasure, excitement, empowerment, or fear to bring them over to your position. Persuasive writing can do many things, and it can be organized many different ways, but its purpose is always the same: to bring about a change in readers. An argument may change what they understand to be true (their beliefs), what they approve of or prefer (their attitudes), or what they believe to be right and moral (their values). In addition, it may change what they do (their behaviors). An argument is considered effective if it inspires *some* change in thinking or action—it is the rare argument that inspires radical change.

The kind of change you can effect in readers will depend in part on where they already stand. Each reader will fall somewhere along a continuum defined by these three terms:

1. Receptive readers

2. Neutral readers

3. Unreceptive readers

Receptive readers. Readers who are sympathetic to you personally or to your point of view usually will be open to your ideas. You can bring such readers into further agreement by emphasizing your shared feelings and concerns, by using rousing and inspirational language, and by reminding readers of the evidence. A reasonable objective with receptive readers is to move them into action. You can do this if you clearly state what needs to be done and specifically ask them to do something.

Neutral readers. Some readers may have no opinion about you, and they may not have considered the issue or decided how they feel about it. These readers may not even care about the issue. A reasonable objective with neutral readers like these is to persuade them to be open to your point of view. You can do this by capturing their attention, informing them of the issue, and showing how it relates to their concerns and values.

Unreceptive readers. Some readers may be defensive or even hostile because they have negative feelings about you or your point of view. A reasonable objective with such readers is to inspire a willingness to accept you or to rethink the issue. You can achieve this goal by demonstrating that you are trustworthy, acknowledging their beliefs and values, emphasizing the areas of agreement, and addressing their arguments with diplomatically worded counterarguments.

Write Now (2)

Several scenarios are listed in the chart below. For each scenario, decide if the audience is probably receptive (R), neutral (N), or unreceptive (U)—or some combination. Also decide on a reasonable objective for the writer. After you have completed the chart, discuss with your classmates how your assumptions about each audience affect what you believe to be reasonable objectives.

Writer	Audience	Probable Audience Position	Reasonable Objective
1. minister writing a sermon about the path to salvation	church members		
2. mother writing a letter of advice	wayward son		

Writer	Audience	Probable Audience Position	Reasonable Objective
3. newspaper editor writing editorial urging city to repair much traveled bridge	newspaper subscribers		
4. scientist presenting a radical new theory in a scientific journal	scientific colleagues		
5. college student writing essay complaining about the cafeteria food	other college students		

Building an Argument

When building an argument, you can make use of four types of statements:

1. Statements of fact

2. Statements of value

3. Statements of policy

4. Statements of conjecture

Statements of fact. Statements that are either true or false are statements of fact. Some statements of fact are easy to prove, but others require evidence and logical reasoning to convince readers that they are true. Statements of fact are rational appeals. They seek intellectual agreement from readers. Examples include:

The rate of births to teenagers is declining.

There was a lot more snow in the winter when I was a child.

Inexperienced drivers have more accidents.

Statements of value. Expressions of opinion are statements of value. These kinds of statements cannot be proven. Rather, they seek emotional agreement from readers. Examples include:

This tax proposal is ludicrously unfair to the middle class.

I love this cold and treeless mountain ridge.

Democracy is America's greatest export.

Statements of policy. Statements that call for a change in the way people act or are governed are statements of policy. Such statements often (but not always) include the word "should." Examples include:

Children should no longer be required to recite the Pledge of Allegiance.

People should be allowed to raise chickens even in the suburbs.

Women must be able to walk alone at night without fear.

Statements of conjecture. Expressions of possibilities about what could have happened, is happening, or may happen are statements of conjecture. Like statements of value, statements of conjecture reveal the writer's opinion. Unlike statements of fact, statements of conjecture are not provable. They can be used to inspire an emotional reaction in readers, such as hope or fear. Examples include:

Without vaccinations, many of us would not be alive.

There is a government conspiracy to control the weather.

Someday soon we will have a colony on Mars.

To present a full and persuasive argument, you may need to make use of all four types of statements—fact, value, policy, and conjecture. Also, it helps to be aware of these four types of statements because then you can better analyze opposing arguments and defend against them.

Write Now (3)

Read the statements below. Indicate whether each is an argument of fact (F), value (V), policy (P), or conjecture (C).

1. _____ It feels good to be alive!

2. _____ Sport utility vehicles should be held to the same fuel efficiency standards as automobiles.

3. _____ The square footage of new homes is increasing.

4. _____ Every year people drown at this bend of the river.

5. _____ Don't you find television soap operas fascinating?

6. _____ We should each open our home to a homeless person.

7. _____ The end of the world is near.

8. _____ Analog recordings (such as the vinyl LP) offer better sound than digitized recordings (such as the compact disk).

9. _____ Risk-taking and flaunting of safety are good for the soul.

10. _____ Descendants of African Americans held in slavery should receive reparations from the government.

Write Now (4)

In small groups, select one of the statements from Write Now (3). Working independently, write four statements on the same topic that express your knowledge and opinion. An example has been provided.

Example:

Topic based on statement #7: *the end of the world.*

Statement of fact: *Some people believe the end of the world will come in their lifetimes.*

Statement of value: *It is frightening to think how easily our planet could be destroyed by nuclear weapons.*

Statement of policy: *We should take seriously the threat of global warming, because it could destroy life as we know it.*

Statement of conjecture: *An asteroid will probably collide with earth someday and smash it to pieces.*

Topic based on statement #____: _____

Statement of fact: _____

Statement of value: _____

Statement of policy: _____

Statement of conjecture: _____

    Next, share your statements with others in your group. Take notes of statements by others in the group that

Support your statements: _____

_____

_____

Oppose your statements: _____

_____

_____

Are neutral: _____

_____

_____

Keep these notes because you may use them in a later activity.

Problem-Solution

One of the most commonly used formats for organizing an argument is **problem-solution**. This is a very simple format, as its name indicates. First you state what is wrong; then you propose how to fix it. An essay organized in this format might, for example, draw attention to the problem of lead poisoning and call for greater efforts at prevention. To create an effective argument, you must clearly define the situation and show how it is a problem rather than an inconvenience or fact of life. You also need to relate the problem to the concerns of readers. Then you must show that your solution is logical, workable, and the best alternative. This format is useful with readers who have not considered the issue before. It also is useful with receptive readers because it can reinforce their commitment and move them into action on the specific solution you propose.

The following selection demonstrates the problem-solution format used in an opinion column on the possibility of new, noncommercial, low-power FM stations. The author, a famous consumer activist, first attracts readers' attention with questions framed to get them nodding "yes." Next he identifies the problem, taking care to demonstrate its relevance to readers. Then he presents his solution and argues why it is such a good one.

Statements of value (in question form) express the problem.

Ever wonder why radio generally has become so canned, flat and insipid, bereft of local news, and stuffed with commercials, mercantile values, and the same old, tired junk? Not to mention the downright offensiveness of Howard Stern and the other shock jocks?

Statements of fact explain the cause of the problem.

First, for years, more than 90 percent of all radio time has been composed of entertainment (music) and advertisements. Second, in the last three years, diversity in radio-station ownership has been collapsing.

The Telecommunications Act of 1996 raised the number of radio stations that any single corporation may own in a particular market. This loosed a flood of radio-company mergers. So, not only is station ownership concentrated in fewer corporate hands, but formulaic programming puts the few reporters left, and local coverage, in the backseat as well.

A statement of value is quoted to demonstrate how others share this concern.

Two conglomerates own more than 400 radio stations each, all over the country. One woman complained about the sameness of Cleveland radio following two huge radio-company mergers: "It's as though McDonald's bought every restaurant in town, and all you could get was a Big Mac."

The purpose of these corporate-radio megaconglomerates is to maximize profits by reducing costs of reporters and editors—not to enrich public discourse or cover the news in their areas. Market forces have not led to a vigorous radio culture, or thoughtful programming, or programming that gives voice to the community. In their quest for larger audiences, more advertising, and greater profits, commercial broadcasters cater to the basest standards, with ever more blatant effusions of crassness, sex talk, and nihilism.

Commercial rewards drive the creation, production, and marketing of ever more Howard Sterns, Greasemans, and the rest of the shock jocks. This inevitably leads to a coarsening of our culture, which has particularly harmful effects on children. Even "public" radio is becoming commercialized. National Public Radio now carries ever longer "underwriting messages"—which are a form of advertisement.

> Statements of value and fact connect the problem to the concerns of readers.

Meanwhile, the public is mostly silent on the airwaves that we legally own. Radio is supposed to serve the ends and purposes of the First Amendment. That means protecting public discourse, which is essential to our form of democratic self-government. But the current regulatory regime for radio serves to thwart the First Amendment rights and the interests of most Americans. We speak little, if at all, on our own airwaves, while the wealthy may speak through radio by controlling who uses their stations and for what purposes.

What good is freedom of speech if nobody can afford it? Is speech truly free if only the wealthy can buy it?

Here's the good news: At last, the Federal Communications Commission (FCC) may come to the rescue. Right now the FCC is considering whether to set up noncommercial, low-power FM (LPFM) radio stations of up to 100 watts, with a range of a few miles. That's a big deal. Imagine the new voices that could flourish on these microstations—service and advocacy groups, universities, community and civic organizations, ethnic groups, arts organizations, seniors groups, and others.

> Statements of value, fact, and conjecture present the solution.

That could really liven up the radio dial. They could give us some choices. But it is not enough merely to authorize LPFM service. The FCC should allocate more spectrum for low-power radio broadcasting and introduce it when radio switches from analog to digital signals.

> A statement of policy expands upon the solution.

These small stations could enrich the public's understanding of civic issues and social problems. They could be a modest but important step toward more cohesive communities, a renewed public discourse, and a richer and more realistic culture. It is not often that a federal agency can achieve so much with so little effort . . .

> Statements of value express why the solution is a good one.

Radio Sucks—and the Only Way to Stop It
Is to Unleash the Low-Power Stations
Ralph Nader

Write Now (5)

Review the previous reading to answer the following questions.

1. How would you summarize Nader's argument?

_____

_____

_____

2. What other solution can you propose to solve the problem of low-quality radio content?

_____

_____

_____

3. Do you agree with Nader that the FCC should license noncommercial low-power FM radio stations? Why or why not?

_____

_____

_____

4. What other First Amendment (freedom of speech) issue is of concern to you?

_____

_____

_____

Analyzing a Problem and Its Solution

To write in problem-solution format, you first need to define the problem (see Chapter 11 for more about defining). Then use a question-and-answer approach to think through your ideas. Questions you might ask yourself are

- For whom is this a problem?

- What are the causes of this problem, and what are the effects?

- Where is it a problem?

- When is it a problem?

- Why is it a problem?

- How is it a problem for my readers?

Make a list of possible solutions; then pick the one that seems most defensible. Think it through by clustering or by using a question-and-answer approach. Questions you might ask yourself include:

- Who can be a part of the solution?

- What cause or effect will this solution repair?

- Where will the solution be implemented?

- When can this solution solve the problem?

- Why is this solution the best one?

- How can readers participate in the solution?

To think through a problem on computer, just type up a list of questions, then scroll up and down the list, inserting answers as you think of them.

A Problem-Solution Outline appears in Figure 14-1. Study the example of the outline to see how it was used to work through the issue of plastic grocery packaging. Then use it as a guide when developing your own argument in problem-solution style.

Figure 14–1: Problem-Solution Outline
Photocopy this form before using.

Part A

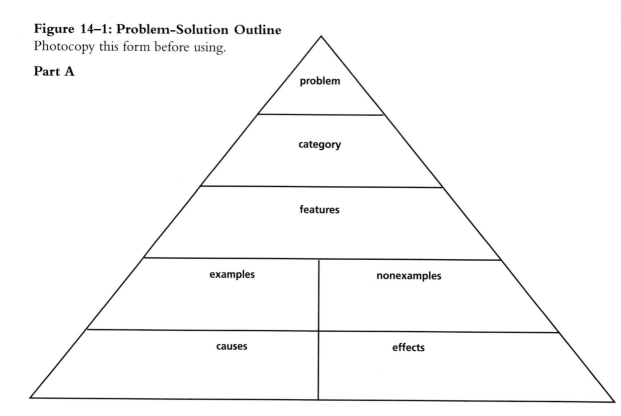

Part B: To continue outlining your problem, phrase a question with each word and then answer it:

(Who)   Question: _____

Answer: _____

(What)   Question: _____

Answer: _____

(When)   Question: _____

Answer: _____

(Where) Question: _____

Answer: _____

(Why)   Question: _____

Answer: _____

(How)   Question: _____

Answer: _____

Part C: Make a list of possible solutions. Use clustering to expand on one or more ideas.

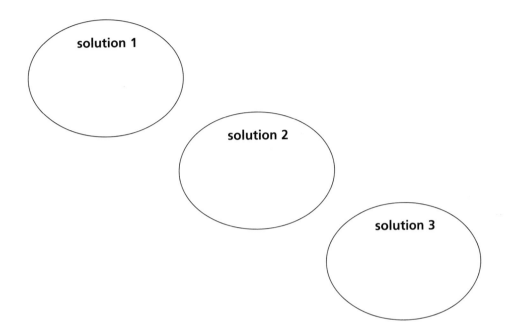

Part D: Pick one solution that you think is most defendable. Put a star next to it. Continue outlining this solution by phrasing a question with each word below. Then answer your questions.

(Who) Question: _____

Answer: _____

(What) Question: _____

Answer: _____

(When) Question: _____

Answer: _____

(Where) Question: _____

Answer: _____

(Why) Question: _____

Answer: _____

(How) Question: _____

Answer: _____

Figure 14–2: Example Problem-Solution Outline

Part A

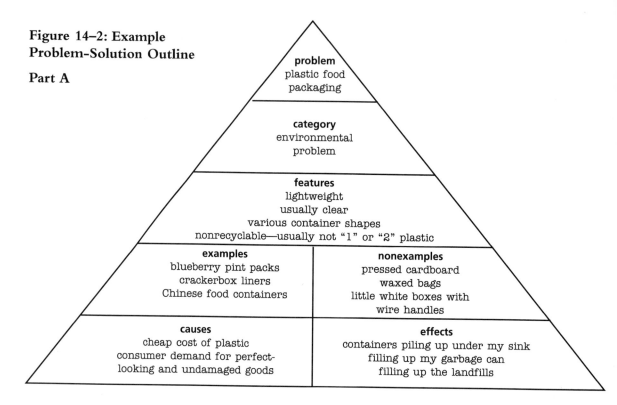

Part B: To continue outlining your problem, phrase a question with each word and then answer it:

(Who)   Question: Who likes this plastic packaging?

         Answer: Grocers, I guess, consumers, plastics manufacturers.

(What)   Question: What can I do with all this plastic packaging?

         Answer: Use when I pack lunches, for children's art projects maybe?

(When)   Question: When did everything go plastic?

         Answer: Seems like in the last couple of years.

(Where)   Question: Where is the plastic made?

         Answer: Don't know—need to find out.

(Why)   Question: Why are these plastics not recyclable?

         Answer: Maybe they are, but not in my community (need to find out?)

(How)   Question: How do other consumers feel about all this plastic?

         Answer: Need to ask.

Part C: Make a list of possible solutions. Use clustering to expand on one or more ideas.

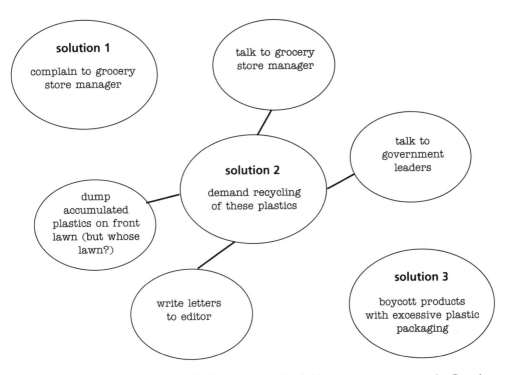

Part B: Pick one solution that you think is most defendable. Put a star next to it. Continue outlining this solution by phrasing a question with each word below. Then answer your questions.

(Who)   Question: Who can be part of the solution?

            Answer: Grocers, consumers.

(What)   Question: What can we do first?

            Answer: Inform public of issue.

(When)   Question: When could we expect to see any response?

            Answer: Don't know, maybe just need a "push" from consumers.

(Where)   Question: Where is plastic recycled?

            Answer: Don't know—need to find out.

(Why)   Question: Why is recycling the best solution?

            Answer: Probably more realistic than expecting food industry to eliminate plastic packaging.

(How)   Question: How would recycling work?

            Answer: Curbside pickup, or drop-off at grocery stores.

Write Now (6)

Think of an issue to explore using the problem-solution format. The issue could be the one you identified in question 4 of Write Now (5), or it could be some other issue, such as:

a regulatory policy; for example, taxing Internet commerce

a cultural issue; for example, the use of cell phones in public places

a media issue; for example, images of violence in film and on TV

Then explore your topic using the Problem-Solution Outline in Figure 14–1. Just work on the outline—you do not need to draft anything at this time. Keep this work because you may use it in a later activity.

Cause and Effect

In the newspaper column quoted earlier, Ralph Nader claims that radio content is a problem and that corporate mergers are responsible. This is a cause-and-effect analysis. Cause and effect is often used in argument to draw connections between events. A cause-and-effect format also can be used to explain a theory, for example, on what led to the extinction of dinosaurs. In addition, it can raise consciousness, for example, showing how weight gain can be triggered by underlying medical disorders and not just by overeating. (For more about cause and effect, see Chapter 13.) The cause-and-effect format is used throughout the column excerpted below. The author, a political commentator associated with the Libertarian Party, presents an accumulation of evidence to show that the availability of guns is *not* a cause of so-called school shootings (the shooting of people on school grounds by youthful assailants):

It's called propaganda: Simplify your lie down to an easily-recalled slogan, repeat it often enough, and people will eventually get it down by heart and accept it as fact.

Take: "The cause of all these school shootings is the too-easy availability of guns." Prior to the National Firearms Act of 1933, there was no law to discourage a veteran of the Great War from keeping a fully-operational souvenir machine gun in the bedroom closet. There were few towns in America where the local lads didn't know the location of at least one such weapon. Yet none was ever used in a "school shooting." *Cause leading to … … (non) effect.*

As late as the 1960s, it was not unusual in rural America for young boys to carry their .22 rifles to school with them, parking them in the principal's office until needed for the target matches after school. At age 49, I am no doddering old-timer, but I can remember young lads walking the country roads of Ohio and Connecticut after school with their rifles (or bicycling home with the weapons across their handlebars), hoping to pick off some predatory bird with the full encouragement of area farmers. A neighbor might chide you about watching where your bullets went if you missed, but no one ever called the police to report "the Jones boy is heading down the road with his gun; come arrest him!" *Cause leading to … … (non) effect.*

When I went away to Eaglebrook School in Massachusetts in 1962 at the age of 12, I took my rifle. We fired for accuracy at the range on Saturdays. I daresay we could have snuck them out of the lockers down at the gym for some mayhem if it ever crossed our minds. . . but it never did… . *Cause leading to … … (non) effect.*

This focus on "the availability of guns"—ignoring the fact they were far more accessible only 40 years ago, when you could order a 20-mm Lahti anti-tank gun through the mail from an ad in the back of a comic book—is intended not only to advance the prior agenda of those who want a disarmed and enslaved citizenry, but also to distract us from asking what it is about the mandatory behavior modification labs (public schools) which creates such rage and frustration in our incarcerated adolescent. *Cause leading to … … effects.*

It also diverts attention from the perfectly relevant question of how many of these shooters had been on drugs known to affect the judgment, like Ritalin and Luvox, prescribed and administered by their government wardens … . *… effect.*

To Prevent a Life of Crime, Buy Your Kid a Gun
Vin Suprynowicz

Write Now (7)

Review the previous reading to answer the following questions.

1. How would you summarize Suprynowicz's analysis?

_____

_____

2. Suprinowicz suggests two possible causes of school shootings and one likely effect of blaming guns. What do you think might be another cause or effect associated with this issue?

_____

_____

3. Do you agree with Suprynowicz that the availability of guns is not a cause of school shootings? Why or why not?

_____

_____

4. What other Second Amendment issue (the right to bear arms) is of concern to you?

_____

_____

Analyzing for Cause and Effect

A cause-and-effect argument relies on careful analysis. Clustering is a useful device for thinking through causes or effects, or both. A cause-and-effect cluster appears in Chapter 13. Study this example to see how it was used to explore the causes of low-birthweight babies. Then use this technique when developing your own cause-and-effect argument.

Write Now (8)

Think of an issue to explore using the cause-and-effect format. The issue could be the one you identified in question 4 of Write Now (7), or it could be some other issue such as:

- a safety issue; for example, campus security
- a behavior issue; for example, adolescent rebellion
- a governing issue; for example, the legal drinking age

Then explore your topic using clusters. Just work on the cluster—you do not need to draft anything at this time. Keep this work because you may use it in a later activity.

Point-Counterpoint

In his opinion column, Vin Suprynowicz states a position he opposes ("the cause of all these school shootings is the too-easy availability of guns") so that he can take it apart through cause-and-effect analysis. This kind of **point-counterpoint** is often called "refutation" because "refute" means to prove wrong. It is useful for reinforcing receptive readers who are aware of an opposing opinion. It also can be used to win over unreceptive readers because it acknowledges their points of view. It is less effective with neutral readers who may become confused by the back-and-forth discussion. The following opinion column uses a point-counterpoint strategy. The author, a member of the National Association of Black Social Workers, acknowledges several points raised by advocates for transracial adoption and then argues against them:

When black children are cut off from their roots, that's a form of cultural genocide. White families can love a black child, but love is not enough. They can provide that child with a good education or a nice home, but that's not enough either. Because being raised by someone of a different race cuts a child off from a sense of historical continuity. They have no sense of who they are as African Americans.

Points leading to . . .

. . . counterpoints.

We transmit our culture at an unconscious level. As we raise our children we don't wake up saying, "What will I tell them today that's culturally significant?" It's like breathing. I'm talking about language and behavior that can only get transmitted within a black family. You might call it cultural paranoia, but it stems back to slavery. We have always prepared our kids to live in a white-dominated society as a way of protecting them.

Many blacks adopted into white families love their families, but they didn't know they would have problems in the world once they left home. The world sees them as black adults, and now they're having difficulty adjusting.

Point and counterpoint.

Counterpoint to point (unstated) that there are not enough black families to adopt.

The main reason I'm against transracial adoption, though, is that it's unnecessary. There are plenty of black families who would love to adopt a child, but there are barriers built into the system. For many black families, putting a price tag on a baby is reminiscent of slavery. Then, too, agencies are headed predominantly by whites. They don't know the black community. Studies have shown that when agencies are sensitive to African American families they have no trouble finding enough black families to adopt black children.

Should White Families Be Allowed to Adopt African American Children? No.
Alice G. Thompson

Write Now (9)

Review the reading above to answer the following questions.

1. How would you summarize Thompson's analysis?

_____

_____

2. Thompson acknowledges these arguments *for* transracial adoption: that whites can be good parents, that black adoptive children love their families, and that there are not enough black families to adopt. What do you think might be another argument in favor of transracial adoption?

_____

_____

3. Thompson offers these arguments *against* transracial adoption: that white parents cannot transmit black culture, that black children raised in white families have trouble adjusting in adulthood, and that many black families are in fact willing to adopt. What do you think might be another argument against transracial adoption?

_____

_____

4. Do you agree with Thompson that white families should not be able to adopt black children? Why or why not?

_____

_____

5. What other family issue is of concern to you?

_____

_____

Analyzing for Point-Counterpoint

To plan an argument using the point-counterpoint format, make a two-column list. In the left column, list the opposing side's arguments. List possible responses in the right column. You also can reverse the exercise. List your arguments in the left column and think of counter-arguments that might be presented by opponents. This can help you anticipate and deflect criticism in your essay. Here is an example of several counterpoints to a point Thompson makes about transracial adoption. These counterpoints come from an essay published alongside Thompson's essay and presenting the opposing point of view:

To think through a point-counterpoint argument on computer, format the page for two columns. That way the points and counterpoints will line up side-by-side.

Point	Counterpoints
black families can better help black adoptive children adjust to living in a racist society	it is better to be adopted into a white family than to sit in foster care
	black adoptive children will tell you their white parents do a fine job
	20-year study proved it's not true
	there is no real evidence that transracial adoption is bad

Write Now (10)

In small groups, decide on an issue to explore using the point-counterpoint format. The issue could be the one you identified in question 5 of Write Now (9), or it could be some other issue, such as:

a childrearing issue; for example, the use of pacifiers

a racial issue; for example, intermarriage

a policy issue; for example, foster parenting

Then explore your topic using a point-counterpoint strategy. Think of an argument on one side of the issue; then come up with one or more responses. Do this for three or four points. Just make a list of points and counterpoints—you do not need to draft anything at this time. Keep a copy of this work because you may use it in a later activity.

Demonstrating Credibility, Dynamism, and Integrity

No matter what kind of audience you have, and no matter how you organize your argument, to be persuasive you must convince readers that you are someone who can be believed and who is qualified to write on the issue. In other words, the key to persuasion is **credibility.** You can establish your credibility directly by referring to your life experience and educational credentials. Often, however, you establish it indirectly: by demonstrating knowledge of the subject and sound judgment and by drawing upon credible evidence. In addition, the more you can convince readers you are just like them, the more they tend to find you an honest source. Finally, there is "borrowed credibility." You obtain it by quoting from authorities that your readers believe to be reliable.

Another key to successful persuasion is **dynamism.** Dynamism is energy and enthusiasm that carries readers along. It shows in your word choice and the rhythms of your sentences. Dynamism is revealed in the attention-grabbing opening and in the way that you build up your presentation to a clinching finale. Dynamism develops most naturally when you feel strongly about your position.

A third key is **integrity**. If you have integrity, you are honest with the facts and you do not try to persuade readers to believe something you know to be false or against their interests. It also means that you fight fairly, that is, you do not resort to unfair emotional appeals. This last point is important because, while all persuasive writing is emotional in some regard, you must guard against extreme emotional charges that fall apart under scrutiny. Some common pitfalls when using emotional argument include:

- The "ad hominem" attack ("ad hominem" means "against the person")—attacking the person directly instead of refuting his or her argument: *Do not believe his budget figures because he is really slippery with numbers.*

- Using "loaded" language—words that trigger highly emotional responses: *This building project is a stinking cesspool of corruption, and the politicians are in it up to their necks.*

- Holding the high ground—suggesting that persons with opposing views have inferior values: *It is irresponsible and immoral to support the incumbent for re-election.*

- The snob appeal—appealing to readers' desires to fit in: *You should join the boycott—everybody else is joining.*

- Using hyperbole—exaggerating: *The budget over-runs are sky-high and if we don't reign in the spending, they'll head out of orbit.*

Write Now (11)

Work in groups to connect the statement to the error.

A. The ad hominem attack

B. Using "loaded" language

C. Holding the high ground

D. The snob appeal

E. Using hyperbole

1. Everybody skips classes now and then—it's normal.
2. Unwashed and ignorant immigrants have always burdened our shores.
3. People who support abortion rights are selfish and anti-children.
4. Media violence is rotting the brains of our youth.
5. Many naïve solutions have been proposed, but the only effective response would be to fire the manager.

Write Now (12)

As a class, review the arguments presented by Nader, Suprynowicz, and Thompson. Use evidence from the essays to support your answers to these questions:

Which authors display credibility?
Which authors display dynamism?
Which authors display integrity?
Which authors use emotional arguments?

Pause from the group discussion to summarize your opinion of each author, based on the essay he or she wrote.

Nader: _____

Syprynowicz: _____

Thompson: _____

Finally, discuss this question:
To what extent is your opinion of each author affected by your agreement or disagreement with his/her position?

Summing Up

1. What kind of writing is an "argument"?

   _____

2. An argument can change readers in terms of their beliefs, attitudes, values, and behaviors. Define these four dimensions:

   beliefs _____

   attitudes _____

   values _____

   behaviors _____

3. Make four statements about this issue: "taking a position."

   a statement of fact _____

   a statement of value _____

   a statement of policy _____

   a statement of conjecture _____

Second Thoughts

Review the poster that opened this chapter; then think about or discuss these points:

1. What is a statement of fact suggested by this poster? a statement of value? a statement of policy? a statement of conjecture?

2. What rational or emotional appeals does the artist use?

3. Do you agree or disagree that "the fate of the planet is your fate"? Explain your position.

4. If you were to turn this poster into an essay, how could you organize the argument?

   Based on what you learned in this chapter about taking a position, how has your reaction to the poster changed? Write your thoughts in the *Responses* section of your journal.

4. Consider the three strategies for organizing an analysis presented in this chapter: problem-solution, cause and effect, and point-counterpoint. Underline the strategy that you tend to use most often. Why do you tend to use it?

_____

_____

5. Circle the strategy you find most difficult. What is one thing you can do to take greater advantage of this strategy when you argue a position?

_____

_____

6. As a result of completing this chapter, what change can you make in your writing to become a more persuasive writer? Write your response in the *Habits for Life* section of your journal.

Write Now: Composing an Essay That Takes a Position

Select a topic from the issues you worked with in Write Now (1), (4), (6), (8), and (10). Write an essay in which you take a position on the issue. To begin, identify your readers as primarily receptive, unreceptive, or neutral. Plan your purpose with those readers in mind. Use one or more outlining strategies presented in this chapter. Decide on the format for your draft: problem-solution, cause and effect, point-counterpoint, a combination of these formats, or some other format. Share your draft with readers to see whether the essay has the effect that you intend. Use their feedback to strengthen your argument. Use both the Writing Checklist and the Essay Scoring Guide from Chapter 8 to help you revise. Prepare a final copy of the essay.

382 | Taking a Position

Avoiding Weak and Useless Words

The best ideas will fail to persuade if they are presented in weak language. You especially want to avoid:

1. clichés

2. slang

3. jargon

4. vague words

5. needless words

Clichés are stale, overused expressions. The first time you hear them they are clever, but repetition causes them to lose their special charm. Clichés get their name from a French word meaning "stereotype," which is a set way of thinking about an idea. Examples include:

It's a long story but, *in a nutshell,* we lost everything.

I know I'll get the job—*it's in the bag.*

Calm down and don't *lose your head.*

The river should be cleaned up because it *stinks to high heaven.*

That chest I bought at the auction *isn't worth a sack of potatoes.*

Slang is casual, informal speech. It does not transfer favorably to writing because it usually is vague, quickly becomes dated, and may not be familiar to many readers. Examples include:

High-top sneakers were *in* last year, but now they're *out.*

Look at those Wall Street *wannabes* in their polyester suits and clip-on ties.

Cisco's *cool*—he's *my main man.*

The manager told me that waitresses make good tips here, but that was *bull.*

I *flipped out* at the landlord when he told me he was *jacking up* the rent.

Jargon is the specialized language shared by members of a group or profession. Jargon is a shorthand way of saying things that is often only intelligible to insiders. Anyone outside the group or profession may not know what it means. Examples include:

The *NLRA* board is involved in the strike negotiations.

An *integrative, contextual approach* to drug treatment works better than an *externally structured focus on pathologies.*

Nobody caught the *typos* before the issue was *sent to bed.*

The *EMD* contract must be funded with *RDT and E3600* funds.

The judge ruled against the *plaintiff's dispositive motion to dismiss.*

Vague words are words that are not specific, precise, or clear. It is not wrong to use vague words, but other words will make your writing far more interesting. Examples include:

The movie was *good.*

The truck started up and *went away.*

The *whole thing* was *special.*

That *man* was *big.*

I have *a lot of stuff* growing in my backyard.

Needless words are words that add no value. They would not be missed if you cut them out or substituted shorter phrases. Examples include:

My point is, we need to work together on this project.

In order to buy a cup of coffee, you have to order food, too.

It is not a good idea, *if you know what I mean.*

I think the future will be better.

I received a *free* gift with my purchase.

Exercise

Put a line through the clichés, the slang, the jargon, and the vague and needless words in the following essay. Select three sentences and rewrite them using words that offer more precise detail and originality.

Recently I read this op-ed piece in the local rag that really got my goat. A Generation-Xer was griping about the fact that women were putting off motherhood until they were in their thirties or—Lord preserve us—their forties. She thinks this is a bum deal for kids because older moms don't have the get-up-and-go that younger moms do. Maybe she has a point there, but listen to this. What really freaks her out is that older moms have lost their looks! For real! That was her main beef! Like we don't have bigger things to worry about than kids being raised by wrinklebags?

Let me tell you. My mom was forty-seven when I was born. Sure, she was a gray-haired fatso in a housedress, but she was, like, awesome. I would not replace her for a million bucks.

The fact is, your mom is your mom. Even if she's not drop-dead gorgeous, and even if she is a little low in the energy department, you love her. The chick who wrote that article needs to get her head screwed on straight.

Sentence Revision #1 _____

_____

_____

_____

_____

Sentence Revision #2 _____

_____

_____

_____

_____

Sentence Revision #3 _____

_____

_____

_____

_____

The Great Cities Have Lost Their Night Skies

By P. N. J. Haworth

Check out the International Dark-Sky Association at www.darksky.org

You can see something very unusual in downtown Tuscon, Arizona, at night: a starry sky. Above most cities of the world, the stars are barely visible. The reason Tuscon is different is that it has adopted policies that reduce the amount of light headed into the sky.

Tuscon is home to the International Dark-Sky Association (IDA), founded in 1988 with the goal of reducing light pollution and other environmental factors (such as space debris) that limit the view of the universe from earth. The association produces newsletters, handouts, slide shows, and information sheets to help communities organize for more efficient and less obtrusive outdoor lighting.

Information Sheet 119 was first published in the Toronto Globe and Mail *and is reprinted here. It is followed by an excerpt from Information Sheet 139, written by an IDA member from New Mexico who has been active in the campaign for lighting ordinances. As you read, notice how the two authors take the same position on light pollution but use very different styles of argument.*

"When did the stars disappear from our cities?" I asked my parents. It was something I had long meant to inquire of them. They were in town for a visit, so I asked. It took some time to get them to grasp what I was after. The stars have not disappeared, I know. However, to the dwellers of the great cities of the world they may as well have. We have blotted them out. Our incandescents, our fluorescents, and our neons have swiped them from the skies. Only the very brightest, or closest stars can spur their light to us through the glare of our electrical glow. The Dippers survive, barely. Orion's belt, the North Star, and a smidgen more. They are our last touch of the celestial. They are mighty enough in their power to reach us, but paltry in numbers compared to what is out there.

Well, my father thought some on my question, and then pronounced: fifty years. Between fifty and forty years. He remembered the city lights of his youth. You would walk down a street from circle of street lamp through the inky dark to the next street lamp. The street lamps were markers of your way, hardly illuminators. If you were to step off the common road, into a park say, the pitch black awaited you. Maybe on a moonlit night you might dare to pick your way over hill and dale

What happened 40 to 50 years ago?

without becoming lost and panicked by sudden inclines, water at your feet, and branches snapping at your eyes. I gather the effects of city light were somber; so it would seem to our eyes today. And yet above you were the heavens.

Don't you think it pitiable? Either you're listening to someone fresh from their latest two week cottage rehabilitation, or the very same words are coming out of your own mouth, "My God it was so amazing to see the stars!" Not that it was amazing to get out of the city to see the elk or the bear or wolverine, but the stars. Perhaps we might have counted on banishing the wildlife from our lives in the name of safety, and even efficiency. Had we counted on losing the heavens as well? I myself was painting a cottage this last summer, and when the elderly folks were fast asleep snug in their beds I would steal down to the lips of the lake, cast off my shorts and swim out into the wild dark. Above me for the first time I saw the great dome of the heavens. Not just the shimmer of the many millions, not merely the glaze of our galaxy dusted across those spikes of light, but the shape of it all, rounded to my eye, enveloping me. More sky than that daily fare from sun up to sunset. Here is eternity.

Eternity is my point. For some forty, fifty odd years, for the first time ever in human history, the great cities of the world are cut off from the wonder of the night sky. From the beginning of human consciousness it has been at once the inspiration of the human soul to break beyond the bounds of this gritty existence, and the majestic beacon to warn us that human affairs are light fare, hardly worth the tears, under the canopy of the cosmos. Take that away and what have you got?

I'll tell you. Step outside from a frantic evening of friends, maybe some gorgeous laughs, maybe some regrets of misspeech that caused pain, maybe some tug of fear at one's inadequacies keeping up in this game of our economic existence, and perhaps even the enticement of someone's eyes glistening in interest. On the threshold of the farewells we feel the night air swarm around us on the way to the car. Look up, and all we see is the weather. Clear or cloudy. Rain or wind or both. Tomorrow should be nice. Nice is nice. And as we wend homewards we are robbed of the shock of the stars. Our city sky assures us that city life is where it's at. We doubt not that what took place at the gathering was important. Status, money, fame, and friend and family all march merrily

What does it mean to be "robbed of the shock of the stars"?

along under the soothing lid of the starless sky.

I'll say it again. They, the star spangled skies, tell the two things of life. Our travail here is fantastically minor. They laugh at the vanity of our struggle for power and wealth. The greatest monarchs and the lowliest peasants stared up to the stars and felt what they truly were: equals in affliction, equals in glory. Even time is shattered by these glimmers, millions of years in arriving. Modern astronomy had an astonishing announcement for us. The light we see may well have travelled towards us before there was even human life on Earth. The light that starts to us now may not find us or our planet when it passes by. The sense of space atomizes us. We are a spit in the wind.

And then the thoughts rebound upon themselves and the ecstasy and joy of life and consciousness stir us to feelings of gratitude and generosity: to be alive. Naked we are, in a naked heavens of white lights set upon a thick black void. Naked yet undeniable. Scrabbling out our existence, we can yet aspire to this sense of infinity.

Who would have it any other way?

So now, as we make our way cut off from this experience of our ancestors when they gazed across the universe, lo, religion has shrunk to a sideshow. A materialistic society has spread its grasp. Its gospel is the here and now. Buy and be happy. So much now contrives to keep our eye on the bottom line. Television is obsessed by merchandise. It has made our world still smaller: not just in speed of transmitting information, but in our vision of humankind's scope. We know information, facts, all kinds of the stuff, but little knowledge or wisdom. Our stars, the ones we follow, they live in Hollywood. You've heard all this before.

And then away from our civilisation for two of the fifty-two weeks, sitting out among the stars, our eyes wincing from the cataclysm of them, our souls shied by the import of them, we glance up quickly, mention their beauty, and resume our conversation of the whatnot.

What is the meaning here of the word "naked"?

What happens when you see the stars only when you are on vacation?

Why Should a City Government Be Concerned About Light Pollution?

By John Gilkison

Light pollution represents a waste of a magnitude that almost no home-owner would allow inside their homes. Interior lights bounce off of all the room's surfaces, providing for good general illumination. Only small amounts of light will escape out of the windows. How strange it is, then, that when we attempt to light the outdoors, we often carelessly allow a large percentage of light to escape unused.

With our older outdoor lighting, we often see up to 50% or more of the light going directly up into the sky or at such shallow angles that it is not useful. Like a driver driving toward the light of the setting sun, such unshielded lighting creates glare and diminishes visibility. In engineering terms, this is known as a poor "coefficient of utilization."

Our tolerance of wasted light means most lighting fixtures are oversized by at least a third in wattage. Many light sources are of an older, less efficient type, which means that opportunities often exist to significantly reduce energy consumption by switching to a newer, more efficient type of light source in a fixture with good control of the light output and proper shielding. Using $10 a year as the average cost for outdoor lighting per person, from $3 to $5 is being wasted. Collectively, for a municipality with a population of 100,000, from $300,000 to $500,000 is being lost to the sky every year.

This results in not only the loss of the stars, but an avoidable economic loss to the community as well. Uncontrolled lighting often creates a garish landscape, with a confusing tangle of lights that shine into citizens' eyes rather than onto the ground, where it is needed. The term for this obtrusive light is "ceiling glare," and we are paying extra for it, each and every night the fixture is in use. We can do better!

This inability to see well in our already over-lit nightscapes due to glare leads to ever more lighting. The eye is designed to function effectively both day and night. But in our cities, our eyes have to run the gauntlet from lit areas that are intensely illuminated to areas of dark shadows caused by those glary lights. The eye will naturally adjust to the brightest portion of a given scene, often leaving quite adequately lit areas nearby looking dark.

In what ways are older lights inefficient?

What does the $300,000 to $500,000 figure represent?

Glare and over illumination are thus counterproductive. The more light we use in one area, the more we need everywhere else because the iris in the eye stops down, letting less light in. Adjacent areas (including streets) with formerly adequate illumination now look relatively dim as we ratchet up the light levels in one particular location. Interestingly, a lower illumination level provided by a white light source in a fully-shielded fixture would allow the eye to naturally adapt to the lower light level, and we could adequately illuminate parking lots with less than one footcandle of illumination.

A disturbing new trend seen in some national chains of convenience stores and gas stations has been to ratchet up the light level under the canopy to very high levels (10,000 times as much illumination as provided by a full moon!) in an effort to attract customers and provide "a safer, more secure" environment for their employees. For their patronage, customers now can have the delightful experience of trying to blindly navigate their vehicle for a few seconds onto the much darker streets while their eyes readapt. No one wins these escalating "light wars" and our aesthetic environment deteriorates by the year. Rather than improve safety, these "ratcheteers" have in fact compromised safety.

It is time to halt this unnecessary and counterproductive escalation in lighting that affects us all whether we own the lighting system or just live near it. After all, it's not rocket science—it's good lighting science. Outdoor lighting should be regulated for the public good, just like signs, billboards, and noise pollution are.

What recent trend has escalated the problem of light pollution?

THINK AND RESPOND

1. Haworth describes several effects on the human spirit caused by the disappearance of the stars over cities. Describe the effect on you.

   _____

   _____

2. What kind of readers (receptive, unreceptive, or neutral) do you think Haworth is addressing and what kind of change do you think he hopes to make in them?

   _____

   _____

3. Haworth's essay contains many statements of value. Copy one of them.

   _____

   _____

4. Gilkison uses a problem-solution format. How does he define the problem, and what solution does he propose?

   _____

   _____

5. What kind of readers (receptive, unreceptive, or neutral) do you think Gilkison is addressing and what kind of change do you think he hopes to make in them?

   _____

   _____

6. How would you compare the styles of the two authors?

   _____

   _____

7. Provide synonyms or definitions for these words from the essasys, and add at least two of them to the *Words Worth Remembering* section of your journal:

    smidgeon _____

    celestial _____

    pitiable _____

    gritty _____

    travail _____

    scrabbling _____

    cataclysm _____

    whatnot _____

    myopia _____

    ratchet _____

8. If you liked this reading, make a record of it in the *Readings Worth Remembering* section.

COMPARING VIEWS

Do you ever look at the stars? How important are they? Do you agree or disagree that light can be a form of pollution? After discussing this topic with others, continue to explore it on your own, in your journal—if you are intrigued by this topic. You may be able to use material from the discussion and your journal in a future writing activity.

APPLIED WRITING

Haworth describes the starlit sky as humbling and inspiring. In what ways has nature been humbling and inspiring to you? Or do you live a "natureless" existence? Write an essay taking a position on the role of nature in modern life. Use the techniques in this chapter to explore your argument. You may choose to model your draft on the style and form of argument of either Haworth or Gilkison. Use both the Writing Checklist and the Essay Scoring Guide from Chapter 8 to help you revise. Prepare a final copy of the essay.

UNIT 4

EXPANDING YOUR WRITING SKILLS

Chapter 15	**Writing the Research Paper**
Chapter 16	**Developing Habits for Life**

In this unit, you will learn how essay skills are applied in a key form of academic writing and in many other aspects of everyday life. Goals of the unit are to help you:

- Understand the function and form of the research paper.

- Familiarize yourself with key information sources.

- Develop and follow a plan for completing a research paper.

- Continue to review and apply grammar principles.

- Learn habits that can help you continue to learn on your own.

- Set new writing-related goals.

Activities in Chapter 15 will guide you through the process of writing a research paper, which is similar to but more substantial than writing an essay. Activities in Chapter 16 have you practice a variety of self-teaching techniques. They also direct you to look back at the writing you have done over the past few months, and to look forward to what you hope to accomplish with writing in the coming months and years.

The Endurance at Night
Frank Hurley

CHAPTER 15

Writing the Research Paper

These are the **key ideas** of this chapter:

- A research paper is a large project that requires an organized approach.

- To do research, you need to know where to look and how to focus your search.

- Documentation of sources is critical because it gives proper credit and it leads other researchers to the sources you found useful.

Picturing Meaning

Examine the photograph on the opposite page; then think about or discuss these questions:

1. What is odd about what you see in this photograph?

_____

_____

2. What questions do you have about it?

_____

_____

3. Where could you find the answers?

_____

_____

In the *Responses* section of your journal, write down your thoughts about this photograph.

Write Now (1)

Think of an episode in history where people got themselves into a difficult situation. How did they get into the jam, and how did they get out of it? What does the incident reveal about human nature and human abilities? Write down what you know about the incident. Also write a list of questions about the incident that you would be interested in having answered. Keep this work because you may use it in a later activity.

Understanding the Scope of the Project

The essay and the research paper are similar, but they have several key differences. The typical essay tends to be much shorter than the typical research paper. The essay contains one or more opinions supported by some facts, while the research paper presents many facts, from a variety of sources, as evidence in support of one major opinion. In a research paper, that opinion is called the thesis. As you may recall from Chapter 2, a thesis is the main idea of a paper that expresses a claim. A research paper, therefore, is often referred to as a **thesis paper.**

The thesis is an opinion, but it must be an opinion that can be supported with evidence. An example of a thesis is:

Children who learn to read at ages four and five do not grow up to be better readers than children who learn to read at ages six and seven.

Another example is:

Shakespeare's play *Romeo and Juliet* is 400 years old, but it remains relevant.

The thesis is your point of view, but in a research paper you must present it straightforwardly and without emotion. You must discuss it objectively and defend it with evidence. You must carefully select and organize your evidence so that readers are persuaded to agree with your thesis. In these ways, writing a research paper involves the same techniques as writing a persuasive essay (see Chapter 14 for more about writing persuasively).

When you write a research paper, you must document the sources of your evidence in the paper itself. You also must list your sources at the end of the paper. Careful documenting is important because when you write a research paper, you join the academic world's ongoing discussion of ideas. Part of the way you convince readers that your thesis is correct is by showing that you have used believable sources that others can check to confirm your findings. Furthermore, some readers may use your research as a starting point for their own research. If so, they will want to know your sources so they can use them also.

If it takes you a week to write an essay of three to five pages, you probably will need at least two weeks to write a research paper of the same length. If you are like most people, you need at least a month to write a research paper of ten pages or longer. Having a plan that divides the work into parts makes the task manageable. It also helps prevent you from leaving too much to do until right before your deadline. Here is a sample plan for a research paper that you have four weeks to complete:

TASK	COMPLETED BY
Receive the assignment	
Get organized	
Focus on a general topic	
Research and read up on that topic	
Narrow the topic to one question	End of first week
Conduct additional research	
Develop a thesis	
Outline the paper	End of second week
Draft the paper	
Do final research	End of third week
Revise the paper	
Prepare documentation in appropriate form	
Proof final draft	
Prepare final copy	
Turn in paper	End of fourth week

If you will do your note taking and writing on a word processor, create a separate, new folder for your research paper. Save each file related to that paper into that new folder.

One of the first steps on the timeline is to get organized. This is simple to do but essential. Get a notebook and folder with pockets for this project. You also may want to purchase index cards for note taking (some people find it easier to draft from note cards than from notes in a notebook). Make a time line and keep it in your folder.

Write Now (2)

Find out from your instructor the required length of your research paper and the time frame you have for completing it. In small groups, review the plan below and estimate when you should have each step accomplished. You may choose to group the tasks into three or four deadlines, as was done with the example on the previous page.

TASK	COMPLETED BY
Receive the assignment	
Get organized	
Focus on a general topic	
Research and read up on that topic	
Narrow the topic to one question	
Conduct additional research	
Develop a thesis	
Outline the paper	
Draft the paper	
Do final research	
Revise the paper	
Prepare documentation in appropriate form	
Proof final draft	
Prepare final copy	
Turn in paper	

After completing the time line, discuss these questions:

- Which steps in the process will take the most time?

- On average, how many hours per day will you have to work?

- What should you do if you fall behind schedule?

Knowing Where to Find Information

Essays and research papers require the same writing skills, but research papers require you to apply information-finding skills as well. A tremendous amount of information already exists on practically any topic you choose to research, but the challenge is finding it. Here are three important sources of information:

1. Libraries

2. The Internet

3. Unpublished sources

Libraries. Libraries are one of the great inventions of civilization. These spaces contain vast holdings of books, other print materials, and information in nonprint media, such as CD-ROM, microfiche, and video—all available for looking at or borrowing if you have a library card (which is usually free). Your educational institution has a library, and your community probably does also. In addition, medical centers, academic research centers, historical societies, law firms, large corporations, and trade associations have libraries that may be open to the public. Libraries that do not have what you need usually can obtain it for you from another library (this is called an interlibrary loan). They also have another treasure: real, live human beings whose job is to help you find the answers to your research questions. Some libraries have staff available twenty-four hours a day, in person or by phone, to guide you to the appropriate sources or simply to help you track down that one last fact you need.

The Internet. The worldwide network of computers known as the Internet contains a huge amount of new and historical information, and the content increases every day at an astounding rate. Magazines, newspapers, entire books, indexes, graphics, movies, and music are just some of the material available on the Internet. In addition to its lode of source materials, the Internet can put you directly in touch with experts working in various fields, and it can lead you to online discussion forums having to do with your subject. Many research sites are accessible through the Internet, but the most well traveled avenues are on the linked pages of the World Wide Web. The Web is a gold mine, but it is also a land mine. It is loaded with opinion, propaganda, and misleading information from individuals who may not necessarily have any authority on their subjects. Publishers evaluate material before printing it, and librarians screen material before putting it on their shelves, but much of what is on the Internet has not been judged for its value by anyone. When using the Internet, therefore, you must be especially cautious in evaluating your sources.

Unpublished material. Miscellaneous documents—letters, diaries, copies of speeches, locally distributed reports, press releases, transcripts of television or radio programs, billboards, posters, ledger books, and an infinite number of other kinds of papers—are valuable to the researcher. The original materials that you find are called **primary sources**. The program from a play is a primary source, while a review of the play is a secondary source because it is an interpretation of the play and not from the event itself. Original material that you generate yourself—from personal interviews, experiments, surveys, and eyewitness observations— is called **primary research**. Primary sources can be hard to find, and primary research can be time-consuming, but both are valuable because they present direct evidence, unfiltered by outside opinion.

Write Now (3)

Take the quiz *Are You A Savvy Researcher?*, which appears in Figure 15–1. After completing the quiz, discuss your answers with classmates. How can you strengthen your research skills? Which classmates would be good mentors in this area?

Figure 15–1: Are You a Savvy Researcher?

Part 1. How strong are your library research skills? Instructions: Circle *yes* or *no* for each question.		
1. Do you know how books are organized on library shelves?	Yes	No
2. Have you ever asked a librarian for help?	Yes	No
3. Have you ever phoned a reference librarian to find the answer to a question?	Yes	No
4. Have you ever used a computerized library catalog system?	Yes	No
5. Have you ever placed a book on reserve?	Yes	No
6. Have you ever used the interlibrary loan system?	Yes	No
7. Are you familiar with the library's loan policies on reference materials?	Yes	No

8. Have you ever used a computerized database at a library for research?   Yes   No

9. Do you know how to gain access to your library's collection of primary materials?   Yes   No

10. Have you ever taken an official tour of a library or taken a course on using the library?   Yes   No

Part 2. How strong are your Internet research skills?
Instructions: Circle *yes* or *no* for each question.

1. Can you name at least three search engines?   Yes   No

2. Do you know how to bookmark?   Yes   No

3. Do you know how to organize your bookmarks into folders?   Yes   No

4. Do you know how to move back and forward in a search?   Yes   No

5. Have you ever visited an online writing center for research advice?   Yes   No

6. Have you ever visited an online magazine, journal, or newspaper?   Yes   No

7. Have you ever used an online encyclopedia?   Yes   No

8. Have you ever visited the Library of Congress Web site?   Yes   No

9. Have you ever visited the Gutenberg Project or the Bartleby Project (full texts of classic works)?   Yes   No

10. Have you ever taken a guided tour of the Internet or taken a course on using the Internet?   Yes   No

Part 3. How familiar are you with different resources?
Instructions: Place a checkmark next to each resource you have ever used for a research project.

1. ____ *Library of Congress Subject Headings* (an official guide used by indexes to organize their materials—it can be a useful starting point to find out what key words to use in your search through other sources)

2. ____ *Books in Print* (a listing of books available in the United States)

3. ____ *Readers Guide to Periodical Literature* (an index of magazine and journal articles listed alphabetically by topic, author, and media)

4. ____ *Facts on File* (summaries of news stories reported in the national press)

5. ____ Encyclopedias (compendiums of information on a broad range of subjects, arranged alphabetically; some encyclopedias cover a range of subjects within a specialized topic)

6. ____ Microfiche collections (materials, such as old magazines and newspapers, preserved on microfilm that can be read using special microfiche machines)

7. ____ Special indexes (listings of magazine and journal article titles that relate to the index's topic)

8. ____ Abstracts (summaries of academic papers and published articles)

9. ____ Atlases (collects of maps, tables, or charts)

10. ____ Unpublished materials (diaries, letters, etc.)

Scoring the Quiz: If you scored 7 or more points in each section, your research skills are strong enough for you to be a research mentor to other students (a mentor is a friendly advisor and teacher). If you scored 4 or more points in each section, you have a good base of research skills. Use your next research paper assignment to improve these skills. If you scored fewer than 3 points in each section, find yourself a research mentor!

Narrowing a Topic

After getting organized, the next step in writing a research paper is to identify a topic. Usually when you write a research paper, the general topic has been assigned to you. For example, in a class on world religions, the general topic for student research papers almost certainly will be religion or some **subtopic** (topic within a topic) of religion. Fifteen to twenty pages may seem like a lot to write, but for a huge topic such as Islam or Christianity, it is not much at all. Your task is to narrow the topic, again and again, until you identify one piece of it that meets these three criteria:

You can research it within your timeframe.

You can explore it thoroughly within your page limit.

It interests you.

One way to narrow a topic is to make a cluster with your general topic in the center circle. In circles connected to the main circle, write subtopics. In circles connected to each subtopic, write sub-subtopics. Keep exploring until the paper is covered with discrete, specific ideas. Here is an example of a cluster that only begins to explore the many subtopics related to the topic of the stock market:

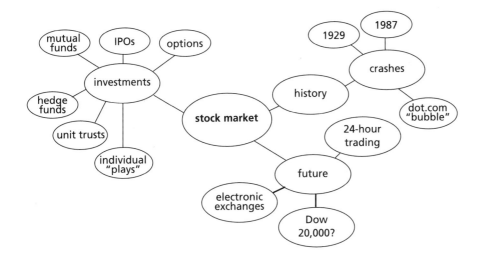

Another method for narrowing a topic is to use the Topic Exploration Outline which appears in Figure 15-2. Study the example of the outline (Figure 15-3) to see how it was used to think through tap dance as a possible research paper topic. Then use the outline to explore your own topic.

Figure 15–2: Topic Exploration Outline
Photocopy this form before using.

Possible topic for your paper

Your connection to the topic or reason for being interested in it

What you know about it	What you would like to find out

Other words, phrases, and names associated with your topic

Where you could find more answers (specific people, places, & materials)

Figure 15–3: Example Topic Exploration Outline

Possible topic for your paper:
tap dance

Your connection to the topic or reason for being interested in it:
taking a tap exercise class

What you know about it	What you would like to find out
many kinds of tapping jazz tap Irish step dancing Appalachian clogging South African gum boot black fraternity and sorority stepping routines flamenco	Who were the very first tappers? Why does tap go in and out of popularity? How beneficial is tap as a form of exercise? How do the different tap cultures (African, African American, Irish, Appalachian, etc.) interact? Is there an international language of tap? How much of tap is choreographed, how much is improvised? Who are the greatest tappers of all time?

Other words, phrases, and names associated with your topic
Bo Jangles, Shirley Temple, Damien Glover, Riverdance, the "shim sham"

Where you could find more answers (specific people, places, & materials)
my tap instructor an encyclopedia on tap or a "history of tap" book university dance programs movies and videos

Once you have decided on the specific topic for your paper, phrase it as a question and write it in large letters on the first page of your notebook. Use it to direct your research. Here is an example of a research question stemming from the previously shown cluster of the stock market:

How does an electronic exchange differ from live trading?

Write Now (4)

Move into pairs. For each general topic listed below, think of a subtopic. Next, think of a subtopic of that subtopic. An example has been provided. Finally, phrase the focused topic as a research question.

1. Topic: Democracy

    Subtopic: *democracies in Africa*

    Subtopic of that subtopic: *democracy in Namibia*

    Focused research question: *Is democracy taking hold in Namibia?*

2. Topic: Endangered species

    Subtopic: _____

    Subtopic of that subtopic: _____

    Focused research question: _____

    _____

3. Topic: Astronomy

    Subtopic: _____

    Subtopic of that subtopic: _____

    Focused research question: _____

    _____

4. Topic: Dinosaurs

    Subtopic: _____

    Subtopic of that subtopic: _____

    Focused research question: _____

    _____

5. Topic: Photography

    Subtopic: _____

    Subtopic of that subtopic: _____

    Focused research question: _____

    _____

Write Now (5)

Continue working with your partner from Write Now (4). Select one of the topics from that activity and draw a cluster to generate a dozen or more subtopics. Finally, pick one subtopic that interests you and phrase it in the form of a research question. Keep this work because you may use it in a later activity.

Write Now (6)

In small groups, select a topic to explore for a research paper. The topic could be:

a historical moment; for example, the era of the conquistadors
a place; for example, the Bermuda Triangle
a person; for example, the author Chenua Achebe
a human activity; for example, in vitro reproduction
a natural phenomenon; for example, a solar eclipse

Discuss the topic among yourselves, and scan any resources you have in the classroom (such as the Internet or an encyclopedia). Take notes on the Topic Exploration Outline (Figure 15–2). Put a star next to the one question that most interests you. Keep this work because you may use it in a later activity.

If you explore your topic using the Internet, conduct searches using key words from your Topic Exploration Outline. Bookmark any useful pages, and organize those bookmarks together on your bookmark pulldown menu.

Conducting the Research

When you have a workable topic, framed as a question, take your cluster or topic exploration outline with you to the library to do some initial, exploratory research. Do a search in the library's catalog using key words. These are specific words having to do with your topic that you generated when brainstorming. In your notebook, write down the location information of all the relevant materials you find (start a section in the back of your notebook called "Resources" for this information). If your library has a computerized catalog system, you can easily print out location information of relevant sources. By taking these steps, it will be easier to find these resources later. After doing your own search, go to a librarian, show him or her what you have found, and ask for help finding additional resources that address your research question. Then check out the most interesting or relevant books or periodicals and scan through them.

This initial search may lead you to modify your research question. You may discover that there is not enough information to be found on your original question, so that you have to broaden the question or find a new angle. Or, you may find too much information, in which case you must make the question more specific. Sometimes your research will lead you to an even more interesting question.

When you are comfortable with your research question, begin an outline of your topic. The traditional outline form (using Roman numerals, letters, and numbers) is well suited to the research paper. Here is the start of an outline for a research paper on the U.S. merchant marine:

Research Question: How was Morse code used by the U.S. merchant marine in WWII?

    I. Brief history of Morse code
   II. Establishment of a worldwide network of radio stations
  III. Role of merchant marine
  IV. How Morse code helped merchant marine fulfill its role

A Research Paper Outline appears in Figure 15-4. Study the form to see how it was used to make a detailed outline for researching the role of Morse code in the merchant marine during World War II.

When researching on the Web, evaluate each source. Who is the author? What is the institution? Is the author presenting findings or opinions? Is the material current? Is the site approved by any credentialing organizations?

Figure 15-4: Research Paper Outline

Photocopy this form before using.

Research Question:
Short Outline

I. _____

II. _____

III. _____

IV. _____

Extended Outline

Thesis Statement: _____

I. _____

    A. _____

        1. _____

        2. _____

        3. _____

    B. _____

        1. _____

        2. _____

        3. _____

    C. _____

        1. _____

        2. _____

        3. _____

Note: Continue your outline in this format on another sheet of paper.

Figure 15-5: Example Research Paper Outline

Research Question: How was Morse code used by the U.S. merchant marine in WWII?

Short Outline

I.   Brief history of Morse code

II. Establishment of worldwide network of radio stations

III. Role of merchant marine in war

IV. How Morse code helped merchant marine fulfill its role

Thesis Statement: Morse code was an indispensible form of communication for the U.S. merchant marine in World War II.

Extended Outline

I.   Brief history of Morse code
   - A. Development of electricity
   - B. Development of a code by Samuel F. B. Morse
   - C. Demonstration by Marconi of wireless transmission
   - D. Installation of radio transmitters & receivers on commercial merchant ships

II. Establishment of a worldwide network of radio stations
   - A. Privately owned commercial ships (M.M.) outfitted with Morse-code- based radio communications equipment
   - B. Operating under a common set of rules

III. Role of the U.S. merchant marine in war
   - A. Carried food and fuel supplies for the Allied forces
   - B. Delivered war material and personnel to the war fronts
   - C. Supported amphibious landings in all theaters of war

IV. How Morse code helped merchant marine fulfill its role
   - A. Morse was the primary (or sole) communications method
     1. To and from merchant and naval ships at sea
     2. Between ships at sea and control organizations on shore
   - B. Morse was reliable
     1. Signals could transmit longer distances than voice
     2. Less susceptible to distortion and interference than voice
   - C. Morse was a universal code
     1. Used by merchant mariners and naval vessels of many nations
     2. Ensured effective coordination of complex activities

After you have made your initial outline, look at your list of resources. Go first to the ones that appear likely to provide what you need: background information that readers will need to understand the question, as well as information that will answer the question. Also, go to the best resources. These are the ones that have the most authority on the subject and that offer the most current analyses. Use the table of contents and index of any material you are scanning to find the relevant pages.

Create a **bibliography** in your notebook to record the specific resources from which you take notes. Write down the author, title, publisher, publisher location, and date of publication of each resource you use. For example:

Bibliography
Beverly Hungry Wolf
Daughters of the Buffalo Women: Maintaining the Tribal Faith
Canadian Caboose Press, Skookumchuck, B.C., Canada, 1996

To take notes, give each separate idea a heading. Then, summarize in your own words, or paraphrase, the main ideas. When copying word-for-word (even short phrases), use quotation marks so that you later remember that it is a direct quotation. Double-check for accuracy when copying direct quotations. After each set of notes, record the author and page. Here are some notes taken from the book in the bibliography example above:

Indian boarding school—"love-hate experience" for many Indians—in 1890s a voluntary system—author's grandmother first in family to go. By 1920s a requirement—author's mother forced to attend. Government workers, priests searched villages for children. Roman Catholic and Anglican churches competed for the children "whom they considered morally doomed unless they were given the severe indoctrination that was expected to turn them from ordinary Indians into 'civilized' and God-fearing wards of the government." Hungry Wolf, p. 24.

The reason that you must carefully document your notes is because you must give credit to your sources in your final paper. If you do not— if by mistake or on purpose you make use of the unique ideas and phrases of others without mentioning your source—then you are stealing. This kind of stealing is called **plagiarism**, and the penalty for plagiarism is often a failing grade or expulsion.

On the other hand, you do not need to credit the sources of information that is **common knowledge.** Common knowledge is information you can find from several sources; for example, it is common knowledge that President John Kennedy was assassinated on November 22, 1963, while in an open convertible that was part of a parade motorcade through Dallas, Texas. If you mention these facts in a research paper, you do not need to give credit to a source. If, however, you make use of an author's distinct interpretation of that day's events, you must give credit.

If you take notes on computer, be sure to add quotation marks around any information cut and pasted from sources. Also be sure to record the original location of the information.

If you photocopy materials in order to take notes from them, remember also to photocopy the copyright page, because it contains the reference information you will need. An easy way to take notes with photocopies is simply to use a highlighter to mark the useful information and quotations. Make a brief note of this information and the source in your notebook, such as:

Indian boarding school experiences, Hungry Wolf, pp. 24-42 (see photocopy)

Write Now (7)

Read each research question. Put a checkmark next to each resource that might be useful when researching the question. Put an "X" next to any source that probably would not be useful. Explain why you think a source would be useful or not useful.

1. Research Question: How did Adolph Hitler arrive at his philosophy?

Source	Reasoning
_____ Hitler's book *Mein Kampf*	_____
_____ Web site of a white supremacist	_____
_____ A book by a World War II historian	_____
_____ A novel set in World War II	_____

2. **Research Question: How are children's sleep patterns affected when their parents work night shifts?**

Source	Reasoning
_____ A survey you conduct of parents who work the night shift	_____
_____ The newsletter of an association of early childhood educators	_____
_____ A textbook on sleep habits and research	_____
_____ A research paper evaluating evening and nighttime childcare options	_____

3. **Research Question: Is Minnesota's frog population endangered?**

Source	Reasoning
_____ A zoo worker who specializes in amphibians	_____
_____ The University of Minnesota zoology department	_____
_____ A frog lover's Web site	_____
_____ A state study documenting changes in wetland acreage	_____

Write Now (8)

Working in small groups, select a research question to outline for a research paper. The question may relate to the topic you explored in Write Now (1), (5), or (6), or it may stem from another topic. Use the Research Paper Outline (Figure 15–4). Work together to phrase the question and to create an initial outline (using Roman Numerals I, II, III, IV, and so on). If you can, add extra details to your outline (using A, B, C, 1, 2, 3, and so on). Keep your work because you may use it in a later activity.

Writing the Paper

Begin drafting when you have pulled together enough information to attempt an answer to the research question. Start this work by turning your question into a thesis statement. For example, a research question, "Is gene therapy a cure for disease?," could become this thesis statement:

> Many researchers believe that someday soon gene therapy will be a revolutionary way to treat disease, but its benefits remain unproven.

Then work on your initial outline to flesh it out with additional points and subpoints. Before drafting, stop to consider the structure of a research paper. Just like an essay, the research paper has three important parts:

1. Introduction
2. Body
3. Conclusion

Introduction. The opening paragraph or paragraphs present the purpose of the paper. This introduction contains the thesis statement, which often appears as the last sentence or sentences of the section. The goal in an introduction is to grab readers' attention so that they continue reading to find out how the opening claim is defended.

Body. The body is the longest part of the paper. It contains background evidence that readers will need to understand the thesis. It also presents an analysis of the research that has been conducted. This analysis should be presented in such a way that it builds a strong case of support for the thesis (for more on analyzing, see Chapter 13).

Conclusion. The conclusion restates the thesis, but with some final insights based on the evidence presented. When well written, the conclusion leaves readers convinced that the topic is important and the thesis is correct.

The research paper has one additional section that an essay does not: the **documentation of sources,** with full bibliographic information for each source that you quote from or refer to in your paper. This list is included at the end of the paper.

Use your thesis statement as a guide when writing your introduction. Use the outline as a guide when writing the body. You will discover your conclusion as you write. In this way, drafting a research paper is essentially no different from drafting an essay. It is a bigger project, however, and therefore can be more intimidating. Here are some tips for making the process go smoothly:

- Use the strategy of "divide and conquer." Work on the draft one section at a time.
- Another strategy is to freewrite the entire first draft. Carefully review your outline, then set it aside and write a full draft without stopping. Do not worry about including all the specific facts in this draft or making the words flow beautifully. Your goal is simply to create a framework that you can flesh out in subsequent drafts.
- Do not feel obliged to work through your draft in a strict order from the beginning to the conclusion. Try starting with your

introduction, but skip over the sections that are difficult or that require you to do more research. Go back later to fill them in.

- Familiarize yourself with the documentation style that you will be required to follow in your final paper. (If you are not clear on the requirements, ask your instructor.) Follow those style rules as you draft. This vastly simplifies the revising process. It also ensures that you have properly credited your sources in all places.

- After you have completed your first draft, revisit your thesis. Does your analysis actually lead toward a different conclusion? Revise the thesis as necessary. In fact, be prepared to revise your thesis several times.

- Also review your first draft to see if there are any holes in your analysis. You may need to do additional research to fill in the gaps.

- To ensure that you are writing effectively, check each draft against the Writer's Checklist in Chapter 8.

- When you have a near-final draft, double-check your direct quotations for accuracy.

- Choose a title when you have a final draft and will make no more changes to the thesis. The title of a research paper is usually a phrase that refers to the thesis.

- For the final copy, create the list of documented sources that will go at the end of your paper. Look at your paper side-by-side with the bibliography in your notebook. Put a star next to each resource you actually quoted from or credited. Then type them up in proper order, using proper formatting.

Write Now (9)

Decide on the research question that you will pursue for your paper. The question may relate to the topic you outlined in Write Now (8), or it may have to do with some other topic that you have explored and briefly outlined. Write that research question on a piece of paper, then exchange papers with a partner. Discuss with your partner these questions:

   Is the research question interesting?
   Is it sufficiently narrow?
   Is it sufficiently large?
   How will you conduct your research?
   How will you begin your draft?

Finally, with your partner, turn your research question into a possible thesis statement.

Summing Up

1. How is the research paper similar to, and different from, an essay?

   _____

   _____

2. Define thesis.

   _____

   _____

3. Why is it a good idea to start your research by focusing on one question?

   _____

   _____

4. Name two reasons why it is important to be especially organized when writing a research paper.

   _____

   _____

Second Thoughts

Review the photograph that opened this chapter and then think about or discuss these questions:

1. What general research topics are suggested by this photograph?

2. How could you narrow those topics into specific research questions?

3. Describe how you would research each of those questions.

   Based on what you have learned in this chapter about researching, what do you think of this photograph (and other visual images) as a good starting point for a research paper? Write your thoughts in the *Responses* section of your journal.

5. Briefly describe the main steps in writing a research paper.

   _____

   _____

6. Define plagiarism and explain why it is wrong.

   _____

   _____

7. Name two situations outside of school where you might be called upon to do research or write a research report.

   _____

   _____

8. As a result of reading this chapter, what one change will you make to improve your skills in writing research papers? Write your resolution in the *Habits for Life* section of your journal.

Write Now: Composing the Research Paper

Write a research paper on the thesis statement you developed in Write Now (9). Get page length and deadline requirements from your instructor. Organize for the project by obtaining the necessary materials (such as a notebook) and by preparing a time line. Conduct focused research to gather information. Before drafting, revisit your thesis statement: can you support it from your research? Expand your outline based on the information you have collected. Draft the paper so that it has an introduction, body, and conclusion. Review your draft to make sure that readers can understand the thesis and will be convinced by your analysis that the thesis is correct. Use both the Writing Checklist and the Essay Scoring Guide from Chapter 8 to help you revise. Proof your final draft to make sure you have properly cited and accurately quoted all sources.

Using MLA Documentation Style

Research papers on subjects in the humanities (such as for courses in literature, art, drama, or music) often are required to follow MLA style. This is the style developed by the Modern Language Association.*

To follow MLA style in the body of the paper, provide the author and page number wherever you quote, paraphrase, or summarize from another source. Put this information in parentheses:

> While schooling is a form of cultural reproduction, there is opportunity for change within the education process (Freire 126).

If the author is named in the text, then only the page number is required:

> "I believe this space for change, however small, is always available," says Freire (39).

Underline (or italicize) titles of books, plays, magazines, films, and so on. Put in quotation marks titles of poems, articles, short stories, and other works that appear within larger works. These rules about underlining or using quotation marks apply when naming works in both the body of the paper and in the "Works Cited" section, which is a list of every source that you cite. This list goes on a separate page at the back of the research paper. Entries in the "Works Cited" list go in alphabetical order by the author's last name. If there is no author, the first word of the title is used.

MLA style dictates exactly how to reference all of the possible sources you may use in a research paper, including books, magazines, Web sites, CD-ROMs, videos, and unpublished material. A few sample formats are listed here. For more information, ask at your library for the *MLA Handbook for Writers of Research Papers.* Another useful resource is *The Columbia Guide to Online Style* by Janice R. Walker and Todd Taylor, published by Columbia University Press.

---

* Research papers on subjects in the social sciences (such as for courses in history, sociology, or psychology) often are required to follow APA style, developed by the American Psychological Association. Medicine, mathematics, the branches of science, and other fields each have their own documenting system. Ask at your library for assistance in finding the appropriate style guidelines.

Book with one author

Italics can be used in place of underlining.

A colon separates the city from the publisher and date of publication.

Freire, Paulo. <u>Pedagogy of the Oppressed</u>. New York: Continuum, 1981.

Comma after first author.

Book with two authors

Do not put last name first for the second author.

Freire, Paulo, and Donaldo Macedo. <u>Literacy: Reading the Word and the World</u>. South Hadley: Bergin & Garvey, 1987.

Indent five spaces when reference continues onto another line.

Don't forget the periods.

Use "ed." without the "s" if there is only one editor.

Book with one or more editors

Borgerhoff Mulder, Monique, and Wendy Logsdon, eds. <u>I've Been Gone Far Too Long: Field Trip Fiascoes and Expedition Disasters</u>. Oakland: RDR Books, 1996.

Newspaper article

Use international style for dates.

Chang, Leslie. "Teenage Band Tries to Rock China." <u>Wall Street Journal</u> 21 July 1999, late edition: B1+.

Section and page number—the plus sign indicates that the story continues on other pages.

A work from a collection

Lisker, Roy. "Science as Credo." <u>Suppressed Inventions and Other Discoveries</u>. Ed. Jonathan Eisen. New York: Avery Publishing Group, 1999. pp. 179–185. —— Include page numbers of work.

Journal article

Kossor, Mike. "A Doppler Radio-Direction Finder." <u>QST: Official Journal of the American Radio Relay League</u> 83.6 (1999): 37–40.

Include the volume and issue number (this is volume 83, issue 6).

Magazine article

Vogel, Shawna. "Why We Get Fat." <u>Discover</u> Apr. 1999: 96–99.

Personal interview

Miller, Kate Finn. Personal Interview. 21 Sept. 1999.

Online database

Include date of publication or most recent update.

Electronic Resource Center. April 1998. EMC Corporation. May 2001. <http://www.emcp.com>.

Give the complete Internet address.

include name of sponsoring organization.

Also include the date you accessed the database.

CD-ROM

Covey, Stephen. Lessons in Leadership. CD-ROM. Pasadena: Covey Leadership Center, Inc./EarthLink Networks, 1996.

Formatting Your Paper, MLA Style

Put identifying information in upper left margin.

Indent each paragraph 5 spaces or add an extra line of space between paragraphs.

Use standard 8-1/2" x 11" white paper.

Use 1" margins on all sides.

Dunbar 1

Robert Dunbar

Brooke

Careers in Health

May 4, 2000

New Career Opportunities in Alternative Medicine

After being ignored or disparaged for centuries by the Western medical establishment, alternative therapies have begun to receive widespread public acceptance (The American Medical Association Family Medical Guide 753). In the past decade, millions of people in North America have turned to alternative medical therapies to alleviate pain and other maladies (Trends in Health 166). Physicians also are coming to see alternative therapies as expanding their range of treatment choices for patients (Harvard Health Letter 4). One effect of this trend is the creation of many new career opportunities in health care.

Three alternative approaches that are creating new career paths in the health industry are herbalism, acupuncture, and homeopathy. Herbalism is an ancient art that uses plants for prevention of diseases and for the treatment of pain and illnesses.

Dunbar 2

Barks, leaves, roots, berries, flowers, and seeds form the basis of

hundreds of salves and potions used to treat patients. For example,

aloe vera gel (made from fibers of the aloe plant) is used to treat

sunburn, cuts, and burns (New Choices in Natural Healing 222).

Chamomile, ointments, and tinctures are used for treating a range

of conditions from rashes to indigestion (New Choices in Natural

Healing 58). The ancient Egyptians fed garlic bulbs to their slaves

in the belief that it kept them healthy. Today, garlic is thought to

lower blood pressure and blood cholesterol.

Put your name and page number in every corner 1/2" from top of page.

Exercise

Format the following sources in MLA style.

1. Book
    Title: Using America Online
    Authors: Jean Steinberg and John Stroud
    Publisher: Que Corporation
    Publisher location: Indianapolis, Indiana
    Date: 1994

    _____

    _____

    _____

2. Newpaper article
    Title: Still Exploring the Vast Unknown
    Author: George (Pinky) Nelson
    Newspaper: Star Tribune
    Page: Section B, Page 1
    Publisher location: Minneapolis, Minnesota
    Date: July 22, 1999

    _____

    _____

    _____

3. A work from a collection
    Title: Privacy and the Control of Genetic Information
    Author: Madison Powers
    Collection title: The Genetic Frontier: Ethics, Law, and Policy
    Pages: 77-100
    Editors: Mark S. Frankel and Albert H. Teich
    Publisher: American Association for the Advancement of Science
    Publisher location: Washington, D.C.
    Date of publication: 1994

    _____

    _____

    _____

4. Magazine article
    Title: Building Awareness So Children Get the Vaccines They Need
    Magazine title: Children's Magazine
    Publisher: Children's Hospitals and Clinics
    Publisher location: Minneapolis, Minnesota
    Date: July 1999
    Pages: 8-9

    _____

    _____

    _____

5. CD-ROM
    Title: Columbia World of Quotations
    Publisher: Columbia University Press
    Publisher Location: New York, New York
    Date: 1996

    _____

    _____

    _____

Useful Web Sites

MLA Style

www.mla.org
The Modern Language Association of America answers basic questions about MLA documentation style, particularly documentation of Web sources. From the home page, select "MLA Style."

The Writer's Handbook on Grammar and Style

www.wisc.edu/writing/Handbook/Documentation.html
Maintained by the University of Wisconsin–Madison Writing Center, this page includes general information on documentation. It also leads to summaries and examples for several documentation styles, including MLA and APA, as well as guidance on documenting Web sources.

Research Papers

owl.english.purdue.edu/writers/by-topic.html#research
"Handouts" listed on this page provide comprehensive information on researching, outlining, writing, documenting, and all other tasks associated with research papers.

Music Education: A Much Needed and Important Discipline

by Danielle M. Trasciatti

Like many others in the academic world, Dr. Kathleen Nulton Kemmerer, assistant professor of English at Pennsylvania State University, now has a presence on the World Wide Web. Her Web site has the usual fixtures of a college instructor: course descriptions, a schedule of office hours, her "curriculum vitae," and a list of her publications. In addition, her Web site offers material for students of writing not enrolled in her classes—pages such as the simple-to-follow instructions for building a Web site, the concise and amusing "Laws of Learning," and a more extensive "Help for Desperate Writing Students."

Dr. Kemmerer's Web site also includes a Writing Hall of Fame that was developed as a Web project by a student. The writers featured here are actually not famous—they are simply students who produced work in Dr. Kemmerer's classes good enough to serve as models. Among the work in this Hall of Fame is the following short research paper on music education. As you read Danielle Trasciatti's paper, consider whether her thesis is convincing, and also consider this question: What new ideas for research are suggested by her conclusions?

Check out Dr. Kemmerer's Web site at www2.hn. psu.edu/Faculty/ Kkemmerer/main. htm#projects. At the bottom of the home page, select "English— Writing Hall of Fame."

"A nation that allows music to be expendable is in danger of becoming expendable itself," said Richard Dreyfuss during the Grammy Awards broadcast on the 28th of February (National Coalition for Music Education 14). This is a very interesting statement because it involves something that is related to everyone—school curriculum. When school budgets have to be cut, the music classes are usually the first ones to be removed. Ironically, music is one of the most important areas of study because of its positive effects on students' creativity, learning and growth, and everyday life. Since music education has such an important impact on students' academic and personal growth, it should not be removed from students' learning curriculum.

Why is school curriculum "related to everyone"?

What claims are made for music education's impact on students?

The first important aspect of music is the amount of creativity and originality it brings out in students. Music has a way of letting everyone express him/herself personally, with others, and even for others. Personal expression through music is such a beautiful experience, and yet it happens so naturally. As John Dewey wrote, "In great art, there is no limit set to the individualization. . . ." (204). Experiencing music with others is another magnificent way of expression, but the opportunities must be there for it to happen. Also, expression in music for others is related to this because it can be done alone or with others. Learning about music is beneficial, because it lets students learn about themselves as they learn about music. Students learn to work together, to use teamwork, and to take responsibility. According to *Music Educators Journal*, Jacquelyn Dillon-Krass, president of the American String Teachers Association, said in an interview, ". . . Through the arts, especially through active participation in music, children learn the sort of discipline that enables them to become better organized, to work as members of a team, and most importantly, to be more sensitive people than they might otherwise be" (8).

Nurturing students' growth is another important aspect of music. Music gives students a comfortable niche in which to grow, for everyone is welcome and capable of making music. After trying and participating, students feel pride in their very own accomplishments through music. Working with peers of the same musical interests and talents is a healthy experience. The idea of teamwork appears again because it is so important. Students working together in something as challenging and wonderful as music can give them more than adequate training for life's future situations. As Eiji Oue, conductor of the Minnesota Orchestra, wrote in *Teaching Music,* "They can take the good experience from their hard work—the discipline, the practice, and the accomplishment of being unified in an ensemble—and apply it to whatever they want to accomplish later in their lives" (45). Also, students mature as a group the more they work together. Helping each other as they grow through music is an experience found nowhere else.

Another important aspect of music is that it is beneficial in everyday life. Music helps with learning other subjects and performing daily activities because making and learning about music involves so much. In *Teaching Music,* Bear Irwin, instrumental music supervisor for Mill High North in Vermont, said in an interview, "In music we're working in many areas—the cognitive domain, the affective domain, the physical domain.

What does it mean to "nurture growth"?

What parts of the body and brain are used when making music?

We synthesize, create and interpret, compose and improvise—everything related to the rest of life pertains to music education in a sense" (87). Using all of the domains to perform these activities strengthens students' skills to perform other tasks. Another quality gained through music is confidence. In doing all that Irwin spoke about, like creating, interpreting, and improvising, students feel good about themselves. Making something beautiful like music is definitely something to be proud of. Students learn to feel confident in all that they do, whether it be scholastics or sports. As a result of this, they tend to excel in doing just about anything.

In conclusion, Music Education should not be removed from students' learning curriculum. It is evident that music is more than beneficial; it is needed. Students should be given the opportunities to grow and mature to their greatest potential. Music can give students these opportunities. When music is considered as expendable from the curriculum, students do not get a chance to experience all the wonderful things music has to offer, and skills, talents, and dreams are wasted. As Michael Mark summed it up, "Living life to the fullest suggests providing an environment for acquiring the skills needed for creative living. Creativity is latent in the human at birth. The environment of the child can stimulate or suppress its development. It is the school's responsibility to establish an environment that encourages creativity and provides outlets for it" (46).

How does music relate to "living life to the fullest?"

Works Cited

Dewey, John. *Art as Experience*. New York: John Dewey, 1934.

Dillon-Krass, Jacquelyn. Interview. "Music is Key." *Music Educators Journal* March 1996:8–14.

Irwin, Bear. Interview. "Members Speak Out." *Teaching Music* April 1996: 76.

Oue, Eiji. "Giving Kids a Classical Choice." *Teaching Music* February 1996: 44–46.

Mark, Michael L. *Contemporary Music Education*. New York: Shirmer, 1978.

National Coalition for Music Education, The. "Dreyfuss Defends School Music at Grammy Awards." *Music Educators Journal* May 1996: 14–15.

THINK AND RESPOND

1. Which sentence in the first paragraph presents the thesis?

   _____

   _____

2. In such a short research paper, Trasciatti was not able to include
   background information on her subject. For example, she does not
   define "music education." How would you define it?

   _____

   _____

3. Trasciatti presents several arguments in favor of music education.
   Summarize two of them.

   _____

   _____

4. Name one source the author uses and explain whether it is credible.

   _____

   _____

5. How does the conclusion in paragraph five expand on the thesis in
   paragraph one?

   _____

   _____

6. If you wanted to write a paper with the thesis that music education
   is unnecessary, how would you conduct your research? (Consider
   primary as well as secondary sources.)

   _____

   _____

7. Provide synonyms or definitions for these words from the essay, and add at least two of the words to the *Words Worth Remembering* section of your journal.

expendable _____

curriculum _____

individualization _____

beneficial _____

ensemble _____

cognitive domain _____

affective domain _____

physical domain _____

pertains _____

latent _____

8. If you liked this reading, make a record of it in the *Readings Worth Remembering* section of your journal.

COMPARING VIEWS

What is the role of music in your life? How has music education (or the lack of it) affected you? How is your experience like or different from others' experiences? Come up with a list of questions relating to music education that might be interesting to research. After discussing this topic with others, continue to explore it on your own, in your journal—if you want to pursue this topic. You may be able to use material from the discussion and your journal in a future writing activity.

APPLIED WRITING

In her research paper, Trasciatti focused on one aspect of schooling— music education. She then presented evidence to support her thesis that music education is necessary to education. Others have made similar arguments about physical education, summer breaks, year-round schooling, computer skills, recess for elementary school children, and later school starting times for high schoolers. What do you think is essential to a good education? How do educators fit all of the "essentials" into the school calendar? Write a short research paper having to do with one essential purpose of school. Use the guidelines from this chapter for selecting a topic, outlining, researching, and writing the paper. Use both the Writing Checklist and the Essay Scoring Guide from Chapter 8 to help you revise. Prepare a final copy of the essay.

The Art Student: A Self Portrait
Elizabeth Torak

CHAPTER 16

Developing Habits for Life

These are the **key ideas** of this chapter:

- Writing is a skill that can be improved through independent effort outside of the classroom.
- By expanding your vocabulary, you can become a more effective writer.
- Setting goals can help you continue to progress as a writer.

Picturing Meaning

Examine the self-portrait on the opposite page; then think about or discuss these questions.

1. What is the artist doing?

   _____

   _____

2. How is a person taught to paint?

   _____

   _____

3. How does one teach oneself to paint?

   _____

   _____

4. What does this portrait reveal about the skills and habits the artist has?

   _____

   _____

   In the *Responses* section of your journal, write your thoughts about this self-portrait.

Write Now (1)

How does a *writer* create a self-portrait? In your journal or elsewhere, jot down your ideas. Think about what your self-portrait would be like. How would you present yourself, and why? How would your self-portrait reveal the writing skills and habits you have? Keep this work because you may use it in a later activity.

Learning from Models

How will you continue developing your writing skills once you have moved beyond this textbook? You can take more classes, of course, but you also can be your own teacher. Consider this popular saying: "Educated people educate themselves."

One way to continue your training is to read and study good models of writing. Just looking at words on a page, however, will not help you understand what makes them work as a whole. You must actively get inside the structure. Here are four techniques for doing so. These are not new ideas—they are traditional, proven techniques that many students of writing have used to teach themselves:

1. Listen to writing read aloud.

2. Transcribe passages of other writers' works.

3. Transcribe from memory.

4. Use good writing as a template.

Listen to writing read aloud. Listening to good writing makes you more sensitive to the rhythm of words. It helps you learn to distinguish between smooth-flowing sentences and awkward-sounding ones. It trains your ear to be a better tool when you do your own writing. There are many ways to listen to good writing. Find something you like and read it aloud to yourself. Have a friend read to you. Rent books on tape from the library. Attend poetry readings and "slams." Listen to radio essayists, such as the ones who appear on public news programs. Listen with a studious ear to speeches and sermons. You probably have some of your own ideas on where you can hear good writing.

Transcribe passages of other writers' works. To **transcribe** means to make a written copy. You can improve your writing skills by transcribing from good texts, just like the student artist who paints copies of works done by the old masters. Transcribing without thinking does not teach you anything, but transcribing attentively does. Select a passage you admire. As you copy it, notice the words. Notice how one idea is connected to the next, and notice any stylistic devices (such as repetition or parallelism). Notice how the topic is introduced, developed, and concluded.

Transcribe from memory. With this technique, you experience the same issues that another author has resolved successfully—such as how to make a transition or how to phrase a complex point. Take a passage that you admire and make a brief outline of its key points. Set this outline aside for some time, even a day or more, so that your recollection of the passage has a chance to fade. Then use the outline to try to rewrite the original passage. Compare your copy to the original.

Use good writing as a template. A **template** is a pattern or mold, usually made of a rigid material. Using good writing as a template can be instructive in the same way you might learn how a clock works by taking one apart and putting it back together. Take a paragraph you think is well written. Use it as a model for a new paragraph on a different topic. Replace words in the paragraph with others from the same category—verbs for verbs, nouns for nouns, adjectives for adjectives, prepositions for prepositions, and so on. The first paragraph from an essay written with a great deal of style, "How to Poach an Egg," is a good template for this exercise (the entire essay appears in Chapter 6):

> Poaching is the nicest way to treat an egg, provided you know the nicest way to poach. Eggs don't respond well to random acts of culinary violence. Cast them about like a raft at sea in water that's too hot and too rough, and they will get revenge by tightening, toughening, getting stringy, and falling apart.

Below is a new paragraph that has a new topic but the same structure. The underlined words are new, but they are of the same kind as the ones they replaced:

> Dieting is the surest way to lose some weight, provided you know the surest way to diet. Bodies don't respond well to severe restrictions on culinary pleasures. Beat them down like a prisoner of war with food that's too fatless and too sugarless, and they will get revenge by obsessing, craving, getting hysterical, and falling apart.

This is a difficult task, but it can be very satisfying, and it can teach you a lot. If you dislike such a rigid exercise, allow yourself more flexibility in adding and substituting words or phrases.

If you copy your paragraph onto a disk, save it. You can use it again for Write Now (3) and (4).

Write Now (2)

With a partner, look through the *Readings Worth Remembering* section of your journals to find a piece of writing that you both particularly enjoyed. Identify a one-paragraph passage from this piece that you agree is particularly well written. Read it aloud to your partner, then listen while your partner reads it aloud to you. Next, copy the paragraph. Discuss with your partner what it is about the words and the way they are put together that makes the paragraph effective.

Write Now (3)

Use the same paragraph you selected for Write Now (2). Make a brief outline of its key points. Allow time to pass. Then, using your outline, try to rewrite the paragraph word for word. Compare your copy to the original. What did you learn about the paragraph's structure?

A word processor helps with this technique. Copy and paste the passage, one copy below the other. Keep the first copy untouched, as your model, and replace words in the second copy.

Write Now (4)

Use the same paragraph you selected for Write Now (2) and (3). Use it as a template for a paragraph about another topic. Follow the structure of the original, replacing words with others from the same category as much as possible. Then share your new paragraph with classmates, to get their reactions on the style of your composition.

Building Your Vocabulary

Words are the writer's raw materials. The more words you know, the richer your writing will be. Here are three techniques for building your vocabulary:

1. Mark up your dictionary and thesaurus.

2. Keep a word list.

3. Find opportunities to learn and use new words.

Mark up your dictionary and thesaurus. When you look up a word in the dictionary, mark it with a highlighter pen. (This advice assumes the dictionary belongs to you.) The next time you are searching through the dictionary, your eyes will be drawn to the previously highlighted words. This reinforcement helps those words stay in your working vocabulary.

Keep a word list. Your journal contains a section called *Words Worth Remembering*. If you have been following this textbook's instructions, you have added words to that section. Keep this up. Writing down new words actively exercises your brain, which helps you remember the words. Furthermore, every time you go back to that word list to add something new, you will see the words already there, and this will enhance your recall of them. To reinforce this learning, put the new words on flashcards with the definitions on the reverse side. Keep those flashcards in a convenient place and, whenever you have an extra moment, quiz yourself as to their meaning.

Find opportunities to learn and use new words. If you pay attention, you will realize that you hear new words every day. Take notice of these words. Jot them down and then, when you have time, look up their meanings and record them in your journal. You also can seek out new words. Buy yourself a "word-a-day" flashcard set or calendar. Also remember to use any new word you learn. The standard advice for remembering a person's name is to repeat it at least three times right after hearing it: "Hello, Jules. Nice to meet you, Jules. Have you been here before, Jules?" The same advice applies to learning new words. Use them as soon as you can and repeat them often in writing and in conversation.

Many dictionary, thesaurus, and other language-related Web sites offer "word of the day" features. Bookmark one of these pages and check it out whenever you are on the Web.

Write Now (5)

Read the list of words below. Working with a partner, pick a word that you do not know. Look up the word in a dictionary. Highlight the word, if the dictionary belongs to you, or make a flashcard. Also add the word to the *Words Worth Remembering* section of your journal. Working separately from your partner, write the word in a sentence that reveals its meaning. Finally, take turns reading your sentences aloud. Repeat these tasks with at least two more words. In a discussion with the whole class, take turns sharing one new word. Explain when or where you might be able to use that word in the near future. Finally, as a group, discuss with the class the effect this process might have on your ability to remember new words.

adumbrate	attenuate	austere	automaton
bastion	blatherskite	defalcate	deft
deleterious	dilettante	disingenuous	exasperate
fibula	gazetteer	glossolalia	homily
lugubrious	mercurial	mukluk	obsidian
ort	perspicacious	prosaic	recondite
reiterate	sanctum	sartorial	sycophantic
vitiate	voluble	wrangle	zephyr

Continuing a Journal

People express themselves by singing, dancing, painting, and other arts. Another way that all sorts of people express themselves is by keeping journals. Farmers, homemakers, doctors, scientists, truck drivers, telemarketers: people of all types keep journals because they choose to and not because anyone tells them they must. These ordinary people, who may or may not be great writers, take pleasure from transforming their ideas into a structured pattern of words. For these people, keeping a journal helps them think. It also helps them remember, analyze, understand, and learn.

In the past few months, you have experimented with keeping a journal. Look back through your journal. Is it an expression of yourself? Does writing in a journal help you think, remember, analyze, understand, and learn?

Write Now (6)

Review your journal. As a class, discuss these questions:

- **Did you give journal writing a fair try? Why or why not?**
- **Which sections did you use or enjoy the most?**
- **How did journal writing, by itself, affect your progress as a writer?**
- **What form of journal, if any, do you think you will keep after this class?**

   After the discussion, write in your journal your intentions for it after the class ends. Will you keep it or throw it away? Will you keep writing in it, or start a new one?

Writing for Life

Hundreds of years ago, people told time by church bells, learned songs by hearing them sung, discovered the news from the town crier, and signed their names with X's. Much has changed since then, but what has particularly changed has been the function of the written word. In the contemporary world, knowledge in written form—not wheat, steel, or even oil—is the supreme commodity. Words are what people work with now, and if you do not have the skills to do this kind of work, increasingly you are left out or left behind. Distance learning, telecommuting, e-commerce: these are just a few of the ways that transactions formerly done physically now occur in writing.

   The second-to-last question in the "Summing Up" section of each chapter in this textbook asked you to think of circumstances in your present or future life where you must apply writing skills. Look back and review your own responses to these questions. Are you ready as a writer?

Write Now (7)

As a class, make a list of everyone's responses to the second-to-last questions from the "Summing Up" section of each chapter. Using one of those circumstances to focus discussion, address these questions:

- What are the features of the writing that will be required for this situation? (Answer in terms of quality, style, format, language, and other features.)
- What writing skills will be necessary?
- Are you prepared with those skills?
- What skills do you need to continue developing in order to be prepared?

Repeat this discussion focusing on several more circumstances.

Reviewing Progress and Setting New Goals

The first chapter of this textbook introduced five habits writers should have. They were:

1. Observe.

2. Read.

3. Be organized.

4. Write often.

5. Have goals.

By now you should have a very clear sense of what it means to have these habits. This course, this textbook, your classmates, your instructor, and your own experiences and reflections have all given you ideas on how to incorporate these habits into daily life. You have practiced these habits over the last few months. Now you need to decide how to continue reinforcing these habits so that your writing skills become even stronger.

Re-examine your writing folder—the outlines, drafts, and completed works that you have accumulated throughout this course. Also, re-examine your journal. As you scan over this material, think about the progress you have made as a writer. Ask yourself such questions as:

- Are you more organized?

- Are you more efficient?

- Are you thinking more creatively?

- Are you having an easier time getting started?

- Are you better able to produce longer works of writing?

- Are you a better critic of your own work?

- Are you producing better writing?

Consider your strengths and accomplishments; then direct yourself forward with new goals. What do you hope to accomplish in the next month, the next three months, and the next year? At the end of your lifetime, what do you hope to be able to say about yourself as a writer? These are questions that take hard thinking, but answering them can help you set new goals. As with any skill, the more you set goals and work to achieve them, the better you become at that skill.

Write Now (8)

Review your journal and writing folder. Then complete each of the sentences below.

1. One way I can become a better observer is to

_____

2. One thing I can do to increase the amount of reading I do is

_____

3. One thing I can do to be better organized for writing is to

_____

4. One way I can begin to write more is to

_____

5. One thing I can do to focus on my new writing goals is to

_____

Compare your responses above to those you gave in Write Now (4) of Chapter 1. How have your responses changed? Why? What does this tell you about your progress as a writer?

Write Now (9)

Complete the Inventory of Your Writing Habits that appears in Figure 16-1. Then compare your responses to the ones you gave in Write Now (10) of Chapter 1. How have your responses changed? Why? What does this tell you about your progress as a writer?

Figure 16-1: Inventory of Your Writing Habits—Revisited

Instructions: Put an X on each line somewhere between the two endpoints. For example, on item 1, if you dislike writing, put your X close to the left end of the line. If you like to write, put your X close to the right end of the line. Put your X somewhere in the middle if your feelings about writing are somewhere between like and dislike.

1. I dislike
   to write.
   _____
   I like
   to write.

2. I write only when
   required to do so
   by others.
   _____
   I often write for
   my own purposes.

3. For any writing
   task, I write as little
   as necessary to get by.
   _____
   For any writing
   task, I write until
   I am satisfied with
   my work.

4. I live each day
   without looking for
   writing ideas.
   _____
   I collect writing
   ideas from the
   events in my day.

5. I read very little
   each day.
   _____
   I read a great deal
   each day.

6. I have no specific
   place for writing.
   _____
   I have an
   organized location
   where I can write.

7. I write very little
   each day.
   _____
   I write a great
   deal each day.

8. I do not keep
   a journal.
   _____
   I keep a journal.

9. I do not use
   a word processor.
   _____
   I effectively use a
   a word processor.

10. I do not use
    the Internet.
    _____
    I effectively use
    the Internet.

11. I have no
    particular goals for
    myself as a writer.
    _____
    I have clear goals
    for myself as a
    writer.

12. I do not think of
    myself as a writer.
    _____
    I think of myself
    as a writer.

Write Now (10)

In the concluding activity of Chapter 1, you wrote a letter to yourself that you gave to your instructor for safekeeping. Obtain that letter back and read it. How did the reality of this course compare with your expectations? To what degree did you accomplish your goals? Now write a second letter to yourself. Describe what you expect your challenges to be as a writer in the coming months. Describe the new writing goals you have set for yourself. Seal the letter inside an envelope, address it to yourself, stamp it, and turn it in to your instructor. Your instructor will mail it back to you after an interval of time.

If the instructor supplies an e-mail address, you may send the letter electronically, and the instructor will return it the same way.

Write Now (11)

Go through your writing folder to organize it and turn it into a portfolio. Save the essays you like best. Staple together the outlines and drafts of those essays, to keep as a reminder of the effort that went into them. Keep a separate file or paste into your journal other interesting scraps of writing worth keeping. Throw away everything else. If your instructor requires a portfolio as a final submission, review and follow the class instructions on what to keep and how to present it. Finally, if your instructor requires it, write a short analysis of your portfolio.

Summing Up

1. What can you learn from studying good writing models?

    _____

    _____

2. Name one advantage to adding words such as *vitriolic, etymology,* and *barbarous* to your vocabulary.

    _____

    _____

3. In this chapter, you have been prompted to review your progress as a writer and to set new goals. Name the next point at which you plan to reflect on progress and goals.

    _____

    _____

Second Thoughts

Review the self-portrait that opened this chapter; then think about or discuss the following:

1. What kinds of models do you think this artist has studied?

2. What is the artist's equivalent of "vocabulary"?

3. What do you think are habits a painter needs to have?

4. How might an artist like this one practice those habits?

5. What goals do you think this artist might set for herself?

   Based on what you have learned in this chapter about habits and goals, answer this question: In what ways is this portrait a portrait of you? Write your thoughts in the *Responses* section of your journal.

4. Name three situations in your life where you might decide to write for your own purposes (as opposed to being required to write by an instructor or in a work situation).

   _____

   _____

5. As a result of completing this textbook, what is one change you can make in the way you approach writing overall? Write your response in the *Habits for Life* section of your journal.

Write Now: Composing an Essay about You as a Writer

Write an essay about your development as a writer. To plan the essay, review what you wrote for Write Now (1) of this chapter, the self-assessment exercises from Chapter 1 and this chapter, the letter you wrote to yourself at the beginning of this course, and your portfolio. Review also your journal and reflect on the different textbook assignments you have completed. You also may interview people who know you as a writer, such as a classmate or your instructor. Describe the changes you have seen in yourself that have occurred in the past few months. What new strengths do you have? What challenges remain? Address the issue in terms of both your skills and your attitude. Use the thinking and planning tools you have learned and apply the writing strategies you have practiced. Review and edit your essay without input from others, and complete a final copy.

Learning Suffixes, Prefixes, and Roots

Why learn one word when you can learn ten? Learn the meaning of prefixes, suffixes, and roots, and you will be able to deduce the meaning of a great many more words. **Prefixes** are syllables attached to the front of words that help define their meaning. **Suffixes** are syllables attached to the end of words. **Roots** are words or parts of words that stem from the ancient Anglo-Saxon, Latin, and Greek languages and are part of many English words. Use the charts below to learn some of these word parts.

Common Prefixes

Prefix	Meaning	Sample Word	Meaning of Word
ante	before	antechamber	room before another room (such as a waiting room)
anti	against, opposed	antifreeze	a liquid that is combined with another liquid to prevent its freezing
auto	self	autobiography	a book written about oneself
bi	two	bifurcate	divide into two
bio	life	biodegrade	capable of being broken down by living organisms
com	with	company	people working with each other
de	down, off, away, not	deplane	get off the plane
di, dis	against, not	dissemble	not tell the truth
mis	bad, wrong	misbegotten	wrongly done (illegitimate)
non	not	nonstarter	something that did not work
poly	more than one	polygamy	having more than one spouse
pre	before, in front	prefixes	syllables attached to the front of words that help define their meaning
re	back, in reverse	reimburse	pay back
sub	under	submerge	move under
un	not, opposite	uncover	take off the cover

Common Suffixes

Suffix	Meaning	Sample Word	Meaning of Word
able, ible	able to be or do	fixable	able to be fixed
ar, er, or	one who	predator	one who preys on others
ful	full	awful	full of awe (fear)
ic	relating to	psychic	ability relating to the mind (psyche)
ify	make more of	deify	make into a godlike object of worship
ile	like	infantile	like an infant
in	not	inconsequential	not important
ish	approximately	sevenish	approximately seven o'clock
less	without	peerless	without equal
ling	small	gosling	baby goose
logy	body of knowledge	etymology	knowledge of how words evolve
ly	like	ghastly	like a horrible ghost
ment	state, act, result	amusement	state of being entertained
sion, tion	act, process, result	television	the sending of visual images
wise	in the manner of	clockwise	movement to the right, down, and around (in the manner of clocks)

Common Roots

Root	Meaning	Sample Word	Meaning of Word
audi, audio	to hear	audit	exam or hearing to review accounts
base	bottom, starting point	baseboard	board at the bottom of a wall
derm	skin	hypodermic	under the skin
dict	say	verdict	a stated judgment
grad	step, stage	upgrade	move to a higher level
graph	write	holograph	a document handwritten by the author
leg, lect	to read	legible	able to be read
mobil	moveable	bloodmobile	a van equipped to collect blood donations
quer,ques,quir	ask, seek	inquiry	investigation
photo	light	photon	a small particle of light
put	think, argue	reputation	how others think about a thing or person
scop	look at	microscope	device to look at small objects
scrib, scrip	write	prescription	a written order for medicine
spect	to look at	inspection	a careful look
vid, vis	to see	video	a moving visual recorded image
vigor	energy	invigorate	to make energetic

Exercise 1

Move into pairs. As a class, divide the chart below into equal sections for each pair. Work with your partner to fill in your assigned section of the chart. Most prefixes and suffixes are listed in the dictionary. Some root words also are listed in the dictionary. You also can deduce meaning by thinking of several words containing the prefix, suffix, or root. Share your work with the class so that everyone ends up with a completed chart.

More Prefixes	Meaning	Sample Word	Meaning of Word
a, ab	_____	_____	_____
con	_____	_____	_____
e, ef, ex	_____	_____	_____
ob	_____	_____	_____
pro	_____	_____	_____
pseudo	_____	_____	_____
pyro	_____	_____	_____
quasi	_____	_____	_____
trans	_____	_____	_____
ultra	_____	_____	_____

More Suffixes	Meaning	Sample Word	Meaning of Word
ally	_____	_____	_____
ance, ence	_____	_____	_____
ate	_____	_____	_____
en	_____	_____	_____
cede, ceed	_____	_____	_____
ise, ize	_____	_____	_____
ism	_____	_____	_____
ity, ty	_____	_____	_____
like	_____	_____	_____
ous	_____	_____	_____

More Roots	Meaning	Sample Word	Meaning of Word
anthropo	_____	_____	_____
centi	_____	_____	_____
cred	_____	_____	_____
fin	_____	_____	_____
memo	_____	_____	_____
morph	_____	_____	_____
neur	_____	_____	_____
techno	_____	_____	_____
tele	_____	_____	_____
vari	_____	_____	_____

Exercise 2

Using your chart from Exercise 1 and the previous charts, guess the meaning of the words below. Check your answers against the dictionary definitions.

1. amorphous _____

2. baseless _____

3. incredible _____

4. disputation _____

5. anthropology _____

6. misanthropic _____

7. neurology _____

8. telephoto _____

9. predecessor _____

10. variegated _____

Useful Web sites
http://www.etymologic.
com/
"The toughest word
game on the Web"
presents quizzes on word
origin and definition.

http://webster.commnet.
edu/writing/writing.htm
A directory of useful
links for writers—to
grammar guides,
dictionaries, on-line
writing labs, and more.
Maintained by
Dr. Charles Darling of
Capital Community-
Technical College.

A Lighthouse Keeper's Wife

By Jeanne Marie Laskas

Life for women has changed dramatically in the past hundred years. A century ago, women were restricted by corsets and long hemlines, they did not have the vote, they were excluded from positions of power in the labor force, and they did not have today's technological conveniences. Though women growing up a century ago did not have the kinds of choices that today's women have, they still managed to create interesting and fruitful lives.

Twenty-five such women are profiled in a book sponsored by Good Housekeeping Magazine *and written by journalist Jeanne Marie Laskas. The book is called* We Remember: Women Born at the Turn of the Century Tell the Stories of Their Lives in Words and Pictures. *The following profile is of Connie Small, who lived as a lighthouse keeper's wife. As you read Small's story, consider what she had to learn* after *she stopped going to school.*

For twenty-eight years Connie Small, ninety-seven, lived as a lighthouse keeper's wife on the rocky coast of New England. It was a life of extraordinary isolation—and adventure. She would sometimes go four months without seeing a human being other than her husband.

"I remember one day feeling so sad," she says, sitting in the small room she occupies today in the Mark Wentworth Home in Portsmouth, New Hampshire. "It was Easter. And I had on my wedding suit, and the most beautiful blouse, embroidered with flowers. And a hat that had peacock feathers." Newly married, she was living in her first lighthouse, Avery Rock, three miles from the mainland midway up the coast of Maine, and her husband had gone to shore—a forty-five minute rowboat ride away—for groceries and household supplies.

"And here I was sitting on a rock pile in the middle of nowhere," she says. "I was so alone. And I remember I looked down, and there was a little puddle between the rocks, with a little sea urchin in there." She picked up the urchin.

Why was Small wearing her wedding suit?

"I can see the water today, going through my fingers," she says, cupping her hands. "And I looked at that little animal and I thought, 'Why should I feel sorry for myself when I've got the world right in my hand?'" A world to explore and investigate.

"That," she says, "was a turning point."

She was born Constance Scoville in Lubec, Maine, the easternmost point of the United States. One of five children, she grew up next to the sea. Her grandfathers had been sea captains, her uncle was a lighthouse keeper, and two other uncles had been lost at sea together. Her father worked for the U.S. Life Saving Service, a precursor of the U.S. Coast Guard.

"You could see the ships crash on the rock and the vessel would be destroyed," she recalls. "And I can remember my father at the cannon and the beautiful brass powder can." The cannon would shoot a special lifesaving buoy and float to shore. "He saved many, many sailors," she says.

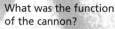

What was the function of the cannon?

When Connie turned thirteen, she developed debilitating asthma. "I would be in bed with it, very, very ill, for many weeks at a time, and so I couldn't go to school because I couldn't keep up. Back then they didn't know about allergies." Years later she would learn that her condition was actually an allergic reaction to the family's Chihuahua.

Her sheltered and lonely life improved considerably when, at seventeen, she met Elson Leroy Small, a tall, blond Merchant Marine serving in World War I, who was home on a brief leave. It was love at first sight. "Just as soon as we walked into each other's life," she says, "We knew we wanted to stay there."

When the war ended about a year later, he came back for her and she accepted his marriage proposal. Then he said, "But do you love me enough to go live in a lighthouse?" He had been offered the caretaking job from the U.S. Lighthouse Service (which, in 1939, was incorporated into the U.S. Coast Guard).

"Well, I had to stop a minute with that one. But I looked at him, and I had to say yes."

They moved into the Avery Rock lighthouse in 1922. Connie was twenty-one, and Elson was twenty-five. "We had no telephone, no electricity, no refrigerator," she says. "We couldn't keep fresh food. Elson

Why would Small be scared by the thought of running out of food?

would buy fresh meat, and we'd put it in the sink in the water. We could keep it for a couple of days. I learned to can. I canned everything. I was so frightened of running out of food."

It was a test of survival for the young couple. Connie remembers a blizzard that came suddenly one night. "I had to run," she says. "I had to shut all the shutters, three inches thick, so the waves wouldn't come through the glass and bury us right in the sea. And Elson was violently ill. And I had no knowledge of sickness, but I took his temperature and it was a hundred and three. He became delirious and I couldn't do a thing with him until he spent his energy and collapsed in bed. He was in a coma for three days. And here I was all alone. And not able to tell anybody we were in trouble. And I had to keep the light burning."

It was the lighthouse keeper's mission, his duty to the world. And her duty, as his wife. Lighthouses (which are now automated, no longer requiring live-in personnel) have been used to safeguard mariners since early times. Constructed at important points on a coastline, the lights guide ships sailing on coastal waters. An extinguished light could spell disaster. Maintenance of the light was a complicated task requiring exacting attention to a system of weights and pulleys that kept the sophisticated crystal lens turning and flashing at precise intervals. As a lighthouse keeper's wife, Connie learned how to work the equipment. She was not on the payroll. She would never receive a pension.

What was the alcohol for?

She believed that her husband was dead, during that blizzard at Avery Rock. Her task now was to figure out how to preserve the body. She remembered her mother saying you used alcohol to do this. She got the alcohol. "And I stood outside his door for twenty minutes trying to get up the courage to go inside," she says. When she finally did, she heard something, a faint voice. "I'm hungry."

"That was my miracle," she says humbly.

Connie and her husband lived at Avery Rock for four years before moving on to other lighthouses along the New England coast. It wasn't until she and Elson moved to St. Croix River Light Station on a small island on the St. Croix River, near the United States/Canada border, that she found paradise. There were sandy beaches, and tourists who visited for picnics. She had a garden, chickens for fresh eggs, and a cow providing milk.

"It was a playground," she says.

World War II interrupted their heaven on earth, however. Elson was called to serve. Another lighthouse keeper was brought to work the lighthouse, which meant that Connie would have to leave her paradise.

She was forty. She was forced to move into a hotel, then a boardinghouse, and then was taken in by a friend of her mother's for the duration of the war.

When her husband was released from the service, the two went back to the St. Croix River Light Station. Soon, they moved to their last lighthouse, Portsmouth Harbor Light in New Castle, New Hampshire.

Elson retired as a lighthouse keeper in 1947 after the U.S. Coast Guard assumed responsibility for that lighthouse. The couple moved to a modern house in Eliot, Maine.

Elson died of cancer in 1960, when Connie was fifty-nine. "He's still here," she says. "To me, he's going to open that door someday and walk in." With no pension, Connie had to make a life for herself. She could hear him encouraging her, as he had so many years before, telling the girl with asthma that she could do anything she set her mind on. She got a job at a department store, then as a resident in a dorm at Farmington State College, in Farmington, Maine, eventually taking on duties as substitute dean of students. When she was eighty-five years old, she published a book, *The Lighthouse Keeper's Wife* (University of Maine Press, 1986), and began lecturing about her days on the edge of the sea. At ninety-seven, she is still at it.

"So far I've delivered 521 lectures," she says.

Sometimes she tells people about the time she and her husband were introduced to their first electric lighthouse, the one in New Castle, New Hampshire, in the 1940s. It was quite a modern invention compared to the old kerosene-powered ones that required a full twenty minutes to light.

"And now it was just a button!" she recalls. "And I was so excited to push that button." And so she did.

"And. . . I didn't feel anything," she says. This was strange. The light had come on, as she predicted. But where was the thrill? She had expected her first experience with electricity to be more exciting than this.

"I wondered about that for a long time," she says. "And then I realized that before we had to put twenty minutes of ourselves into lighting that light. But now, to just push a button? It didn't mean anything. We hadn't given anything.

"You have to give of yourself to have anything important."

What did Small do after her husband died?

THINK AND RESPOND

1. Small says she learned to adjust to life in remote lighthouses by changing her attitude. How exactly does a person do that?

   _____

   _____

2. As a lighthouse keeper's wife, Small had to learn how to work the equipment. She also had to learn how to run a household without modern conveniences and far from stores and other people. How do you think she learned to do these things?

   _____

   _____

3. Small was fifty-nine when her husband died. For the first time in her life, she had to live on her own and find a paid job. What skills and habits do you think she drew on to do these things?

   _____

   _____

4. At age eighty-five, Small wrote a book about her life as a lighthouse keeper. What skills and habits do you think she drew on to write a book so late in life?

   _____

   _____

5. When the book was published, Small began lecturing about her life as a lighthouse keeper. How do you think she learned to do that?

   _____

   _____

6. Why do you think she likes to tell the story about her first experience with an electric lighthouse?

   _____

   _____

7. Provide synonyms or definitions for these words from the essay, and record at least two of them in the *Words Worth Remembering* section of your journal:

sea urchin _____

precursor _____

debilitating _____

incorporated _____

delirious _____

coma _____

mariners _____

exacting _____

pension _____

duration _____

8. If you liked this reading, make a record of it in the *Readings Worth Remembering* section of your journal.

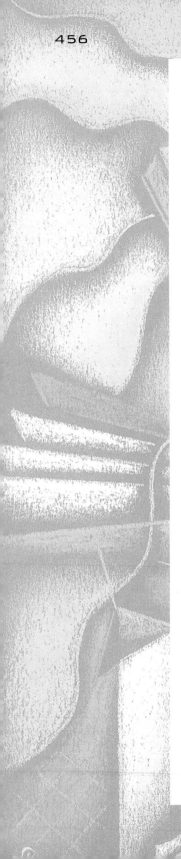

COMPARING VIEWS

Living apart from the mainstream has its advantages and disadvantages. Could you live in a lighthouse or some other remote location? Do you have the self-reliance? What attitude and skills would you need to have? How would you learn, on your own, what you need to know to survive? After discussing this topic with others, continue to explore it on your own, in your journal—if the questions intrigue you.

APPLIED WRITING

A willingness to learn can make life more interesting—and can make you more interesting to others. Using the profile of Connie Small as a guideline, write an essay about a fascinating person who has been a lifelong learner. If your subject is alive and available, interview him or her. If your subject is famous, do research to learn about his or her life. Interview others who know your subject. Make notes of any recollections you have of this person. Try to discover the skills and attitudes your subject used to cope with circumstances and learn new things. To write your essay, draw on the planning, interviewing, drafting, essay development, revising, and evaluating strategies you have learned in this course. Use both the Writing Checklist and the Essay Scoring Guide from Chapter 8 to help you revise. Prepare a final copy of the essay.

UNIT 5

MASTERING LANGUAGE ESSENTIALS

This unit serves as a supplement to the main text, providing instruction and exercises in the principles underlying Standard Written English (for more about Standard Written English and other forms of English, please refer to Chapter 1). Goals of the unit are to help you:

- Review the conventions (generally accepted rules) of grammar and mechanics.

- Test your proficiency in these conventions.

Chapters (and exercises within each chapter) can be worked on in any order, so that you may selectively focus on those skills needing reinforcement.

CHAPTER 17

The Simple Sentence

This chapter provides a general overview of the sentence. Read and do the exercises in this chapter if you need help understanding:

- What a sentence is.

- What goes into a sentence.

- How to recognize a sentence when you see one.

This chapter covers only the bare essentials of what makes up a sentence. Further details and refinements are covered in other chapters. At each step along the way, you will see references to these other chapters. Turn to them as needed.

A Sentence Defined

Imagine reading this textbook if it were presented as one unending string of words. For example, try to read the following paragraph:

a journal is a written record of your everyday thoughts and events a journal is for yourself there are no rules and there are no limits to a journal you decide the function of your journal and you decide what to put in it no one reads your journal without your permission and no one has any right to judge what is in it but you

You may understand what it says, but you have to put extra effort into reading because everything runs together. Now read the paragraph again:

A journal is a written record of your everyday thoughts and events. A journal is for yourself. There are no rules and there are no limits to a journal. You decide the function of your journal and you decide what to put in it. No one reads your journal, without your permission, and no one has any right to judge what is in it but you.

The same set of words becomes easier to read when it is shaped into sentences. The definition of a **sentence** is this:

A sentence is a group of words expressing a complete thought and containing at a minimum a subject and a verb.

A writer indicates where each sentence begins by starting it with a capital letter. A writer indicates where each sentence ends by concluding it with a punctuation mark. Shaping words into sentences helps readers because it creates a visual break where a normal pause in the reading occurs. This is important because a reader will not see the writer's face or gestures or hear the tone of voice, which all help convey meaning in spoken communication.

One of three kinds of punctuation marks is used to end a sentence. A period (.) closes a sentence that is a statement; for example:

This is a sentence.
It is a short sentence.

Sentences that ask a question end with a question mark (?):

Do you understand?
Is this clear?

An exclamation point (!) closes a sentence that states a command. This punctuation mark is also used to close a statement that conveys energy, enthusiasm, or passion:

Learn this!
I shall not forget it!

Note that the **comma** (,) does not indicate the end of a sentence. It only indicates a short pause within a sentence. For example:

Commas, I confess, confuse me.
Fear not, for you will grasp it soon enough.

Unlike some other languages, English does not ever use punctuation at the beginning of a sentence:

Spanish: ¿Es una oración?
English: Is this a sentence?

Punctuating compound and complex sentences, Chapter 6.
Using commas, Chapter 23.
Other punctuation marks, Chapter 23.
Other functions of capital letters, Chapter 24.

Exercise 1

In the paragraphs below, draw lines between the sentences. There are eleven sentences, so you should draw ten lines.

I feel as if I could not write again. Words seem to break in my mind like sticks when I put them down on paper. I cannot see how to spell some of them. Sentences are covered with leaves, and I really cannot see the line of the branch that carries the green meanings.

I must put out my hands and grasp the handfuls of facts. How extraordinary they are! The aluminum balloons seem nailed into the sky like those bolts which hold together the radiating struts of a biplane between the wings. The streets become more and more deserted and the West End is full of shops to let. Sandbags are laid above the glass pavements over basements along the sidewalk. Last night during the blackout there was a tremendous thunderstorm. We stood at the bottom of Regent Street in the pouring rain, the pitch darkness broken up intermittently by flashes of sheet lightning which lit up Piccadilly Circus like broad daylight.

The Thirties and After
Stephen Spender

Exercise 2

Create ten sentences from the following string of words. Add capital letters to indicate the beginning of each sentence and punctuation marks to indicate where each sentence ends.

the only rule for your journal is to date your entries there are no other rules a journal can be more than a record of each day's events your journal can include any information you wish to put in it your journal is your private book you can record your thoughts and observations in your journal you can put your goals in your journal you can write down facts and quotations in your journal you can use a journal as a daily reminder of things to do what you put in your journal is up to you

Exercise 3

Create ten sentences from the following string of words. Add capital letters to indicate the beginning of each sentence and punctuation marks to indicate where each sentence ends. Use four periods, four question marks, and two exclamation marks.

have you ever kept a journal if your answer is "no," now is the time to start you can keep your journal on paper or on a computer some people keep their journal on loose scraps of paper how do you decide at some point you have to make a decision have you thought about how you will keep your journal private certainly you don't want other people nosing into it the hardest part about keeping a journal is getting started, isn't it get started now

Verbs in Sentences

A vital ingredient in a sentence is the **verb**. See what happens when you take the verbs out of the paragraph on journals:

A journal a written record of your everyday thoughts and events. A journal for yourself. There no rules and there no limits to a journal. You the function of your journal, and you what in it. No one your journal, without your permission, and no one any right to what in it but you.

You can pick out some of the meaning of this paragraph, but not all of it.

Action verbs. Verbs make it clear what is happening in the sentence. Verbs express action, for example: No one *reads* your journal. Other examples of action verbs include

write	I *write* every day.
break	Oscar *breaks* his pencil from writing so hard.
reveal	You *reveal* your soul in your words.
put	Do you *put* your best effort into your work?
print	Tamika *prints* a hard copy of her computer journal.

State of being verbs. Verbs also express conditions of being or of relationship, for example: a journal *is* for yourself. The verb *is* and its other forms (*are*, *was*, and *were*) are the most common state-of-being verbs. Other examples of verbs expressing condition include:

has/have	She *has* (or I *have*) strong feelings about this.
fear	I *fear* being judged for what I write.
seem	Some writers *seem* to go into a trance as they write.
feel	It *feels* good to get something down on paper.

Verb tenses. Besides indicating what is happening in a sentence, verbs have another function. They indicate *when* it is happening. To indicate whether a sentence is about the past, the present, or the future, the verb changes form. For example:

I *wrote*. (about the past)
I *had written*. (about the past, before something else happened)
I *write*. (about the present)
I *do write*. (about the present, with emphasis)
I *will write*. (about the future)
I *could write*. (about a possibility in the future)

Note that there is more than one way to express a verb in past, present, or future tense. The different choices help to express intention. Also note that sometimes **helping verbs** are added to the main verb to form a phrase like "I *had written*" or "I *could write*."

Negative verbs. A verb's opposite meaning is indicated when the word *not* or *never* appears next to it. For example, the two sentences below have the same verb, *is*, but have opposite meanings:

A journal *is* for yourself.
A journal *is not* for anyone else to read.

Other examples of verbs expressed negatively include:

She *did not* write in her journal today.
You *never know* what will happen when you start to scribble.
We *do not realize* the power of our own imagination.

Simple verb tenses, Chapter 18.
Helping verbs, Chapter 18.
Verb contractions, Chapter 23.

Exercise 4

In the list of fifty words below, thirty can be used as verbs. Circle the verbs. *Hint: Try using the words "I" or "we" or "she" in front of each word to see if it will work as a verb.*

fluctuate   shout   lemon   revise
invention   veer   punctuate   paragraph
television   but   compute   invent
compose   habit   write   by
only   explain   automobile   become
are   decide   envision   organize
participate   understand   grovel   indicate
scan   desk   seize   music
make   have   and   is
illustrate   there   goals   enter
open   while   that   mouse
create   ten   throw   language
carry   calendar

Exercise 5

Circle the sixteen verbs in the sentences below.

A pigeon nest is usually constructed on covered building ledges that resemble cliffs. They also nest and roost on support structures under bridges. They build their nests with small twigs. A male brings the nesting material to his mate, one piece at a time, and she builds the nest. Nests are usually well hidden and hard to find. Pigeons usually lay two white eggs. The parents take turns keeping their eggs warm (incubating). Males usually stay on the nest during the day; females stay on the nest at night. Eggs take about 18 days to hatch. Both male and female parents produce a special substance called "pigeon milk," which they feed to their hatchlings during their first week of life.

Project Pigeon Watch
Cornell Laboratory of Ornithology

Exercise 6

Circle nine verbs in the sentences below.

This seemingly empty land is busy with inhabitants. Low to the ground (are) bullsnakes, rattlers, mice, gophers, moles, grouse, prairie chickens, and pheasant. Prairie dogs (are) more noticeable, as they (denude) the landscape with their villages. Badgers and skunk (lumber) busily through the grass. Jackrabbits, weasels, and foxes (are) quicker, but the great runners of the Plains (are) the coyote, antelope, and deer. Meadowlarks, killdeer, blackbirds, lark buntings, crows, and seagulls (dart) above the fields, and a large variety of hawks, eagles, and vultures (glide) above it all, hunting for prey.

Dakota, a Spiritual Geography
Kathleen Norris

Nouns in Sentences

Another important element in sentences is the **noun**. Look at what happens when the nouns disappear from the paragraph about journals:

A is a written of your everyday and. A is for. There are no and there are no to a. Decide the of your and decide what to put in. Reads your, without your, and has any right to is in it but.

Without nouns, it is difficult to even guess at meaning. Nouns name persons, places, or things. Examples include:

journal	event	modem	ink
record	paper	site	illustration
desk	instructor	notebook	computer
classroom	student	library	book

Nouns also name states or qualities. Examples include:

thought	function	planning	frustration
limit	reality	patience	ecstasy
imagination	dream	capacity	idea

Many words that are used as verbs also can be used as nouns. Here are some examples:

rules	There are no *rules* to a journal. (noun)
	Creativity *rules!* (verb)
limit	There is no *limit* to a journal. (noun)
	Limit your distractions. (verb)
read	This book is a good *read*. (noun)
	No one *reads* your journal but you. (verb)
dreaming	*Dreaming* gives me ideas for writing. (noun)
	I am *dreaming* of an easier time. (verb)
living	I write for fun, not for a *living*. (noun)
	As long as I am *living*, I will write. (verb)

How do you tell if a word is a noun? Usually, if you can put "the" in front of it and use it to start a sentence, you have a noun, as in:

The *thought* of producing twenty pages is overwhelming.
The *patience* required of an artist appears to be great.
The *frustration* of writing has overcome me.

Note that actual names, such as "America" or "Mario," are nouns, but you do not usually put the word "the" in front of them. These kinds of nouns are called **proper nouns.**

Nouns that represent one thing are called **singular nouns.** Nouns that represent more than one thing are called **plural nouns.** Nouns usually change slightly when they are made into plural:

site = sites	folly = follies	box = boxes
ink = inks	thought = thoughts	ax = axes

Nouns made from verbs (gerunds), Chapter 18.
Capitalization of proper nouns, Chapter 24.

Exercise 7

In the list of fifty words below, thirty can be used as nouns. Circle the nouns. *Hint: Try using the word "the" or "a" in front of each word to see if it will work as a noun. This hint does not work with proper nouns.*

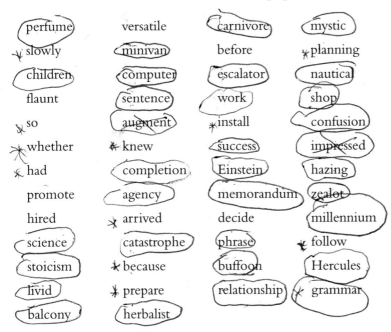

perfume   versatile   carnivore   mystic
slowly   minivan   before   planning
children   computer   escalator   nautical
flaunt   sentence   work   shop
so   augment   install   confusion
whether   knew   success   impressed
had   completion   Einstein   hazing
promote   agency   memorandum   zealot
hired   arrived   decide   millennium
science   catastrophe phrase   follow
stoicism   because   buffoon   Hercules
livid   prepare   relationship grammar
balcony   herbalist

Exercise 8

Circle the twenty-six nouns in the excerpt below.

Our guidebook provides information on airfares, hotels, motels, rental cars, restaurants, and entertainment. Members will receive discounts on reservations made through our organization. Mail this coupon to the address shown at the top of the page. Be sure to include your name and address. A copy of our monthly newsletter will be sent to new subscribers along with our book on top-rated vacations. This special offer expires at the end of the current year.

Nouns as the Subjects in Sentences

Nouns perform many functions in sentences. An important function is to serve as **subjects.** Here is the paragraph on journals with all the subjects missing:

> A is a written record of your everyday thoughts and events. A is for yourself. There are no and there are no to a journal. Decide the function of your journal and decide what to put in it. Reads your journal, without your permission, and has any right to judge what is in it but you.

The subject is the focus of the sentence. It is the person(s), place(s), or thing(s) about which an assertion is made. The subject is directly connected to the action or condition expressed by the verb. When the subject is missing, the meaning of a sentence becomes unclear. An example of a subject connected to an action verb is "*Everybody* reads." Other examples include:

> *Jason* holds the pencil.
> *Veronica* types.
> A *girl* sings.

An example of a subject connected to a state-of-being verb is "a *journal is*." Other examples include:

> My *journal has* a leather binding.
> Her *journal appears* to be nothing more than scraps of paper.
> *I seem* to be making an effort at writing.

Some sentences have more than one subject connected to the verb. An example is "*Rules* and *limits* have no place in journal writing." Other examples include:

> *Poems* and *songs* can be recorded in a journal.
> *Observations* and *thoughts* can be recorded in a journal.
> *Dreams* and *goals* can be recorded in a journal.

Subject-verb agreement, Chapter 6 and Chapter 18.

Exercise 9

Circle the eight subjects in the paragraph below.

The (Dayton Hudson Credit Co.) is responsible for the proprietary credit offered to our customers. The (Collection area) is responsible for the payment of past due debt on this credit. (Collection) (Supervisor positions) are currently available in a variety of collection areas. Qualified (candidates) should possess strong leadership skills and project management experience. A college (degree) is desirable. Previous (experience) is a plus. Current (schedules) available include day, mid-shift, and evening with weekend rotation. Base (salary) is negotiable.

Adapted from an ad placed by Dayton Hudson Credit Co.
Star Tribune (January 19, 1999)

Exercise 10

Fill in the blanks with subjects to construct sentences that make sense.

1. _____Judy_____ nibbles on her pencil thoughtfully.
2. The _____girl_____ filled his dreams.
3. The _____dog_____ is always good.
4. The pink _____carpets_____ look good with the navy blue sofa.
5. _____Dan_____ is the man behind the mask.
6. _____She_____ is about to bungee off the bridge!
7. _____James_____ and _____Kyle_____ are not here yet.
8. The _____play_____ was horrible.
9. _____Students_____ are always late.
10. The _____soup_____ is too shoddy for my taste.

Exercise 11

Make sentences by having a subject operate with each verb below.

1. observe _The lions observe their prey at night_

2. read _I read the paper every day._

3. organize _Organize the paper!_

4. write _Write me a letter!_

5. imagine _Imagine what paradise looks like!_

6. mail _Did you receive mail._

7. inspire _I inspire others._

8. practice _Can you practice three times a week?_

9. know _Do you know your name?_

10. improve _Try to improve your foul shot._

Pronouns as Substitutes for Subjects

Another whole category of nouns is the pronoun. A pronoun is used in this riddle:

First I walk on four legs. Then I walk on two legs.
Later I walk on three legs.
Then I do not walk at all. Who am I?

Ancient Greek Riddle

The word "I" is a subject pronoun. It is a substitute word for the subject. In this case, the subject is the answer to the riddle. The answer is: a human being. Pronouns that can stand in place of singular subjects are:

I   you   she   he   it   this

Pronouns that can be used in place of plural subjects are:

we   you   they   there

Other pronouns that can be used in place of singular subjects include:

anybody	anyone	anything	what
much	everybody	everyone	everything
nobody	no one*	nothing	somebody
someone	something	each	either
much	that	one	another
who	which		

*Notice that the words are separated.

Other pronouns that can be used in place of plural subjects are:

neither	none	any	both
which	that	what	few
many	several	who	

Pronouns and the subjects they replace must *agree*. This means they must be of the same number (singular or plural) and they must be of the same gender (male, female, or neutral). Examples of pronouns used as subjects in sentences include:

We think that this is crazy.
Everyone has agreed to meet at midnight.
Who is not coming?
Something is in the air.
Nobody can say what it is.
She and *I* think that something mysterious is happening.

Indefinite pronouns, Chapter 18.
Noun and pronoun agreement, Chapter18.

Exercise 12

Circle the seven pronouns below.

In the morning (it) was bright, and (they) were sprinkling the streets of the town, and (we) all had breakfast in a café. Bayonne is a nice town. (It) is like a very clean Spanish town and (it) is on a big river. Already, so early in the morning, (it) was very hot on the bridge across the river. (We) walked out on the bridge and then took a walk through the town.

The Sun Also Rises
Ernest Hemingway

Exercise 13

Circle the sixteen subjects in the poem below. Some are nouns and some are pronouns. Do not circle nouns or pronouns that are not operating as subjects.

The moon is so high it is
Almost in the Great Bear.
I walk out of the city
Along the road to the West.
The damp wind ruffles my coat.
Dewy grass soaks my sandals.
Fishermen are singing
On the distant river.
Fox fires dance on the ruined tombs.
A chill wind rises and fills
Me with melancholy. I
Try to think of words that will
Capture the uncanny solitude.
I come home late. The night
Is half spent. I stand for a
Long while in the doorway.
My young son is still up, reading.
Suddenly he bursts out laughing,
And all the sadness of the
Twilight of my life is gone.

"I Walk out into the Country at Night"
Lu Yu
One Hundred Poems from the Chinese
Kenneth Rexroth, Trans.

Sentence Length and Sentence Fragments

A sentence can be as short as one word:

Beautiful.
No?
Help!

Sentences this short break the rule that applies to most sentences—that is, a sentence must have a subject and a verb. If either the subject or the verb is left out, the sentence is incomplete and has no clear meaning. This construction is called a **sentence fragment** and should be avoided. Examples of sentence fragments include:

After Rob and I.	My broken arm.
Raining so hard.	A good day.
A written record.	Pulled out of a drawer.

Most sentences go far beyond the minimum requirement of one subject and one verb. In fact, for style reasons writers sometimes create sentences that go on at great length. Readers may need to read these sentences several times to grasp all the information. Consider this example:

When I first saw New York I was twenty, and it was summertime, and I got off a DC-7 at the old Idlewild temporary terminal in a new dress which had seemed very smart in Sacramento but seemed less smart already, even in the old Idlewild temporary terminal, and the warm air smelled of mildew and some instinct, programmed by all the movies I had ever seen and all the songs I had ever heard sung and all the stories I had ever read about New York, informed me that it would never be quite the same again.

"Goodbye to All That"
Slouching Toward Bethlehem
Joan Didion

In addition to a subject and a verb, a sentence may include words or phrases that add meaning and detail to either the subject or the verb. These words and phrases are called **modifiers**, and they can modify either the subject or the verb. A modifier can be a single word or an entire phrase. For example: "A journal is a *written* record." Other examples include:

When I first saw New York I was twenty.
The warm air smelled of *mildew*.

Longer sentences are also made by linking shorter sentences together using words such as *and* or *but*. These transitional words are called **coordinating conjunctions**. For example: "You decide the function of your journal, and *you* decide what to put in it." Other examples of two sentences linked together to make one are:

When I first saw New York I was twenty, *and* it was summertime.
Ivan was a good linguist, *but* still he was unable to understand the dialect.

Words that modify verbs (adverbs), Chapter 20.
Words that modify nouns (adjectives), Chapter 20.
Compound sentences, Chapter 6 and Chapter 21.
Coordinating conjunctions, Chapter 21.

Exercise 14

Of the ten items below, only five are complete sentences. The rest are sentence fragments. Put a check next to the complete sentences.

_____ 1. How you feel about writing.

__✓__ 2. Positive feelings about writing will help you.

__✓__ 3. Negative feelings may get in your way.

_____ 4. To get something out of this course.

_____ 5. Effective writing skills.

__✓__ 6. What does it mean to "define yourself" as a writer?

_____ 7. Organizes words into a recorded form.

_____ 8. When you are a writer.

__✓__ 9. The end product makes the struggle worthwhile.

__✓__ 10. You must think of yourself as a writer.

Exercise 15

Underline the eight sentence fragments in the following journal entries.

July

1. The Adams and we are going to spend the Independence Day in the village to see the holyday fun. Father hopes to buy a horse on that day.

2. Thunder shower before sunrise, I dug new potatoes.

3. More rain. It cleared tonight, and tomorrow should be clear for our going to town.

4. Never heard so many bells and cannon shots. Several wagonloads were on their way as we walked to the village. Last year poor Daniel drove us in. Mr. Adams was reading the Declaration of Independence when we arrived and Mr. Grimes said a long prayer. Sarah looked very pretty. Father bought a horse and a waggon! We shall collect them on Saturday.

5. Began making ready for Bang. Father says a horse will jump over such fences as ours so we began making them higher.

6. A most exciting Saturday. We went to the village to collect Bang and the waggon. Bang is faster on the road than Daniel; we arrived home in less than ten minutes. Bessie would have none of Bang and she kicked her stall through. We shall leave Bang at pasture until the two animals become better friends.

7. Went to Meeting in the new waggon. It is great enjoyment to drive a horse.

8. Brilliant warm day. Father and Mr. Beach squared new timbers for the mill machinery. Tried my hand at the squaring axe while Father and Mr. Beach chizelled.

Diary of an Early American Boy: Noah Blake 1805
Eric Sloane, Ed.

Exercise 16

Make these fragments into complete sentences by attaching the fragment to a sentence or by supplying a missing subject or verb. The first one is done for you.

1. After I inherited some money from my uncle.

   <u>After I inherited some money from my uncle, I bought a new car.</u>

2. Since we both like dancing.

   <u>Since we both like dancing, I signed-up for dance classes.</u>

3. Unfortunately cannot go to the concert this evening.

   <u>Unfortunately Kyle cannot go to the concert this (he) evening.</u>

4. Plans to go to business school after she gets her degree.

   <u>She plans to go to business school after she gets her degree.</u>

5. We hoping to start a dry cleaning business.

   <u>We are hoping to start a dry cleaning business</u>

6. Need money from investors.

   <u>We need money from investors.</u>

7. The car in the accident.

   <u>The car in the accident, rolled seven times.</u>

8. Very excited about their new home.

They are very excited about their new home.

9. My friends and I camping at Glacier National Park.

My friends and I were camping at Glacier National Park.

10. Taken to the hospital in the ambulance.

He was taken to the hospital in the ambulance.

CHAPTER 18

Simple Verb Tenses and Subject-Verb Agreement

Verbs change form, or tense, to indicate when the action in a sentence is taking place. The verb tenses covered in this chapter are called **simple tenses**:

- **present tense**—what is happening now, for example, *I talk*
- **past tense**—what happened before, for example, *I talked*
- **future tense**—what will or may happen, for example, *I will talk*

This chapter also provides practice in creating **subject–verb agreement**, which means matching verbs with subjects so that the two agree in number (singular or plural) and in person (first person *I* or *we*, second person *you*, or third person *he, she, it,* or *they*). Writers must pay attention to subject-verb agreement for all verbs in the present tense and for the verb *be* in the past tense. It is not an issue in the future tense.

Present Tense

In the present tense, most verbs add *s* when used with a singular noun or *he, she,* or *it* (the third person singular):

> He *runs* away.
> The woman *grieves.*
> The fish *stinks.*

Most verbs that end in *tch, sh, ss,* or *x* add *es* for the third person singular:

> Antwan *catches* the ball.
> She *rushes* to get ready.
> The older sibling *bosses* the younger ones.
> Donnell *boxes* at the community gym.

Verbs that end with *y* change the *y* to *i* and add *es* for the third person singular.

> Mr. Litchfield *envies* you.
> Vinton *applies* for a scholarship.
> The bathing suit *dries* in the sun.

If the *y* follows a vowel, however, it does not change to *i* before *es* is added:

enjoy	enjoys
delay	delays
portray	portrays

The verbs *do* and *go* also add *es* for the third person singular:

> Kaita *does* the dishes.
> The babysitter *goes* to the door.

The verb *to be* follows a unique pattern. Notice that the singular form changes while the plural forms remain constant:

	Singular	**Plural**
first person	I *am*	we *are*
second person	you *are*	you (all) *are*
third person	he, she, it *is*	they *are*

The verb *have* also is unusual. The third person singular does not add *s*. Rather the word changes to *has*:

> She *has* meningitis.

Exercise 1

Fill in the blanks with the present tense form of the verb. Make sure that subject and verb agree.

1. The candidate for Senate _____ an outline for his speech. (sketch)

2. The students _____ for more parking. (campaign)

3. The manager _____ about the decline in sales. (worry)

4. Tram _____ our paychecks. (hold)

5. The demonstrator _____ away. (go)

6. Several boats _____ passengers between the two shores. (ferry)

7. The assistant _____ the packages from the front desk. (fetch)

8. He always _____ around in the morning before work. (rush)

9. This cleanser _____ a good job of removing grit. (do)

10. Wanting it to be perfect, she _____ over the final details. (fuss)

11. She _____ with the crowd. (mix)

12. The woman _____ up her garage sale receipts. (tally)

13. You _____ to get more sleep. (need)

14. The painter _____ the hole with some plaster. (patch)

Exercise 2

Fill in the blanks with the present tense form of the verb. Make sure that subject and verb agree.

1. In the film *Dr. Doolittle*, a veterinary surgeon _____ to the animals. (talk)

2. *For Whom the Bell Tolls* _____ a story about partisan fighters in the Spanish Civil War. (tell)

3. In *Citizen Kane*, a reporter _____ the newspaper tycoon's friends to discover the meaning of his last words. (interview)

4. The tramp in *City Lights* _____ a millionaire and falls in love with a blind girl. (befriend)

5. In the film *Murder on the Orient Express*, Hercule Poirot _____ a murder on a snowbound train. (solve)

6. In *King Kong*, a film producer _____ back a giant ape from a safari. (bring)

7. In *Snow White*, the wicked stepmother _____ an evil potion with which to destroy her young rival. (mix)

8. In *Dr. Strangelove*, a mad air force general _____ out a nuclear attack on the Russians. (carry)

9. In *East of Eden*, a wild adolescent _____ against his stern father and discovers that his mother, believed dead, runs a nearby brothel. (rebel)

10. In the *Bridge of San Luis Rey*, five people die when a Peruvian rope bridge _____. (collapse)

11. In *Brief Encounter*, a suburban housewife _____ a love affair with a local doctor. (develop)

12. In the film *Dazed and Confused*, high schoolers _____ all night long after the last day of school. (celebrate)

13. At the end of *The Sound of Music*, the governess _____ the father of the children. (marry)

14. In John Sayles's *Matewan*, West Virginia coal miners _____ to unionize. (struggle)

15. In *Being There*, Peter Sellers's character _____ a lot of television but later becomes president. (watch)

Exercise 3

Fill in the blanks with the correct present tense form of the verb *be* or *have*. Make sure that subject and verb agree.

1. Manatees, or sea cows, _____ a gentle nature.

2. We _____ right, of course.

3. The financial statements _____ ready.

4. This Kodiak bear _____ nine feet tall.

5. She _____ a nose ring and dyed black hair.

6. I _____ the facilitator today.

7. You and your sister _____ welcome.

8. That corporation, which is owned by a family, _____ an excellent reputation.

9. You _____ no excuse.

10. Slip, loop, square, and bowline _____ names of knots.

11. The man with the deep voice _____ quite a temper.

12. Lymphoma _____ another word for tumor.

13. You _____ the winning ticket holder.

14. Here _____ the maps.

15. The doctor _____ the test results now.

Simple Present Tense with Helping Verbs

Verbs used with other verbs to help indicate time are called **helping verbs**. Verbs that help form simple present tense sentences include *can, could, may, might, must, shall, should, will,* and *would.* These helping verbs turn a present tense sentence into a statement about possible action:

> You *can achieve* great things if you set goals.
> They possibly *could say* yes.
> The door *might fall* off its hinges in the next big wind.

The verb *do* and its third person singular form *does* also operate as helping verbs for simple present tense sentences. *Do* and *does* add emphasis to the present tense:

See? They *do have* all the luck.
She *does love* me, after all!

Note that the verb after a helping verb does not change form for subject-verb agreement (for example, *love* does not become *loves*).

Exercise 4

In each sentence, underline the subject. Then select the correct form for the second verb in each sentence. *Hint: Since these verbs follow helping verbs, their form does not change for subject-verb agreement.*

1. Cecil can (have, has) the tickets for tomorrow's game.

2. Ron and Jane may (go, goes) to Puerto Rico next fall.

3. You can (be, are) anything you want for the costume party.

4. From now on, you must (follow, follows) your own instincts.

5. My child shall (have, has) everything when I am rich.

6. Would your uncle (do, does) such a terrible thing?

7. This medicine does (help, helps) his arthritis.

8. I might (be, am) late.

9. He should (realize, realizes) that the lender he is talking to is offering him a poor rate of interest.

10. I will (finish, finishes) the marathon even if I have to crawl the last mile.

11. We must (eat, eats) before the food gets cold.

12. The music started, so shall we (dance, dances)?

Exercise 5

Circle the eighteen helping verbs and underline the verbs they assist.
Hint: Sometimes the helping verb and the verb it assists are separated by other words.

I do not have time to watch TV, but my roommate can watch TV all he wants because he does not work. He does not realize how much the TV bothers me. I will say to him, "The program is over. Can I turn the TV off?" Unfortunately, he will always say, "No, I must see what's on next." If the situation does not change, I may go crazy with that tube blaring all the time. I guess I should just ignore the noise. I think that he should look for a job instead of watching so much TV. Last month, he could not pay the rent. He must earn some money eventually. You can live off savings only so long. We do like each other except for this one issue, but if the situation does not change, I may look for a new place to live.

Past Tense

Most verbs follow a standard formula to indicate past time. These verbs are called **regular verbs**. But a number of exceptions to these rules also occur. The exceptions are called **irregular verbs**.

Regular verbs. Many verbs show the past tense by adding *ed*:

bargain	bargained
call	called
enter	entered

Verbs that end in *e* add only a *d* to form the past tense:

barge	barged
hope	hoped
live	lived

Verbs ending in *y* form the past tense by changing the *y* to *i* and adding *ed*:

carry	carried
copy	copied
cry	cried

If the *y* follows a vowel, however, it does not change to *i* before *ed* is added:

enjoy   enjoyed
delay   delayed
portray   portrayed

Irregular verbs. Irregular verbs break the regular patterns outlined above. Instead, each of these verbs follows its own unique pattern to create the past tense. For example:

buy   bought
drive   drove
go   went

The verb *be* follows a unique pattern in the past tense. Note that the singular form changes while the plural form remains constant:

	Singular	**Plural**
First person	I *was*	we *were*
Second person	you *were*	you (all) *were*
Third person	he, she, it *was*	they *were*

Many verbs are irregular. A list of common irregular verbs and their past tense forms appears in Figure 18–1.

Figure 18–1: Irregular Verbs

Present Tense	Past Tense	Past Participle (used with a helping verb)
1. arise	arose	arisen
2. awake	awoke	awoke, awaked
3. be	was, were	been
4. bear	bore	born
5. beat	beat	beaten
6. become	became	become
7. begin	began	begun
8. bend	bent	bent
9. bite	bit	bitten
10. blow	blew	blown
11. break	broke	broken
12. bring	brought	brought
13. broadcast	broadcast	broadcast
14. build	built	built
15. burn	burned, burnt	burned, burnt
16. burst	burst	burst
17. buy	bought	bought
18. catch	caught	caught
19. choose	chose	chosen
20. cost	cost	cost
21. cut	cut	cut
22. do	did	done
23. dig	dug	dug
24. dive	dived, dove	dived
25. draw	drew	drawn
26. dream	dreamed, dreamt	dreamed, dreamt
27. drink	drank	drunk

Figure 18–1: Irregular Verbs (continued)

Present Tense	Past Tense	Past Participle (used with a helping verb)
28. drive	drove	driven
29. eat	ate	eaten
30. fall	fell	fallen
31. feed	fed	fed
32. feel	felt	felt
33. fight	fought	fought
34. find	found	found
35. fly	flew	flown
36. forget	forgot	forgotten
37. freeze	froze	frozen
38. get	got	got, gotten
39. give	gave	given
40. go	went	gone
41. grow	grew	grown
42. hang*	hung	hung
43. have	had	had
44. hear	heard	heard
45. hide	hid	hidden
46. hit	hit	hit
47. hold	held	held
48. keep	kept	kept
49. know	knew	known
50. lay	laid	laid
51. lead	led	led
52. leave	left	left
53. lend	lent	lent
54. let	let	let

*Hang meaning "to kill by suspending from a rope" is regular (hang, hanged). Hang in any other sense is irregular.

Figure 18–1: Irregular Verbs (continued)

Present Tense	Past Tense	Past Participle (used with a helping verb)
55. lie**	lay	lain
56. lost	lost	lost
57. make	made	made
58. mean	meant	meant
59. meet	met	met
60. pay	paid	paid
61. put	put	put
62. quit	quit	quit
63. read	read	read
64. ride	rode	ridden
65. ring	rang	rung
66. rise	rose	risen
67. run	ran	run
68. say	said	said
69. see	saw	seen
70. sell	sold	sold
71. send	sent	sent
72. set	set	set
73. shake	shook	shaken
74. shoot	shot	shot
75. shrink	shrank	shrunk
76. shut	shut	shut
77. sleep	slept	slept
78. sing	sang	sung
79. sink	sank	sunk
80. sit	sat	sat
81. speak	spoke	spoken
82. spend	spent	spent

**Lie meaning "to tell an untruth" is regular (lied, lied). Lie meaning "to rest, to recline in a prone position" is irregular.

Figure 18–1: Irregular Verbs (continued)

Present Tense	Past Tense	Past Participle (used with a helping verb)
83. spread	spread	spread
84. spring	sprang, sprung	sprung
85. stand	stood	stood
86. steal	stole	stolen
87. stick	stuck	stuck
88. sting	stung	stung
89. stink	stank, stunk	stunk
90. swear	swore	sworn
91. sweep	swept	swept
92. swim	swam	swum
93. swing	swung	swung
94. take	took	taken
95. teach	taught	taught
96. tear	tore	torn
97. tell	told	told
98. think	thought	thought
99. throw	threw	thrown
100. understand	understood	understood
101. wake	waked, woke	waked, waken
102. wear	wore	worn
103. win	won	won
104. withdraw	withdrew	withdrawn
105. write	wrote	written

Spelling, Chapter 22.

Exercise 6

Fill in each blank with the present or past tense form of the verb that makes sense in the story. *Hint: For present tense verbs, pay attention to subject-verb agreement. For past tense sentences, add* d *or* ed *to the verb.*

1. I _____ into a two bedroom apartment recently. (move)

2. Now that I am settled in, the apartment _____ me very much. (suit)

3. Before I moved here, I _____ in a co-op. (live)

4. I did not like the co-op because everyone always _____ into my room without an invitation. (walk)

5. Finally, I _____ this very nice apartment near the college. (locate)

6. Now it _____ so quiet here by comparison! (seem)

7. I _____ to get away from the noise and confusion. (move)

8. I once _____ noise but not anymore. (enjoy)

9. Now I _____ without unwanted interruption. (live)

10. My mother wants me to move back home, and she _____ when I refuse. (cry)

11. Each time she asks I explain that I _____ to be independent. (need)

12. I _____ for five courses, so I must have a quiet place to study. (register)

13. I _____ that my mother will accept this. (hope)

14. She finally _____ to take in a student boarder after I moved out. (decide)

15. I _____ her every Sunday so she won't be too lonely. (visit)

tenses

Exercise 7

Review the past tense forms of irregular verbs in Figure 18–1 to complete the following lists.

1. Find five verbs that do not change for the past tense.

Present tense	Past tense
_____	_____
_____	_____
_____	_____
_____	_____
_____	_____

2. Find ten verbs that form the past tense by changing just one letter.

Present tense	Past tense
_____	_____
_____	_____
_____	_____
_____	_____
_____	_____
_____	_____
_____	_____
_____	_____
_____	_____
_____	_____

3. Find five verbs that form the past tense by removing one letter.

Present tense	Past tense
_____	_____
_____	_____
_____	_____
_____	_____
_____	_____

4. Find five verbs that form the past tense by changing the last letter *d* to *t*.

Present tense   **Past tense**

_____   _____

_____   _____

_____   _____

_____   _____

_____   _____

5. For each set of verbs listed below, think of another pair that follows the same pattern of vowel change. The first one is done for you.

	Present tense	**Past tense**
bring, brought	think	thought
break, broke	_____	_____
drive, drove	_____	_____
lay, laid	_____	_____
sink, sank	_____	_____
wear, wore	_____	_____

tenses

Exercise 8

Fill in the blanks with the past tense form of each verb. *Hint: All the verbs are irregular, so refer to Figure 18–1 as needed.*

1. Yesterday, I _____ to my bus because I got up late. (run)

2. Last week, I _____ a new stereo. (buy)

3. Walking home, we _____ the sunset. (see)

4. Monday, while peeling vegetables, I _____ my finger. (cut)

5. After six weeks of skiing lessons, the two women _____ (quit)

6. She _____ to stay with her grandmother for at least six months. (mean)

7. I _____ Li would not be late again. (think)

8. While I was recovering, I _____ several novels. (read)

9. My friends _____ some magazines to me. (bring)

10. My coworkers _____ my cold. (catch)

11. Long after the argument, I finally _____ her point of view. (understand)

12. The procedure did not _____ as much as I feared it would. (hurt)

13. The campers _____ to the pontoon in the middle of the lake. (swim)

14. True fans are those who _____ in line all night to get the first tickets. (stand)

15. Without being told, we _____ immediately what had happened. (know)

Exercise 9

Fill in the blank with the correct past tense form of *be* (either *was* or *were*).

1. Lee and Joni, where _____ you yesterday?

2. My son _____ well behaved as a child.

3. The cousins _____ close growing up.

4. The puppies _____ very hungry all the time.

5. You _____ late yesterday.

6. The firefighters _____ on the truck.

7. The CD that I threw away _____ damaged.

8. Sweenie _____ good at adding things in her head.

9. The telemarketer _____ very persuasive.

10. The defendant _____ pleased by the verdict.

11. _____ you cold last night?

12. Vinton's dream _____ very disturbing to him.

Future Tense

A sentence in the future tense is formed with the helping verb *will* along with another verb:

Junius *will succeed* as a computer technician.
I *will be* first in line when the store opens.
She *will find* a new job after she graduates.
This job *will improve*.

Note that the helping verb *will* always comes before the other verb. Note also that the second verb does not change form for subject–verb agreement (for example, *succeed* does not become *succeeds*).

Exercise 10

Add *will* plus a verb from the list below to make future tense sentences. *Hint: Remember that in future tense sentences, the second verb does not change form for subject-verb agreement.*

debate	cover	prepare	trade	help
meet	arrive	enjoy	be	visit

1. Library patrons _____ next month's discussion topic.

2. We _____ the issues surrounding light-rail transit for our city.

3. My loans _____ most of my education costs this year.

4. If you win the lottery, you _____ one set of money troubles for another.

5. Our career center _____ you to research different employment fields.

6. I _____ several job sites before I make any decisions.

7. I _____ my resume before I apply for any positions.

8. We _____ at the airport in time to get our connecting flight.

9. We _____ the VIPs in the reception hall.

10. This _____ enough gift wrap to take care of all these presents.

Subjects Separated from the Verb or after the Verb

Subjects and their verbs must agree, even when separated by other words:

> The *bailiff* at the back of the courtroom *comes* forward.
> *Sales staff* in each department *conduct* the inventory.

Subjects and their verbs must agree, even when the subject comes after the verb:

> Out the door *runs* the *cat*.
> When *was* the *tournament*?
> There *is* the *snake*.

Exercise 11

Underline the subject in each sentence. Then circle the correct form of the verb. *Hint: In each sentence, the subject is separated from the verb or is after the verb.*

1. Hundreds of unmarked bills (was, were) found inside the envelope.

2. How (is, are) your father?

3. The candles in the window (glow, glows) brightly.

4. What (is, are) your names, please?

5. The hostess of the party (hurry, hurries) to open the door.

6. The pencils in the drawer (was, were) sharpened.

7. Who (was, were) those handsome fellows?

8. Under this bridge (run, runs) a little stream.

9. Here (is, are) our rooms.

10. Will your hairdresser also (do, does) your color?

Exercise 12

Using the following list, pick a verb for each sentence that agrees with the subject in the sentence. You may use some verbs more than one time.

    was   were   meet   meets   need   needs   cost   costs

1. Our house _____ to have a new roof.

2. The tornadoes in our area _____ very destructive last year.

3. One of my neighbors _____ injured by a falling tree.

4. The tickets to the concerts _____ us twenty-five dollars each.

5. Where _____ the concert?

6. Living under our house _____ a cat with her kittens.

7. My friends, along with their mothers, _____ taking a trip to Florida.

8. Two of my classes _____ on Saturday.

9. The books that I am reading _____ written by American authors.

10. Kathy, one of the twins, _____ a newspaper editor in New York.

Compound Subjects

When a sentence has more than one subject joined by *and*, the verb takes the plural form:

Mel and *I exchange* recipes.
The *Cowboys* and the *Packers were* in the stadium.

When a sentence has two subjects joined by *or, either . . . or, neither . . . nor,* or *not only . . . but also*, the verb form is determined by the closest subject:

The students or the *teacher prepares* all the refreshments.
Neither my sisters nor *I hope* that happens.
Not only the officer but also his *lieutenants were* in full military regalia.
Either the pair of them or *Chi goes* first.

Exercise 13

Circle the correct form of the verb in each sentence below. Pay attention to the word joining the subjects (such as *and* or *or*) to decide whether to use the singular or plural form of the verb.

1. Neither Isabel nor Corinna (return, returns) today.

2. Cassettes and compact disks (is, are) old technology.

3. Some players, a flat field, a ball, and a bat (make, makes) a baseball game.

4. Neither the dress nor the hat (match, matches) the shoes.

5. My younger sister and my little cousins (play, plays) together.

6. Either the coach or her players (has, have) the trophy.

7. My brother and I (settle, settles) our dispute.

8. Where (was, were) the tools and the instructions?

9. Not only the watch but also these necklaces (need, needs) repair.

10. Angel and I (photocopy, photocopies) the notices.

11. The people going in and the people going out (shove, shoves) past each other.

12. Neither my sister nor I (has, have) our brother's new address.

13. The two kittens and the puppy (tackle, tackles) each other playfully.

14. Not only cake but also chocolate ice cream (is, are) out on the table.

15. The pilot and the flight attendants (has, have) similar uniforms.

Indefinite Pronouns

Pronouns that refer to an unspecified number of persons or things are called **indefinite pronouns**. As the subject of a sentence, the following indefinite pronouns are singular:

anybody	everybody	nobody	somebody	each
anyone	everyone	no one	someone	either
anything	everything	nothing	something	neither

Anybody *was* eligible for the contest.
Nobody *likes* to be late for the performance.

Each of the following pronouns can be either singular or plural, depending on whether the subject it stands for is singular or plural:

any	most	some
all	more	none

None of the *candy is* for you.
None of my *friends are* here.

The following pronouns take the verb form:

both	many	several
few	others	

Both of them *leave* at the same time.
Few of us *read* the fine print.

Exercise 14

Circle the correct form of the verb in each sentence below. Pay attention to the indefinite pronoun to decide whether to use the singular or plural form of the verb.

1. Everybody (is, are) welcome at the party.

2. Some of my friends (like, likes) to vacation in Jersey.

3. Some of these doughnuts (was, were) stale.

4. Nobody (dress, dresses) like she does.

5. Most of the employees (go, goes) to the company picnic.

6. These flowers bloom early, but some (bloom, blooms) later in the spring.

7. Neither door (is, are) locked.

8. The puppies are all female, but none (is, are) spayed yet.

9. Few of the residents (own, owns) a pet.

10. Some of us (go, goes) to the meetings on a regular basis.

11. My great-aunt helped me plant the flowers, and most (was, were) in bloom when she came back to visit.

12. All of the boys stand nearby, and several (watch, watches) the fight.

13. A lot of land around here is for sale, and some (go, goes) up for auction tomorrow.

14. Stop making sandwiches because enough (is, are) on the table to feed an army.

15. Some guests left today and the others (depart, departs) tomorrow morning.

Collective Nouns

A noun that represents a group of people or things, such as *team, jury,* or *family,* is called a **collective noun.** Collective nouns usually take a singular verb form to indicate that the group of people or things is acting as one body. However, when the collective noun refers to several individuals in a group, you may use the plural verb form instead:

> The *club has* a membership meeting today. (singular)
> The *synagogue needs* a larger building. (singular)
> The *staff prefers* the four-day work week. (singular)
> The *staff are* demanding their wages. (plural)

Exercise 15

Circle the correct form of the verb in each sentence below. Pay attention to whether the subject is a singular or plural noun.

1. The audience (clap, claps) hard after the performance.

2. The biggest fans in the audience (stand, stands) for an encore.

3. The project leadership (decide, decides) who will work on which project.

4. Project participants (is, are) each assigned to one project.

5. Septima's parents (has, have) strict rules for their daughter.

6. The couple (permit, permits) her to date only once a week.

7. Our company team (play, plays) softball after work.

8. The team pitchers (throw, throws) excellent curve and fast balls.

9. The church (run, runs) a day-care center for our children.

10. Many churchgoers (send, sends) their children to the center.

11. The staff (attend, attends) first aid training at 3:00.

12. The staff members (was, were) eager to take the training.

13. The union (begin, begins) collective bargaining next week.

14. Union members (pay, pays) dues to support this effort.

Gerunds

Gerunds are nouns that are formed by adding *ing* to a verb. When a gerund is the subject of a sentence, it is singular:

River *rafting is* great fun.
Community *policing wa*s effective.

Gerunds operating as nouns should not be confused with gerunds operating as verbs:

We ate chicken with stuffing. (*stuffing* is a noun)
Cindy is stuffing envelopes. (*stuffing* is a verb)

Exercise 16

Circle the correct form of the verb in each sentence below. *Hint: If a gerund is the subject of the sentence, the verb must be in the singular form.*

1. Her writing (have, has) greatly improved.

2. They (was, were) writing their congressional representatives.

3. Laughing (is, are) good for your health.

4. Everyone (was, were) laughing at the comedian's stand-up routine.

5. The lighting (seem, seems) dim in here.

6. The waiters (was, were) lighting the candles.

7. Walking (has, have) helped me lose weight.

8. Studying (help, helps) me to earn good grades.

9. Scuba diving (thrill, thrills) me.

10. Diving into deep waters (is, are) great fun.

11. What filling (is, are) in these doughnuts?

12. The maintenance workers (is, are) filling the pool for the new season.

13. This frosting (is, are) chocolate.

14. The cold evening air (is, are) frosting our windowpanes.

CHAPTER 19

Progressive and Perfect Verb Tenses

The last chapter explained how verbs operate in the simple tenses for present, past, and future. This chapter provides practice in the use of other tenses, called **progressive** and **perfect**:

- Progressive tenses describe action that is ongoing (present tense), was ongoing (past tense), or will be ongoing (future tense).

- Perfect tenses describe actions that are completed (present tense), were completed (past tense), or will be completed (future tense).

Present Tense (Progressive and Perfect)

Be in the present tense (*am, is, are*) acts as a helping verb to form present tense sentences:

> I *am splurging* on a big dinner.
> She *is fasting* for religious reasons.
> They *are competing* against each other.

This tense is called **present progressive**. It expresses ongoing action. Note that the verb after *be* is in the *ing* form. This verb form is called the **present participle**.

Have in the present tense (*have, has*) may be used to form another kind of present tense sentence:

> The equipment *has deteriorated*.
> The injured runners *have withdrawn* from the race.

This tense is called **present perfect**. It expresses action begun in the past that continues into the present (or that was completed at some unspecified, recent point in time). Note that the verb after *has* in the first example above is in the *ed* form. This is called the **past participle**. In the second example, the verb after *have* does not end with *ed* because its past participle is irregular. Past participles for irregular verbs are listed in Chapter 18, Figure 18–1.

Exercise 1

Underline the eleven verb phrases that are either present progressive or present perfect. *Hint: Remember that the present progressive is formed by* am, is *or* are + *present participle (*ing *verb) and the present perfect is formed by* have *or* has + *past participle (*d, ed, *or irregular verb).*

The Internet has had a major impact on the way people buy cars. Researching and even buying a car over the Internet is becoming the method of choice for smart consumers. From car-buying services such as Autobytel and Carpoint, consumers are obtaining specific price information such as factory invoice. These car-buying services also have made available financing, insurance, and warranty information and purchasing opportunities. From dealer Web pages, consumers are finding regularly updated inventory information on vehicles in stock. From manufacturer Web pages, consumers are viewing on-screen the available models, colors, and options. Car auctions also are cropping up on the Internet. All of this is putting consumers in a much better bargaining position. The Internet is allowing customers to research and even purchase cars without leaving their homes or offices. These days, you are setting yourself up for a bad deal if you go into a dealership unprepared. A consumer who has done the research almost always gets a better price and has a better purchase experience.

Exercise 2

Review the past participles of irregular verbs in Chapter 18, Figure 18–1, to complete the chart:

1. Find ten verbs for which the past tense and the past participle are the same.

Past tense	Past participle
_____	_____
_____	_____
_____	_____
_____	_____
_____	_____
_____	_____
_____	_____
_____	_____
_____	_____
_____	_____

2. Find ten verbs that have a past participle ending in *en*.

Past tense	Past participle
_____	_____
_____	_____
_____	_____
_____	_____
_____	_____
_____	_____
_____	_____
_____	_____
_____	_____
_____	_____

3. Find five verbs for which the past participle is formed from the past tense by changing *a* to *u*.

Past tense   **Past participle**

_____   _____

_____   _____

_____   _____

_____   _____

_____   _____

4. Find five verbs that have two acceptable ways of forming the past participle.

Past tense   **Past participle**

_____   _____

_____   _____

_____   _____

_____   _____

_____   _____

5. For each set of verbs listed below, think of another pair that follows the same pattern of vowel change.

                    Past tense   **Past participle**

drank, drunk   _____   _____

kew, known   _____   _____

rang, rung   _____   _____

shook, shaken _____   _____

Exercise 3

Fill in the blanks with a verb in the present progressive tense. Remember that the present progressive tense suggests that an action is occurring now. The first one is done for you.

1. The dog _____is hiding_____ his bone from us. (hide)

2. We _____ everywhere for it. (look)

3. The volunteers _____ their time very generously. (give)

4. I _____ my daughter go to the dance with her friends. (allow)

5. What academic program _____ you _____ in college? (study)

6. We _____ since our furnace went out. (freeze)

7. My parents _____ to move to Florida when all the children are grown. (plan)

8. They _____ to Tokyo on Northwest Airlines. (fly)

9. Jackie _____ all her friends about her wedding plans. (tell)

10. I _____ my new employees every two weeks. (pay)

11. You _____ way too much money on clothing and entertainment! (spend)

Exercise 4

Fill in the blanks with a verb in the present perfect tense. Remember that this verb should suggest that an action has just been completed. The first one is done for you.

1. They _____have spent_____ all their money on the trip to Africa. (spend)

2. We _____ our tax form in time for the April 15 deadline. (mail)

3. Lindsay _____ a new dress for her daughter's wedding. (buy)

4. They _____ plans with their travel agent. (make)

5. She _____ all the maps in preparation for her trip. (order)

6. I _____ a lot of history for my trip to Mexico. (read)

7. We _____ a party for them, but they changed the date of their return. (plan)

8. We already _____ the invitations. (address)

9. My instructor _____ all of our papers and _____ the grade list. (grade, prepare)

10. You _____ a beard; it looks good on you. (grow)

Exercise 5

For each verb and noun, create two sentences. One should be in the present progressive tense to suggest that the action is going on *now*. The other should be in the present perfect tense to suggest that the action *has been completed*. As needed, use Figure 18.1 in Chapter 18 to find the past participle for irregular verbs. The first one is done for you.

1. brush, teeth They are brushing their teeth in the bathroom now.

   They have brushed their teeth and now they are going to bed.

2. cut, wood _____

_____

_____

3. exterminate, cockroaches _____

_____

_____

4. transmit, fax _____

_____

_____

5. interrogate, suspect _____

_____

_____

6. varnish, table _____

_____

_____

7. sweep, porch _____

_____

_____

_____

8. bring, appetizers _____

_____

_____

9. go, baseball _____

_____

_____

10. swim, pool _____

_____

_____

verb tenses

Past Tense (Progressive and Perfect)

Be in the past tense (*was* or *were*) acts as a helping verb to form past tense sentences:

> He *was talking* about her as she entered the room.
> We *were walking* along when the stranger stopped us.

This tense is called the **past progressive**. It expresses action in the past that was ongoing. Note that the verb after the helping verb is in the present participle (*ing*) form.

Have in the past tense (*had*) can be used to form another kind of past tense sentence:

> The machine *had failed* twice before repair personnel were notified.

This tense is called the **past perfect**. Past perfect sentences express an action that happened prior to another action. Note that the verb after *had* is in the past participle (*d, ed,* or irregular) form.

Exercise 6

Fill in the blanks with a verb in the past progressive tense. *Hint: Put was or were before any present participle (ing verb form) to form the past progressive.* The first one is done for you.

1. They _____were taking_____ off their coats when I came in. (take)

2. The usher _____ latecomers down the aisle when the music started. (lead)

3. The children _____ in the garage. (hide)

4. I _____ you would visit me in the hospital, but you never did. (hope)

5. The last time I saw her, she _____ on stage. (sing)

6. You lost your job because you _____ your work. (neglect)

7. When I last heard them, they _____ out back. (play)

8. When I saw him, he _____ down the freeway in a reckless manner. (drive)

9. The electricity cost a lot, because we _____ our air conditioner all the time. (run)

10. We _____ on weight, so we decided to start exercising. (put)

Exercise 7

Fill in the blanks with a verb in the past perfect tense. *Hint:Put* had *before any past participle (d, ed, or irregular verb form).* The first one is done for you.

1. They already _____had taken_____ off their hats and gloves. (take)

2. He _____ me to my seat a few minutes earlier. (led)

3. We _____ our key under the mat. (hid)

4. I _____ that you would visit me in the hospital, but you never did. (hope)

5. She _____ her solo and was doing a duet. (sing)

6. You lost your job because you _____ your work. (neglect)

7. Dean claimed he _____ several bull's-eyes with his eyes closed. (shot)

8. He _____ bad fish and was sick all the next day. (eat)

9. She _____ infatuated with the rock star. (become)

10. Marla always _____ very casual clothes, but that changed when she began working in the law office. (wear)

Exercise 8

For each verb and noun, create two sentences. The first sentence should be in the past progressive tense to suggest that the action was ongoing. The second sentence should be in the past perfect tense to suggest that the action was completed. The first one is done for you.

1. shut, water

   The last time I checked they were shutting off the water to fix the pipes.

   They had shut off our water for four hours in order to do the repairs.

2. look, keys

   _____

   _____

3. ride, bronco

   _____

   _____

4. ring, buzzer

   _____

   _____

5. deposit, cash

   _____

   _____

6. buy, lottery tickets

   _____

   _____

7. think, ideas

   _____

   _____

8. beat, record

   _____

   _____

9.   fight, war

_____

_____

10.   teach, Spanish

_____

_____

Future Tense (Progressive and Perfect)

Will plus *be* can be used as helping verbs to form future tense sentences:

> We *will be jumping* for joy if we succeed.
> He *will be throwing* fits when he hears about the dent.

This tense is called the **future progressive**. It expresses action that will be ongoing at some future point. Note that the third verb is in the present participle (*ing*) form.

Will plus *have* can be used with other verbs to form another kind of future tense sentence:

> I *will have finished* my coursework by the time of the wedding.
> The virus will *have infected* our software by now.

This tense is called the **future perfect**. Future perfect sentences express an action that will be completed prior to another action. Note that the third verb is in the past participle (*d, ed*, or irregular) form.

Exercise 9

Fill in the blanks with a verb in the future progressive tense. *Hint: A present participle (ing verb) should follow* be. The first one is done for you.

1. I _____will be leaving_____ soon. (leave)

2. They _____ the goods tomorrow. (ship)

3. The director _____ before the evening performance. (rest)

4. We _____ a memorial service for my mother. (have)

5. I _____ German better after spending this summer in Berlin. (speak)

6. I _____ by train to my cousin's house. (go)

7. I _____ two weeks with my cousin and his family. (spend)

8. They _____ me back at the end of the two weeks. (drive)

9. You _____ all my family at the reunion in May. (meet)

10. I _____ reservations for you at a good motel. (make)

Exercise 10

Fill in the blanks with a verb in the future perfect tense. *Hint: A past participle (d, ed, or irregular verb) should follow* will have. The first one is done for you.

1. I _____will have missed_____ the train by now, so I will catch a ride with Suze. (miss)

2. They _____ each package carefully before putting them in the shipment. (wrap)

3. The program _____ by now. (finish)

4. She _____ the encore by now. (play)

5. I _____ German for two years before I actually go to Germany. (study)

6. You _____ a lot of Russian after you have lived in Russia for two years. (learn)

7. They _____ their dinner by the time we get there. (finish)

8. The airplane _____ by now. (leave)

9. Our friends _____ before we get there. (arrive)

10. I _____ all the arrangements by the time you arrive. (complete)

verb tenses

Exercise 11

For each verb and noun, create two sentences: one in the future progressive and one in the future perfect. Write the future progressive sentence to suggest that the action will be going on. Write the future perfect sentence to suggest that the action will be completed before something else happens. *Hint: For the future progressive, use* will + be + *present participle (ing verb), and for the future perfect use* will + have + *past participle (d, ed, or irregular verb).* The first one is done for you.

1. start, party _She will be starting the birthday party promptly at noon._

    She will have put up all the decorations by then.

    _____

2. look, antique _____

    _____

    _____

3. speak, girlfriend _____

    _____

    _____

4. defrost, meat _____

    _____

    _____

5. sell, coins _____

    _____

    _____

6. fly, vacation _____

    _____

    _____

7. gossip, rumors _____

    _____

    _____

8. eat, snack _____

_____

_____

9. leave, town _____

_____

_____

10. do, best _____

_____

_____

verb tenses

CHAPTER 20

Adjectives and Adverbs

This chapter provides practice in the use of adjectives and adverbs. These words add details that help readers visualize the objects (nouns) and the actions (verbs) of a sentence. They help make vague or general sentences more specific.

Adjectives

An **adjective** adds information that limits (modifies) the meaning of a noun, making that noun more specific:

> the *big* ship
> the *foreign* ship
> the *only* ship

Adjectives can provide information about quantity:

> the *many* faces
> my *three* friends

They can add descriptive details:

> the *confusing* plan
> the *outrageous* performance

They also can specify which particular item is being identified:

> the *left* hand
> the *last* bite

More than one adjective can be used to describe a noun:

> the *angry little* boy
> a *crumbling cement* staircase

Adjectives go before the noun, unless they are linked to the noun by a verb:

> The path is *long*.
> The rainbow grows *faint*.

Exercise 1

Underline the twenty-three adjectives in the paragraph:

My new apartment has high ceilings, faded curtains on large windows, and beige carpeting with a worn patch near the entry. The walls are plain white and they are clean, although there are several big holes in the plaster. There are a few crooked but charming pictures on the walls. There is little furniture except for several comfortable cushioned chairs and a big round table beneath an old chandelier. The atmosphere is shabby but friendly.

Exercise 2

Fill in the blanks with adjectives from this list to create sentences that make sense. Use each adjective only once.

pretty	red	excellent	hot	dented
stimulating	funny	delicious	noisy	frightening
braided	plaid	cluttered	fast	many

1. The _____ letter sent me into gales of laughter.

2. The steak and shrimp dinner is _____.

3. Luther said that he heard an _____ concert the other night.

4. The little girl held the _____ balloon tightly.

5. I watched the _____ motorcycles as they raced around the track.

6. The _____ traffic made me nervous.

7. _____ photographs decorated the walls of their home.

8. The _____ coffee burned my lips.

9. Ed had a _____ conversation with his instructors.

10. The haunted house's 3-D effects are _____.

11. Her hair is _____.

12. The _____ chair was the most noticeable piece of furniture in the room.

13. My desk is _____ with letters, books, and food.

14. The repair shop finally fixed my _____ bicycle.

15. The hospital patient was worn out by her _____ visitors.

Exercise 3

Pair each noun with an adjective that makes sense. Do this twice for each noun. You may use adjectives more than once.

Adjectives

cold	close	distant	evil	horrid
chatty	difficult	historical	medical	vague
sensible	excellent	northerly	true	long
deplorable	scientific	painful	awesome	ancient
powerful	horrible	beautiful	poor	scary

Nouns

1. _____ story _____ story

2. _____ novel _____ novel

3. _____ friend _____ friend

4. _____ experience _____ experience

5. _____ dictator _____ dictator

6. _____ evidence _____ evidence

7. _____ facts _____ facts

8. _____ information _____ information

9. _____ ride _____ ride

10. _____ wind _____ wind

11. _____ directions _____ directions

12. _____ movie _____ movie

13. _____ girl _____ girl

14. _____ storm _____ storm

15. _____ adventure _____ adventure

Exercise 4

Use the supplied nouns, verbs, and adjectives to create ten sentences. Use each word only once. The first one is done for you.

Nouns	Verbs	Adjectives
wind	seems	logical
picture	grows	hot
statement	is	blurry
cap	sounds	bitter
evidence	appears	weak
sun	becomes	strong
puppy	blows	hateful
plan	feels	soft
dinner	tastes	delicious
medicine	smells	small

1. The plan seems logical. _____

2. _____

    _____

3. _____

    _____

4. _____

    _____

5. _____

    _____

6. _____

    _____

7. _____

    _____

8. _____

    _____

9. _____

    _____

10. _____

    _____

Exercise 5

Make a list of ten adjectives and ten nouns from this paragraph. Match each adjective with a noun and write ten new sentences. The first one is done for you.

Most of the dwellings are fairly spacious farm houses in the customary white, with wide wraparound porches and tall narrow windows, though there are many of the grander kind—fretted, scalloped, turreted, and decorated with clapboards set at angles or on end, with stained-glass windows at the stair landings and lots of wrought iron full of fancy curls—and a few of these look like castles in their rarer brick. Old stables serve as garages now, and the lots are large to contain them and the vegetable and flower gardens which, ultimately, widows plant and weed and then entirely disappear in. The shade is ample, the grass is good, the sky a glorious fall violet; the apple trees are heavy and red, the roads are calm and empty; corn has sifted from the chains of tractored wagons to speckle the streets with gold and with the russet fragments of the cob, and a man would be a fool who wanted, blessed with this, to live anywhere else in the world.

In the Heart of the Heart of the Country and Other Stories
William Gass

	Adjective	**Nouns**	**New Sentence**
1.	spacious	porches	Old-fashioned houses often had spacious porches.
2.	_____	_____	_____
3.	_____	_____	_____
4.	_____	_____	_____
5.	_____	_____	_____

6. _____ _____ _____
_____

7. _____ _____ _____
_____

8. _____ _____ _____
_____

9. _____ _____ _____
_____

10. _____ _____ _____
_____

Adjectives That Compare

Adjectives may be used to compare two or more things. Most adjectives of one syllable can be used to compare by adding the suffix *er* for the comparative form or *est* for the superlative form:

> Marc's car is *big*.
> Marc's car is the *bigger* of the two cars. (comparative adjective)
> Marc's car is the *biggest* one in the whole show. (superlative adjective)

Notice that the final consonant, *g*, gets doubled in the comparative and superlative forms of *big*.

For two-syllable adjectives ending in *y*, the *y* changes to *i* before *er* or *est* is added:

> Jake was *silly*.
> Jake was *sillier* than the other boys.
> Jake was the *silliest* of them all.

For other adjectives of more than one syllable, use *more* and *most* to compare:

> Lorna is *efficient*.
> Lorna is *more efficient* than Liza.
> Lorna is the *most efficient* of all the employees.

The adjectives *good* and *bad* follow a unique pattern when used to compare. The patterns are *good, better, best* and *bad, worse, worst*:

Food at Manny's is *good*.
Food at Teja's is *better* than at Manny's.
The food at La Cantina is the *best* of all the Mexican restaurants around here.

The acting in *Cyrano* was *bad*.
The acting in *Hamlet* was *worse* than in *Cyrano*.
The acting in *Othello* was the *worst* of all.

In the examples above, note the use of the words *than* and *of* to form the comparisons.

Exercise 6

Write the comparative and superlative forms of these adjectives.

	Adjective	Comparative	Superlative
1.	quick	_____	_____
2.	high	_____	_____
3.	tremendous	_____	_____
4.	bright	_____	_____
5.	lazy	_____	_____
6.	excellent	_____	_____
7.	large	_____	_____
8.	offensive	_____	_____
9.	small	_____	_____
10.	brutal	_____	_____
11.	gigantic	_____	_____
12.	nice	_____	_____
13.	rich	_____	_____
14.	interesting	_____	_____
15.	happy	_____	_____

Exercise 7

Fill in the blanks with the comparative and superlative adjectives that make sense.

1. (sick) Rags was the _____ puppy in the litter.

2. (weak) He was _____ than any of the other pups.

3. (small) Rags was the _____ dog in the local animal shelter.

4. (frisky) After Rags received good care at the shelter, he became one of the _____ animals there.

5. (affectionate) He also became the _____ puppy you ever saw.

6. (wonderful) He was adopted by the _____ family.

7. (large) The shelter can handle a _____ number of animals now that the facilities have been improved.

8. (rich) Last year, the _____ woman in town gave $50,000 to renovate the shelter.

9. (large) That was the _____ gift the shelter had ever received.

10. (great) It was a _____ contribution than the shelter management expected to receive.

11. (generous) Our benefactor really was the _____ woman in town.

12. (quick) _____ than you could imagine, the shelter was renovated.

13. (few) There were _____ problems during the renovation than we had anticipated.

14. (functional) The shelter is _____ than before.

15. (outstanding) Now it is the _____ shelter in the area.

Exercise 8

From the adjectives supplied, circle the one that makes sense.

1. I am suffering from a (bad, worst) cold today.

2. My cold is (worse, worst) than it was yesterday.

3. This has been the (worse, worst) year for me in terms of health.

4. I am trying to make a (good, best) translation of this poem.

5. It sounds (better, best) in Spanish than in English.

6. French is the (good, best) language of all for romantic poetry.

7. The patient's blood pressure is (worse, worst).

8. These are the (worse, worst) numbers she has registered.

9. Her situation is (worse, worst) than it was before she went on the medication.

10. This kind of fish makes a (good, better) main course.

11. It will taste (better, best) baked than fried.

12. Grilling is the (better, best) of all methods for cooking fish.

13. That is a (bad, worse) spot for your garden because it is too shady.

14. Over here would be a (better, best) spot for the garden.

15. Homegrown tomatoes taste (better, best) than store-bought ones.

Adjectives Formed from Verbs

Many adjectives are created by adding the suffix *ed* or *ing* to a verb:

> The *thrilled* winners received their *thrilling* prizes.
> The *bored* audience listened to a *boring* speech.
> The *interested* listeners surrounded the *interesting* visitor.

In some cases, the past participle form of irregular verbs may serve as adjectives. These past participles are listed in Chapter 18, Figure 18–1.

> He lingered by the *frozen* lake.
> *Forgotten* memories returned to her.

Adjectives formed this way are used in the same way as other adjectives. Both are used to provide extra information about the nouns they modify.

Exercise 9

Make adjectives out of the verbs in the list below by adding the suffix *ed* or *ing*. Complete this paragraph by filling in the blanks with these adjectives. Use each word only once. *Hint: Remember that one-syllable words ending in* e *drop the final* e *before adding these suffixes.*

dine   sing   write   frost   whip   give   entertain   cut

I write a local food column, and I often use my laptop computer to find new recipes. The other day I found one for an orange cream cake that looked good, but it called for a cup of _____ cream. Unfortunately, I didn't have any cream. However, I was able to borrow some from my neighbor lady who is a very _____ person. It turned out so well that I took her a piece of the _____ cake.

I am really happy with this laptop computer that represents _____ edge technology. It is so convenient that I even use it at restaurants to take notes on the food. For example, Saturday night I dined at a very _____ restaurant that had a _____ waitstaff. While I was there, I was able to get the recipe for one of their specialties. The computer enables me to complete my _____ assignments for the magazine very quickly. Most fine _____ establishments are usually quite agreeable about sharing their recipes.

Exercise 10

From the adjectives supplied, circle the one that makes sense in the sentence.

1. The (torn, tearing) pages of a book were scattered down the street.

2. The accident was a (terrifying, terrified) experience.

3. Our flight was (delayed, delaying) so we went to the airport cafe for some coffee.

4. I went to bed with a (throbbed, throbbing) headache.

5. I had to replace a much (loving, loved) pair of shoes.

6. Her (ached, aching) ankle hurt so much that she had to go to the doctor.

7. My grandfather's (declining, declined) health required that he enter a nursing home.

8. The car came charging toward the (shocking, shocked) pedestrians.

9. She was using (delayed, delaying) tactics to avoid turning in the project.

10. The (broken, breaking) faucet needs a new gasket.

Adverbs

Adverbs modify the meaning of verbs by adding description or information. Many adverbs end in *ly*. Adverbs can go before or after the verb they modify:

Jan writes *quickly*.
Emil *happily* eats.
Wael and Khalid speak *often*.

Never and *not* are two commonly used adverbs:

We are *not* attending.
Never insult your coworkers.

Adverbs also modify adjectives:

The presentations were *very* pertinent.
Joleen had a *really* enjoyable evening.
The argument was *quite* loud.

Adverbs also modify other adverbs:

The train moved *unusually* slowly.
She retraced her steps *very* quickly.
They worked *too* hard.

Note that when adverbs modify adjectives or other adverbs, they usually go before the word they modify.

Adverbs should not be confused with adjectives that are similar:

    Adj.   *Noun*
The <u>brave</u> firefighters saved the children. *(adjective modifies noun)*

    Adv.   *Verb*
They <u>bravely</u> fought the flames. *(adverb modifies verb)*

Exercise 11

Circle the adverb or adverbs in each sentence and draw a line to the word(s) modified.

1. The sports car suddenly stopped for the red light.

2. I write slowly when I do my first draft.

3. I have a really crowded schedule next week.

4. Most patrons in the library speak very softly.

5. The brick complex was sturdily built.

6. The men and boys' choir sang the national anthem clearly.

7. The young thief ran swiftly.

8. The enthusiastic audience clapped vigorously after the last act.

9. He really speaks with very little accent.

10. The lab instructor stated her instructions quite carefully.

Exercise 12

Circle the adjective or adverb that should be used in each sentence.

1. The line for the show moved (slow, slowly).

2. Despite the good reviews, we found it to be a (slow, slowly) movie.

3. The doctor (grim, grimly) told us the news.

4. Our father's chances of surviving the operation were (grim, grimly).

5. We hired a (careful, carefully) driver.

6. He (careful, carefully) negotiated the mountain's hairpin turns.

7. Magdalena is a (fine, finely) artist.

8. She produces (fine, finely) drawn etchings.

9. The minister's boys dress (smart, smartly).

10. They are very (smart, smartly), too.

Exercise 13

Write ten sentences that make use of the nouns, pronouns, verbs, and adverbs from the list below. Use each word only once. The first one is done for you.

Nouns and Pronouns	Verbs	Adverbs
I	go	often
you	make	again
chef	purchase	never
classmates	eat	truly
it	enjoy	always
we	prepare	really
riders	happen	quickly
twins	recognize	barely
colleague	schedule	not
the others	work	rarely

1. I always schedule appointments for Fridays. _____

2. _____

_____

3. _____

_____

4. _____

_____

5. _____

_____

6. _____

_____

7. _____

_____

8. _____

_____

9. _____

_____

10. _____

_____

The Adverbs *Well* and *Badly*

Well and *badly* are adverbs that are easy to confuse with the adjectives *good* and *bad*. Use *well* and *badly* to modify verbs. If the sentence expresses a state of being or refers to state of health, use the adjective *good* or *bad*.

Marie sings *well*.
Eduardo skates *badly*.
She is a *bad* sport.
Shanna doesn't feel *good*, so she went home.

Exercise 14

Fill in the blank with the adverbs *well* or *badly* or the adjectives *good* or *bad*.

1. I enjoyed the play because it was _____ acted.

2. The apples are sour, but these bananas taste _____.

3. The puppy is behaving _____ and we need to train her.

4. It is a _____ thing you went to the emergency room when you did.

5. The staff was disappointed that the meeting had been so _____ handled.

6. The new worker is _____ liked by the others on the line.

7. There is little turnover in this department because it is _____ run.

8. I did _____ in the swimming meet.

9. Give me one _____ reason to stay, and I will stay.

10. The schedule did not work because of _____ timing.

11. Andreas is feeling _____ because he has a migraine headache.

12. Are you feeling _____ enough to attend tonight?

13. The party was a great success, and the guests had a _____ time.

14. The papers were _____ confused, and it took hours to order them.

15. The silk shirt feels _____ against the skin.

CHAPTER 21

Compound and Complex Sentences

Simple sentences that are well written can be very effective, but often writing is enhanced by using more complicated and varied sentence structures. Whether you know them by name or not, you often speak, read, and write using two kinds of sentences: compound sentences and complex sentences. Both of these sentence forms build on the simple sentence, which was the topic of Chapter 17.

This chapter provides practice in

- Creating compound sentences using coordinating conjunctions, semicolons, and transition words.

- Recognizing and correcting two kinds of sentence errors, the comma splice and the run-on.

- Building complex sentences using subordinating conjunctions and relative pronouns.

Compound Sentences

A **compound sentence** contains two or more simple sentences that are related in thought. As covered in Chapter 17, a simple sentence has a subject and a verb and expresses a complete idea. It is also called an **independent clause** because it can stand alone. Here are two simple sentences:

Subject   Verb
Thouraya wrote the report in longhand.

Subject   Verb
William typed it on the computer.

Joining these two simple sentences results in a compound sentence:

Subject   Verb   Subject   Verb
Thouraya wrote the report in longhand, and William typed it on the computer.

Using Coordinating Conjunctions to Make Compound Sentences

In the example above, the two simple sentences are joined by the word *and*, which is one of the seven connecting words called **coordinating conjunctions**. The seven conjunctions are:

and   but   or   so   nor   yet   for

When you use coordinating conjunctions, you indicate to readers that the two independent clauses connected by the conjunction are of equal importance. Note that a comma always comes before a coordinating conjunction:

The detectives worked on the case for several years, *but* it was never solved.

Jon will deliver the letter, *or* I will send it by express mail.

I will not be going to the wedding, nor will I attend the shower for Rita.

Mary arrived long after the concert began, *so* I had to head for our seats alone.

The taxi was very expensive, *yet* I decided to take it anyway.
The doctor ordered a liquid diet for Tim, *for* he was badly dehydrated.

Notice that *nor* means the opposite of *or*. When you use *nor*, you need to reverse the subject-verb order of the second clause and remove the word *not*.

I am not stupid. I am not ignorant.
I am not stupid, *nor* am I ignorant.

Exercise 1

Circle the coordinating conjunctions in these sentences.

1. I did not feel well yesterday, (yet) I still went to work.

2. We could not get hotel reservations, (so) we had to delay our trip.

3. Many people buy raffle tickets, (but) very few ever win a prize.

4. You need to reserve a seat soon, (or) you will not get one.

5. The weather was hot and dry (yet) it was not unpleasant.

6. Janice will bring the hot dish, (and) Sonja will bring the dessert.

7. We took the plane to Dallas, (for) it would have been too long a trip by car.

8. I will not sign the petition, (nor) will I attend the rally.

9. Today is a school holiday (so) we are going to the state fair.

10. We did not go to the concert, (for) the tickets were too expensive.

Exercise 2

Insert a coordinating conjunction between each pair of simple sentences. Choose a conjunction that makes sense. Be sure to put a comma before the conjunction.

1. The dinner was served very quickly, _____yet_____ it was not very hot.

2. The waiter was apologetic, _____so_____ he offered to return the food to the kitchen.

3. This restaurant has received good publicity, _____but_____ it never seems to attract a big crowd.

4. We really look forward to eating out, _____so_____ we try to eat out at least twice a month.

5. My sister works at a very elegant restaurant, _____and_____ she gets good tips.

6. I once thought running a restaurant would be fun, _____but_____ now I am not so sure.

7. I think it would be interesting to be a food critic, _____so_____ I could eat out often at little cost.

8. My friend Elsa likes to cook at home, _and_____
she also likes to eat out at good restaurants.

9. I cut recipes out of the newspaper _, and_____ I
put them in a file for future reference.

10. I never learned to cook as a child, _yet_____ I
have a great interest in cooking.

Joining Independent Clauses with Semicolons

Another way to join closely related independent clauses is by using a
semicolon(;). The semicolon suggests a slightly shorter stop than a
period and a slightly longer stop than a comma and conjunction. Do not
capitalize the word following a semicolon, unless it is a proper name.
Be cautious with semicolons. Be sure that you use them only to join
independent clauses that are close in meaning. Overusing this
punctuation mark can be distracting to the reader. Study the following
examples:

Sabastine worked hard all afternoon. He finished his report.
(two complete sentences)

Sabastine worked hard all afternoon, and he finished his report.
(a compound sentence joined by a coordinating conjunction)

Sabastine worked hard all afternoon; he finished his report.
(a compound sentence joined by a semicolon)

All three sentences have essentially the same meaning, but the last one
emphasizes the connection between Sebastine's hard work and its result.

Exercise 3

Circle six semicolons in this paragraph. Then read the paragraph out loud
and listen for the "shorter stop."

I have grown fond of semicolons in recent years. The semicolon tells you that there is still some question about the preceding full sentence; something needs to be added; it reminds you sometimes of the Greek usage. It is almost always a greater pleasure to come across a semicolon than a period. The period tells you that that is that; if you didn't get the meaning you wanted or expected, anyway you got all the writer intended to parcel out and now you have to move along. But with a semicolon there you get a pleasant little feeling of expectancy; there is more to come; read on; it will get clearer.

"Notes on Punctuation"
Lewis Thomas
From *Medusa and the Snail*

Exercise 4

Find six pairs of sentences that can be joined by a semicolon. Make the independent sentences into compound sentences by changing the period ending the first sentence to a semicolon and replacing the uppercase letter of the first word in the second sentence with a lowercase letter.

Nora was very excited; she had been made supervisor of her department. She had worked there for only six months, so she didn't expect the promotion so soon. The company has been purchased by a competitor. Many employees feared they would lose their jobs. Some employees left the company; others decided to stay and see what would develop. Unfortunately, Al was afraid his job would be eliminated; he took a job with another company. Actually no jobs were eliminated; the company even hired more employees. The company is growing. Revenues are 50 percent higher this year. Now Al regrets leaving the company; his new job is not nearly as interesting. The company may rehire him; they are looking for a person with his skills.

Joining Independent Clauses with Transition Words

Another way to link independent clauses is by joining them with **transition words**. These words help make a smooth connection from one idea to the next. The following words are common transitions and phrases:

actually	instead	as a result
also	meanwhile	for example
besides	moreover	in addition
consequently	nevertheless	in fact
furthermore	therefore	in other words
however	thus	of course
indeed	unfortunately	on the other hand

All three of the following examples are essentially equivalent in meaning:

I still had a lot of work to do. Nevertheless, I went to the movies.
I still had a lot of work to do; nevertheless, I went to the movies.
I still had a lot of work to do; I went, nevertheless, to the movies.

Note that a transition word after a semicolon is not capitalized (again, because the transition occurs within a compound sentence). Also note that when the transition word is used in the middle of a clause (such as in the third example above), commas are used in front and back of it.

Exercise 5

Make compound sentences by inserting semicolons, transitional phrases, and commas. Transitional words and phrases that you can use include:

as a result	for example	however	actually
in addition	in fact	therefore	unfortunately

1. I like to travel; _in fact,_ I am planning a trip to Africa next summer.

2. I have some friends who want to join me, _actually (therefore)_ several have already made plans to go.

3. One of my friends is nervous about flying; _however,_ he still plans to go on the trip.

4. The Internet has information on Africa; _as a result,_ I am spending a lot of time on the Internet.

5. I checked airline ticket prices on the Internet; _in fact,_ I got a very inexpensive round trip ticket.

6. I plan to keep a journal on this trip; _unfortunately_ it may be difficult to write every day.

7. I will take a portable laptop computer with me; _in fact,_ I hope to write articles for a magazine.

8. Most often we will stay in inexpensive hotels; _for example,_ sometimes we will stay in youth hostels.

9. I am studying many travel books; _in addition;_ I am watching a lot of travel videos.

10. I have to get my passport; _however (in addition)_ I have a lot of things to do before the trip.

Exercise 6

Create compound sentences by composing a sentence to link onto each sentence below. Use transition words from the list below to join the sentences. *Hint: Put a semicolon after the first sentence, do not capitalize the transition word, and put a comma after it.*

therefore	as a result	in addition
however	for example	in fact

1. I used to exercise every day; *as a result, I have a nice midline.*

2. I go to school twenty hours a week; *in addition, I work 20 hours a week*

3. I really prefer to watch television in my spare time; *however, I don't have a lot of it*

4. The weather was very bad; *in fact, the state highways have been closed*

5. Some days I am full of energy; *therefore I can get all of the chores done.*

6. I enjoy old movies; *in fact, I own the whole series to Bonanza.*

7. The ice was very thin; *therefore, we couldn't go ice skating.*

8. My good friend exercises every day; *in addition, she has a well balanced diet too.*

9. I like to go to the gym; *however, I usually don't have time too with my hectic work schedule*

10. Some days I have to work overtime; *in fact I worked till 2:00 a.m. yesterday*

The Comma Splice

A **comma splice** occurs when two independent clauses are linked by a comma and are thus treated as one sentence. An independent clause has a subject and a verb and can stand alone. Comma splices interfere with communication. The reader wonders if words have been left out of the sentence or if the two clauses should be considered separate sentences. Comma splices can be corrected in several ways:

- Joining the clauses with a comma and a coordinating conjunction.
- Joining the clauses with a semicolon.
- Making the independent clauses into two separate sentences.

Examples of comma splices include:

My dog got Lyme disease, she was sick for six weeks.
Her medicine was very expensive, it made her well.

Ways to correct the comma splice include:

My dog got Lyme disease, and she was sick for six weeks. (comma and coordinating conjunction)

My dog got Lyme disease; she was sick for six weeks. (semicolon)

My dog got Lyme disease. She was sick for six weeks. (two separate sentences)

Exercise 7

Underline the five places in each letter where two sentences are joined with a comma splice.

Dear Suzi:

It was so good to hear from you. Yes, I do know where the whirling dervishes perform, they appear twice a week at the Ghuri Palace. The performances are on Wednesday and Saturday evenings, they are free. It is a good idea to get there early, the seating is limited. You will be amazed at the skill of the dancers, they wear very colorful and elaborate costumes. The main dancer whirls for about thirty minutes without stopping, I don't see how he can do it without getting dizzy. I know you and your friends will enjoy the performance.

Best regards,
Yuri

Dear Yuri:

Thank you for your information about the whirling dervishes. I took my friends there last Friday, we had a wonderful evening. After the performance, we went to the Egyptian Pancake House, they make pancakes that are like crepes. As we were eating, a man offered to shine our shoes, now we all have clean shoes! Next week I am taking these same friends for a cruise on the Nile River. I hear that the food is not very good on these cruises, it is pretty bland. Nonetheless, the magnificent scenery makes up for the poor food. The entertainment includes a belly dancer, it should be a great evening!

Best regards,
Suzi

Exercise 8

These sentences contain comma splice errors. Correct these sentences by forming two independent sentences, joining the clauses with a comma and a coordinating conjunction, or joining the clauses with a semicolon. Several variations are possible.

1. My brother lives in Europe, he is a world-relief worker.

   _____

   _____

2. My stepsister is an exceptionally good tennis player, she has qualified for the Olympics.

   _____

   _____

3. Omar was promoted to head manager, everyone was happy for him.

   _____

   _____

4. My sister is a very talented writer, she has authored two books.

   _____

   _____

5. We live in Chicago, our apartment is near Lake Michigan.

   _____

   _____

6. The play is scheduled for this weekend, tickets are already on sale.

   _____

   _____

7. Cocker spaniels are good pets, some say inbreeding has made them too nervous.

   _____

   _____

8. My nephew will be married in August; he will move to Alaska in September.

_____

_____

9. I like to write poetry; everyone encourages me by praising my efforts.

_____

_____

10. My dream is to travel to the Middle East; the airfare is very expensive.

_____

_____

Run-ons

The **run-on sentence** is similar to the comma splice sentence except that there is no comma separating the independent clauses. The run-on sentence has two or more independent clauses that simply run into each other without any punctuation. This makes it hard for the reader to know where a thought starts or ends. The run-on sentence may be corrected in the same way that comma splice errors are corrected:

- Joining the clauses with a comma and coordinating conjunction.
- Joining the clauses with a semicolon.
- Making the independent clauses into two separate sentences.

Two examples of run-on sentences are:

Our house is not very new it needs a lot of repair.
We took our vacation at the lake we had a good time.

Ways to correct the run-on include:

Our house is not very new, and it needs a lot of repair. (comma and coordinating conjunction)

Our house is not very new; it needs a lot of repair. (semicolon)

Our house is not very new. It needs a lot of repair. (two separate sentences)

Exercise 9

Draw a line under the four run-on sentences in this letter.

Dear Mr. Aquilla:

Thank you for your request for an application form I am enclosing some company literature and an application form. Please complete the form as thoughtfully and as completely as possible. Your profile will be entered into our computerized search system. The profile will be only as informative and accurate as the information you provide. You should make sure that the information is clear, specific, and easy to understand "key words" are an important tool in our computer search process. They help us find the applicants who most closely fit the particular specifications of our position openings.

We will keep your application on file for one year after that you should call us if you are still interested. Then we can discuss keeping your file active. Thank you for your application we appreciate your interest in our company.

Sincerely,
Elaine M. Kawasaki

Exercise 10

Correct the errors in the following run-on sentences. Rewrite the sentences using any of the three methods just discussed.

1. Individuals are very different from each other in learning styles, some students need smaller school settings that feel more like families.

   _____

   _____

   _____

2. Some students need hands-on experiences in order to internalize learning; still others need to feel ownership of governance and decision making.

   _____

   _____

   _____

3. Others feel trust in whatever system serves them. Some need very special arrangements or services.

   _____

   _____

   _____

4. It is important to understand that students have unique needs; they learn in different ways.

   _____

   _____

   _____

5. Some students who are not challenged drop out of school. They do not develop their full potential.

   _____

   _____

   _____

6. Some communities have started charter schools, *and* they focus on the individual needs of their students.

   _____

   _____

   _____

7. Some students feel more comfortable in the smaller charter school settings; some teachers also thrive in the smaller, more intimate settings.

   _____

   _____

   _____

8. Some charter schools are very structured, *o*thers offer expanded opportunities for creativity or involvement in self-governance.

   _____

   _____

   _____

9. Some charter schools have been very successful, *but* others have had problems.

   _____

   _____

   _____ *in addition*

10. Their success often depends on the degree of community support, it also depends on how much financial aid they receive from the state.

    _____

    _____

    _____

Complex Sentences

A **complex sentence** contains two clauses: an independent clause and one or more **dependent clauses**. A dependent clause contains a subject and a verb, but it cannot stand by itself; its meaning "depends" or relies on the independent clause to which it is connected. The dependent clauses are italicized in these examples:

Zachariah studied diligently for his exam *after he walked around the park.*

Because her dog was getting restless, Marla took him for a walk.

Using Subordinating Conjunctions to Make Complex Sentences

In the example above, a connecting word is used to join a dependent clause to an independent clause. These connecting words are called **subordinating conjunctions**. Subordinate means "of a lower order" or "secondary." Subordinating conjunctions add secondary information to a main idea. The following words are important subordinating conjunctions:

after	although	as	as though
because	before	even though	how
if	in order that	since	so that
though	unless	until	when
whenever	where	while	who
whoever	whose		

The dependent clause can go before or after the independent clause. When the dependent clause comes first, a comma is used to separate it from the independent clause. Usually no comma is necessary when the dependent clause follows the independent clause.

Exercise 11

Underline the eight dependent clauses in this paragraph and circle the linking subordinating conjunctions.

Although television provides entertainment for millions of people, many experts believe that too much television viewing is bad for young children. When the television is used as a babysitter, children are deprived of human interaction. Children's imagination and creativity may be stunted because watching television is a passive activity. If you think your child is watching too much television, keep a daily log of viewing hours. After you log the hours, make a note of the program content. Whenever you notice programs inappropriate for your child, suggest an alternative program or activity. Take time to explain why it is a poor choice so that your child understands your concerns about the program. Work with your child to plan special activity days without television viewing.

Exercise 12

Create complex sentences by adding a subordinating conjunction.

1. Alternative medicine is becoming more accepted by the medical profession _____though_____ many traditional doctors remain skeptical.

2. _____Unless_____ the medical school of a major university is opening a department of alternative medicine, alternative medicine is still not accepted by many people.

3. Researchers have still not proven that vitamin C helps prevent colds _____even though_____ it sure works for me.

4. Max refuses to see a doctor _____although_____ he has a severe illness.
   (until)

5. I, on the other hand, go to the doctor _____when_____ I have the slightest problem.

6. Yvonne gets headaches _____when_____ she has to give a speech.

7. _Although_ yoga isn't for everyone, many people who practice it believe that it helps them to relax and stay fit.

8. _Since_ some health insurance plans now cover acupuncture, more people are willing to try it.

9. _When_ I was in China, I studied herbal medicine.

10. _So that_ I can be well informed on alternative therapies, I read two alternative medicine journals each month.

Exercise 13

Create a complex sentence by adding a dependent clause before each independent clause. Remember that a dependent clause starts with a subordinate conjunction and has a subject and a verb. Remember also to use a comma after each dependent clause. The first one has been done for you.

1. After driving all night to the slopes, we went skiing.

2. _When I sliced my finger with the knife_ they took me to the hospital.

3. _Even though I broke my toe,_ I was able to walk again in three weeks.

4. _While I was in Russia living,_ I took a six-hundred-mile motorcycle trip.

5. _Even though I trained daily,_ I found that I didn't have as much stamina as before.

6. _Whenever Scott goes on a trip he does everything_ he does not like deep sea diving.

7. _They didn't give up until,_ they climbed the Matterhorn.

8. _As an obese person,_ I need to work out three times a week.

9. _Even though I hate school,_ I am taking a computer course and a math course.

10. _Whenever a tornado hits you personally_ you have great respect for the power of tornadoes.

Joining Clauses with Relative Pronouns

A dependent clause also can be joined to an independent clause using a **relative pronoun**, which substitutes for a noun and is placed next to the noun to which it refers. In the following examples, the dependent clause is in italics and the relative pronoun is underlined:

Dr. Lee is an excellent history teacher *who lived in China during the Cultural Revolution.*

The teacher gives "A's" to the students *whose papers are most complete and informative.*

Zachariah studied hard for the exam *that he needed for certification.*

Frequently used relative pronouns are:

who	*refers to persons*
whose	*refers to ownership by persons*
that	*refers to persons or things*
which	*refers to things*

When the dependent clause is not essential to the meaning of the independent clause but merely interrupts it, it should be separated by commas. The dependent clause is **nonessential** if the rest of sentence makes sense without it, as in the following examples:

Kirinee Stevens, *who starred in the television commercial,* is my neighbor.
I am the guardian of the Smith girls, *whose parents died.*

If a dependent clause starting with a relative pronoun is **essential** to the meaning of the independent clause, then no commas are necessary.

Kirinee Stevens is the neighbor *who starred in the television commercial.*
Those girls *whose parents died* are coming to live with us.

The relative pronouns *which, who,* and *whose* may be used to introduce both essential and nonessential clauses. The pronoun *that* only introduces essential clauses. Therefore, commas are never used to separate dependent clauses beginning with *that.*

This is the Mustang *that I rebuilt.* (essential—no comma needed)

I am selling this furniture, *which is made of mahogany.* (nonessential—comma needed)

People *who are never on time* really irritate me. (essential—no comma needed)

Exercise 14

Determine which sentence of each pair contains a nonessential clause. Add commas to separate the nonessential clauses. *Hint: Start by underlining the* dependent clause *beginning with the* relative pronoun. *Then read the sentence out loud and determine whether the meaning conveyed by the* relative clause *is important to the meaning of the sentence or is simply additional (nonessential) information.*

1. Lana who will be my roommate next fall lives in Alaska. Fortunately, the roommate who was so sloppy is moving out.

2. A new volunteer at the hospice is Jodi who is an honor student. Most of the volunteers who work in the summer are still in high school.

3. The insurance policy which I bought from my friend has a hundred thousand dollar payout. This is the policy that my financial planner advised me to purchase.

4. The work clothes which I had ordered from Spiegel finally arrived today. They will replace the outfits that I have outworn.

5. My friend who is our neighbor gave me a good recommendation for a restaurant. The other neighbor who is going there with us had never heard of it before.

6. I needed a new computer to replace the one that crashed. My new computer which I bought from a discount house is a Pentium III.

7. The day manager is the person who oversees the entire staff. Zack who has worked for us for three years holds that position.

8. Fady who was born in Iran speaks Arabic and French fluently. He is the consultant who helped with those translations.

9. Dr. Betts who will perform your surgery is out of town this week. Dr. Betts is the same surgeon who did my brother's knee surgery.

10. The movie which had a huge budget was a total flop. It starred actors who commanded multimillion dollar salaries.

Exercise 15

Use a relative pronoun (*who, whose, which,* or *that*) to add a dependent clause to each independent clause below. Separate with commas those clauses that are nonessential. The first one has been done for you.

1. Microsoft is a huge software company

   <u>that has been extremely successful.</u>

2. I know of some software developers

   <u>That don't really like their job.</u>

3. I also have friends,

   <u>who work for these companies.</u>

4. I also know some people

   <u>who would die to work for these companies</u>

5. Laptop computers <u>which are very high-tech,</u>
   are becoming increasingly popular.

6. The employees <u>whose job is to design the computer,</u>
   have a very good health plan.

7. Investors often will take a risk on new start-up companies

   <u>which helps the inventors work out flaws.</u>

8. I would like to be an inventor

   <u>whose invention ended up making millions</u>

9. I want to take the kind of computer courses

   <u>that teach you the basics,</u>

10. Computer programmers <u>that go to the right school,</u>
    usually get paid well.

Exercise 16

Make a complex sentence from each pair of sentences. Make the second sentence into a dependent clause introduced by *which* or *that*. Remember to separate the clause with commas if it does not add essential information. The first one is done for you.

1. Mozart wrote many symphonies and operas.
   They have lived on long after his death.

   <u>Mozart wrote many symphonies and operas that have lived on long</u>

   <u>after his death.</u>

2. George Frederic Handel wrote *Messiah*.
   It is often sung in church at Christmas and at Easter.

   George Frederic Handel wrote Messiah, which is often sung in church on christmas and at Easter.

3. Antonin Dvořák, a Czech composer, wrote the *New World Symphony*, *which*
   ~~It~~ was composed while he was living in Spillville, Iowa.

   _____

   _____

   _____

4. Camille Saint-Saëns wrote *Carnival of the Animals*, *which*
   ~~It~~ is enjoyed by both children and adults.

   _____

   _____

   _____

5. The processional played at many graduation ceremonies is *Pomp and Circumstance*, *that*
   ~~It~~ was written by Edward Elgar, a British composer.

   _____

   _____

   _____

6. George Gershwin wrote music, *that*
   ~~The~~ music has a definite American flavor.

   _____

   _____

   _____

7. Some modern music uses an atonal scale, *that*
~~It~~ doesn't sound melodic to some people.

_____

_____

_____

8. Edvard Grieg based many of his compositions on folk melodies, *which*
~~He~~ learned ~~these~~ melodies as a child in Norway.

_____

_____

_____

CHAPTER 22

Spelling

It is easy to make spelling mistakes in English because words are not always spelled as they sound. For example, the *f* sound in a word might be spelled using an *f*, a *ph*, or a *gh*. An *s* sound might be spelled using an *s* or a *c* or even a z. In addition, many pairs of words that sound the same—such as *there* and *their*—have different spellings and meanings. You cannot depend on the spelling checker on your computer to tell you if you are using the correct word. For example, it will not flag the word *hole* (opening) when the word you need is *whole* (entire). In many cases, the only way to know how a word is spelled is by memorizing the spelling of that specific word.

Fortunately, many English words, including long words, follow predictable spelling patterns. By learning these patterns, you can increase your spelling accuracy. In this chapter you will:

- Review the most useful spelling rules and their exceptions.
- Identify some commonly misspelled words.
- Learn some tips to help you spell difficult words correctly.

i before *e*

The trick for correctly spelling words that have an *ie* or *ei* vowel combination is to learn this rule:

> *i* before *e*
> except after *c*
> or when the sound is like *ay*
> as in *neighbor* and *weigh*

Words that use the *ie* combination include:

> ach*ie*ve
> br*ie*f
> n*ie*ce

Words that use the *ei* combination after *c* are:

conceive
deceit
receipt

Words with the *ei* combination that sounds like *ay* include:

neighbor
sleigh
weight

Exceptions. If the *c* sounds like *ch* or *sh*, the *ie* combination is used.

ancient
deficient
sufficient

Other words that do not follow this rhyming rule include:

caffeine	protein
either	seize
height	sleight
leisure	stein
neither	weird

Exercise 1

Copy the words below into the appropriate section of the chart.

niece	ancient	conceive	vein	caffeine
deceit	beige	freight	veil	grief
weigh	receive	thief	seize	relieve
sleigh	efficient	perceive	deceive	neighbor
diesel	weird	sufficient	conceit	yield
receipt	their	conscience	believe	friend

i* before *e	**except after *c***	**sounds like *ay***

***c* sounds like *ch* or *sh* (*ie*)**	**other exceptions (*ei*)**

spelling

Exercise 2

Write the correctly spelled word in the blanks. Put a circle around the vowel combination *ie* or *ei* in each word that you choose.

1. The store gave me a _____ for my purchase. (receipt, reciept)

2. I _____ in my family's values. (believe, beleive)

3. My son likes to watch _____ trains. (freight, frieght)

4. Our walls and carpet are _____. (biege, beige)

5. The _____ in coffee and some other drinks is a stimulant. (caffeine, caffiene)

6. Our _____ is always doing good deeds for us. (neice, niece)

7. Jake's _____ is named Zandra. (friend, freind)

8. I felt a lot of _____ after my dog died. (grief, greif)

9. I try to live my life so that my _____ is clear. (conscience, consceince)

10. Color-blind persons cannot _____ the difference between red and green. (percieve, perceive)

11. I hope to _____ a diploma in two years. (receive, recieve)

12. I _____ too much because I am eating too much junk food. (wiegh, weigh)

13. Science fiction sometimes is pretty _____. (weird, wierd)

14. _____ engines have replaced steam engines. (Diesel, Deisel)

Exercise 3

Draw a line through the word in each pair that is misspelled.

1. neighbor   nieghbor
2. reciept   receipt
3. wiegh   weigh
4. wierd   weird
5. conscience   consceince
6. receive   recieve
7. achieve   acheive
8. conceive   concieve
9. either   iether
10. niece   neice
11. percieve   perceive
12. sufficeint   sufficient
13. stien   stein
14. anceint   ancient
15. thief   theif
16. diesel   deisel

Changing *y* to *i*

When a verb ends in *y*, change *y* to *i* before adding *es* (not just *s*) or *ed*:

cry	cries	cried
apply	applies	applied
deny	denies	denied

When a noun ends in *y*, also change *y* to *i* before making it plural by adding *es* (not just *s*):

pony	ponies
pansy	pansies
nanny	nannies

When an adjective ends in *y*, change *y* to *i* before adding the comparative suffix *er* or *est*:

lovely	lovelier	loveliest
ugly	uglier	ugliest
nasty	nastier	nastiest

Also change the final *y* to *i* when adding other suffixes such as *ful, ly,* or *ness*:

beauty	beautiful
merry	merrily
holy	holiness

Exception: When the final *y* of a verb has a vowel before it, do not change the *y* before adding an ending:

obey	obeys	obeyed
relay	relays	relayed

spelling

Exercise 4

Complete this exercise by writing the correct form for each verb.
The first one is done for you.

Present tense	Third person singular	Past tense
1. defy	defies	defied
2. try	_____	_____
3. employ	_____	_____
4. relay	_____	_____
5. marry	_____	_____
6. pry	_____	_____
7. hurry	_____	_____
8. play	_____	_____
9. bury	_____	_____
10. betray	_____	_____

Exercise 5

Fill in the blank with the correctly spelled plural of each noun.

1. I have finally completed all my _____. (study)

2. The children will participate in the _____ and other races. (relay)

3. According to the myth, Santa Claus comes down your chimney to deliver _____ and other presents. (toy)

4. We have made frequent _____ into the city. (foray)

5. Beethoven wrote nine _____. (symphony)

6. For the writing course, students had to complete several _____. (essay)

7. Diners at the outdoor restaurant were shaded from the sun by _____ that hung from the sides of the building. (canopy)

8. Graduates of the program are sought after by all the best catering _____. (company)

9. _____ are major crimes and the punishments are more severe than for misdemeanors. (Felony)

10. _____ were swarming near the garbage can. (Fly)

11. _____ and coffee were served during the break. (Pastry)

Exercise 6

Draw a line through the word in each pair that is misspelled.

homelier	homelyer
prettyer	prettier
fanciest	fancyest
shyest	shiest
happyly	happily
bountiful	bountyful
fancyful	fanciful
ugliness	uglyness
silliness	sillyness
craziness	crazyness

Dropping the Silent e

When a word ends with a silent *e*, drop it before adding a suffix such as *able*, *ion*, *ing*, and *ous*:

value	valuable
motivate	motivation
give	giving
nerve	nervous

Exceptions. When the silent *e* follows a soft *c* (pronounced like *s*), the *e* is usually kept to signal the soft *c* sound. For example:

noticeable
peaceable
serviceable

Some words retain the final *e* when a suffix is added that begins with a consonant, such as *ful*, *less*, *ly*, *ment*, and *ness*.

care	careful	name	nameless	love
lovely	manage	management	complete	completeness

Exercise 7

Fill in the lines of the chart by combining the root word from the top row with an ending from the column at the left.

	love	grieve	grace*
able	_____		
ion			
ing	_____	_____	_____
ous		_____	_____
ful			_____
less	_____		_____
ly	_____		
ment			
ness			

	fame	use	televise
able		_____	
ion			_____
ing		_____	_____
ous	_____		
ful		_____	
less		_____	
ly			
ment			
ness			

	arrange	advise	mercy
able		_____	
ion			
ing	_____	_____	
ous			
ful			_____
less			_____
ly			
ment	_____		

	lonely	happy
ly		_____
ness	_____	_____

*To combine grace + *ous*, insert an *i*: gracious

Exercise 8

Draw a line through the word in each pair that is misspelled.

1. debateable   debatable

2. motivatieon   motivation

3. moving   moveing

4. famous   fameous

5. homeless   homless

6. completely   completly

7. appropriately   appropriatly

8. peacful   peaceful

9. arrangement   arrangment

10. rudeness   rudness

Doubling Consonants When Adding Endings

In one-syllable verbs, the final consonant is doubled before *ed* or *ing* is added if it follows a consonant and a vowel. In other words, to check whether the final consonant should be doubled, see if the letter pattern is *consonant–vowel–consonant (cvc)*:

cvc		
shop	shopped	shopping

cvc		
strap	strapped	strapping

cvc		
admit	admitted	admitting

Reminder: The vowels are a, e, i, o, u, *and* y *when it has the sound of* i. *All other letters are consonants.*

In two-syllable words, the final consonant is doubled if the letter pattern is a consonant–vowel–consonant *and* the last syllable is stressed. If you are not sure where the stress falls, say the word out loud and notice which syllable is emphasized. Some two-syllable words that are stressed on the second syllable are:

cvc
control   contro__lled__   contro__lling__

cvc
occur   occu__rred__   occu__rring__

cvc
commit   commi__tted__   commi__tting__

cvc
defer   defe__rred__   defe__rring__

Some two-syllable words have a *cvc* pattern, but they are stressed on the first syllable so they do not double the final consonant:

cvc
fasten   fastened   fastening

cvc
open   opened   opening

cvc
ponder   pondered   pondering

cvc
revel   reveled   reveling

Exception. When a one-syllable word ends in *x*, the final consonant is not doubled before adding an *ed* or *ing* ending:

box   boxed
fix   fixed
tax   taxed

Exercise 9

Add the endings *ed* and *ing* to the following words. Remember to double the final consonant if necessary. The first one is done for you.

	ed	ing
1. thin	thinned	thinning
2. admit		
3. open		
4. control		
5. skin		
6. occur		
7. peel		
8. refer		
9. scream		
10. transfer		
11. light		
12. tend		
13. strain		
14. need		
15. narrow		
16. turn		
17. resist		
18. patrol		
19. submit		
20. defer		
21. commit		
22. fax		
23. hex		
24. scan		

Exercise 10

One word on each line is misspelled. Cross out each misspelled word and write the correct spelling below it.

1. occur   occured   occurring

    _____

2. prefer   preferred   prefering

    _____

3. transfer   transfered   transferring

    _____

4. omit   omitted   omiting

    _____

5. commit   committed   commiting

    _____

6. patrol   patrolled   patroling

    _____

7. persist   persistted   persisting

    _____

8. visit   visited   visitting

    _____

9. depart   departed   departting

    _____

10. disappear   disappeared   disappearring

    _____

The Endings *able* and *ible*

The suffix *able* is added to some words that would be complete without a suffix:

avoid	avoidable
depend	dependable
consider	considerable

The suffix *ible* is added to some words that cannot stand by themselves without the suffix:

audible	plausible
edible	terrible
horrible	visible

Exceptions. Some words that break this pattern include:

accessible	digestible
collectible	exhaustible
convertible	flexible

Exercise 11

Draw a line through any of the following words that are misspelled. Write the correct spelling for the misspelled words.

1. breakible _____

2. comfortible _____

3. peaceable _____

4. taxible _____

5. workible _____

6. permissible _____

7. dependable _____

8. visable _____

9. favorable _____

10. readable _____

11. laughable _____

12. noticeible_____

13. perishible_____

14. drinkable _____

15. sinkible _____

16. affordable_____

17. mentionable_____

18. creditable _____

Exercise 12

Fill in the blanks with words ending in either *able* or *ible*. Choose words from Exercise 11, but be sure to spell them correctly. Apply the rules; then look in the dictionary to check your work.

1. No one thought that the Titanic was _____.

2. Sometimes mistakes are not _____.

3. The demonstration was _____.

4. She was a very _____ witness.

5. The manuscript was clear and very _____.

6. He had a _____ hole in the sole of his shoe.

7. Some housing today is too expensive; however, some is
   _____.

8. The lines on the road often are not _____ on
   dark, rainy evenings.

9. Jorge got a _____ grade on his research report.

10. Fresh fruit is _____.

11. Fragile glass is often very _____.

12. My bed in the dorm is not very _____.

13. It was _____ to think I could run the mile in
    less than one minute.

14. My sister always helps me out; she is very _____.

15. My professor said that my thesis statement was not
    _____.

Commonly Misspelled Words

The following list contains 200 words that are frequently used and frequently misspelled.

absence	conscience
acceptable	conscious
accidentally	consequence
accommodate	consequent
accuracy	controlled
acknowledge	convenient
acquire	criticize
across	curiosity
address	customary
adjust	dealt
advertise	definitely
advisory	dependent
amateur	descent
analyze	desert
argument	dessert
ascent	destitute
assassination	descriptive
associate	destroy
argument	develop
athletic	disappear
attendance	disappearance
beautiful	disastrous
because	discipline
behavior	discouraged
belief	dissatisfied
believe	dissolve
bureaucracy	distinction
business	embarrass
calendar	emphasis
cancelled	encounter
capital	envelope
career	environment
change	especially
changeable	equipment
character	exaggerate
choose	excellent
column	excitable
concentrate	excitement

expendable

experience

facility

familiarity

fascinate

fascist

financial

foreign

fortunately

finally

forty

fourth

fulfill

fully

genuine

gorgeous

government

grandeur

grateful

gratitude

handkerchief

hindrance

hindsight

hostility

illogical

immediately

incidentally

individual

intelligent

interfere

involvement

irresistible

jealous

jewelry

knowledge

knowledgeable

legible

leisure

liability

liberation

library

license

limitation

literature

loose

marriage

mimicked

mortgage

municipal

mystery

necessary

ninety

ninth

nonsense

noticeable

nutritious

occasion

occasionally

occur

occurrence

opinion

opportunity

panicked

parallel

permissible

possess

potatoes

precede

preferred

prejudice

prescribe

principal

principle

privilege

probably

procedure

professor

professional

prognosis

pronunciation

propaganda

psychology

really

repetitious

spelling

resemblance
resistance
restaurant
reversible
roommate
rhythm
sacrifice
sandwich
sentiment
separate
similar
specifically
substitute
success
surrounding
swimming
thorough
thought
through
transparent
transportation
tragedy
trapeze
typical
tyranny
unanimous
unnecessary
useful
utility
vacuum
valve
violent
virtue
visible
visual
weather
yearn
yield
yesterday
zinc

Exercise 13

Choose twenty words from the preceding list that are difficult for you to spell. Write each word at the beginning of the line and then compose a complete sentence using each word.

1. _____

   _____

2. _____

   _____

3. _____

   _____

4. _____

   _____

5. _____

   _____

6. _____

   _____

7. _____

   _____

8. _____

   _____

9. _____

   _____

10. _____

    _____

11. _____

    _____

12. _____

    _____

spelling

13. _____
_____

14. _____
_____

15. _____
_____

16. _____
_____

17. _____
_____

18. _____
_____

19. _____
_____

20. _____
_____

spelling

Exercise 14

In the passage below, circle ten words that you find difficult to spell or that you think might be difficult for others. Copy them below. For extra credit, think of a strategy for remembering the correct spellings.

Eighteen months earlier, the Callejón de Huaylas had been the scene of the greatest earthquake-plus-avalanche disaster in Peruvian history and it was only now that its fearful aftermath was beginning to be cleaned up. In a number of towns in this 100-mile-long, densely populated valley every building had been destroyed, and in Ranrahirca alone, 30,000 people had been buried in a single instant under millions of tons of rock, mud and ice. Apart from the tragic spectacle this offered, Walter thought that the huge relief effort invited description, and mentioned that psychiatrists had been sent from all over the world to help cope with the psychological problems of thousands of victims of the catastrophe who had been driven beyond the limits of endurance by their sufferings. Disasters at Huaylas, he said, had occurred regularly throughout history, even being recorded by the Incas. Apart from spectacular loss of life, these terrible events had induced their own medically recognized form of neurosis, prevalent in people doomed to live out their lives waiting for millions of tons of ice to fall on them from the skies.

The World, the World
Norman Lewis

_____ _____ _____ _____

_____ _____ _____ _____

_____ _____

Strategy: _____

_____

_____

_____

Exercise 15

Write a sentence using the word on each line. Underline the word you use. Look in a dictionary if you are not sure of a word's meaning.

1. gracious _____

_____

2. handkerchief _____

_____

3. virtue _____

_____

4. hindsight _____

_____

5. occurrence _____

_____

6. argument _____

_____

7. knowledgeable _____

_____

8. disastrous _____

_____

9. parallel _____

_____

10. develop _____

_____

11. accommodate _____

_____

12. potatoes _____

_____

13. prejudice _____

_____

14. succeed _____

_____

15. conscience _____

_____

Homonyms

Homonyms are words that sound alike but have different meanings and spelling. Errors in the usage of these words will not be caught by the spelling checker on a computer, so you must train your eye to catch them. Here are twenty-eight sets of common homonyms:

air	brake	buy	fair	hear	hole	hour
err	break	by	fare	here	whole	our
its	knew	knight	know	made	passed	peace
it's	new	night	no	maid	past	piece
plain	principal	rain	real	sew	stationary	their
plane	principle	reign	reel	so	stationery	there
						they're
threw	to	wear	weather	who's	write	your
through	too	where	whether	whose	right	you're
	two				rite	

spelling

Exercise 16

Circle the correct word in each of the following sentences.

1. Should I buy plain, white, or flowered (stationery, stationary)?

2. (It's, Its) a great day to go hiking.

3. I bumped into our high school (principle, principal) at the grocery store.

4. My purse seemed to have vanished into thin (air, err).

5. The (rain, reign) of Henry VIII in England was marked by much violence.

6. (Whose, Who's) responsibility is it to keep the coffee room clean?

7. He was the (principle, principal) researcher on the project.

8. (You're, Your) driving way too fast for the traffic conditions.

9. I wish that there could be (peace, piece) in the world.

10. He had a big (whole, hole) in his sock.

spelling

Exercise 17

Fill in the blanks with the correct word. Study the context (meaning of the sentence) to help with your choice.

1. I thought that the plane _____ was outrageously expensive. (fare, fair)

2. _____ suitcase was left behind? (Who's, Whose)

3. England was a powerful nation during the _____ of Queen Elizabeth. (rain, reign)

4. Mr. Torres is the _____ of the school. (principle, principal)

5. Are you sure that you have the _____ directions? (write, right, rite)

6. Alicia _____ biology with flying colors. (passed, past)

7. I want to hear the _____ story! (hole, whole)

8. I dropped my fishing rod in the lake, so I had to buy a new _____. (real, reel)

9. I _____ that you want to take the summer off, but it just isn't possible. (know, no)

10. Is that _____ suitcase and carryall over by the counter? (there, their)

11. When I started my consulting business, I bought new _____. (stationary, stationery)

12. Professor Wang explained the _____ of the combustion engine. (principle, principal)

13. Are you sure that this business venture isn't going to be _____ risky? (to, too, two)

14. I _____ someone who could advise you on how to develop a business plan. (know, no)

15. I _____ that she is reasonable and gives great advice. (hear, here)

16. It is sometimes easy to _____ on the side of caution rather than to explore new areas. (err, air)

spelling

Confusing Words

Some words sound so similar that it is difficult to know which word you need in a particular sentence. Here are fourteen sets of words that can be troublesome.

accept (to receive willingly)
except (exclude or excluding)

advise (to offer advice)
advice (opinion)

affect (to influence)
effect (as a noun means "result"; as a verb, "to cause" or "to accomplish")

among (involving three or more items)
between (involving only two items)

apt (suitable)
likely (possible or probable)

beside (next to)
besides (in addition to)

desert (dry, sandy region)
desert (to abandon)
dessert (comes after a meal)

few (a small number)
less (a smaller amount or quantity)

later (after the expected time)
latter (the second of two items mentioned)

least (lowest in rank or order)
lest (for fear of)

loose (not tight)
lose (unable to find)

quiet (silent)
quite (to the fullest extent)

statue (sculpture of a figure)
statute (law)

than (used to compare)
then (relates to time)

Exercise 18

Put the correct word in the blanks.

1. Jason is much taller _____ his cousin. (then, than)

2. Jann and Jena's mother will not let them have _____ unless they eat all their main meal first. (desert, dessert)

3. The United Nations divides the cost of operation _____ all members. (among, between)

4. I would like to _____ change in my children's behavior. (effect, affect)

5. Law books are filled with the _____ that have been passed by Congress and state legislatures. (statues, statutes)

6. I have _____ tickets for tonight's game. (to, too, two)

7. If you take my _____, you will take every opportunity you get to travel. (advise, advice)

8. The Sahara is a vast sand _____ in northern Africa. (dessert, desert)

9. Manuel's car had engine problems, and so he arrived a lot _____ than he had planned. (later, latter)

10. Everyone came to the office party _____ Rita. (accept, except)

spelling

CHAPTER 23

Punctuation

Punctuation marks help the writer express ideas clearly to the reader. The usage of punctuation is based on rules that have evolved over several hundred years to clarify meaning for readers. When you use punctuation marks according to these standards, you improve the chances that readers will receive the message you intended. This chapter reviews the following kinds of punctuation:

- End marks, which show where a sentence ends and whether it is a statement, a question, or an exclamation.

- Commas, which indicate pauses in thought.

- The colon, semicolon, dash, and parentheses, which are used to set off ideas or to separate items in a list of words or phrases.

- The apostrophe, which replaces the missing letters in words. It is also used to indicate ownership.

- Quotation marks, often used to indicate the exact words a person has said.

End Marks

The end of a sentence is always indicated with a period, a question mark, or an exclamation point. Most sentences end with a period. In fact, more than 95 percent of all sentences end with a period.[1]

> The Declaration of Independence was signed in 1776.
> What year was the Declaration of Independence signed?
> You know your history!

---

[1] *Errors in English and Ways to Correct Them,* Harry Shaw, HarperPaperbacks, 1993, p. 184.

Exercise 1

Supply the correct end stops for each sentence.

1. What planet is closest to the Earth

2. Which planet spins east to west

3. Finally, I can name all the planets

4. Which planet has a moon that is larger than the planet Mercury

5. Mercury and Venus are the two planets closer to the sun than Earth

6. What planet has the most moons

7. How many planets are there

8. Jupiter is the largest planet in the solar system

9. Look, that meteorite just crashed into that field

10. Is Mars the fourth or fifth planet from the sun

Commas to Separate Independent Clauses

In Chapter 21 you learned that an independent clause expresses a complete idea and must have a subject and verb. You also learned that two independent clauses, joined by a coordinating conjunction, can form a compound sentence. When you write a compound sentence, a comma is used after the first independent clause and before the coordinating conjunction. Remember that the coordinating conjunctions are *and, but, or, so, nor, yet,* and *for.*

Last year the tornadoes were very destructive, and many houses were destroyed.

Some people did not have insurance, so they face severe financial hardship.

Exercise 2

Put a comma before the coordinating conjunction that joins two independent clauses. Remember that each independent clause must have a separate subject and verb. Seven of the sentences below need a comma.

1. "Take Your Dog to Work Day" has convinced a few companies to allow employees to bring their dogs to work but most companies still do not allow any pets in the workplace.

2. This is an entirely new concept so it will be interesting to see how many corporations eventually accept this idea.

3. Pet Sitters International is organizing the event and their management believes that this will increase staff morale and productivity.

4. Some companies are waiting to see how the first year goes but they say they will consider joining the program in the future.

5. I have a dog, a cat, and a bird and I don't think it is fair that I can only bring my dog.

6. Ben and Jerry's, the ice-cream maker, currently allows dogs daily in the office yet they won't let employees brings cats or other types of pets.

7. One major company will pay for a pet sitter or kennel when employees have to be away for an extended period.

8. Some people think that having dogs in the office would be distracting and they strenuously object to this idea.

9. People with allergies also oppose this event and have expressed opposition.

10. Do you think that this is an idea whose time has come or just a passing fad that will go away?

Commas to Separate Introductory Phrases and Clauses

Use a comma after a phrase or clause that begins a sentence:

> When the man fell down, the onlookers rushed to help him.

> Because the man was very old, many thought that he had sustained a heart attack.

> As it turned out, he had just fainted.

Exercise 3

Put a comma after each introductory phrase or clause in these sentences.

1. While I was driving home late at night I hit a deer.

2. Because I did not hit the deer straight on the damage was not as bad as I expected.

3. When I surveyed the damage I realized that I was lucky not to be hurt.

4. Scared and trembling I called the Emergency Road Services.

5. After assessing the damage they said they would tow the car to the nearest garage.

6. Since I had borrowed the car from my parents I dreaded going home.

7. Although shocked and upset my parents were very nice about it.

8. When the car was repaired it looked just like new.

9. Whenever I drive on that road I remember the accident.

10. Driving slowing and cautiously I pass the exact spot where it happened.

Commas to Set Off Interrupting Words, Phrases, or Clauses

Commas are used to set off words, phrases, or clauses that interrupt the natural flow in a sentence. Words that interrupt usually are not essential. If the sentence makes sense without these words, they are **interrupters** and should be set off with commas.

Some common words that interrupt are:

actually	by the way
for example	on the other hand
however	as a matter of fact

My father, *for example,* became a successful inventor even though he did not have a technical background.

He was, *as a matter of fact,* the developer of a very successful plastic molding compound that is used in the manufacture of automobile parts.

Nonessential clauses that interrupt the flow of the sentence should be set off with commas. These clauses begin with *who, which,* or *whose:*

Mr. Janeciez, *who owns the factory,* said that I could have a job this summer.

The prefabricated houses, *which are built in his factory,* require hundreds of skilled carpenters.

Exercise 4

Find eight sentences that have interrupters. Supply the commas that are needed. *Hint: Read the sentences aloud to help identify interrupters.*

1. Tibet which is located on one of the highest plateaus in the world has developed a unique lifestyle and culture.

2. Tibet which is an autonomous region of the People's Republic of China occupies a 500,000-square-mile area in China's southwest corner.

3. It is only recently that a few visitors have been allowed access to this ancient land.

4. There are few landing strips for airplanes, and in fact there are no railroads and few highways for automobile traffic.

5. Buddhism which is one of the world's major religions is the dominant religion in Tibet.

6. Most of the people follow the Dalai Lama a God-King who currently lives in India.

7. Chenngu which has wide avenues and traditional houses is one of the most interesting old cities to visit in Tibet.

8. The Jokhang Temple which is one of the oldest temples in Tibet is located in the center of old Lhasa.

9. Traveling to Asia is so expensive that some people feel they cannot afford it.

10. A round-trip ticket to Tibet for example can run as high as $4,000.

Commas to Separate Items in a Series

Use commas to separate three or more items in a series:

New York, Los Angeles, Chicago, and Detroit are the largest cities in the United States.

After dinner I must take my dog for a walk, water my plants, and prepare an assignment.

Our dinner consisted of lamb chops, baked potatoes, green salad, and ice cream.

Exercise 5

Use commas in the following sentences to separate items in a series.

1. My favorite colors are blue lavender and mauve.

2. Jessye Norman Dawn Upshaw and Placido Domingo are famous opera singers.

3. Vegetables in the root family include turnips rutabagas onions and beets.

4. Peru Brazil Argentina and Columbia are countries in South America.

5. I flew to New York took the train to Washington D.C. and then drove to Fort Myer.

6. I gambled lost and wept.

7. Jeb's plan is to graduate from college get a job and marry his girlfriend.

8. Bangkok Tokyo Beijing and Seoul are large cities in Asia.

9. When you take a camping trip, you should always pack insect repellent warm clothing hiking boots and head covering.

10. My diet requires that I reduce calories walk each day and take vitamins.

Commas with Appositives

Appositives are nouns or noun phrases that describe a nearby noun. Appositives are set off with commas whether they appear near the beginning, in the middle, or at the end of a sentence.

Toby, *our rambunctious puppy*, required obedience lessons.

The school board gave our history teacher, *Mr. Jones,* sabbatical leave this semester.

She has two computers, an *Apple* and a *Dell*.

A single word appositive usually does not require commas. Using commas would indicate that the noun refers to a single unit. For example, using commas before and after "Yoko" in the following sentence would indicate the writer has only *one* friend:

My friend Yoko has cut several records.

Exercise 6

Add commas to set off appositives in these sentences.

1. A fifth of America half the West is semidesert.

2. Hoover Dam the project first known as Boulder Dam was built with aluminum, steel, copper, brass, and tons of concrete.

3. Grand Coulee once the world's largest dam supplies power to cities and towns in the Northwest.

4. John Witherspoon a Scottish clergyman immigrant was one of the signers of the Declaration of Independence.

5. Germany, Italy, and Japan the Axis powers fought and lost in World War II.

6. The modern submarine an underwater vessel propelled by nuclear engines can stay submerged for many days.

7. The cavalry fighting men on horseback played an important role in the Civil War.

8. The Taverne a convenient meeting spot is visited by many students in San Antonio.

9. Victoria a city in Canada was named one of the ten most beautiful cities in the world.

10. This city the capital of British Columbia is famous for beautiful flowers, fabulous seafood, and a magnificent view of snowcapped mountains.

Commas to Introduce Quotations

Quotation marks are used to indicate the exact words people are speaking. The placement of the comma depends on where the direct quote is in the sentence.

When an introductory phrase comes before the direct quotation, put a comma after the introductory phrase and before the first quotation mark. Put the ending period inside the quotation marks:

He said, "I'll be attending the concert after work."

When a sentence begins with a direct quotation, put the comma after the end of the quotation and before the quotation mark:

"I haven't finished the book yet," she said.

When the quotation is interrupted, put a comma after a reference to the person speaking:

"I haven't finished the book yet," she said, "but you may borrow it when I am done."

Notice in this last example that a comma is used after the first clause and again after the words that interrupt the sentence.

punctuation

Exercise 7

Add seven commas that are needed in this paragraph to set off direct speech.

The actors were having a huge fight in front of the audience. The man in the tiger costume said "I will never again perform on this stage with you." Immediately, the young girl started crying and screamed "You are just plain mean. I didn't mean to step on your foot." At that point the director came between them, saying "Now let's all calm down. This is not a big deal. Johann I think you should apologize to Amelia." "Okay, I'm sorry" he said "but if it happens again, I'm quitting." Amelia, still trembling, said "You can be sure that it won't happen again." She walked off the stage, turned, and shouted "I'm quitting, goodbye!"

The Apostrophe to Form Contractions

Contractions are used in speaking and in informal writing. A contraction is created when two words are joined and some of their letters omitted. In written language, the omitted letters are indicated with an apostrophe (').

Examples of common contractions include:

I+ am = I'm	she + will = she'll	you + are = you're
I+ have = I've	it + is = it's	they + are = they're
I+ had = I'd	it + has = it's	let + us = let's
I+ will = I'll	is + not = isn't	could + not = couldn't
he + will = he'll	we + are = we're	would + not = wouldn't
do + not = don't	did + not = didn't	was + not = wasn't
who + is = who's	what + is = what's	

Contractions in this list are formed by replacing one or two letters with an apostrophe. Note that the contraction *won't* is an exception:

will + not = won't

Be careful of the contraction *it's* and the possessive pronoun *its*. Never use *it's* to show possession. The proper spelling of the possessive form of *it* is *its*:

It's time to leave for the airport. (*it's* is a contraction for *it is*)

The plane left *its* landing gate promptly at 11:00 P.M. (*its* shows ownership)

You can determine if the contraction *it's* is used correctly by replacing it with the words "it is" in the sentence. If the sentence still makes sense, you should use the contraction form (*it's*). Otherwise, the possessive form (*its*) is required.

Exercise 8

Find twelve places where contractions have been used. Cross out the words and write the two words that form the contraction below.

Well, I don't know what will happen now. We've got some difficult days ahead. But it doesn't matter with me now. Because I've been to the mountaintop. And I don't mind. Like anybody, I would like to live a long life. Longevity has its place. But I'm not concerned about that now. I just want to do God's will. And He's allowed me to go up to the mountain. And I've looked over. And I've seen the promised land. I may not get there with you. But I want you to know tonight, that we, as a people will get to the promised land. And I'm happy tonight. I'm not worried about anything. I'm not fearing any man. Mine eyes have seen the glory of the coming of the Lord.

Martin Luther King, Jr.
Speech in Memphis, Tennessee, April 3, 1968
A Testament of Hope

_____ _____ _____

_____ _____ _____

_____ _____ _____

_____ _____ _____

The Apostrophe to Show Possession

The apostrophe is used to show ownership. When the owner (the noun) is singular, an apostrophe is placed after the last letter followed by an *s*:

Jake's dog is a golden retriever. (The dog belongs to Jake.)

Tara wants to borrow her sister's car. (The car belongs to the sister.)

Everyone's responsibility is to maintain his or her own sidewalk. (The responsibility belongs to everyone.)

James's goal is to be a long-distance runner and to manage an electronics store. (If the word ends in *s*, it is acceptable to either add *'s* or simply an apostrophe.)

Plural nouns and other words ending in *s* show ownership by adding an apostrophe at the end of the word. A second *s* is not added:

Many of our neighbors' homes were damaged by the flood.

The students' complaints about parking problems led to a solution.

The players' new uniforms were delivered to the wrong address, so the game had to be canceled.

Plural nouns that do not end in *s* show ownership by adding an apostrophe and an *s*:

The children's play drew a huge crowd.
The women's basketball team won the tournament.
The geese's flight patterns change in the spring.

Exercise 9

Add an apostrophe to the twelve words where it is needed to show ownership.

1. Sues story is typical of the growing interest in finding a lost relative.

2. In order to locate a relative, it is helpful if you have the relatives last known address or phone number.

3. Computer searches can provide historical and current information about a persons address, drivers license, and past employment.

4. If you have siblings or parents names, you have a better chance of success.

5. The persons age also is helpful along with the date and location of birth.

6. If you decide to use an agency to help with your search, be sure to check on the agencys reputation.

7. My two friends success in locating missing relatives has stimulated my interest in the subject.

8. Sams case was particularly exciting because he thought that his cousin might have died.

9. As it turned out, Sams cousin had moved back to Senegal.

10. The childrens surprise came when they learned that their birth mother was living in the same town.

Exercise 10

Decide which word in each phrase shows possession and underline it. Then write the word with the apostrophe in the blank space to the right. Be careful to note whether the possessive word is singular or plural. The first one has been done for you.

1. after the <u>womans</u> speech   woman's

2. from all the voters ballots   _____

3. because of the books cover   _____

4. to the twins brother   _____

5. from our grandmothers house   _____

6. for my Uncle Joels daughter   _____

7. with the band students uniforms   _____

8. in Mr. Torres classroom   _____

9. to the presidents assistant   _____

10. with the mens bowling team   _____

11. at my two cousins party   _____

12. by our families cabins   _____

13. after Jacks report   _____

14. in the womens cosmetic department   _____

15. before Annettes visit   _____

The Colon

The **colon** in a sentence tells readers that something more is to follow. The colon follows a complete thought and should not be inserted between a subject and verb or before a prepositional phrase. The colon also introduces a list of examples or items that are singled out for emphasis:

The meal that I want to prepare tonight needs the following items: fettuccini, tomato sauce, garlic, lettuce, tomatoes, peppers, cucumbers, and ice cream.

I have one thing to recommend: plastics.

In informal writing, the colon may precede a quotation:

Robert Kennedy said in a speech at the University of Pennsylvania: "About one-fifth of the people are against everything all the time."

The colon separates the hours from the minutes when indicating time of day:

I will meet you at the airport at 2:45 P.M. today.

The colon also is used after the salutation in a business letter (as opposed to the comma that is used in informal letters):

Dear Dr. Morgenstern:
Dear Ms. Tobias:

Exercise 11

Write ten sentences using each set of words below and using a colon.
The first one is done for you.

apples, peaches, apricots, lemons, and oranges

one thirty (use numerals)

"Ask not what your country can do for you, but what you can do for
your country"

joy, anger, fear, love, sadness

eleven forty-five (use numerals)

get enough sleep, exercise regularly, eat healthy foods

Dear Ms. Jackson

Physics, Computer I, Business Communications, and Music History

"What goes up must come down"

Give Peace a Chance, Yellow Submarine, She Loves You, and *All You Need
Is Love*

1. Fruits that grow in North America include the following: apples,

   peaches, apricots, lemons, and oranges.

2. _____

   _____

3. _____

   _____

4. _____

   _____

5. _____

   _____

6. _____

   _____

7. _____

_____

8. _____

_____

9. _____

_____

10. _____

_____

The Semicolon

As explained in Chapter 21, the main use of the semicolon is to join closely related independent clauses. Semicolons also are used to separate a series of phrases that are long and include internal commas. Using commas and semicolons correctly keeps the reader from becoming confused:

> I sent brochures to Morgan and Myers, 7008 Highway 7, Bakersfield, CA 93309; Signature Public Relations, 126 North 3rd Street, Carnegie, PA 15106; Montgomery Press, 2519 Tracy Avenue, Dallas, TX 75205; and The Thoms Group, 121 S. 8th Street, Bedford, MA 01730.

Notice in this example that the company addresses have several commas. Using a semicolon as the end of each address makes it easier for the reader to separate the companies.

Exercise 12

Five of these sentences have used commas where semicolons should be used. Correct the sentences that have errors. If the sentence is correct as written, place a *C* in front of it.

1. _____ I have friends in my class from Italy, Saudi Arabia, Japan, and Brazil.

2. _____ Arianna is from Naples, Italy, Ali is from Riyadh, Saudi Arabia, Tomigi is from Kyoto, Japan, and Maria is from São Paulo, Brazil.

3. _____ These friends, respectively, speak Italian, Arabic, Japanese, and Portuguese.

4. _____ Artists and their style of art are represented by the following, Gauguin, Impressionism, Renoir, Realism, Dali, Surrealism, and Seurat, Pointillism.

5. _____ Glacier Park, Montana, the Grand Canyon, Arizona, Zion National Park, Utah, and Yosemite Park, California are spectacular places to see.

6. _____ Allegro, andante, adagio, and presto are musical terms.

7. _____ The Mississippi, the Amazon, the Yangtze, the Rhine, and the Nile are major rivers in the world.

8. _____ I am looking at job offerings in a suburb of Portland, Maine, a town near Savannah, Georgia, and downtown San Francisco, California.

9. _____ My instructors are the following, Ms. Jones, ethics, Mr. Torres, political science, Ms. Varshavsky, computer science, and Ms. Mugabe, English.

10. _____ English, Arabic, Mandarin, Spanish, French, and Russian are major world languages.

The Dash

The **dash** is used to show a sudden interruption of thought or an aside, which is extra information not necessary to the meaning of the sentence. As a general rule, use dashes sparingly. Often, commas will serve the same purpose. Dashes are used to indicate a more abrupt or a more powerful break:

My feeling—if you will excuse me—is that you are being incredibly rude. (interruption)

I am very happy—in fact I am overjoyed—that you can lend me the money for the down payment on our house. (interruption)

My boss gave me a raise—if you call ten dollars a month a raise—because I completed all my projects on time. (aside)

Most word processing programs have a special symbol for the dash. Otherwise, use a double hyphen with no space before or after it.

Exercise 13

Indicate where dashes should be added to set off interrupted thoughts. The first one is done for you.

1. This is the most difficult job I have ever had, but if you insist I will stick with it to the bitter end.

   This is the most difficult job I have ever had, but—if you insist—I
   will stay with it to the bitter end.

2. I knew although I tried not to admit it that my father was gravely ill.

   _____

   _____

3. Our garden the most beautiful in the neighborhood was full of gorgeous annuals.

   _____

   _____

4. I am telling you and for the last time that I will not pay that much for a new car.

   _____

   _____

5. She fell down actually she collapsed in a heap because the heat was too much for her.

_____

_____

Parentheses

Parentheses are marks used like dashes to enclose information that is not necessary to the meaning of the sentence. Just like dashes, use these marks of punctuation very sparingly. They are asides to the readers and as such may interrupt the flow of reading and distract the reader if overused.

I received a box of chocolates (my very favorite candy) for my birthday.

I read the part on symbolism (Unit 6) yesterday just before class.

Be sure to turn right on the corner of 42nd and Bridgewater (across from the water tower) and then make a sharp left on Maple Avenue.

Exercise 14

Indicate where parentheses should be added to set off interrupted thoughts. The first one has been done for you.

1. I am enclosing directions to my house, which I think (but am not absolutely sure) are quite accurate.

2. You should have no difficulty making the trip in thirty minutes forty if it is rush hour to our house.

3. We plan weather permitting to eat outdoors on our deck.

4. I have invited the Tweeter twins old friends from next door to join us.

5. I am sure they will come they never miss anything along with their older brother.

CHAPTER 24

Capital Letters, Abbreviations, and Numbers

Though editors do not agree on all the uses of capital letters, abbreviations, and numbers, certain basic rules usually apply. One important rule is to be consistent. This chapter outlines some guidelines on when to capitalize letters, when to use abbreviations, and when to spell out or use a numeral for numbers.

Capital Letters to Begin a Sentence

Capitalize the first letter of the first word in a sentence, a direct quotation, or a line of poetry:

Sentence: Hundreds of new words are added to the English language every year.

Quotation: My professor said, "Excellent, well done!"

Poem: Good authors, too, who once knew better words
              Now only use four-letter words
              Writing prose . . .
              Anything goes.

                                        Cole Porter (1893-1964)

Exercise 1

Add eight capital letters where they are needed in this paragraph:

a friend told me that whenever it rained, her grandmother repeated this little two line poem:

sweet April showers

bring May flowers.

that would satisfy her for a while, but then she said she would always ask, "but when will the sun come out?" now she loves rainy days and uses them to catch up on reading and inside projects. most of her friends don't agree with her. they much prefer sunny days.

Capital Letters for Proper Nouns, for the Pronoun *I*, and for Place Names

Names of people and middle initials are always capitalized. The pronoun *I* is always capitalized, but no other pronouns are capitalized unless they begin a sentence. This rule also applies to terms that replace names, such as Dad or Mom, where the writer is addressing that person: "Please call me, Mom, when you get home." Names of cities, states, counties, countries, continents, and large bodies of water are capitalized. Country names used as adjectives also are capitalized. Capitalize the names of languages and the titles of college courses, but not generic subjects such as biology and math.

The book I liked best was the biography of Franklin D. Roosevelt.

My mother teaches English at a community college.

The French painter, Gauguin, lived much of his life in Tahiti.

Leo Tolstoy was a famous nineteenth-century Russian author.

Her new second-semester courses are history, Spanish, and Western Civilization.

Exercise 2

Circle each word that should be capitalized in these sentences. The number of capitals needed in each sentence is in parentheses.

1. james earl carter was the thirty-ninth president of the united states. (5)

2. william clark and meriwether lewis were famous explorers. (4)

3. jamestown was the site of the first permanent english settlement in america. (3)

4. his daughter called and said, "dad, please send money for my rent." (2)

5. marseilles is a city in the south of france on the mediterranean sea. (4)

6. the mediterranean sea is surrounded by europe, asia minor, the near east, and africa. (9)

7. william randolph hearst was an american newspaper publisher. (4)

8. argentina, brazil, columbia, and peru are countries in south america. (6)

9. when i travel to italy next summer, i plan to study italian, of course, but also european art and astronomy. (6)

10. nogales is a mexican city that borders the state of arizona. (3)

Capital Letters in Titles

The nouns in titles of books, magazines, newspapers, reports, films, songs, television shows, stories, and poems are capitalized. Conjunctions, short prepositions, and the articles *a*, *an*, and *the* are not capitalized unless they are the first word of the title:

The House on Mango Street
To Kill a Mockingbird
Sports Illustrated
Seinfeld
Ode on the Death of a Favorite Cat

Exercise 3

Circle each letter that needs a capital. Write the corrected title in the space provided. The number of capitals needed for each line is in parentheses.

1. *new york times, popular mechanics* (5)

   _____

2. *catcher in the rye, autobiography of malcolm x* (5)

   _____

3. *citizen kane, gone with the wind, star wars* (6)

   _____

4. *good morning america, saturday night live* (6)

   _____

5. *the price is right, the x files, law and order* (9)

   _____

6. *the star spangled banner, america the beautiful* (6)

   _____

7. *romeo and juliet* (2)

   _____

8. *u.s. government yearbook on environmental issues* (6)

   _____

9. *national geographic, newsweek, journal of the american medical association* (7)

   _____

   _____

10. *the raven, rime of the ancient mariner, the road not taken* (9)

   _____

   _____

Capital Letters for Organizations, Companies, Political Groups, and Religions

The proper names of organizations, companies, political groups, and religions are capitalized. *Exception*: Small prepositions and the articles *a*, *an*, and *the* usually are not capitalized unless they are the first word of the name or the first word in a sentence.

Chamber of Commerce
General Motors
Socialist Party
Baptist Church

Exercise 4

Circle the first letter of each word that requires a capital letter. Some words are not proper names and do not need capitals. Fifty-eight capital letters are needed.

girl scouts of america	coffee
united farm workers	u.s. senate
american cancer society	park
university	shoes
islam	dairy queen
buddhism	reformed church of america
democratic party	labor party
peace corps	republican party
fascist party	street
hinduism	religion
utah historical society	judaism
court of appeals	league of women voters
chicago grain exchange	seattle
legislature	new york philharmonic
university of arkansas	debate
national anthem	toastmaster's international
state department	trophy

museum   roman catholic

restaurant   bowling alley

common market   university of florida

Capital Letters for Days of the Week, Months, and Holidays

Use capital letters for the days of the week, the names of the months, and holidays. Use small letters for the seasons and for nonspecific places:

Days: Monday, Tuesday, Wednesday . . .

Months: January, February, March . . .

National Holidays: Thanksgiving, Labor Day, Flag Day, Martin Luther King Day, Independence Day, Father's Day, Mother's Day

Religious Days: Easter, Hanukkah, Ramadan, Holy Week, Passover, Lent, Kwanza

Seasons: spring, fall, winter, summer

Nonspecific Places: college, park, church

Exercise 5

Find and circle eighteen capital letters that are needed in this letter.

Dear Zita,

I will be spending a week in new york after easter. I would like to have dinner with you on tuesday evening, april 7. After I leave new york, I will go to pennsylvania to visit old college friends. I try to visit my friends at least once a year, but I have not been in pennsylvania since the winter before last.

This will be a busy travel year for me. In the fall, I will have a business conference in san francisco. After that I plan to spend a few days' vacation in las vegas. This trip will be in early november. In december I will go to florida to be with my parents for christmas.

Please let me know if you can meet me for dinner on april 7.

Love,
Jenny

Capital Letters for Geographical Place Names

Use capital letters for the names of specific places and geographical features, such as cities, national monuments, parks, rives, lakes, dams, and mountains:

Everglades National Park
Atlantic Ocean
Mount McKinley National Park
Little Bighorn River
Hoover Dam

Exercise 6

Capitalize the place names in these sentences. Also capitalize the first word in the sentence. The number of capitals needed in each sentence is in parentheses.

1. zion national park is located in utah. (4)

2. the mojave desert covers 15,000 square miles in california. (4)

3. people travel from all over the world to see the grand canyon. (3)

4. mount rainier national park is a scenic area in the cascade mountains. (6)

5. the great lakes are superior, michigan, huron, erie, and ontario. (8)

6. chateau thierry is a town in france northeast of paris on the marne river. (6)

7. one of the most beautiful lakes in the united states is lake placid in new york. (7)

8. the mississippi river flows 2,350 miles to the gulf of mexico. (5)

9. mykonos is a greek island in the aegean sea. (4)

10. the great sand dunes national monument contains large, sand dunes in colorado. (7)

Capital Letters for Addresses

Street addresses are capitalized. Also capitalize the names of cities, states, and countries:

857 West Maple Avenue, Tampa, Florida
10 Downing Street, London, England
IDS Center, 10th and Marquette, Minneapolis, Minnesota
Hohemarkstrasse 190, 01330 Obersursel, Deutschland

Exercise 7

Add the twenty-five capital letters that are needed to make this letter correct. Remember that proper names and names of the months are always capitalized.

302 cobblestone drive

colorado springs, colorado 80906

november 1, 2001

Dr. john m. gawlik

8200 west france avenue

chandler, arizona 85249

Dear dr. gawlik:

On october 15, I received a bill from you in the amount of $700 for a root canal procedure that was performed on september 24. It was my understanding that this procedure would be under $600.

Your secretary has informed me that you are on vacation until after thanksgiving. I will be leaving for my winter vacation on december 1, and I should like to talk with you about this matter before I leave. Therefore, I plan to call your office on monday, november 29. Please have your secretary let me know if you will be in your office on this date.

I would like to settle this matter before I leave since I will not be back until late spring.

Sincerely,

george s. bender

capital letters

Capital Letters for Historical Events and Cultural Periods

Capitalize commonly used names for historical events and cultural periods:

War of Independence
Civil War
Great Depression
Great Irish Famine
Dark Ages
Renaissance
Roaring Twenties
Jazz Age

Exercise 8

Circle the words that need capital letters, including the first word of each sentence. The number of capitals needed in each sentence is in parentheses.

1. martin luther was the leader of the reformation. (3)

2. naturalism was a literary movement in the late nineteenth and early twentieth centuries and included the following writers: emile zola, stephen crane, and jack london. (7)

3. my brother was a pilot during the korean war. (3)

4. franklin delano roosevelt started the new deal. (5)

5. during the prohibition era, the manufacture and sale of alcoholic beverages was against the law. (3)

6. the classical era is a period in european history when greek and roman cultures flourished. (6)

7. in the first world war soldiers fought in trenches. (4)

8. learning and culture were almost eliminated during certain periods of the middle ages. (3)

9. labor day is a legal holiday in the united states and is celebrated on the first monday in september (6)

10. armistice day is the anniversary of the suspension of hostilities in world war I; today, this day is called veterans' day. (6)

Capital Letters for Product Names

Use capital letters for the trademark or brand names of products but not for the products themselves.

Brand Names	Product Type
Reebok	sneakers
Gillette	shaving cream
Crest	toothpaste
Dove	soap
Heinz	catsup

Exercise 9

In the first column, supply capital letters for the items that are brand names. In the second column, write down a brand name for each item that is not a brand or write down a product type for each item that is a brand. The first two are done for you.

1. pop _____Sprite_____

2. Tide _____detergent_____

3. ford _____

4. puffs _____

5. revlon _____

6. sony _____

7. breakfast cereal _____

8. candy _____

9. soap _____

10. sneakers _____

Exercise 10

Find seventy places where capital letters should be used. Write the capital letters above the words or abbreviations.

molly brooke catering company
3405 south laurel street
port angeles, washington 98362

april 2, 2001

dr. jack zimmer

survey design, incorporated

5100 industrial boulevard

seattle, washington

dear dr. zimmer:

this letter is to invite you to meet with me on april 19 at a time convenient for you. the purpose of this meeting is to discuss your interest in conducting a market survey for our product, *molly babies.*
molly babies are cream-filled cookies made one batch at a time from an original recipe created in my kitchen. my goal is to sell these cookies in specialty food stores and in coffeehouses, such as starbucks, dunn brothers, java express, and caribou.

these cookies have an exuberant lemon flavor. although the exact combination of ingredients is our secret, the main ingredients are flour, butter, whipping cream, lemon juice, milk, lemon, sugar, and shortening. we have received very favorable reviews from numerous groups who have purchased these cookies from us. the ptsa at our local elementary school has ordered sixty-five dozen cookies in the last six months. also, the vfw and the local aaa office have placed orders totaling over 100 dozen in the last twelve months.

although we are located in the state of washington, we have had interest expressed by stores in oregon, idaho, montana, and canada.

we are interested in having a market survey conducted to assist us in our long-range planning. we need to assess the extent of interest by small stores and coffeehouses. also, we need to know the approximate size of weekly orders, and if we could expect larger orders for thanksgiving, christmas, easter, and other holidays throughout the year.

please call me to set a definite time for our meeting on april 19.

sincerely,

molly brooke matthews

Abbreviations

Abbreviations are shortcuts for words. They provide short forms for names of organizations, time periods, academic degrees, geographical terms, and titles.

Organizations. Some organizations become known by the first letters of the words in their titles. These abbreviations do not contain periods between the capital letters. When you are in doubt, check with the organization's administrative office. These common organizations are known by their short forms:

Internal Revenue Service - IRS
U.S. Department of Agriculture - USDA
American Automobile Association - AAA
American Broadcasting Corporation - ABC
Federal Bureau of Investigation – FBI
North Atlantic Treaty Organization - NATO

When abbreviations that do not require periods end a sentence, use a period:

My father works for the USDA.

Time. The most common way to express the time of day is:

A.M. (before noon)
P.M. (after noon)

Using lowercase letters, such as a.m. and p.m., is also acceptable. Just be sure to be consistent within your document. Notice also that these abbreviations use periods. When an abbreviation that uses a period ends a sentence, you do not add a second period:

I told Maxine that I would meet her at 2:00 P.M.

Social or business titles. Social or business titles are abbreviated and are placed in front of a person's name. The most common of these titles are:

Mr.   Mrs.   Ms.   Dr.

Academic degrees. Colleges and universities award a variety of academic degrees based on the completion of program requirements. These degrees are nearly always abbreviated and, when used, are placed after the person's name. In some cases, the abbreviations come from Latin words. A partial list of academic degrees follows:

B.A.   Bachelor of Arts
B.S.   Bachelor of Science
M.A.   Master of Arts
A. S.   Associate of Science
M.B.A.   Master of Business Administration
Ed.D.   Doctor of Education
D.D.   Doctor of Divinity
D.D.S.   Doctor of Dental Science
R.N.   Registered Nurse
M.D.   Doctor of Medicine
Ph.D.   Doctor of Philosophy

When an academic degree follows a person's name, the usual address form of Mr., Ms., Mrs., or Dr. in front of the name is not used:

John M. Jackson, Ph.D.   Olivia S. Banker, M.D.

States and countries. In formal writing, you should spell out the full names of the states. For informal writing and on mailing addresses, however, the postal service abbreviations may be used. Local telephone directories list these two letter abbreviations. The abbreviations are always in capital letters with no periods and no space between the letters:

Pennsylvania   PA   New Jersey   NJ   Massachusetts   MA

Country names are usually spelled out:

Germany   Nigeria   Norway   Peru   Mexico

Country names of two or more words may be abbreviated in informal writing. Some names may be abbreviated in formal writing also:

United States – U.S.   United Kingdom – U.K.

Exercise 11

Circle the incorrect abbreviations in the following sentences and make a correction beneath the error. The number of corrections needed in each sentence is in parentheses. The first one is done for you. *Hint: Some abbreviations need periods in addition to capital letters.*

1. Mr. Salah said that he would meet me at 10 (am) on (Tues) next
    week. (2)   a.m.   Tuesday

2. I plan to visit the u k next summer; after that I will go to Fr. and
    Ger. (3)

3. A dentist may put the initials d.d.s. after his or her name. (1)

4. A graduate of the Univ. of Texas with a master of science degree
    may use the initials m.s. on his or her resume. (2)

5. I always wanted to work for the FBI or the cia. (1)

6. My letter was addressed to Bethany Connor, d.d.S, Tower Office
    Building, Saganaw, Mi. (2)

7. On the weekend, I work from 6:00 am to 7:00 pm. (2)

8. Our minister graduated from the University of Iowa with an ma., and then he switched to theology and earned a d.d. (2)

9. Dr. Salazar is a highly respected physician with multiple academic degrees: PH.D., m.d., and m.s. (3)

10. His practice is in Penn., but sometimes he is invited to Eng. to deliver lectures. (2)

Numbers

Spell out the words for the numbers between one and ninety-nine. Numbers twenty-one through ninety-nine are hyphenated, except for units of ten:

twenty	forty	sixty	eighty
fourteen	twenty-one	forty-two	eighty-six

Use numerals for 100 or larger numbers:

146	2,987	10,000	898,900

Use numerals for percentages and in technical material:

About 50 percent of the class passed the exam.

Always spell out a number that begins a sentence even if it is more than ninety-nine. Or, rewrite the sentence so the number is in a different location:

Forty-two percent of the graduating class returned the survey.
The return rate for the survey of the graduating class was 42 percent.
Nine hundred fifty students attended the protest meeting.
About 950 students attended the protest meeting.
Two thousand fans were screaming for an encore at the rock concert.
Some 2,000 fans were screaming for an encore at the rock concert.

Consistency in the use of numbers is important. If your material contains some numbers that are less than ninety-nine and some that are more than ninety-nine, follow the rule for numbers greater than ninety-nine:

There were 60 students in my grade-school graduating class, 189 students in my high-school graduating class, and more than 950 students in my college graduating class.

Exercise 12

Write the correct form for the numbers in the blank spaces.

1. I am taking _____ courses this quarter at college. (4 or four)

2. I work more than _____ hours each week to help pay for school. (20 or twenty)

3. College tuition increased this year by _____ percent. (6 or six)

4. On our bike ride, I covered _____ miles the first week. (80 or eighty)

5. I covered _____ miles the second week. (120 or one hundred twenty)

6. _____ students attend Dr. Proust's lectures each week. (200 or two hundred)

7. Last week I read _____ pages in my English text. (10 or ten)

8. In addition I wrote a _____-page paper for sociology. (15 or fifteen)

9. My brother-in-law is building a boat that is _____ feet long. (35 or thirty-five)

10. My home town is _____ miles from here. (525 or five hundred twenty-five)

Glossary

abbreviation the short form for names of organizations, time periods, academic degrees, geographical terms, and titles.

adjective a word or phrase that adds information that limits (modifies) the meaning of a noun, making that noun more specific.

adverb word that modifies the meaning of verbs, adjectives, or other adverbs.

agreement consistency in the use of tense, person, number, and other grammatical elements.

analogy a comparison of things that are very different; serves to make a difficult or unfamiliar idea understandable by matching it with something familiar. Analogies are usually extended, going on for several sentences or paragraphs.

analyze to examine critically by dissecting a subject into its essential features. Analyzing usually explores questions of *how* or *why*.

anecdote a brief story.

antonym one of two or more words or phrases that have opposite meaning; for example, *day* and *night*.

apostrophe a punctuation mark that replaces the missing letters in words.

appositive a noun or noun phrase that identifies a nearby noun.

argument writing that takes a position.

bibliography a list of sources used in the preparation of a paper that provides full documentation of each source, including author, title, publisher, publisher location, and date of publication.

body the middle section of an essay containing the paragraphs in which the main idea is explored from different angles or with accumulating details.

brainstorm to generate a large number of ideas that later can be sorted through for their value.

category a group of things that have similarities and share features; also referred to as a *class*.

cause and effect a form of analysis that draws connections between events.

characterization a description of a person; also called a *profile*.

chronological order in narrative writing, a retelling of events in the order in which they occur.

class a group of items that have similarities and share features; also referred to as a *category*.

classify to organize items into classes (groups of like items).

clichés stale, overused expressions.

clustering a brainstorming method that begins by drawing a circle with a key word or phrase inside and then drawing connected circles containing associated ideas. Clustering is also called *diagramming* or *mapping*.

coherence the state of being logically connected and consistent; in writing, coherence is achieved when readers can follow the thoughts within a sentence, from one sentence to the next, and from one paragraph to another.

collective noun a noun that stands for a group of people or things.

colon a punctuation mark used to tell readers that something more follows or to introduce a list of examples or items singled out for emphasis.

comma a punctuation mark indicating a short pause in thought within a sentence.

comma splice two independent sentences incorrectly linked by a comma rather than a coordinating conjunction, a semicolon, or a period.

common knowledge information that can be obtained from several sources; in a research paper, the source of common knowledge does not need to be credited.

compare to show how two or more things or persons are alike.

complex sentence a sentence containing an independent clause and one or more dependent clauses.

compound sentence a sentence containing two or more simple sentences related in thought and joined by a conjunction or a semicolon.

compound-complex sentence a sentence that is compound (contains two or more independent clauses connected together) and complex (contains one or more dependent clauses).

conclusion the final section of an essay, which ties together everything that has been said before to complete the purpose of the essay.

conjunction a word that joins sentences, phrases, or words (example: *and*).

context clues sentences or phrases surrounding a term (its context) that reveal its meaning.

contraction a word created when two words are joined and some of their letters are omitted.

contrast to show how two or more things or persons are different.

coordinating conjunction a transitional word that links shorter sentences together, for example: *and, but, or, so, nor, yet,* and *for*.

credibility in writing, the quality of being believable and having the qualifications to write on an issue.

dash a punctuation mark used to show an abrupt or powerful break in thought.

definition a form of description that explains what something *is*.

dependent clause a clause that contains a subject and a verb and that relies on an independent clause to complete its meaning.

description a full and detailed representation of an object, place, person, or event—a picture drawn in words.

dialect a particular vocabulary, pronunciation style, and grammar structure shared with others from the same community.

dialogue a conversation in writing.

dictionary a reference list of words and their meanings.

documentation of sources the inclusion of full bibliographic information for each source cited in, or consulted for the preparation of, a research paper.

draft to draw up in written form, shaping ideas into sentences and paragraphs.

dynamism energy and enthusiasm that help persuade readers to the author's point of view.

end mark a punctuation mark used to show where a sentence ends and whether the sentence is a statement, a question, or an exclamation.

essay a composition on a theme or subject.

essential clause a clause that is necessary to the meaning of a sentence.

example one item used to represent many items; also called an *illustration*.

exclamation point a punctuation mark used at the end of a sentence to indicate that it should be expressed with energy, enthusiasm, or passion.

explicit fully and directly expressed.

expository writing writing that explains, for example, *what* something is, *how* something works, or *why* something occurs.

figurative language language that creates figures, or pictures, in the mind; also known as *imagery*.

flashback a reference to something that happened earlier.

focused freewriting writing done freely and without conscious effort on a specific topic in order to generate ideas and details.

foreshadowing a reference to something that happens after or at the end of the event being described.

future perfect a verb tense expressing action that will be completed in the future prior to another action.

future progressive a verb tense expressing action that will be ongoing at some future time.

future tense the time of the action in the sentence indicating that it occurs in the future, after the present moment.

gerund a noun formed by adding *ing* to a verb.

guide word a word appearing in the upper left or right margin of a page in a reference book such as a dictionary, indicating the first or last word listed on that page.

helping verb a verb used with other verbs to help indicate time, possible action, or emphasis.

homonym one of two or more words that sound alike but have different meanings and spellings, for example: *there* and *their* or *by* and *buy*.

illustration an example used to make a point.

imagery figurative language.

implicit indirectly expressed.

indefinite pronoun a pronoun that refers to an unspecified number of persons or things.

independent clause a group of words with a subject and a verb; also called a *simple sentence*.

inferences the guesses as to meaning that readers make from *contextual clues*.

integrity the quality of being honest with the facts and fair.

Internet the worldwide network of computers that enables anyone with a connection to access and exchange information.

interrupter a word, phrase, or clause that breaks the natural flow in a sentence.

introduction the first section of an essay or other piece of writing that draws readers in and presents the main idea.

irregular verb a verb that does not follow a regular pattern in forming the past tense and the past participle.

jargon the specialized language shared by a group or profession.

journal a private book in which a writer records thoughts and ideas.

key words words and phrases that are central to the idea being addressed in a piece of writing.

main idea the central subject of a piece of writing; also called a *theme* or *thesis*.

mechanical error a capitalization, spelling, or punctuation mistake in a sentence.

metaphor a statement that one item *is* the other (a direct comparison), or a statement in which the word for one item is used *in place* of the other (an implied comparison).

modifier a word or phrase that adds meaning and detail to either the subject or the verb.

narrative writing writing that describes one or more events—that tells a story.

neutral readers readers with no fixed opinion about the author or the ideas expressed by the author.

nonessential clause a clause that is not necessary to the meaning of a sentence and that is usually set off with commas.

noun a word or phrase that names a person, place, thing, or idea.

number for a noun, the state of being singular (one) or plural (more than one).

outline a brief sketch of the points the writer wants to make in a piece of writing.

paragraph in a piece of writing, an organized set of sentences that develops one idea. A paragraph is indicated by indentation of the first line or by an extra line of space separating it from the next paragraph.

paraphrase to approximate what was said using other words.

parentheses a set of punctuation marks used to set off words and phrases or to separate items in a list of words or phrases.

part of speech a category of words that has a specific function in a sentence. In English, the parts of speech include *noun, pronoun, verb, adverb, adjective, preposition,* and *conjunction.*

past participle a verb form made by adding *ed* or *en* to the base verb except for verbs which form their past participles irregularly.

past perfect a verb tense expressing action that happened in the past, prior to another action.

past progressive a verb tense expressing action in the past that was ongoing.

past tense the time of the action of the verb in the sentence indicating that the action occurred in the past, before the present moment.

perfect tense the time of the action of the verb in the sentence indicating that the action *has been* completed (present tense), *had been* completed (past tense), or *will have been* completed (future tense).

period a punctuation mark used at the end of a sentence to indicate that it is a statement. Periods also are used at the end of an abbreviation, for example, Mr. for the word Mister.

person the point of view used in writing: first person (*I* or *we*), second person (*you*), or third person (*he, she, it, they,* or *one*).

persuasion writing that persuades others to agree; also called *argument.*

plagiarism the use of the ideas and phrases of others without documenting the source.

plural noun a noun that represents more than one person, place, or thing.

point-counterpoint a form of argument in which the opposing position is presented so that it may be disputed.

portfolio a collection of a person's best writing. It also may include samples of a piece of writing through all stages from initial draft to final product.

preposition a part of speech that shows the relationship between an object and the rest of a sentence; for example, *by, into,* and *for.*

prepositional phrase a phrase beginning with a preposition that adds extra information to a sentence.

present participle a verb form made by adding the suffix *ing* to the base verb.

present perfect a verb tense expressing action begun in the past that continues into the present (or that was completed at some unspecified, recent point in time).

present progressive a verb tense expressing action that began in the present moment, is not completed, and is still occurring.

present tense a verb tense expressing action in the sentence that is occurring at that moment.

primary research research conducted by the author of a research paper.

primary sources original documents containing direct evidence.

problem-solution an organizing format for argument in which the author states what is wrong and how it can be fixed.

profile a description of a person; also called a *characterization.*

progressive tense the time of the action of the verb in the sentence indicating that the action *is* ongoing (present tense), *was* ongoing (past tense), or *will be* ongoing (future tense).

pronoun a substitute word for a noun.

pronoun agreement the use of a pronoun that matches the subject it replaces in terms of number (singular or plural) and gender (masculine, feminine, or neuter).

proper noun a noun that is actually a name, for example: *America* or *Mario*.

punctuation marks that help the writer express ideas clearly to the reader.

question mark a punctuation mark used at the end of a sentence to indicate that it is a question.

quotation mark a punctuation mark used in sets to indicate the exact words that a person has said.

random freewriting writing done as thoughts occur on any subject or subjects.

receptive readers readers who are sympathetic to the author or to the ideas expressed by the author.

regular verb a verb that forms the past tense and the past participle by adding *d* or *ed*.

relative pronoun a noun substitute placed next to a noun to which it refers: for example, *who* (or *whom*), *which*, *whose*, and *that*.

research paper a piece of writing that presents evidence in support of a *thesis*.

revise to make changes to a draft in order to improve meaning, structure, and style.

rubric another word for *scoring guide*.

run-on sentence two or more independent clauses that incorrectly run into each other without any punctuation.

scoring guide an evaluation that measures writing against specific criteria. It uses a scale to indicate how well the writing meets the criteria; also called a *rubric*.

secondary sources documents containing someone's intepretation of primary sources or direct evidence.

semicolon a punctuation mark used to join closely related independent clauses or to separate a series of long phrases that include internal commas.

sentence a group of words expressing a complete thought. A sentence contains, at a minimum, a subject and a verb.

sentence fragment a sentence that is incomplete because it does not contain both a subject and a verb.

simile a comparison between two items constructed with the words *like*, *as*, *as if*, or *as though*.

simple sentence an independent clause that contains a subject and a verb and expresses a complete thought.

simple tense the time of the action of the verb in the sentence indicating that the action occurs in the present, past, or future.

singular noun a noun that represents only one person, place, or thing.

slang casual, informal speech.

Standard Written English (SWE) the variety of the English language that is taught for writing in English-language school systems and that is universally accepted and understood by educated people.

statements of conjecture expressions of possibilities about what *could have* happened, *is* happening, or *may* happen.

statements of fact statements that are either true or false.

statements of policy statements that call for a change in the way people act or are governed.

statements of value expressions of opinion.

subject whoever or whatever is directly connected to the action or condition expressed by the verb in a sentence.

subject–verb agreement the use of a singular subject with a singular verb form or a plural subject with a plural verb form.

subordinating conjunction a connecting word used to join a dependent clause to an independent clause.

subtopic a topic within a topic; for example, *winter* is a subtopic of *seasons*.

synonym one of two or more words or phrases that can be substituted for each other because they mean essentially the same thing, for example: *run, scurry, dash,* and *race*.

template a piece of writing that is used as a pattern for writing something new.

tense the indication of time as expressed by the verb in a sentence.

theme the central subject of a piece of writing; also called a *main idea*.

thesaurus a reference list of *synonyms* and possibly also *antonyms*.

thesis the opinion or claim that is made in a piece of writing.

thesis paper another name for a research paper.

tone the mood created through the words used in a piece of writing that reflect the writer's attitude toward his or her subject.

topic the idea under discussion.

topic sentence the sentence in a paragraph that reveals its main idea.

transcribe to make a written copy.

transition word a word that helps readers make the connection from one idea to the next.

unity the state of being united or uniform; in writing, the situation in which all sentences contribute to the same topic.

unreceptive readers readers with negative feelings about the author or the ideas expressed by the author.

verb a word that express an action, a condition, or a relationship.

working draft a legible version of a draft with all the basic elements present.

World Wide Web linked computer sites on the Internet that users can leap back and forth between with simple keystrokes.

writing the act of organizing thoughts into recorded words, usually to communicate those thoughts with others.

writing folder an organizing system for the papers or computer files generated by a writer.

writing process the steps involved in planning, drafting, and revising a piece of writing.

writing ritual a habitual act performed before writing to create a mood for working effectively.

Acknowledgments

ART

Gilbert Atencio, San Ildefonso, *Marie and Blond Tourist Viewing Pottery*. 24146/13. Museum Purchase, Museum of Indian Arts and Culture/Laboratory of Anthropology, Museum of New Mexico. Photographed by Blair Clark.

Vija Celmins, *Ocean Surface Woodcut*, 1992, woodcut, 19-1/4 x 15-1/2 inches. Edition of 50. Courtesy McKee Gallery, New York.

André Cypriano, *Lois on the Bench*. Copyright © 1997 by André Cypriano. Reprinted by permission.

Harvey Dinnerstein, *Underground*. Reprinted by permission of the artist.

Eager Web Page Design, *Building a Custom Home*. Pictures by Elliott A. Gurwitz, Eager Web Page Design. http://www.eagerweb.com. Reprinted by permission.

Lee Friedlander, *Haverstraw, New York*. Courtesy Fraenkel Gallery, San Francisco.

Sidney Harris, *Hunter-Gatherers, North America, Late 20th Century*. Reprinted by permission of the artist.

Frank Hurley, *The Endurance at Night*. Reprinted by permission of the Royal Geographical Society, London.

Brenda Joysmith, *Summer Hats*. Reprinted by permission of Joysmith Studio.

V. Khotianovsky, *The Fate of the Planet Is Your Fate*. Reprinted by permission of Liberation Graphics.

John Loose, *Ozone, Tennessee Outhouse*. Outhouse belonging to Manya Marshall, painted by her daughter, Mikki Riggs (www.jldr.com). Reprinted by permission.

F. Malespin, *Earth Garden*. Reprinted by permission of the Nicaraguan Cultural Alliance.

Jean Marzollo, from *I Spy School Days: A Book of Picture Riddles*. Photographs by Walter Wick. Published by Cartwheel Books, a division of Scholastic, Inc. Text copyright © 1995 by Jean Marzollo, photographs copyright © 1995 by Walter Wick. Reprinted by permission of Scholastic.

Richard Craig Thompson, *This Painter (at 42)*. Reprinted by permission of Adam A. Weschler & Sons, Inc.

Elizabeth Torak, *The Art Student: A Self Portrait*. Reprinted by permission of Adam A. Weschler & Sons, Inc.

TEXT

Mitch Albom, from *Tuesdays with Morrie*. Copyright © 1997 by Mitch Albom. Reprinted by permission of Doubleday, a division of Random House, Inc.

Julia Alvarez, excerpt from "Grounds for Fiction." Copyright © 1998 by Julia Alvarez. Published in *Something to Declare*, Algonquin Books of Chapel Hill, 1998. Reprinted by permission of Susan Bergholz Literary Services, New York. All rights reserved.

American Association for the Advancement of Science, "Brain and Behavior: Mental Disorders and Substance Abuse." Reprinted by permission.

John Andrisani, from *The Short Game Magic of Tiger Woods*. Copyright © 1998 by John Andrisani. Reprinted by permission of Crown Publishers, Inc.

Gloria Anzaldua, "Tlilli, Tlapalli: The Path of the Red and Black Ink" from *Borderland/La Frontera: The New Mestiza*. Copyright © 1987 by Gloria Anzaldua.

Sue Bender, "Gale's Pot," from *Everyday Sacred*. Copyright © 1995 by Sue Bender. Reprinted by permission of HarperCollins Publishers, Inc. Pages 226-228.

Queen Brown, "My Neighborhood." Reprinted by permission of the author.

Douglas Clifford, *From Vietnam: Reflexes and Reflection*. Reprinted by permission of the author.

Edward N. Kelley, "Illegal and Immoral Uses." Reprinted with permission from *Practical Apartment Management*, Third Edition, by Edward N. Kelley, CPM. Copyright © 1990 by the Institute of Real Estate Management, 430 North Michigan Avenue, Chicago, Illinois 60611.

Larry King, from *How to Talk to Anyone, Anywhere*. Copyright © 1994 by Larry King. Reprinted by permission of Crown Publishers, a division of Random House, Inc.

Martin Luther King, Jr. "Eulogy for the Martyred Children," from *A Testament of Hope*. Copyright © 1968 by Martin Luther King, Jr.; copyright renewed 1996 by The Heirs to the Estate of Martin Luther King. Reprinted by arrangement with The Heirs to the Estate of Martin Luther King, Jr., c/o Writers House, Inc. as agent for the proprietor.

Martin Luther King, Jr. "Speech in Memphis, Tennessee, April 3, 1968," from *A Testament of Hope*. Copyright © 1968 by Martin Luther King Jr.; copyright renewed 1996 by The Heirs to the Estate of Martin Luther King. Reprinted by arrangement with The Heirs to the Estate of Martin Luther King, Jr., c/o Writers House, Inc. as agent for the proprietor.

Pee Wee Kirkland, from *Soul of the Game*. Copyright © 1997 by Melcher Media, Inc. Reprinted by permission.

Herbert Knapp and Mary Knapp, from *One Potato, Two Potato: The Folklore of American Children*. Copyright © 1976 by Herbert Knapp and Mary Knapp. Reprinted by permission of W. W. Norton and Company, Inc.

Jeanne Marie Laskas, "Connie Small: A Lighthouse Keeper's Wife," from *We Remember: Women Born at the Turn of the Century Tell the Stories of Their Lives in Words and Pictures*. Text: Copyright © 1999 by Jeanne Marie Laskas. Reprinted by permission of William Morrow and Company, Inc.

Spike Lee, *Do the Right Thing*. Copyright © 1989 by Spike Lee. Reprinted by permission of Simon and Schuster.

Norman Lewis, from *The World, The World*. Copyright © 1996 by Norman Lewis. Reprinted by permission of Henry Holt and Company, LLC.

Erika Lopez, *Flaming Iguanas: An Illustrated All-Girl Road Novel Thing*. Copyright © 1997 by Erika Lopez. Reprinted by permission of Simon and Schuster.

Andre Lyles, "My Neighborhood." Reprinted by permission of the author.

Thomas Lynch, from *The Undertaking: Life Studies from the Dismal Trade*. Copyright © 1997 by Thomas Lynch. Reprinted by permission of W. W. Norton and Company, Inc.

David Mas Masumoto, "Peaches and Prose: Keeping a Journal." Copyright © 1997 by David Mas Masumoto. First appeared in *40 Contemporary Writers and Their Journals* (Sheila Bender, editor) published by Dell Publishing, 1997. Reprinted by permission of author.

William Maxwell, "Nearing Ninety." Copyright © 1997 by William Maxwell, first published in *The New York Times Magazine*, reprinted by permission of The Wylie Agency, Inc.

Diane McClun and Laura Nownes, from *Quilts! Quilts!! Quilts!!!*, copyright © 1997. Reprinted by permission of NTC/Contemporary Publishing Group, Inc.

Robert McCrum, William Cran, and Robert MacNeil, from *The Story of English*. Copyright © 1986 by Robert McCrum, William Cran, and Robert MacNeil. Reprinted by permission for US by Viking Penguin, a division of Penguin Putnam, Inc. Reprinted by permission for Canada by Sterling Lord Literistic, Inc.

N. Scott Momaday, "Native American Christmas Story." From *Circle of Wonder*. Copyright © 1994. Reprinted by permission of Clear Light Publishers.

David Mura, *Turning Japanese: Memoirs of a Sansei*. Copyright ©1991. Reprinted by permission of Atlantic Monthly Press.

Ralph Nader, from *Radio Sucks*. Copyright © 1999. Reprinted by permission.

National Organization for Rare Disorders, Inc. *Narcolepsy*. Reprinted by permission.

Kathleen Norris, excerpts from *Dakota*. Copyright © 1993 by Kathleen Norris. Reprinted by permission of Ticknor and Fields/Houghton Mifflin Co. All rights reserved.

Cynthia Ozick, *The Best American Essays*. Copyright © 1998 by Cynthia Ozick. Reprinted by permission of the author and her agents, Raines and Raines.

Paul Reiser, excerpt from *Babyhood*. Text: Copyright © 1997 by Paul Reiser. Reprinted by permission of William Morrow and Company, Inc.

Daniel Rothenberg, excerpt from "Farmworkers: I Earned That Name," from *With These Hands: The Hidden World of Migrant Farmworkers Today*, copyright © 1998 by Daniel Rothenberg. Reprinted by permission of Harcourt, Inc.

Mark Salzman, *Iron and Silk*. Copyright © 1986 by Mark Salzman. Reprinted by permission of Random House, Inc.

Richard Selzer, *Confession of a Knife*. Copyright © 1974 by Richard Selzer. Reprinted by permission of John Hawkins and Associates, Inc.

Jean Shade, "My Neighborhood." Reprinted by permission of the author.

Chuck Shepard, "News of the Weird." Copyright © by Chuck Shepard. Reprinted with permission of Universal Press Syndicate. All rights reserved.

Eric Sloane, *Diary of an Early American Boy Noah Blake 1805*. Copyright © 1962 originally published by Wilfred Funk, Inc., permission granted by Mrs. Eric Sloane.

Meredith F. Small, "Bringing Baby Back." Copyright the American Museum of Natural History (1999). Reprinted by permission from *Natural History* (March 1999).

Stephen Spender, *The Thirties and After*. Copyright © 1979. Reprinted by permission for US by Random House, Inc. Reprinted by permission for Canada by Ed Victor Ltd.

Kevin Summers, "Army Training." Reprinted by permission of the author.

Vin Suprynowicz, " To Prevent a Life of Crime, Buy Your Kid a Gun," from *Las Vegas Review-Journal* (May 1999). Reprinted with permission of Mountain Media and the *Las Vegas Review-Journal*. Vin Suprynowicz is the author of "Send in the Waco Killers: Essays on the Freedom Movement, 1993-1998," Mountain Media, 1999.

Phyllis Theroux, "Closet Lovers," from *House Beautiful*. Reprinted by permission of the author and the Aaron Priest Literary Agency.

Lewis Thomas, "Notes on Punctuation," from *The Medusa and the Snail*. Copyright © 1979 by Lewis Thomas. Reproduced by permission of Viking Penguin, a division of Penguin Putnam, Inc.

Alice G. Thompson, "Should White Families Be Allowed to Adopt African American Children?" Reprinted by permission from *HEALTH* © 1993.

Danielle M. Trasciatti, "Music Education: A Much Needed and Important Discipline." Comp. Kathleen M. Kemmerer. *Writing Hall of Fame*. Summer, 1996. http://www.hn.psu.edu/Faculty/Kkemmerer/fame.html

Calvin Trillin, "Sign Writing," from *Too Soon to Tell*. Published by Farrar, Straus, and Giroux. Copyright © 1994, 1995 by Calvin Trillin. Reprinted by permission of Lescher and Lescher, Ltd.

TV-Free America, "Organizer's Kit." 1999 National TV-Turnoff Week. Reprinted by permission.

Brenda Ueland, "If You Want to Write." Excerpt copyright © 1987 by the Estate of Brenda Ueland. Reprinted from *If You Want to Write* by Brenda Ueland with the permission of Graywolf Press, Saint Paul, Minnesota.

Tom Vanderbilt, "Sneakers and the Environment," from *The Sneaker Book*. Copyright © 1998 *The Sneaker Book* by Tom Vanderbilt. Reprinted by permission of the New Press.

Wayside Gardens, text adapted from *Complete Garden Catalog* (Fall 1998).

Wired Magazine, "Scream Machine." Copyright © 1999 by The Condé Nast Publications, Inc. All rights reserved. Reprinted by permission.

Thomas K. Wynn, "How Are Mother Influenced Our Family Lives." Reprinted by permission of the author.

Lu Yu, "I Walk Out Into the Country at Night." From *One Hundred Poems from the Chinese* by Kenneth Rexroth. Copyright © 1971 by Kenneth Rexroth. Reprinted by permission of New Directions Publishing Corp.

William Zinsser, *Writing to Learn*. Reprinted by permission.

Notes on the Artists

CHAPTER 1

This Painter (at 42): A Self Portrait
Richard Craig Thompson was born in 1945 in McMinnville, Oregon. He is a painter and lithographer who has taught painting and drawing at several major universities. His paintings are hung in the Harris Gallery, Houston, Texas; the Space Gallery, Los Angeles, California; and the Roischon Gallery, Denver, Colorado.

CHAPTER 2

Summer Hats
Barbara Joysmith is from Memphis, Tennessee. She studied at the Art Institute of Chicago, received a bachelor's degree in fine arts from the University of Chicago, and opened her first studio in 1980. Her work is primarily in pastel and focuses on positive portrayals of African Americans. Her work has appeared on the set of *The Cosby Show* and other television series, is included in many prestigious collections, and is sold in open- and limited-edition prints through many galleries. Other works by Brenda Joysmith may be viewed at www.joysmith.com.

CHAPTER 3

Underground
Harvey Dinnerstein was born in 1929 in Brooklyn, New York. He taught drawing and painting in New York from 1963 to 1980. Throughout his career Dinnerstein received many awards and prizes and his work has hung in numerous galleries. *Underground* is a self portrait. The artist (in glasses and beard) appears at left.

CHAPTER 4

Haverstraw, New York
Lee Friedlander was born in 1934 in Aberdeen, Washington, and is among the most prominent American photographers of the twentieth century. He has held one-man exhibits throughout the world and has received numerous awards for his work. *Haverstraw, New York* is a self portrait taken in 1966.

CHAPTER 5

Ocean
Vija Celmins was born in 1939 in Riga, Latvia. Along with the rest of her family, she was a refugee during World War II. The family eventually settled in Indianapolis, Indiana, where Celmins completed art school. She later received a master's in fine arts from the University of California, Los Angeles, and taught at the University of California, Irvine. She has produced artwork in a variety of media, with many of her works focusing on segments of the ocean, the sky, or the ground. Her works are small in size, yet some have taken up to a year to finish. View another Celmins piece at http://sheldon.unl.edu/HTML/ARTIST/Celmins_V/TL.html.

CHAPTER 6

Lois on the Bench
André Cypriano was born in 1964 in Brazil and, after receiving a college degree, relocated to the United States in 1990. He studied photography in San Francisco and has since completed several projects that have been exhibited in galleries and museums in Brazil and the United States. Mr. Cypriano specializes in photo documentaries, particularly of remote, lesser known communities such as the dogs of Bali and the penitentiary of Candido Mendes in Rio de Janeiro, Brazil. *Lois on the Bench* was displayed at the El Museo del Barrio in New York as part of 1999 S-Files (Selected Files), an annual summer showcase of U.S.-born Latino artists and New York City–based Latin American artists. Mr. Cypriano's work can also be viewed at www.f8.com and at www.pictureeditor.com.

CHAPTER 7

Musculoskeletal System: Anterior View
Created by the Electronic Illustrators Group, Fountain Hills, Arizona, this illustration originally appeared in a textbook titled *Medical Terminology for Health Careers*, published by EMC/Paradigm Publishing, St. Paul, Minnesota.

CHAPTER 8

Untitled photographs
These photographs are from "The Building of a Custom Home," a photo feature by Eager Web Page Design. The Web site, which shows in words and pictures each step involved in constructing a home in San Antonio, Texas, may be visited at www.eagerweb.com/newhome.

CHAPTER 9

Earth Garden
Francisco Malespin is one of many Nicaraguan artists whose images are made available outside Nicaragua through the Nicaraguan Cultural Alliance (NCA) in Hyattsville, Maryland. According to the NCA, "Nicaragua is a poor land, but rich in art and poetry. NCA celebrates this tradition with images that mirror the spirit, pride and resilient hope of the people." This painting and nearly two dozen others by Nicaraguan artists are made available on T-shirts, business cards, and greeting cards. The sales generate income to the artists while also funding development projects in Nicaragua. Images may be viewed at www.quixote.org/nca.

CHAPTER 10

Marie and Blond Tourist Viewing Pottery
Gilbert Atencio (Wah Peen) was born in 1930 and raised in the San Idefonso pueblo in New Mexcio. He was born into a family of artists, so he learned to paint by observing and also by studying painting as part of his education at the Santa Fe Indian School. He served in the U.S. Marine Corps and worked as a medical and technical illustrator, but his primary vocation was as a painter. He began to sell and exhibit his work at a very early age. Mr. Atencio specialized in

painting the traditions and ceremonies of his people. According to Mr. Atencio, as quoted in *When the Rainbow Touches Down* by Tryntje Van Ness Seymour, "I do my paintings both for myself and for other people. Especially for people who enjoy Indians, their way of life, their ceremonies." Mr. Atencio died in 1995.

CHAPTER 11

Ozone, Tennesee Outhouse

This photograph is from the "Outhouses of America Tour" organized by John W. Loose and found on the Web at www.jldr.com. This particular outhouse is on property in Ozone, Tennessee. The outhouse belongs to Manya Marshall and was painted by her daughter Mikki Riggs. The photograph is several years old; according to the Web description, the outhouse was in use "until a tree fell on it."

CHAPTER 12

Levers, Ramps and Pulleys

Walter Wick graduated from the Paier Art School in New Haven, Connecticut, and is a freelance photographer whose pictures have appeared on the covers of more than 300 magazines and books. His photographic games have been featured in *Games* magazine, and he also is the photographer of the best-selling *I Spy* book series. This photograph is from *I Spy School Days: A Book of Picture Riddles*.

CHAPTER 13

Hunters-Gatherers, North America, Late 20th Century

Sidney Harris was born in Brooklyn, New York, "long ago enough," he says, "to have drawn more than 28,000 cartoons." In his long professional career he has never held a regular job, but always freelanced. His cartoons have appeared in the *New Yorker, The Wall Street Journal, Playboy, American Scientist, Discover*, and numerous other periodicals. He has published twenty cartoon collections, the most recent being *49 Dogs, 36 Cats and a Platypus*. You can see science-related cartoons by Mr. Harris at www. ScienceCartoonsPlus.com

CHAPTER 14

The Fate of the Planet Is Your Fate

V. Khotianovsky is an artist of the former Soviet Union, which during its existence had a strong tradition of disseminating education, propaganda, and political ideology through poster art. This poster was published by Plakat Publishers, the official poster publisher of the Communist Party. It was awarded with a special prize "For Peace and Social Progress" at the 1986 International Political Poster Competition.

CHAPTER 15

The Endurance at Night

Frank Hurley was born in Australia in 1890 and is best known for his photographs of the Antarctic and the two World Wars. He was the official photographer of Sir Ernest Shackleton's Imperial Trans-Antarctic Expedition in 1914. Due to unusually severe weather conditions, the expedition ship, the *Endurance* (pictured here), was trapped and crushed in the ice of the Weddell Sea. Expedition members survived by living on ice floes for several months before attempting a daring but successful journey in small life boats across the Drake Passage to an island off the coast of South America. Hurley also made documentary films on topics ranging from aboriginal culture to the Holy Land. He died in 1962.

CHAPTER 16

The Art Student: A Self Portrait

While still in high school, Elizabeth Torak moved from her family home in Princeton, New Jersey, to New York City so she could study at the Art Students League while simultaneously earning a diploma from an in-town school. She received a bachelor's degree in mathematics at the University of Chicago and then returned to New York to continue studying at the Art Students League. Torak now lives in Vermont. Her paintings feature still-lifes, landscapes, figures, and other subject matter. To achieve the special atmospheric quality of her paintings, Torak uses an old-fashioned and painstaking method of preparing canvas and paints. Some of her works may be viewed at www.tilting.com/torak.html.

Index